T … litics of Human Progress

Could Thomas Jefferson claim any consistency in his advocacy of democracy and the rights of man while remaining one of the largest slaveholders in Virginia? This extensive study of Jefferson's intellectual outlook suggests that, once we fully acknowledge the premises of his ethical thought and his now outdated scientific views, he could. Jefferson famously thought the human mind to be "susceptible of much improvement ... most of all, in matters of government and religion." Ari Helo's thorough analysis of Jefferson's understanding of Christian morality, atheism, contemporary theories of moral sentiments, ancient virtue ethics, natural rights, and the principles of justice and benevolence suggests that Jefferson refused to be a philosopher, and did so for moral reasons. This book finds Jefferson profoundly political in his understanding of individual moral responsibility and human progress.

Ari Helo is currently a University Lecturer in History of Science and Ideas at the University of Oulu. He earned his PhD at the University of Tampere in 1999 with a doctoral dissertation examining Thomas Jefferson's political thought. He has taught intellectual history, American studies, and cultural studies at numerous universities since 1996, and he has worked as a visiting researcher at the University of Virginia in Charlottesville. Helo's articles on American intellectual history have been published in Britain, Estonia, Finland, Hungary, Netherlands, and the United States, among them the widely noticed "Jefferson, Morality, and the Problem of Slavery," with Peter Onuf, in *The William and Mary Quarterly* (2003) and a survey article on Jefferson's political thought in *The Cambridge Companion to Thomas Jefferson* (2009).

CAMBRIDGE STUDIES ON THE AMERICAN SOUTH

Interdisciplinary in its scope and intent, this series builds on and extends Cambridge University Press's long-standing commitment to studies on the American South. The series not only offers the best new work on the South's distinctive institutional, social, economic, and cultural history, but also features works in national, comparative, and transnational perspectives.

Titles in the Series

Robert E. Bonner, *Mastering America: Southern Slaveholders and the Crisis of American Nationhood*
Ras Michael Brown, *African-Atlantic Cultures and the South Carolina Lowcountry*
Christopher Michael Curtis, *Jefferson's Freeholders and the Politics of Ownership in the Old Dominion*
Ari Helo, *Thomas Jefferson's Ethics and the Politics of Human Progress: The Morality of a Slaveholder*
Kathleen Hilliard, *Masters, Slaves, and Exchange: Power's Purchase in the Old South*
Scott P. Marler, *The Merchants' Capital: New Orleans and the Political Economy of the Nineteenth-Century South*
Peter McCandless, *Slavery, Disease, and Suffering in the Southern Lowcountry*
Johanna Nicol Shields, *Freedom in a Slave Society: Stories from the Antebellum South*
Brian Steele, *Thomas Jefferson and American Nationhood*
Jonathan Daniel Wells, *Women Writers and Journalists in the Nineteenth-Century South*

Thomas Jefferson's Ethics and the Politics of Human Progress

The Morality of a Slaveholder

ARI HELO

CAMBRIDGE
UNIVERSITY PRESS

CAMBRIDGE
UNIVERSITY PRESS

32 Avenue of the Americas, New York NY 10013-2473, USA

Cambridge University Press is part of the University of Cambridge.

It furthers the University's mission by disseminating knowledge in the pursuit of education, learning and research at the highest international levels of excellence.

www.cambridge.org
Information on this title: www.cambridge.org/9781107687721

First published 2014
First paperback edition 2015

A catalogue record for this publication is available from the British Library

Library of Congress Cataloguing in Publication data
Helo, Ari.
Thomas Jefferson's Ethics and the Politics of Human Progress :
the Morality of a Slaveholder / Ari Helo, University of Oulu, Finland.
pages cm. – (Cambridge Studies on the American South)
Includes bibliographical references and index.
ISBN 978-1-107-04078-6 (hardback)
1. Jefferson, Thomas, 1743–1826 – Relations with African Americans.
2. Jefferson, Thomas, 1743–1826 – Ethics. 3. Slavery – Moral and ethical aspects – United States. 4. Presidents – United States – Biography. I. Title.
E332.2.H46 2013
973.4′6092–dc23 2013013352

ISBN 978-1-107-04078-6 Hardback
ISBN 978-1-107-68772-1 Paperback

To all those Jefferson scholars whose insights on
the topic the author has failed to address

No man can be sovereign because
not one man, but men, inhabit the earth …

Hannah Arendt

The Human Condition (1958) 1998, p. 234

Contents

Acknowledgments

To paraphrase Tacitus, it is more becoming for a historian to remember than to bewail the dead. Many colleagues have asked me what I "truly think" of Thomas Jefferson as a person. I therefore wish to begin this book with a brief answer to that.

Regardless of the many years I have spent reading Jefferson's records and trying to grasp his thinking, I have never thought of him as a model to be embraced or rejected, but rather as a stranger from a strange culture. It was in Karen Blixen's *Out of Africa* (1937) – a book about a strange African culture written from an almost equally strange European perspective of "the olden times" – where I found a short passage best exemplifying how I would estimate Jefferson. The passage is about Blixen's last visit to see a dying great Kikuju chief, called Kinanjui:

> From the look of him, I thought that he had come back from his journey triumphant, and had got all his cattle back with him, in spite of his Masai sons-in-law.... [H]e had plainly, I thought, done his worldly task, gone home, and taken his wages in every sense. If he were clear enough in his mind to look back at his life, he would find very few instances in which he had not got the better of it. A great vitality and power of enjoyment, a manifold activity were at their end here, where Kinanjui lay still.[1]

To turn to the far easier assessments of persons and characters: On getting this book written I owe my biggest debt to a great historian and a great friend, Peter Onuf from the University of Virginia. It was his ceaseless encouragement and belief in the project over many years that made me finish the book. He is also one of those very rare scholars I have met who can discuss any topic in his field of expertise with genuine readiness to reconsider his own position on it.

Another friend and great intellectual, Allan Megill from the University of Virginia, has tirelessly responded to my pleas for critical advice over the years. Anyone familiar with Allan's extensive writings in philosophy and history can guess that critique was sometimes hard, but always helpful.

Other important friends, colleagues, and sparring partners in numerous discussions on intellectual history and Jefferson include Jonathan Lagerquist, Petteri Pietikäinen, Markku Roinila, and Mikko Saikku.

An incredibly long time ago, Kari Palonen gave me the idea to study Jefferson and Seppo Tamminen had the questionable honor to review the first paper I ever wrote on Jefferson. I also wish to express my heartfelt thanks to a number of friends and colleagues for their comments and critical remarks about this manuscript at various stages. They include Robert Bannister, Roger Clarke, Cheryl Greenberg, Erkki Helo, Markku Henriksson, Marjatta Hietala, Maijastiina Kahlos, Petter Korkman, Kenny Marotta, Jeffrey Meikle, Sari Nokkanen, Keith Olson, Riikamaria Paakkunainen, Christoph Parry, Gerald Porter, Kari Saastamoinen, Leonard Sadovsky, Eran Shalev, Frank Shuffelton (d. 2010), Katri Sieberg, Juha Sihvola (d. 2012), Mark C. Smith, Mechal Sobel, Keijo Virtanen, and Brian Yost. For their immensely important editorial help in finishing the book I owe special thanks to Niina Koskipää and David Moltke-Hansen.

Numerous universities and academic institutions have provided funding and other help for my research work, including the Academy of Finland, the International Center for Jefferson Studies at Monticello, and the Leo and Regina Wainstein Foundation. I also thank the faculty and staff of the Corcoran History Department at the University of Virginia for providing me an excellent environment for research and study during the three years I lived in Charlottesville.

To my son Elias I owe special thanks for that patient, and occasionally strangely amused, smile on his face during the years he watched his father writing "that book." Finally, I wish to express my immense debt to two, now passed away, friends and intellectuals, who more than anyone else modified my thinking as a historian: Tapani Hietaniemi (d. 2009) and Matti Viikari (d. 1994).

Abbreviations Used in Notes

AJL	*The Adams-Jefferson Letters: The Complete Correspondence Between Thomas Jefferson and Abigail and John Adams*, Lester J. Cappon (ed.), 2 vols., Chapel Hill: University of North Carolina Press, 1959.
Anthology	*Moral Philosophy from Montaigne to Kant: An Anthology*, J. B. Schneewind (ed.), 2 vols., Cambridge: Cambridge University Press, 1990.
Extracts	*Jefferson's Extracts from the Gospels: The Papers of Thomas Jefferson, Second Series*, Dickinson W. Adams and Ruth W. Lester (eds.), Princeton, NJ: Princeton University Press, 1983.
Ford	*The Works of Thomas Jefferson*, Paul Leicester Ford (ed.), 12 vols. (Federal edition), New York, 1904–1905.
Kames, *Essays*	Kames, Henry Home (Lord Kames), *Essays on the Principles of Morality and Natural Religion*, Edinburgh: 1751, facsimile reprint: London: University Microfilms International, Ann Arbor, MI, 1981.
L&B	*The Writings of Thomas Jefferson*, Andrew A. Lipscomb and Albert Ellery Bergh (eds.), 20 vols., Washington, DC, 1903–1904.
Legal CB	*The Commonplace Book of Thomas Jefferson: A Repertory of His Ideas on Government* [Jefferson's Legal Commonplace Book], Gilbert Chinard (ed.), Baltimore: Johns Hopkins University Press, 1926.
Literary CB	*Jefferson's Literary Commonplace Book: The Papers of Thomas Jefferson, Second Series* [Jefferson's Literary Commonplace Book], Douglas L. Wilson (ed.), Princeton, NJ: Princeton University Press, 1989.

Locke, *Essay*	Locke, John, *An Essay Concerning Human Understanding* (1690, 1700), Peter H. Nidditch (ed.), Oxford: Oxford University Press, 1979.
Locke, *Second Treatise*	Locke, John, *The Second Treatise of Government*, in John Locke, *Two Treatises of Government* (1690, 1698), Peter Laslett (ed.), Cambridge: Cambridge University Press, 1960, 1994, 265–428.
Notes	Thomas Jefferson, *Notes on the State of Virginia* (London, 1787), in *Thomas Jefferson Writings*, Merrill D. Peterson (ed.), New York: Library of America, 1984.
PAPERS	*The Papers of Thomas Jefferson*, Julian P. Boyd et al. (eds.), Princeton, NJ: Princeton University Press, 1950–.
Smith, *TMS*	Smith, Adam, *The Theory of Moral Sentiments* (1759, 6th edition), D. D. Raphael and A. L. Macfie (eds.), [The Glasgow Edition], Oxford: Oxford University Press, 1982.
TJ	Thomas Jefferson
TJW	*Thomas Jefferson Writings*, Merrill D. Peterson (ed.), New York: Library of America, 1984.

Introduction to the Morality of a Slaveholder

JEFFERSON'S IMAGE AND INTELLECTUAL LEANINGS

Thomas Jefferson owned almost 200 slaves when authoring the famous lines of the Declaration of Independence in 1776 that all men are created equal and entitled to the rights of life, liberty, and the pursuit of happiness. After his death on July 4, exactly fifty years later, approximately the same number of slaves at Jefferson's Monticello plantation – as well as the estate itself – were auctioned off in order to clear his huge debts. Nevertheless, this Virginia slaveholder, living beyond his means, remains in American history "the great apostle of democracy and national self-determination" belonging to the "pantheon of American demigods" alongside George Washington and Abraham Lincoln.[1] Thanks to Jefferson's politically skillful advocacy of democratic rights, popular sovereignty, equal elementary education, and religious freedom, all scholars in the field are familiar with James Parton's 1874 exclamation that "if Jefferson was wrong, America is wrong."[2]

Rather than studying Jefferson's importance to the American idea, this book seeks to answer a different question: Could Jefferson claim any consistency in his advocacy of democracy and the rights of man while remaining, throughout his life, one of the largest slaveholders in Virginia? Once we fully acknowledge the premises of his ethical thought, the answer will be that he could. Admittedly, any attempt to find a morality in the mind of a slaveholder is vulnerable from the perspective of absolute moral imperatives. Neither can one compare the bad choices that Jefferson felt he confronted over slavery to the tragic choices that individual slaves confronted when, for example, choosing to run away at the cost of leaving their spouses and children in slavery. Yet, moralizing about Jefferson's racial prejudices and often helplessly old-fashioned scientific assumptions is the shortest route to misunderstanding the ethical dimensions of his thinking. Jefferson's position on slavery was not self-evidently even the weakest link in his egalitarianism. He never suggested full equality of women either.

The problems of interpreting Jefferson's moral thought arise from his confusingly liberal use of such ethical – or ethically charged – concepts as natural rights, natural law, and the state of nature, or such apparently uncomplicated pairs of concepts as justice and benevolence, morals and manners, virtue and vice, and duties and obligations. Jefferson's ethical thought, this study argues, arose from one context only, namely from his well-known belief in human progress. Even if it remained unlikely in his view that "the human condition will ever advance to such a perfection as that there shall no longer be pain or vice in the world," he famously thought the human mind to be "susceptible of much improvement, and most of all, in matters of government and religion."[3]

One should not confuse Jefferson's understanding of progress with any confessedly progressive theory of history. In an attempt to define the latter notion, we would only fall into myriads of controversies about the definitions of progress, history, historicity, or temporality. As this study shows, Jefferson's conception of progress was a worldview, not a theory about history. It provided no guarantee that history, as a simple sequence of human events, would not include retrograde developments. Neither did it rest on any detailed view of what the proper end of progress – the perfection of man – must look like at the end of days.

The context of human progress is all the more important to keep in mind, given that Jefferson is one of those historical figures whose moral convictions have been primarily questioned on the grounds of his actual achievements in putting them into effect. On the slavery question Jefferson attained what most moral philosophers have: He condemned injustices on paper. He considered slavery immoral, unjust, and harmful for both slaves and masters. In the only book Jefferson ever authored, *Notes on the State of Virginia*, he thought it evident that "the whole commerce between the master and slave is a perpetual exercise of the most boisterous passions, the most unremitting despotism on the one part, and degrading submissions on the other."[4]

Most historians today agree with John Chester Miller's 1977 thesis that Jefferson was sincere in his principled opposition to slavery. The same holds true of Miller's central conclusion that, from early on, "it was impressed upon Jefferson that he must choose between the preservation of his political 'usefulness' and his active opposition to slavery."[5] In order to grasp Jefferson's position, one needs to question the implied straightforward opposition between political "usefulness" and "active opposition" to slavery, or to some other moral evil. It is hardly self-evident that Jefferson regarded political action as a simple alternative to some presumably higher notion of moral duty. He famously insisted on "having never believed there was one code of morality for a public; and another for a private man."[6] In fact, he was conspicuously consistent in arguing for a political solution to the slavery question instead of individual manumissions. This calls for some other explanation than that Jefferson simply erred in his own moral thought.

As the title of the book implies, Jefferson's ultimate belief in human progress entailed politics as the single route to any long-standing success. The ethically sustainable method of extending justice was political action – that is, embracing legal reforms, not individual crusades against the contemporary legal order. Progress, alongside increasing material welfare and accumulating scientific knowledge, was about gradually developing shared patterns of morally desirable behavior. No individual could achieve it alone. Enduring steps forward could be taken only through democratically accepted reforms. This is the context in which this study seeks the consistencies both within Jefferson's moral thought and between his thought and his policies. Inconsistencies no doubt remain, but they are considerably fewer than usually presumed.

It is important not to accidentally turn Jeffersonian optimism upside down. It would be a fundamental mistake, for example, to identify his belief in progressive natural sciences with one or another, presumably coherent, eighteenth-century "scientific worldview," and, consequently, with one or another racial theory of the time. Scientific progress, even in Jefferson's eyes, was about continuing research of the unknown. A scientific theory is, by and large, true as long as it cannot be disqualified as a research hypothesis.[7] Its truth-value depends solely on the yet uncompleted research. Anyone believing in cumulative knowledge must doubt its contemporary state. So did Jefferson. Taking this aspect of Jefferson's thought seriously, it is perhaps not such "an odd thing about a man who lived as long as Jefferson" that "he seldom changed his mind about anything," as Stanley Elkins and Eric McKitrick once argued.[8]

In certain important aspects, Jefferson's commitment to human progress does not quite fit with his contemporary fame as "the great philosopher and statesman of the south," nor with his current textbook image as a "philosopher scientist."[9] To be sure, Jefferson gained a well-earned reputation as a man of letters, a part-time scientist, a nationally recognized architect, and a cosmopolitan intellectual. He headed the American Philosophical Society from 1797 to 1814. His foreign contacts included such luminaries as the Marquis de Condorcet, Alexander von Humboldt, Thomas Paine, Richard Price, J.B. Say, and Dugald Stewart. But Jefferson's fame rested not so much on his intellectual achievements as on his exceptionally successful career as the spokesman of democracy and the rights of man.

As a statesman, Jefferson was conspicuously prone to view politics in moral terms. In the immediate aftermath of the War of Independence, one already finds him warning his fellow Virginians not to lose themselves "in the sole faculty of making money." Instead, they should keep close watch of their rulers, who will turn corrupt as soon as the people grow "careless."[10]

How did Jefferson become the American apostle of liberty? In his home state of Virginia, he advocated the abolition of the traditional restrictions on free inheritance of land and authored the famous Virginia statute for religious freedom. In his early drafts of the Northwest Ordinance of 1787 he demanded both universal male suffrage and the prohibition of slavery in the new western territories prior to their accession to the Union.

From where did Jefferson's much-acclaimed liberal constitutional thought arise? As the American minister to France from 1785 to 1789, Jefferson counseled his fellow revolutionaries in their efforts to formulate the French Declaration of the Rights of Man and Citizen. From France he also persuaded his life-long friend and closest political ally, James Madison, to incorporate the Bill of Rights into the newly ratified Constitution.[11]

In 1790, Jefferson joined President Washington's first cabinet as the secretary of state but eventually resigned in bitter opposition to the secretary of the treasury, Alexander Hamilton. The notion of Jefferson as the foremost American spokesman of minimal government has its origins in his struggles with Hamilton, the key figure of the Federalist Party. It was Hamilton's large-scale fiscal program – based on permanent national debt, on the British model – that turned Jefferson's political instincts into moral fury. Hamilton's apparently one-sided favoritism of commerce and manufacture over agriculture threatened to subject Jefferson's beloved American husbandmen to an ever-increasing tax burden needed for the interest payments on the national debt. Moreover, the payments were headed into the pockets of a new hideous monocracy, the government's creditors.

Jefferson's vision of self-sufficient farmers' participatory democracy as the backbone of American freedom is best conveyed in his characterization of "true republicans" as including landholders and all other "labouring" Americans "in husbanding or the arts." These people he contrasted not only to a whole race of "nervous persons," but also to merchants, speculators, bankers, and office-hunters most of whom associated themselves with the principled "tories" of the Federalist Party.[12]

Jefferson's fame as a states' rights advocate, in turn, stems from his famous Kentucky Resolutions of 1798. During John Adams's presidency, the "nervous" Federalists attempted to suffocate criticism of the government through the infamous Alien and Sedition Acts, which appeared to nullify the constitutional right of free speech. These developments led the then Vice President Jefferson to argue that if no other branch of the federal government could put a stop to such an abuse of power, the member states of the Union were entitled to exercise judicial review on their own.

In 1800, Jefferson was elected the third President of the United States with his Democratic-Republicans winning the majority in both houses of the federal congress. This landmark event was, in Jefferson's words, "as real a revolution in the principles of our government as that of 1776 was in its form; not effected indeed by the sword, as that, but by the rational and peaceable instrument of reform, the suffrage of the people."[13]

It was clear to Jefferson that after the catastrophic failure of the French Revolution, America had to stand on its own, in isolation from the superpowers of the time. France had fallen under the yoke of Napoleon, "the greatest of the destroyers of the human race," and Britain remained as unable as ever to include a single "chapter of morality into her political code."[14] From here arises Jefferson's image as the visionary of American exceptionalism.

Where should one look for Jefferson's progressive moral ideals? He was aware of practically every late-eighteenth-century theoretical argument in circulation, whether originating in Antiquity, the Middle Ages, or the Enlightenment. Jefferson's thousands of letters and memoranda reveal a never-fading interest in Epicurus and Cicero and a number of Stoic philosophers. Jesus of Nazareth, in Jefferson's words, had "supplemented" the ancient virtue ethics with the principle of universal benevolence. With equal ease Jefferson embraced such Scottish-Enlightenment-derived notions as common sense, moral sentiments, and the inborn moral sense of man.

Alongside John Locke, Jefferson – a lawyer by education – frequently referred to such prominent authorities in the field of the law of nature and nations as Hugo Grotius, Samuel Pufendorf, and Emer(ich) de Vattel.[15] To be sure, such luminaries as Kant or Fichte do not figure in Jefferson's records. Nor does Rousseau get more than a couple of brief remarks, and even Hume is summarily dismissed as merely a monarchist-minded British historian. But what appears to distinguish Jefferson as an American intellectual of the time was his interest in the apparent anticlericalism of the French Encyclopedists and in their followers, particularly Condorcet, Helvétius, and the less known Destutt de Tracy. Many of these "virtuous atheists" Jefferson described as his allies on the subject of human progress, although he personally remained a deist.[16] Even on moral issues Jefferson's own beliefs should be kept distinct from what he thought all could agree on.

In fact, the most characteristic aspect of Jefferson's intellectual outlook was his Stoic-inspired disregard of theory. This disregard held equally true in theology, natural history, and moral philosophy. In his eyes, the contemporary theoretical debates on morality served only to prove "how necessary was the care of the Creator in making the moral principle so much a part of our constitution as that no errors of reasoning or of speculation might lead us astray from it's observance in practice."[17] From this conviction arose Jefferson's conspicuously eclectic attitude to moral studies as well as to philosophy in general. What he maintained was this:

> I never submitted the whole system of my opinions to the creed of any party of men whatever in religion, in philosophy, in politics, or in anything else where I was capable of thinking for myself. Such an addiction is the last degradation of a free and moral agent.[18]

There is plenty of evidence that everything Jefferson ever claimed about morality emanated from *the absolute primacy of temporality in his intellectual outlook, embodied in this conception of the human being as a free, moral agent.*

To be sure, viewing temporality as the paradigmatic element of Jefferson's moral thought only extends the theme of generational sovereignty in Jefferson scholarship, most forcefully brought to the fore by Richard Matthews and Herbert Sloan.[19] In the simplest terms, Jefferson's principle held that each "generation is as independent as the one preceding" and has therefore "a right to choose for itself the form of government it believes most promotive of its own happiness." In order to link this apparently political conception of human happiness to Jefferson's rights thinking one may resort to the same document also stating that "*the dead have no rights*. They are nothing; and nothing cannot own something."[20] Jefferson's understanding of generational sovereignty was both moral and inescapably linear.

What was the relationship of temporality to the notion of progress in Jefferson's thought? In the simplest form, the answer can be found in his most celebrated law text, the Virginia bill for religious freedom. The bill held that the assembly enacting religious freedom had "no power to restrain the acts of succeeding Assemblies" from revoking that freedom. It could only urge the future assemblies to respect the principle as a natural right.[21] Within Jefferson's self-confessedly progressive moral outlook, temporality did not yield to the modern, linear view of time, whether unfolding progressive or retrograde developments. Insofar as morality is about one's respect for other people, as the term is most broadly defined, it cannot remain in the past. As "free moral agents," our respect for others should recur every day.

Whereas Jefferson's commitment to generational independence is widely acknowledged, this study's central claims about the man himself are highly controversial. First, Jefferson refused to be a philosopher for moral reasons. His statements on the rights of man, on ethics, on race, or on gender issues did not aim at a consistent theory but at keeping ethical discourse alive. Second, if anything, Jefferson was a man of politics. His ethically charged Lockean leanings cannot be grasped in isolation from his belief in free representative democracy as the crucial human innovation in history. Free government provided the very framework in which genuinely progressive steps forward could be taken. Third, and the most controversial point, is that the image of Jefferson as an advocate of only minimal government is a misconception.

These claims run counter to dominant voices in the field of Jefferson studies. But it is equally notable that philosophers and intellectual historians disagree about Jefferson's inconsistencies. Jefferson has been described as a moral rationalist, a moral sentimentalist, and an Epicurean, as well as a modern libertarian.[22] Particularly in relation to the problem of slavery, Jefferson has often been accused of sheer self-deception.[23] No doubt, he attempted to provide himself with an argumentative moral niche from which to blame others. But his alleged failures and simplicities in formulating his position have been unnecessarily exaggerated.

Historians, as if by occupational hazard, insist on finding Jefferson maturing in his thought over time. Again, they often disagree on the direction of the presumed changes – most of which, as this study argues, never occurred.[24] The central suggestion of the present study is that Jefferson usually aimed at circumventing rather than resolving philosophical and scientific problems because of his faith in democratic political discourse in solving peacefully such concrete, contemporary ethical predicaments as slavery.

JEFFERSON THE POLITICIAN

Scholars also disagree on whether Jefferson matured into a more Liberal, Libertarian, or Republican political thinker over the years.[25] Even in this respect his views changed much less than is commonly presumed. The scholarly disagreements arise as much from methodological as from political or purely historical grounds. Consider Carl Becker's classic claim that, in Jefferson's eyes, "the only thing to do with political power, since it is inherently dangerous, is to abate it."[26] Is this not an extraordinary conclusion in view of Jefferson's exceptionally long and energetic career as a diplomat, a legislator, a governor, a national party leader, the president of the United States, and a widely recognized political eminence until the end of his life?

In fact, the fundamental problem lies in keeping the analysis of Jefferson as an American founding father distinct from his image as a politician. Gordon Wood's well-balanced studies on the impact of classical republicanism on the founders' thought deserve their status as standard textbooks on the Revolutionary era. Regardless of his interest in the so-called republican tradition, Wood has always subscribed to the fundamentally Lockean-liberal thesis of the historical meaning of the founding. As early as 1969 he argued that, in adopting the Constitution, "Americans had retained the forms of Aristotelian schemes of government but eliminated the substance, thus divesting the various parts of the government of their social constituents."[27] The American revolutionaries broke with this decidedly premodern tradition, Wood argues, because of their Lockean-derived, modern notion of free society, based on the principle of equal opportunity.[28]

As a large-scale generalization, Wood's view may well be acceptable. But what is not is his further inference regarding Jefferson's ethical convictions, which suddenly begin to appear elementarily indifferent, if not hostile, to the concept of politics. According to Wood, the "Jeffersonian modern virtue" that "flowed from the citizen's participation in society, not in government" must be distinguished from the classical notion of virtue arising out of "participation in politics."[29] From this summary one easily infers that Jefferson's virtue ethic was distinctly modern in being antigovernment, if not entirely antipolitical – as if "citizen participation in society" had nothing to do with the power relations within the so-called free government. The notion of civil society as in anyway related to political discourse does not enter the picture.

To question the popular notion of "Jefferson's antigovernment ethos,"[30] one hardly needs to take sides in the outdated historiographical struggle over the true meaning of the American founding between the John Pocock–inspired republican school and neo-Lockeans, such as Joyce Appleby and Isaac Kramnick.[31] As Daniel Rodgers once brilliantly summarized the debate, eventually the Lockean-liberal school "prevailed by raising the stakes of what counted as *meaningful* conflict, until every conceivable demonstration of conflict short of Jacobin or Bolshevist revolution vanished in the all-pervasive liberal consensus."[32]

Indeed, in order to study Jefferson as a politician of his time, one needs the concept of meaningful conflict. Without going into distinctions between, say, "politicizing" a given issue and "politicking" for it, consider the textbook notion that there is a political aspect to every social phenomenon in which one may discern even a potential conflict.[33] The notion of conflict as the salient feature of human life was far from alien to Jefferson. As he contended, "an association of men who will not quarrel with one another is a thing which never yet existed, from the greatest confederacy of nations down to a town meeting."[34]

By letting go of the oddly common view that conflict is inherently contradictory to human sociability, it is easier to see the myriad ways that power relations permeate everyday life. Power relations are in play in every family disagreement over whose turn it is to take the dachshund out, and in every instance the dachshund pulls on the leash in disagreement with his walker about the proper route. None of this means submitting to some 1970s notion that "everything is political." The notion of politics as public discourse does not run counter to the fundamental tenet of modern liberalism that individuals are generally capable of handling their private-life conflicts without public interference. The suggestion is simply that social phenomena can always be, and often become, politicized.

Methodologically, social developments can be viewed as a series of conflicts and conflict resolutions and, hence, studied as political phenomena. Whenever violence occurs, politics has failed. Here arises the modern notion of civil society as the discursive basis for conflict solving and as an integral part of what is properly called free government. In fact, all standard definitions of "civil society," from Tocqueville onward, involve its function as the site of discourse and, thus, also as a political site for anyone with an agenda. That, after all, is why textual (or discourse) analysis of anyone's sayings is applicable to political studies. In this standard, extended meaning of politics, it definitively belongs to civil society. There one finds politics as an everyday occurrence, practiced by NGOs, the media, political parties, congressmen, courts, corporations, lobbyists, ad hoc pressure group coalitions, and the like. Hence, governmental action, whether taking place on its own initiative or in response to so-called popular pressure, is only one aspect of the constant political action that is one of the most characteristic features of civil society.[35]

To grasp how deeply all this involves Jefferson's image as the foremost ideologue of the founding, one need only visit the Jeffersonian Memorial in Washington, DC. On the wall there is an inscription of Jefferson's statement on black slaves from 1821: "[N]othing is more certainly written in the book of fate than that these people are to be free." Omitted, however, is Jefferson's qualification in the very next sentence: "Nor is it less certain that the two races, equally free, cannot live in the same government."[36]

The time-honored notion of American free society is not mentioned at all in this clumsy appraisal of freedom's application to all races. What makes it so strikingly non-Jeffersonian? Strictly speaking, racial equality was not at issue here. Jefferson averred that no matter how inferior one race may appear in comparison to another, white and black people should become "equally free." It was only that they were not to become so under Jeffersonian "government." Nothing was said about either Lockean or post-Lockean free society. Jefferson's use of the terms "equality" and "government" comprises the whole problem.[37]

At least in 1821, Jefferson's abolition plan entailed compulsory removal of the entire African-American population from the United States. As this study shows, it was the only solution to slavery to which Jefferson ever subscribed. If that makes Jefferson untrue to the Jeffersonian legacy, the reason is that the legacy is derived from historians' later definition of it. The problem is historical. No sane person today would agree with Jefferson's racist grounds for arguing that African Americans should establish themselves as a distinct nation. Neither do many people share Jefferson's outspoken belief that rocks grow.[38]

To track a genuinely power-centered view of society in the Jefferson archive, one may resort to his definition of "pure republic." It consisted of "a state of society in which every member of mature and sound mind has an equal right of participation, personally, in the direction of the affairs of society."[39] This power-derived perspective on the very concept of society arose from the notion that potential conflicts of interests permeate all social life. None of this prevented Jefferson from subscribing to the core conception of modern liberalism that, by and large, individuals are capable of solving conflicts without public control. To what extent Jefferson thought such an ideal to be in the grasp of the America of his day is another question. As noted, he never made up his mind about whether women are by nature entitled to equal political rights with men.

Jefferson never won enough public support to put his emancipation plan into effect. But neither did he win his battle for universal, white male suffrage in his home state of Virginia. As early as 1776, his draft constitution for the state of Virginia suggested that all "male persons" with 25 acres of land and other residents having paid "scot and lot to government the last [two years] shall have right to give their vote in the election of their respective representatives." They were also to be qualified for office. This demand was supplemented with the initiative of appropriating 50 acres of land for all men without property, which in essence would have guaranteed universal male suffrage.[40] The Virginia legislators ignored Jefferson's draft. Against his ceaseless demands to rectify the situation, approximately half of the white, free male Virginians were excluded from the ballot well after Jefferson's death in 1826.[41]

What was Jefferson's personal "consent" to contemporary American democratic discourse like, whether Lockean or otherwise? In seeking consistencies in his ethical convictions, one should begin with the stunning number of compromises he was ready to make in order to remain loyal to contemporary majority rule after the Revolution. Jefferson's faith in an equal white men's democracy in Virginia remained a mere hope, because the majority of the politically empowered were uninterested in the idea. Apparently, Jefferson could compromise even that goal in order to keep his personal loyalty to government intact.

Politics is about the future, not about keeping the world from coming to its end. Even less does it have to do with the view that ethically sound politics should be capable of correcting past injustices. To give an example, Affirmative Action is often (mis)understood in terms of encouraging the employers to take "positive measures to recruit minorities, thus *compensating for past injustices*."[42] This kind of metaphysics of leveling the playing field (in the name of the equal opportunity principle) in the past alongside the present may appear morally valid to many. Such aspirations have nothing to do with Jefferson's future-oriented thought of generational independence.

The standard lamentation that Jefferson was not outspoken enough in all his wishes is out of touch with what successfully playing politics is all about. Rather than speaking his mind, Jefferson regularly urged Madison and other friends to go public with issues he personally could not touch when attempting to acquire power. Jefferson's harsh language about his political opponents was not that surprising given all the abuse he himself had to endure. Over the years, he was accused of being not only an atheist, but also an effeminate liberal idealist with secret abolitionist ambitions, who also kept a black concubine, thus undermining his fame as a genuine racist.[43]

But most conspicuously, it is difficult to view Jefferson's huge number of political initiatives stemming from some essentially antigovernment ethos. Perhaps Max Edling's reading of the founding era, well captured in the title of his book, *A Revolution in Favor of Government*, pertains to Jefferson as well.[44] As to Jefferson's preferences, his purchase of the Louisiana Territory in 1803 not only doubled the size, but also increased the debt of the nation, this despite the fact that he earlier had attempted to get rid of that debt. As Jefferson's opponents argued, the consequent congressional authorization of the president as the single authority over the Louisiana area made "the minimal government Jefferson" a practical "Grand Turk" of the West.[45] Again, his 1808 embargo policy severely restricted free commerce and consumption, thus contradicting the image of Jefferson as the spokesman of only small government. To solve the problem of slavery, Jefferson devised a terribly expensive, fifty-year long program to gradually send the whole African-American population out of the country. In addition, he openly advocated public investments for creating an elementary educational system in Virginia. Neither does his late initiative to establish a whole system of municipal "ward republics" alongside the county administration, the state government, and the federal government appear unequivocally nonpolitical.

ON THE METHODS AND THE THESIS

What can a historical study explain about the morality of a given historical figure? To offer a preliminary insight into what is at stake in Jefferson's case, consider for example A.J. Beitzinger's conclusion – offered after an elegant summary of all the complexities of Jefferson's ethics – that "finally, in practice" Jefferson "proceeded on his belief that what is practicable must often control what is pure theory and that no maxim can be regarded as applicable to all times and circumstances." The author does not explicate the meaning of this, but one may read it as saying that, in the final analysis, Jefferson had neither a moral theory nor any moral maxim to even turn into practice, given that his true belief consisted of expediency only.[46]

As in all academic endeavors, methodology circumscribes the present study's essential findings. Being a large-scale reinterpretation of Jefferson's progressive worldview, this book does not offer a new perspective on early American history, except in the spirit of Joyce Appleby's apt characterization that the "true Jeffersonian legacy is to be hostile to legacies."[47] Neither does it provide any definite views of what the Enlightenment was truly about. Each and every aspect of discourse on natural and moral sciences is discussed in relation to what it appears to have meant for Jefferson's thinking. The reader is not asked to either believe or disbelieve in Jefferson. None of the arguments are presented for the purpose either of praising Jefferson as an early advocate of participatory mass democracy or of accusing him of being a racist slaveholder. He was both.

Studying Jefferson's thinking does not necessarily entail addressing his implicit or imagined responsibility for later historical developments, such as the Jeffersonian legacy of states' rights used by Confederate leaders at the outbreak of the Civil War. Notably, some political scientists discern in politics what historians have traditionally discerned in history – namely, that its results are hardly ever intended. The reason is that no individual's intentions shape a social reality in which not one, but many agents act in common with different intentions – provided that people generally act intentionally to begin with.[48] The present study does not even aim to unfold Jefferson's self-interested, perhaps subconscious, motives in formulating his positions. Instead, it aims at a more articulated understanding of his outspoken moral stance. His stance may appear philosophically invalid, but only once one knows what it approximately was.

Entering the process of interpretation of the Jefferson archive requires prejudgment, for no one enters any such process without one. But a historical interpretation may amount to more than that. Consider, for example, Jefferson's antislavery stance resting entirely on his political program to achieve abolition through deportation. Without any further interpretation, one may both explain and assess Jefferson's ethical position as embarrassingly reminiscent of that of modern neo-Nazis. At their very best, these latter-day racists would subscribe to universal humanity only with a global "separate but equal" principle, and argue that all ethnicities should live in their countries of "origin." In fact, Jefferson did not quite argue that this must always be the case, just that such a position was prudential in his own time and thus ethically defensible.[49]

The method of clinging to Jefferson's own words about his intentions does not entail the view that he could not err in his logic. Nevertheless, most of the time Jefferson was much more circumspect in his formulations than later commentators have allowed. As to haphazard contextualization, it is notable that Jefferson's probably decades-long liaison with his slave mistress, Sally Hemings, does not appear to have had any impact on his racist opinions about African Americans. Historians often find Jefferson subscribing to some fixed positions and then changing his mind about them. More philosophically oriented scholars tend to consider Jefferson's beliefs as equally fixed, so as to compare them to what one now should think of science, ethics, ethnicity, and democracy. In fact, the crucial consistencies appear to lie in Jefferson being constantly disappointed in his largely political expectations about the promotion of material, intellectual, and ethical human progress.

The fundamental presumption of this research is that Jefferson's keen awareness of living in an ongoing history helped him distinguish various extra-historical assumptions about the human condition from the assumptions based on historical evidence. Both kinds of assumptions remained equally distinguishable from his progressive assumption that humankind may experience genuine novelties.

Indeed, Jefferson appears to have kept his ethical convictions about universal justice and benevolence distinct from the historically verifiable notion of conflict-ridden human sociability. Such extra-temporal conceptions as natural law and providential benevolence remained for him non-disprovable hypotheses. However, history showed that human understanding had already gone through significant ethical changes. Jefferson discerned development in both the generally shared patterns of proper behavior as well as the literary definitions of such patterns. Thus, one finds Jefferson disagreeing with many authorities on the law of nature and nations, who still considered African slavery morally defensible. People obviously could transcend historically sanctioned forms of inequality.

The remedy was nothing less than the eighteenth-century ideal of free, representative democracy. Under democratic majority rule, justified violence could count as an acceptable method to preserve justice among equals. At the same time, extending justice to those still deprived of it demanded politics of benevolence on the part of the empowered, those currently endowed with equal political rights. But Jeffersonian progress offered no guarantees against temporary setbacks in even enlightened, democratic majority opinion. Eventually, Jefferson's conception of individual self-determination remained subordinate to the simple practice of renewing one's commitment to justice and benevolence every day, here and now, in concert with others.

In sum, one should understand Jefferson's optimism about the future in political rather than in utopian terms. The politician's present is equally future-oriented with that of a utopian. But the utopian needs only to define the desirable end result, not a policy for moving forward from here and now. The difference, therefore, arises with the politician's attitude to the present as a result of the past and, thus, as the meaningful context of one's future orientation. Changes may be imposed only on the current results of history, meaning for example, that the legal institution of slavery must be made illegal politically. As noted, whenever violence occurs, politics has failed.

It is one thing to suggest an interpretation and another to validate it – the goal of the book at hand. The first out of the following five chapters begins by drawing a distinction between Jefferson's conceptions of history and progress. His commitment to progress arose from the triumvirate of Lord Bacon, John Locke, and Isaac Newton. These intellectual giants had unfolded the possibilities of developing human knowledge. Jefferson could well reconcile this concept of progress with what he called "true religion" – a term he used not to refer to religious truths, but to a set of epistemological notions compatible with increasing human knowledge in both natural and moral sciences. This position also connects to Jefferson's adherence to prudence as the key classic virtue of a man acknowledging the limits of contemporary knowledge. Eventually, the Jeffersonian idea of progress appears to have rested on a conscious, human effort to increase knowledge, material welfare, and general sensitivity to ethical issues among humankind. But the crucial innovation in human history, since the Christian notion of universal benevolence, was that of free government. It alone provided the basis for benevolence to shape the common standards of ethically commendable behavior in terms of open discourse and peaceful reforms. This notion also underlies Jefferson's position on slavery.

Chapter 2 focuses on Jefferson's ultimate understanding of scientific progress. This has little to do with his personal, philosophical position as a materialist and a deist. Belief in scientific progress entails nothing more than acknowledging the imperfection in the current state of knowledge. Progress – resting on the notion of accumulative human understanding – stems from the realization that some aspects of the proverbial "whole truth and nothing but the truth" remain unknown. Jefferson's own scientific beliefs contained very few demonstrable truths drawn from either natural or moral sciences. His much-discussed belief in the inborn moral sense of man did not figure as a moral truth in his thinking. Rather, the moral sense concept remained subordinated to the observable, historical changes in people's actual morals and manners and in their commonly shared contemporary standard of universal justice.

At the core of Jefferson's moral faith, one finds a Stoic-inspired Epicurean virtue ethicist. Chapter 3 examines morality as a matter of faith for Jefferson, and demonstrates that his faith in virtue fully complied with his intellectual outlook. Jefferson's adherence to the ancient ideal of the wise and virtuous man reflected his conviction that individual self-determination means constantly seeking to better oneself. Eventually, his virtue ethics appear to have rested on the notion of an individual's right, even obligation, to cultivate one's intellectual and moral capacities.

Chapter 4 explores Jefferson's conceptions of justice and of justified violence. The reason why Jefferson's rights thinking is fully addressed only in this late chapter is that the essentially extra-temporal natural rights doctrine played a much less important role in his moral thought than scholars tend to assume. In essence, Jefferson's natural rights remained imperfect rights within his conflict-laden view of humanity. Justice derived from the conception of equal rights. Equal rights, in turn, applied only to the living, those who voluntarily give up, or even disclaim, their innocence when assuming moral responsibility for both maintaining and extending those rights. This is why studying Jefferson's adherence to "the consent of the governed" as the historically verifiable basis for the common standards of justice and fair play tell one much more about his actual ethical convictions than any purely theoretical approach to his rights thinking.

Chapter 5 will demonstrate that Jefferson's conceptions of moral equality and benevolence remained inextricably linked to his political thought. In order to discern the embedded inequalities of eighteenth-century America, one did not need to view any of the colonies, much less the Union, as a replica of one or another European society of orders. In Jefferson's eyes, his America – with its striking inequalities in property, in voting qualifications, and in organized systems of free and unfree labor – was still a society of distinct political orders in need of thorough reforms.[50] Given Jefferson's numerous suggestions about progressive taxation, the distribution of vacant lands to the unemployed, public funding for a large-scale emigration of slave children, and establishment of a public elementary educational system, it is equally difficult to consider him an advocate of only minimal government.

As this study shows, Jefferson's conception of benevolence should be viewed as distinct from his conception of justice and, yet, as equally political. Justice could require justified violence, as when free Americans fought to preserve their rights in 1776. Benevolence, as concomitant with sound politics, called for the peaceful extension of justice to those still deprived of political or social equality. The Jeffersonian moral agent could never let go of the practice of benevolence toward all those who, for whatever reason, remained incapable of taking advantage of equal opportunity. This is why the Jeffersonian polity remained a moral construction.

Finally, a word of warning is in place. To those who value historical truths as justification for kicking tombstones in moral indignation, this book will offer little satisfaction. Let me therefore, at this early point, offer the single moral message I had in mind when writing the book. One may readily question Jefferson's ontological maxim that "the dead are not even things" and claim instead that whatever was, never ceases to be part of our more-or-less spatio-temporal understanding of existence. Even the dead Jefferson exists as a possible object of historical scrutiny. Morally speaking, the historian's professional obligation is to depict the past as correctly as possible, whereas the historian's moral judgments have no more authority than those of anyone else. After all, moral judgments should mainly apply to the living. They alone might make the world better or prevent it from getting worse.[51] Nevertheless, let us turn from private musings to history.

1

History, Progress, and Politics

SOMETHING NEW UNDER THE SUN

In 1800, Thomas Jefferson was elected the third President of the United States, and his Democratic Republicans won the majority in both houses of Congress. Reflecting on the significance of this electoral victory, he famously proclaimed: "We can no longer say that there is nothing new under the sun."[1] With something genuinely new under the sun, history must have ceased merely repeating itself. Innovations appeared possible. What kind of innovations Jefferson dreamed of is the subject of this chapter.

Jefferson believed in the improvement of "the human mind, in science, in ethics, in government," and in various other fields, and spoke favorably of genuine "philanthropists" committed to the idea of the practically "indefinite perfectibility of man."[2] To one of the hundreds of his lesser-known correspondents, William Green Munford, Jefferson stated in 1799: "I consider man as formed for society, and endowed by nature with those dispositions which fit him for society. I believe also, with Condorcet, as mentioned in your letter, that his mind is perfectible to a degree of which we cannot as yet form any conception."[3]

Indeed, the Enlightenment notion of progress has often been seen as exemplified by Condorcet's all-embracing optimism about the human condition. It is difficult to determine whether the optimism in question represented a simple replacement of the Christian expectation of heavenly redemption by a utopian vision of humankind creating heaven on earth. No doubt, the progressives of the time differed in their views, just as people still disagree about what counts as progress.[4] Nevertheless, Jefferson viewed human perfection as something "of which we cannot yet form any conception." Even the desirable end result of human progress remained unforeseeable. Jeffersonian progress was open-ended.

There were two particular areas of life in which genuine changes were to be sought: Religion and politics. Shortly before the landmark elections of 1800, Jefferson thundered against the "present despots of the earth" who apply their "cowardly" conservative ideas "especially to religion & politics."[5] On another occasion he labeled the Federalists as "bigots in religion & government," who thought that "we are to look backwards instead of forwards for the improvement of the human mind."[6] A year later, he celebrated his party's electoral victory as nothing less than a triumph over "bigotry in Politics & Religion."[7] As late as 1816, one finds him musing that although it is unlikely that "the human condition will ever advance to such a perfection as that there shall no longer be pain or vice in the world," the human mind is definitely "susceptible of much improvement, and most of all, in matters of government and religion."[8]

This twofold notion of improvement is the key to Jefferson's progressive thought. It was grounded on the ideal of free government in which genuine individual moral responsibility could take root, because even after voluntarily submitting to majority rule, everyone could question the current majority opinion. Participation in open discussion on both political and religious issues was to remain every man's right.

This is also why Jefferson's personal religious convictions should not be confused with his faith in the moral progress of man. His 1814 letter to Miles King provides an illuminating example of how he related religion to such crucial concepts as happiness, honesty, benevolence, and natural rights. His statement begins with the simple presumption that God "has formed us moral agents." That is not to say, he elaborates, "that, in the perfection of his state, he [God] can feel pain or pleasure from any thing we may do: he is far above our power." But, according to Jefferson, as "moral agents," each of us

> may promote the *happiness* of those with whom he has placed us in society, by acting *honestly* towards all, *benevolently* to those who fall within our way, respecting sacredly their *rights* bodily and mental, and cherishing especially their freedom of conscience, as we value our own. I must ever believe that *religion* substantially good which produces *an honest life*.[9]

This passage includes all the essential elements of Jefferson's moral outlook, beginning with the undefined notion of "happiness." Moral concerns are clearly concerns about a given agent's regard for the happiness of that agent's closest fellow human beings. The means for promoting happiness, in turn, consist in the agent's inner commitment to honesty and universal benevolence. Natural rights come into play in the agent's respect for the independence of other agents. First and foremost, this entails conscious respect for individual freedom of conscience. Jefferson's notion of religion is as individualistic as his moral outlook, subordinated as it is to an honest life.

In Jefferson's view, the only reliable, interpersonal standard for judging an agent's inner vocation – the moral philosophers' typical concern about the quality of the motives of action – was exclusively secular. All knowledge others could attain about that inner vocation was to be inferred from the agent's life-long manifestation of it in outwardly visible action. This standard was not far from the ancient, eudaimonistic notion of the man of virtue leading an individually satisfying and morally good life. Regardless of his personal deistic convictions, the ethics that Jefferson thought recommendable to others was of purely social character.

It is a conspicuous feature of Jefferson's moral thought that he never defined the term "happiness." His refusal to answer this theoretical question marks the point where we may gain an image of Jefferson as a champion of modern, individualistic humanity – but only at the cost of viewing him as a philosopher. Neither did he claim to be one. He was a politician, who preached the gospel of free, democratic government in which all free men would equally exercise individual moral responsibility.

What, then, was new under the sun after the revolution of 1800? The novelty consisted in the "mighty wave of public opinion" producing a "peaceable & legitimate" change within the already republican form of government through popular elections. This new phenomenon, superseding "all appeal to force," consisted of an electoral "recovery from delusion" into which the nation had almost fallen under the yoke of the Federalist "bigots."[10] In contrast to the revolution of 1776, this revolution was "not effected indeed by the sword, as that, but by the rational and peaceable instrument of reform, the suffrage of the people."[11] Resisting the backward-looking "bigots in religion and politics" in the name of general enlightenment could succeed only by providing the citizenry with elementary education and general male suffrage. This is the core of Jefferson's absolute commitment to civil government, which, in his progressive worldview, was not the problem but the solution.

The rest of this chapter aims to offer a more detailed overview of how Jefferson's progressive worldview was linked to his faith in free democracy. Jefferson's optimism rested on the recent intellectual revolution brought about by his celebrated triumvirate of Francis Bacon, John Locke, and Isaac Newton. The novel, Baconian notion of increasing knowledge meant that a man of the Enlightenment was constantly dealing with imperfect knowledge. From such a fundamentally temporalized epistemological position arose Jefferson's extended concept of "true religion" as equally reconcilable with Christian benevolence and with Newtonian physics. By the same token, his embrace of the ancient virtue of prudence kept him from claiming his personal deism as an absolute, and it also kept his worldview consistent with belief in intellectual and ethical improvement of mankind. Finally, Jeffersonian progress did not run on autopilot.[12] Both the utopians and the traditionalists were bound to miss the point of progressive politics: Steps forward would be permanent only when achieved by democratic, piecemeal reforms – including the gradual abolition of American slavery. However, in order to grasp the link between Jeffersonian progress and his faith in free government, it is important to first distinguish the political concept of progress from the disciplinary notion of history as knowledge of the past.

PROGRESS IN HISTORY

In defining Jefferson's progressive view of history we need to distinguish the concept of progress from the concept of history. As a modern academic discipline, history offers us knowledge of the past. In doing so, the discipline tends to suspend judgment about the future. It may concede that, in the future, humankind will undergo new revolutions as epoch-making as once were the Copernican Revolution, the industrial revolution, the birth of modern quantum mechanics, or the invention of nuclear weapons. But one may always ask whether, for example, the invention of nuclear weapons was a progressive event or only an inescapably significant event. This is why most present-day historians prefer to keep their distance from the idea of progressive history.[13] Distinguishing what is progressive from what is not progressive cannot rest on historical contemplation. It arises from value choices. And to the degree that these value choices have to do with our shared human future, they are also political.

Examining Jefferson's belief in the presumably progressive history, one needs first to distinguish it from his dismissal of certain kinds of historiography for purely political reasons. "History in general," Jefferson asserted, "only informs us what bad government is."[14] He famously dismissed David Hume as a too monarchist-minded historian, who wasted his undeniable elegance in discrediting "the good principles of the government."[15] For similar reasons, Jefferson fiercely opposed John Marshall's openly Federalist interpretation of the history of the Revolution and sought desperately to find a historian to set the record straight.[16]

Neither should one draw hasty conclusions from Jefferson's recommendation that schoolchildren study history in order to "qualify them as judges of the actions and designs of men," and not only men of the past but also "of the future."[17] The notion that history can provide information about the future suggests that history repeats itself. At first glance, Jefferson's recommendation appears to have drawn on the ancient idea of history as the preceptor of life (*magistra vitae*), revealing all essential elements of human life as they have been and always will be. Yet, had Jefferson taken this paradigm as the sum of all history, he would have found the very idea of progress inconceivable. Jefferson was recommending a much more restricted view – the view that even in the course of progressive history humankind is unlikely to rid itself of the undesirable aspects of human nature.[18]

That Jefferson saw the undesirable aspects of human nature playing an important role in history is sufficiently demonstrated in his 1810 lamentation about the Napoleonic Wars:

> It has been peculiarly unfortunate for us, personally, that the portion of history of mankind, at which we were called to take a share in the direction of their affairs, was such an one as history never before presented.... [T]he hurricane which is now blasting the world, physical and moral, has prostrated all the mounds of reason as well as right. All those calculations which, at any other period, would have been deemed

honorable, of the existence of a moral sense in man, individually or associated, of the connection which the laws of nature have established between his duties and his interests, of a regard for honest fame and the esteem of our fellow men, have been a matter of reproach on us, as evidences of imbecility.[19]

This passage gives a fairly complete picture of Jefferson's understanding of history. First, Jefferson situated himself in a particularly unfortunate "portion of history of mankind," referring to the lengthy European power struggle, which had turned dreadfully dangerous to Americans as well. This world conflagration had nothing do with the American revolutionary legacy, nor even with the remnants of French revolutionary ideals. As Jefferson made clear in the same letter, it was a mere power struggle between Napoleon, the chief "apostle of the desolation of men and morals" on land, and the British nation, "the tyrant of ocean."[20]

To gloss Jefferson's view of man and history in light of this letter, it is useful to consider what he there assumed about the extra-historical human condition. The European struggle had eventually turned into a "hurricane which is now blasting the world, physical and moral." It had, moreover, not only "prostrated all the mounds of reason and right" but also all honest "calculations" of "the existence of a moral sense in man, individually or associated, of the connection which the laws of nature have established between his duties and interests."[21] In the spirit of ancient Stoics, Jefferson here depicted the human condition as inherently related to the idea of seeking conformity with the natural as well as the moral ordering of the world. As a natural creature, man was endowed with reason and moral sense reflecting that fundamentally twofold ordering of reality.

Jefferson's remark about the "existence of a moral sense in man, individually or associated," conveys the crucial point of his personal moral faith, namely that such a sense provides us with the notion of the "laws of nature" as having established a link between "our duties and interests."[22] In the Napoleonic wars Jefferson witnessed yet another human failure to accommodate to this twofold ordering of the world. The responsibility for such failures he placed, not on any extra-human agency in history, but on the shoulders of human beings alone.

Jefferson's most famous statement bespeaking a progressive view of history occurs in his 1824 letter to William Ludlow. There the American continent appears as an exemplary case of the then-commonplace four-stage scheme of history, speaking to the "progress of man from the infancy of creation to the present day."[23] Jefferson's landscape of progressive history unfolded with a "philosophic observer" making an eastward journey through the American continent.

First, the philosopher encountered "the savages of the Rocky Mountains." Clothed in "skins of wild beasts," they represented the most primitive, "earliest stage of association" among humans. What followed, moving eastward, was "the pastoral state" of some more advanced Indian nations. The third stage was represented by "the pioneers of the advance of civilization," while the fourth, the "most improved state" of man was located in the American seaport towns. Here Jefferson clearly subscribed to the standard, eighteenth-century theory of society proceeding from primitive associations of hunting and gathering through pastoral and agricultural stages up to the commercial phase of society. This historicized image of the American landscape hardly qualifies as testimony to any genuine cultural pluralism on his part.[24]

But the Ludlow letter conveys a good deal more about Jefferson's intellectual outlook than merely his commitment to the four-stage theory of history. Three points are worth attention here. First, Jefferson's passing remark about the seaport towns as the cradle of civilization does not highlight any Adam Smith–inspired economic thesis of increasing productivity as the crucial criterion for human progress. The seaport towns linked America to the international Atlantic world of Western civilization, and the four-stage theory of history held commerce, not industrialization, as essential to the rise of civilization.[25]

Second, in view of Jefferson's outspoken "moral and physical preference of the agricultural, over the manufacturing man,"[26] the most striking feature of the Ludlow letter is that the white pioneer settlers – Jefferson's otherwise idealized husbandmen – comprised but a class of "our own semi-barbarous citizens." One may infer that Jefferson saw a potential, Turnerian closing of the frontier as implicating that both the savage and the semi-barbarian pioneer were already subjected to the grand process of civilization.

Third, the letter offers no definition of even the desirable end result of that process. It is about a man of Enlightenment in history, not about the end of history. This is best seen in Jefferson's almost ironically self-centered remark that "this march of civilization advancing from the seacoast" was about civilization manifesting itself in "increasing our knowledge and improving our condition." Expanding on this point, he declared that "we are at this time more advanced in civilization here than the seaports were when I was a boy." In other words, the once most advanced phase of civilization in the colonial seaports had been surpassed even in inland Virginia during Jefferson's own lifetime.

This much Jefferson claimed about history as an observable past from the perspective of his own present. About the future he stated: "Where this progress will stop no one can say." This ambiguously both moderate and bold prophecy about the future is worth a closer look. He formulated the case more fully thus: "Where this progress will stop no one can say. Barbarism has, in the meantime, been receding before the steady step of amelioration; and will in time, I trust, disappear from the earth."[27] The elimination of barbarism is where Jefferson's vision and hopes merged into each other.

What, then, did barbarism represent for Jefferson? Ancient Greek philosophy could exclude barbarians as simply uninteresting because of their incapacity to emulate the apparently natural, polis-centered Greek civilization.

Jefferson, by contrast, was convinced that a universal turn toward "amelioration" among humankind had taken place. Still, throughout his life he needed to resist barbarism. For example, Native American women appeared to be "submitted to unjust drudgery," which Jefferson maintained was "the case with every barbarous people."[28] He also spoke of the "barbarism of our Indian aborigines," who opposed "by ignorance the overwhelming mass of light & science."[29] Certainly under the British influence, Jefferson contended, they "will relapse into barbarism and misery."[30] In an 1812 letter to John Adams, Jefferson gloomily noted that the Native Americans' "steady habits permit no innovations, not even those which the progress of science offers to increase the comforts, enlarge the understanding, and improve the morality of mankind."[31] Here one has arrived at the Jeffersonian threefold conception of progress, consisting of the economic, educational, and moral improvement of humankind.

In addition to the savage way of life among the Indians, Jefferson found various other modes of barbarism that should recede "before the steady step of amelioration." In discussing the American Colonization Society's goal of sending slaves back to Africa, he held that even a small portion of former slaves, trained and educated in America, could prove to be a "blessing in the end to that country." Emigrating "from a country possessing all the useful arts," they could "carry back to the country of their origin, the seeds of civilization."[32]

Barbarism also abounded in international relations. Jefferson once considered that "morality occupied an honorable chapter in the political code of nations" until the "barbarous government" of Russia for the first time divided Poland with Prussia and Austria in the middle of the eighteenth century. These developments had eventually turned into the world conflagration between the British and the French – to the extent that in 1816 one "saw the moral world thrown back again to the age of the Borgias, to the point from which it had departed 300. [sic] years before."[33]

Worse still, barbarism continued to flourish in the heartland of Jefferson's progressive America. There were much more dangerous barbarian groups than Native Americans, African Americans, and the semi-barbarous white pioneers of the West. In the heyday of the Revolution of 1800, Jefferson referred to the group of "barbarians" seeking to "bring back the times of Vandalism, when ignorance put everything into the hands of power & priestcraft."[34] These barbarians comprised all antirepublican American "tories" organized in and around the Federalist Party.[35] They were the backward-looking bigots who thought it best to "recur to the annals of our ancestors for what is most perfect in government, in religion & learning."[36] Their reactionary temperament arose from a doctrinaire denial of "the improvability of the human mind, in science, in ethics, in government etc."[37] Jefferson rejected such pessimism: "I shall not die without a hope that light and liberty are on a steady advance." Hence, "science and liberties" appeared in simple opposition to "barbarism and despotism."[38]

In sum, barbarism served as shorthand for everything that opposed Jefferson's Enlightenment-inspired hope for human improvement in understanding, in material welfare, and in moral conduct. It is not surprising, then, that Jefferson constantly contrasted the "ignorance, poverty and vice" of urban masses with the positive forces of the Enlightenment era that eventually "liberated the ideas of those men who read and reflect."[39] In the Ludlow letter he spoke of the progress of "our knowledge" and "our condition," but without setting any point at which such amelioration would stop.[40] Obviously, he was dealing with something more than just an image of the past. Progress characterized an essentially ongoing experience. History – or, to be more precise, Jefferson's personal experience of human time – had a direction.

Given that Jefferson believed in human progress, the fundamental question to be asked about his image of history is whether progress had been there all along. Jefferson knew of numerous earlier civilizations that had flourished and collapsed. He definitely shared the conventional view that the Renaissance led Christendom "out of Gothic darkness" by revitalizing ancient Greco-Roman philosophy and political thought.[41] The fall of feudal society around 1500 marked the great transition to the early modern era together with such other epoch-making events as the Reformation, the introduction of print and gunpowder in Europe, and the European discovery of the New World.[42]

Jefferson was also aware of the transient nature of great civilizations beyond Europe, as is indicated by the extracts from Voltaire that he copied into his legal commonplace book. It was noted in the extracts, for instance, that the Chinese had invented gunpowder well prior to its introduction in Europe and that their highly developed geometry predated the Euclidian one.[43] Yet, these genuinely remarkable human achievements deserved only passing notice in Enlightenment-era world history. Given this evidence of transience, which developments had "locked" human history so that universal degeneration was no longer likely to recur?

In the records of world history even Jefferson found only one "compleat [sic] eclipse of the human mind," the standard image of the dark Middle Ages. Its origins lay in the equally standard notion that "Northern barbarians" invaded and destroyed "the countries and governments of the civilized world" from the year 400 onward.[44] Should such a complete eclipse recur, however, Jefferson wrote, "the art of printing alone, and the vast dissemination of books, will maintain the mind where it is, and raise the conquering ruffians to the level of the conquered, instead of degrading these to that of their conquerors."[45] He attributed this monumental achievement to the influence of the ever-widening "republic of letters" within Western civilization.

Yet genuinely innovative progress, already transcending ancient philosophy and hopefully continuing into the future, could not be about a mere revival. It was Jefferson's sacred triumvirate of Francis Bacon, John Locke, and Isaac Newton that had brought about this notion of a continuous, human improvement. He contrasted these "three greatest men the world had ever produced" with Hamilton's antirepublican, if not downright childish, suggestion that the greatest hero of human history was Julius Caesar.[46] In the most fundamental terms, Jefferson claimed that his triumvirate had "laid the foundation of those superstructures which have been raised in the Physical & Moral Sciences."[47]

Even though this new foundation of all sciences maintained the ancient division between natural and moral knowledge, it made knowledge itself progressive. The Baconian man of science was supposed to explore yet unknown natural phenomena rather than to regard Aristotle's metaphysics as a fixed system incorporating everything worthy of human contemplation.[48] The Newtonian law of gravity was natural in a strikingly new sense. It was a law of nature equally true of the planets as of every natural being on earth. Regardless of certain ambiguities in Jefferson's commitment to John Locke's philosophy, it is clear that he considered Locke, first and foremost, as the forefather of empirical science and of the systematic exploration of the human mind. Moreover, Jefferson thought this approach fundamental to modern moral sciences.

Locke's influence is of course present throughout Jefferson's ethical thought, beginning with the Declaration of Independence as an unequivocal expression of the most enduring Lockean legacy in political science, the right to armed resistance. What made Locke a crucial innovator in moral sciences were certain decidedly secular aspects of his philosophy, aspects that related ethics to political thought in a new manner.

THE NEW PARADIGM OF MORAL THOUGHT

It is hardly in question that Jefferson saw John Locke as a contributor to the progress of ethics, namely as a follower of the so-called natural lawyers' new paradigm of moral science. To grasp the linkage, it is useful to begin with Jefferson's ethical conception of Christianity. "In developing our duties to others," Jefferson thought, the ancient moralists had been deficient. While correctly embracing "the circles of kindred and friends" and teaching genuine patriotism and justice toward one's fellow citizens, the Greeks and the Romans had failed "to embrace with benevolence the whole family of mankind."[49] Universal benevolence was the unique innovation that the historical Jesus had introduced to moral studies. But things had gone wrong with the "superstructures" that had been laid in moral sciences after Jesus and prior to Locke's "new foundation."

The historical Jesus, Jefferson insisted, had provided "the purest system of morals ever before preached" in human history.[50] Unfortunately, according "to the ordinary fate of those who attempt to enlighten and reform mankind," Jesus soon fell victim to the conservative, religious establishment.

Neither had "the course of his preaching, which was but of about 3. [sic] years, presented occasions for developing a compleat [sic] system of morals."[51] Even if Jesus had a complete system, it could not be found in the New Testament. Jefferson was convinced that Matthew, Mark, Luke, and John were too simple and uneducated to grasp Jesus's message entirely, not to mention the later "corruptions of Christianity by the over learned" – that is, the Catholic Church fathers.[52]

The problem of the genuinely Christian system of morals derived in part from the dark medieval interim in the development of Western civilization. Pierre Bayle's famous *Dictionary* made fully clear that during the Middle Ages, Christian moral philosophers had thoroughly corrupted what was "natural" in the Christian religion, namely the inherent, human capacity to respect all mankind as God's creation on earth. Jefferson, who owned Bayle's book as a student, lamented the fact that "millions of innocent men, women, and children" had been "burnt, tortured, fined, imprisoned," and otherwise mistreated in the name of Christianity.[53]

Jean Barbeyrac's renowned preface to Samuel Pufendorf's *The Law of Nature and Nations* offers one a good insight into how medieval failures in developing Christian philosophy were related to moral science. Jefferson, as one might expect from an eighteenth-century lawyer, owned this volume in both English and French editions.[54] In his prefatory essay, titled "An Historical and Critical Account of the Science of Morality," Barbeyrac concluded that "Morality" was "almost banish'd out of the World by the public ministers of Religion" in the Middle Ages, and therefore "took Sanctuary amongst the Laics." Lawyers, in other words, took the lead in developing moral science so as not to "confound the Duties of Mankind in general, with the particular Duties of a Christian."[55]

What was this novel field of moral sciences like? Samuel Pufendorf's famous subscription to the traditional tripartite division of moral duties into those owed to God, to others, and to oneself also suggested a standard set of disciplines to study them. Theology revealed the duties to God, natural jurisprudence examined one's duties to others, and the more or less Christianized version of ancient virtue ethics explored one's duties to oneself.[56] Of these, natural jurisprudence was the primary field of study for an eighteenth-century lawyer, such as Thomas Jefferson.

From Pufendorf's famous predecessor Hugo Grotius onward, the so-called natural lawyers had developed a whole range of theoretical systems articulating a roster of minimal rules for peaceable social life. In view of the European religious wars, these lawyers understood it as their fundamental challenge to distinguish moral argumentation from religious disagreements among different Christian denominations. Regardless of all other motives, no religious reason qualified as an even formal justification for warfare any more. From this paradigmatic starting point of seventeenth-century academic jurisprudence arose, in turn, a theoretical scheme of human sociability under the moral law of God, prior not only to specific governmental arrangements, but also to any specific religious code of salvation. In Jefferson's citation of Montesquieu it thus appeared unproblematic to hold that one should not derive from the divine laws (*les loix divines*) the laws of men (*les loix humaines*), whereas the latter should not contradict natural law (*la loi naturelle*).[57]

Barbeyrac's history of moral science teemed with references to John Locke as the latest theoretician in the field of natural law. Locke's adherence to the commonplace natural jurisprudence of the time is worth keeping in mind when considering Jefferson's Lockean leanings. In *An Essay concerning Human Understanding*, Locke concurred with the natural lawyers that, even though sociable by nature, different people and peoples could embrace various "sorts of happiness."[58] The problem was that mere sociability did not at all self-evidently equal the Christian golden rule – "*To do as one would be done to.*" Locke's most provocative example of the asymmetry between mere sociability and the golden rule was to point out that some savages customarily treated their female captives of war as sex slaves and devoured their children in cannibal sacrifices. This abominable example was supposed to demonstrate that peacefully ordered societies could still violate the universal moral law.[59] In the Declaration of Independence, the American colonists expressed horrified indignation toward "the merciless Indian Savages, whose known rule of warfare is an undistinguished destruction of all ages, sexes and conditions." The primitive savages appeared ignorant of the Christian golden rule that applied to all mankind – a rule that, according to Locke, dictated the saving of the *innocents*, even in war.[60]

It is illuminating to consider briefly the moral rationale of Jefferson's revolutionary thinking in view of these concepts of innocence and warfare under natural law. In essence, the law of nature, in Locke's well-known phrase, provided every man with the rightful power "*of doing whatsoever he thought fit for the Preservation of himself* and the rest of Mankind."[61] Thus, the fundamental dictate of the law of nature involved both a man's right to self-preservation and the duty to respect the whole rest of mankind in terms of their universal rights to life, liberty, and property. Because of inherent human selfishness, Locke further argued, "it is unreasonable for Men to be Judges in their own Cases," which was why "God hath certainly appointed a Government to restrain the partiality and violence of Men."[62]

Were the government itself to violate the rights of men, men had the right to justified violence in the form of armed resistance. In resorting to war against the British regime, the American revolutionary slaveholders – such as Madison, Monroe, Jefferson, and Washington, for example – hardly qualified as innocents. Throughout the founding era, the status of innocents was reserved, not for those who in 1776 consented to fight for the goal of regaining their liberties, but for women, slaves, and children. These latter remained bystanders with regard to the kinds of conflicts the civil government was originally supposed to solve peacefully – political disagreements on taxes, on representation, on slavery, and the like. By contrast, every free man forfeited his innocence by his consent to the idea of government, under which he also protected the innocents.

In view of this, it is hardly surprising that the Revolution appeared to Jefferson as primarily a legal crisis caused by the British government's deviation from its own, Lockean principles of free government. As early as 1775, Jefferson proclaimed his first wish to be that of "a restoration of our just rights."[63] In his original draft of the Declaration of Independence, the rationale for resorting to armed resistance was expressed in terms of "the preservation of life, & liberty, & the pursuit of happiness."[64] The claim arose from the essentially juridical reciprocity of the rights of free men, a conception that necessarily marginalized all innocents as outsiders in peace and war equally. When Jefferson, years later, portrayed the nation as comprised of "constitutionally and conscientiously democrats," he also portrayed himself as a founding father loving them with parental affection. This did not mean that he regarded them as innocent infants. Instead, he saw them "as adults whom I freely leave to self-government."[65]

Even if the Revolution was only about regaining just government based on popular sovereignty, politics remained what it always had been – peaceful discussion on the needs of legal reforms. Consider, for example, how Jefferson occupied himself throughout the years of the Revolution. From 1774 onward, he served as a member of Virginia house of delegates, writing pamphlets on the meaning of the British constitution; in 1776, in addition to authoring the Declaration of Independence in the Continental Congress, he drafted his own suggestion for the constitution of Virginia; then he served as governor of the state; after that, he embarked on a thorough revision of Virginia's civil legislation and slave codes.

Regardless of Jefferson's occasional appraisal of rebellions as "medicine of the sound health of government,"[66] he never imagined that free government could be permanently based on any other citizen activity than constant, "peaceful deliberation," hopefully reflecting "the voice of the whole people." All questions of justice were to be "fairly, fully and peaceably expressed, discussed, and decided by the common reason of the society" in order to prevent any utopian crusaders from turning society back into a state of morally justified violence.[67] This is also why seizing the power from the Federalist "barbarians" in peaceful elections in 1800 was "as real a revolution in the principles of our government as that of 1776 was in its form."[68]

Jefferson viewed American democracy as a moral, human endeavor among other civilized nations seeking to achieve control of human selfishness. All human predicaments relating to justice and benevolence were to be solved democratically on a national level by taking into account the whole civilized Atlantic world – ideally the true empire of the law of nature and nations capable of genuine universal progress in religious freedom and governmental sciences. In this respect, Americans fared well in comparison to most others: according to Jefferson, the American "government, as it cherishes most it's duties to it's citizens, so is it the most exact in it's moral conduct towards other nations."[69]

As for the moral ramifications of all this, Jefferson never encountered a fully reliable theory of morality beyond the simple natural-law-derived notion that human sociability can be conceived of as moral insofar as it remains compatible with equal justice and benevolence toward the innocents – all those deemed outsiders in the conflicts of power among those deemed equals. For Jefferson, the human sense of justice was thus the key to distinctly human sociability, as opposed to forms of group coherence among social animals. This is how he formulated the case in 1787: "Man was destined for society. His morality therefore was to be formed to this object. He was endowed with a sense of right and wrong merely relative to this."[70] Or consider Jefferson's 1816 comment that "Man was created for social intercourse; but social intercourse cannot be maintained without a sense of justice; then man must have been created with a sense of justice."[71] Deep down, man was but an "an animal destined to live in society."[72] Jefferson also associated the human sense of justice with an instinctive moral sense of right and wrong. Such a moral sense, he claimed, belonged to the definition of man, even if it was not given in exactly equal strength to every individual.[73]

Moreover, Jefferson's socio-moral conception of man appears to have rested on the ancient, Stoic-inspired idea of there being a "connection which the laws of nature have established between" our "duties and interests."[74] It therefore appeared unproblematic to presume that "so invariably do the laws of nature create our duties and interests, that when they seem to be at variance, we ought to suspect some fallacy in our reasoning."[75] With this premise Jefferson embraced "but one system of ethics for men & nations": By simply remaining "faithful to all engagements and under all circumstances," an individual would promote "in the long run even the interests of both."[76]

With equal ease Jefferson mended the Lockean definition of "commonwealth" by equating civil rights with human interests. In his memorandum on Locke's commonwealth concept, Jefferson set the "rights" into parentheses and replaced them with "interests" so as to make commonwealth denote "a society of men constituted for preser[ving] their *civil (rights) interests*."[77] To his nephew Peter Carr, Jefferson explained that, by and large, it would be unproblematic "to pursue the interest of your country, the interests of your friends, and your own interest also, with the purest integrity, the most chaste honor."[78] But he held to his idea that duties equate with interests without any pretension that the tenet was scientifically demonstrable and thus true on any genuinely interpersonal level.

In sum, the seventeenth-century methodological turn of moral philosophy had distinguished questions of the afterlife from the moral law of nature as applicable to secular human life. This new natural law paradigm also provided the fundamental intellectual framework for Jefferson's famous wall of separation between church and state.[79] Notably, even his favorite eighteenth-century Scottish moralists held that an individual's religious convictions comprised the final stage of moral understanding rather than the starting point.[80] The wall was necessary for free government, which would never interfere with individual freedom of conscience.

"TRUE RELIGION"

Understanding Jefferson's belief in the progress of the human mind, "in matters of politics and religion," demands a radically expanded notion of religion itself.[81] Jefferson regularly associated the term "religion" with conceptions drawn from Baconian induction, Newtonian physics, and Lockean philosophy. Like all other fields of study, the realm of faith was to be kept open to new findings. "Had not the Roman government permitted free enquiry," Jefferson once mused, "Christianity could never have been introduced."[82] In 1821, he lamented the conservative revivalism occurring in Europe in the aftermath of the Napoleonic Wars. The Holy Alliance of Russia, Prussia, and Austria arising out of the ruins of the French revolution represented to him a new "cloud of barbarism and despotism," threatening to "obscure the science and liberties" of the civilized world.[83]

By and large, Jefferson's "religion" applied to a given individual's entire worldview, in both its naturalistic and its moral aspects. In his long discussion of "true religion" in the *Notes on the State of Virginia* he contrasted the term, not with skepticism or atheism, but with "religious slavery." Jefferson began the passage with the famous exclamation that "it does me no injury for my neighbour to say there are twenty gods, or no god." "Reason and free enquiry" were to be viewed as the "agents" for testing any particular precept of an individual's whole belief system. True religion was a foe of "error only."[84] As Jefferson formulated the case forty years later, a religious belief consisted in "the assent of the mind to an intelligible proposition."[85]

Most conspicuously, Jefferson's account of religion in the *Notes on the State of Virginia* involved both physical and moral branches of human understanding. Unlike religious slavery, true religion could well include Galileo's findings in the field of physics, reject Descartes's vortex theory of the universe, and embrace Newton's gravitation as an "article of necessary faith." This article of faith, Jefferson elaborated, was more firmly established on the basis of reason than it could ever be were any government to declare it so.[86] His intent here was not to contrast governmental authority and human reason, but to affirm the view that free government is one that abstains from defining reasonable research hypotheses.

A man of the Enlightenment needed first to acknowledge the Baconian distinction between the spirit of systematic examination and the spirit of system building, as the famous precept was put forward in the Preface to the French Encyclopedia.[87] Or, as the restrictions of contemporary scientific knowledge were formulated by Dugald Stewart, the most prominent representative of the Scottish Enlightenment personally known to Jefferson: "Whether, for example, the cause of gravitation be material or immaterial, is a point about which two Newtonians may differ, while they agree perfectly in their physical opinions."[88] What is more, the proverbial whole truth and nothing but the truth did not need to yield to human inquiry. Jefferson held that "Truth can stand by itself."[89]

The essential point about Jefferson's legendary optimism lies in its commitment to the Baconian notion of increasing knowledge. Even the conservative revivalist is future-oriented. In the eternal now of constantly advancing time, the conservative yearns for the recovery of the good-old times, tomorrow. By contrast, the progressive's present gains its meaning from the notion that something significant, now unknown, remains in the essentially unforeseeable future. This is why the person who believes in increasing knowledge claims to know less rather than more.

To illustrate the seminal importance of the distinction between knowing and believing in Jefferson's thought, let us consider his 1823 letter to John Adams. The letter includes Jefferson's most unequivocal assertion of an intelligent agent – or intelligent design – behind observable, constantly regenerating nature (and the apparently endless circulation of matter in innumerable forms in the universe). This exceptionally outspoken statement about the true character of the world starts off with Jefferson lamenting "that every Christian sect gives a great handle to Atheism by their general dogma that, without a revelation, there would not be sufficient proof of the being of a god."

Yet Jefferson's list of all possible evidence of God's existence does not lay claim to the status of truth, but only of the "more probable." After listing a number of "evident proofs of the necessity of a superintending power to maintain the Universe in it's course and order," Jefferson suddenly changed the perspective altogether. He turned the problem into one between two hypotheses rather than two truth claims – the first one held by Christians and deists and the second one held by a handful of atheists:

> So irresistible are these evidences of an intelligent and powerful Agent that, of the infinite numbers of men who have existed thro' all time, they have believed, in the proportion of a million at least to Unit, in the hypothesis of an eternal pre-existence of a creator, rather than in that of a self-existent Universe. Surely this unanimous sentiment renders this more probable than that of the few in the other hypothesis.[90]

In other words, there were two fundamental hypotheses, one of a divine ordering of the universe and the other of a self-existent universe. Considering the probability of each in terms of majority opinion gave preference to the design hypothesis. But Jefferson was not arguing that knowledge is a matter of majority opinion. He had no intention to deny that empirical induction was commonly viewed as the simplest, scientifically valid method of seeking the truth. Indeed, in this same letter he concurred with atheists' skepticism about a "Creator of the world, a being whom we see not, and know not, of whose form substance and mode or place of existence, or of action no sense informs us."[91] In sum, neither hypothesis had anything to do with what an empiricist could hold certain.

Jefferson's reasoning about "the more probable" hypothesis, based as it was on common consent only, was distinguishable from what a given individual should consider reasonable to believe. As one of his favorite philosophers, Lord Kames, argued, it is "less difficult to conceive one eternal unchangeable being who made the world, than to conceive a blind chain of causes and effects." Yet even to Kames the crucial point was that as "we cannot find any inconsistency in the latter supposition, we cannot justly say that it is demonstrably false."[92] There was no way to distinguish between the reasoning of two individuals disagreeing on a subject on which both lacked undeniable empirical evidence. This is why Jefferson distinguished his own beliefs from those of others solely in terms of his own reasoning.

Indeed, Jefferson was remarkably consistent in distinguishing his personal beliefs about human essence and morality from that on which he thought all should agree.[93] Although he could consider individual happiness as the very "aim of life," he never defined happiness.[94] He sometimes referred to the secular, Epicurean notion of "tranquility" as "the greatest good of life,"[95] but could just as easily proclaim that every American is free to aspire to "the happiness of man here and his greater happiness hereafter."[96] In sum, Jefferson neither denied his own belief in the afterlife nor insisted that the concept of human happiness entails such a belief.[97]

On the fundamental premises of such a position, Jefferson argued that he could personally refute even the Christian doctrine of the trinity and still "claim a right to believe in one god, if so my reason tells me."[98] Or, as he lectured his young protégé, Peter Carr: "Your own reason is the only oracle given you by heaven" for considering religious issues, even if you would end up with "a belief that there is no god." The moral point could hardly be made more explicitly than Jefferson did when insisting that on this issue "you are answerable not for the rightness but uprightness of the decision."[99]

The doctrine was simple. If you do not, first of all, remain true to yourself, you will be untrue to others. In view of such an appeal to an individual's conscience alone, Jefferson's claims about the human essence were decidedly modest. They did not depend on whether or not the human being has a soul to be saved. Personally Jefferson claimed to be a Christian. But when depicting himself as "a free moral agent," he insisted, above all, on having "never submitted the whole system of my opinions to the creed of any party of men whatever in religion, in philosophy, in politics, or in anything else."[100]

Jefferson's moral outlook was resolutely and exclusively secular – regardless of his own religious convictions.

As has been shown, Jeffersonian "true religion" emanated from a general, inductive approach to different philosophical views about truth. In full accordance to that position, Jefferson's belief in scientific progress rested on the simple tenet of not holding to be true what could turn out to be untrue upon future investigation.[101] This temporalized epistemology was inherently linked to his commitment to the ancient virtue of prudence.

PRUDENCE AND PROGRESS

The Stoic-inspired, Epicurean ideal of the wise man, whose key virtue was prudence, was precisely what kept Jefferson's intellectual outlook consistent regarding the flip side of progressive knowledge, the yet unknown.[102] There is ample evidence that Jefferson found the ancient Epicurean, eudaimonistic virtue ethics personally important at least as far back as the early 1780s. His most famous endorsement of Epicureanism, however, occurs in his 1814 letter to William Short.[103]

Jefferson's summary of Epicurean morality in the Short letter begins with a view of human happiness as nothing less than the very "aim of life." Virtue was "the foundation of happiness," representing the sole "means" for attaining it, and "Utility [was] the test of virtue." At the end of the syllabus one encounters the classical catalog of the four cardinal virtues common to Plato, Cicero, and Epicurus, among many others: prudence, temperance, fortitude, and justice. The opposites of these Jefferson listed as "1. Folly. 2. Desire. 3. Fear. 4. Deceit."[104] The opposition of prudence to sheer "folly" indicates that it was an intellectual rather than a moral virtue, although related to an ethically charged notion of human happiness as the very aim of life.

An illuminating example of Jefferson's use of the concept of prudence appears in his advice of 1814 to one Doctor Jones on what to write about George Washington's character in American history books. Jefferson's historical assessment of the greatest hero of the Revolution began with an unlikely comparison of Washington to "a Newton, Bacon, or Locke." Rhetorically, the comparison belittled Washington's intellect in order to underline the idea that "the strongest feature in his character was prudence." Prudence epitomized Washington's disposition of "never acting until every circumstance, every consideration, was maturely weighed; refraining if he saw a doubt." After adding that the president's "integrity was most pure, his justice the most inflexible I have ever known," Jefferson concluded that one could see in Washington "in every sense of the words, a wise, a good, and a great man."[105]

Prudence was distinguishable from Washington's intellect as well as from his admirably inflexible sense of justice. Washington's personal disposition to consider all circumstances from a standpoint of rational doubt, together with his admirable sense of justice, sufficed to make him a genuinely wise man. Clearly, in this usage, prudence meant one's permanent disposition to adhere to a kind of overall precautionary principle. The principle underlies Jefferson's most characteristic epistemological assertions – made time and time again in the *Notes on the State of Virginia* – that error is worse than ignorance and that any naturalistic or moral truth claim must bear the test of "reason and free inquiry." In Jeffersonian individualism, virtue remained an individually acquirable moral character trait, always associated with wisdom. Wisdom was not knowledge, but an intellectual, prudent attitude to all human claims about truth. Under free government, an individual's submission to contemporary majority opinion was always qualified by the prerogative to openly question the truth value of that opinion.

Even a look at the Declaration of Independence suggests some of the ethical ramifications of prudence. Only the "long train of abuses" by the British crown could convince the colonists that "it is their right, it is their duty, to throw off such Government." The previous sentence held that "Prudence, indeed, will dictate that Governments long established should not be changed for light and transient causes."[106] Prudence was needed in real-life ethical considerations whenever the exact dictates of natural law remained debatable. As late as 1824, Jefferson suggested that the general, constitutional balance between American state governments and the federal one arose from "the prudence of both parties."[107]

The most telling example of Jefferson's adherence to prudence can be found in his retrospective account of the French Revolution, written to Lafayette in 1815. As Jefferson reminisced, in 1789 he had thought it best for the French to compromise with the king so as to secure at least limited political and civil freedom. He now readily admitted that Lafayette had been right to insist that the French were ripe for a truly constitutional monarchy of the mode of 1791. Unfortunately, the well-meaning radicals – whom Jefferson viewed as "closet politicians merely, unpracticed in the knowledge of men" – took over only to lose their good cause to Robespierre and eventually to Napoleon. But the core point of Jefferson's apparent compliment to Lafayette's political instinct of 1789 lay in the rationale he offered for his own, seemingly too timid stand at the time. As he explained it, his intention was to gain time for "the amelioration of the condition of the people," until they would be "capable of more." While radicals' "imprudence of giving up the certainty of such a degree of liberty" proved disastrous, Jefferson's prudence, even if at first bordering on cowardice, was wiser in leaving open the possibility of moving further later on.[108]

The peaceful deliberation of all questions of justice and fair play among free men was requisite of sound politics even in Jefferson's confessedly progressive worldview. He held that "[s]uch indeed are the different circumstances, prejudices, and habits of different nations, that the constitution of no one would be reconcilable to any other in every point." The guiding principle thus remained the "judicious selection of the parts of each suitable to any other" that comprised "all which prudence should attempt."[109] Neither was Jefferson alone in his conviction that free government was of mere human creation. "All government is but an imperfect remedy for the deficiency" of human "wisdom and virtue," Adam Smith opined.[110]

INNOVATIONS IN POLITICAL SCIENCE

In order to cast light on Jefferson's conviction that modern, representative government was nothing but a government of law by the consent of the ruled and a moral concept at that, it is useful to consider briefly how the contemporary innovations in political and social sciences fit into the picture. James Madison characterized the great Montesquieu not as "a Newton or a Locke, who established immortal systems, the one in matter, the other in mind," but as the leading figure in the "particular science" of politics comparable to "Bacon in universal science."[111]

Montesquieu was a conceptually magnificent empiricist who pointed out that regardless of all the erudite distinctions between different historical forms of governments, the basic point in political science was to distinguish despotic, corrupt governments from the monarchist and the republican forms of government. Even his celebrated theoretical division of governmental powers into the legislative, the executive, and the judicial drew on the already existing British constitutional system.

Montesquieu's apparently relativist distinctions between the monarchist principle of honor, the republican principle of virtue, and the despotic principle of fear did not go unnoticed among his contemporaries. A lesser-known French scholar, Destutt de Tracy, dedicated his *A Critical Commentary and Review of Montesquieu's Spirit of Laws* to prove many Montesquieu's doctrines morally untenable. Jefferson not only helped translate Destutt's book-length critique of Montesquieu from French into English, but also preferred the volume to Chipman's and Priestley's political writings, as well as to *The Federalist Papers*. He considered this book the best "in the world" in political science, particularly as it was "equally sound and corrective of political economy."[112] Destutt de Tracy's critique arose from Montesquieu's association of honor and virtue with different governmental forms, as if true honor was not as distinguishable from false honor as virtue was distinguishable from vice. Hence, despotism should have been defined not as concomitant with the principle of fear, but simply as abuse of just governmental powers.[113]

Destutt de Tracy – who considered it obvious that "the human mind is progressive in the social as in all other sciences" – provided Jefferson's imagination with much more than a mere critique of Montesquieu. He discerned only three phases of civilization, all of them epitomizing certain general patterns of thinking and the corresponding political modes of society.

According to de Tracy, "democracy or despotism were the first governments imagined by men, and mark the first degree of civilization." In this phase, it was "ignorance which governs or force that dictates." At the second stage of history, "opinions are formed, and religion has the greatest power," so as to procure "aristocracy under one or more chiefs, whatever name may be given to it." Only once "reason begins to prevail and philosophy has more influence" may people attain a "representative democracy under one or several delegates." In sum, it was representative democracy that comprised the "new invention, which forms and constitutes the third degree of civilization."[114]

Destutt de Tracy thus argued that sheer ignorance may bring about pure democracy just as well as pure despotism. This ambiguity resulted from his central claim that, not democracy, but representative democracy is the regime by which man may gain control over the future course of the human condition. "The introduction of this new principle of representative democracy," Jefferson famously held, "has rendered useless almost everything written before on the structure of government."[115]

Not at all surprisingly, Jefferson's views of Native-American nations appear compatible with Destutt de Tracy's threefold concept of progress as related to the varying modes of human associations. "The present state of the several Indian tribes, without any public order of priests," sufficed to convince Jefferson that they were free from the spell of theocracy. Instead, all their ceremonies, public and private, were customarily held by "the worthies of the nation."[116] Occasionally Jefferson also found Indian nations embracing democracy, with "parties among them adhering to different leaders, and governed by their advice, not by their command."[117] But only in 1812 did he find some of the once merciless savages so much "advanced in civilisation" as to be capable of instituting "regular representative" governments among themselves.[118] Again, one encounters Jefferson's commitment to free, representative government as the requisite of human progress.

Progress would prevail over backward developments only insofar as the politically empowered remained willing to countenance the further extension of equal justice to all free men and to show benevolence to all others. There is no need to portray Jefferson as a minimal-government ideologue in order to grasp the fundamentals of his progressive politics. His apparently liberal animosity to excessive government was not inspired by any distinctly antigovernment convictions. It grew solely out of hostility toward the early modern society of orders, often called the *ancien régime*.

By and large, the European society of orders was based not on the equal rights of all men, but on exclusive privileges apportioned according to the presumably natural orders of men. Such privileges ranged from royal concessions of monopolies to shoemakers to innumerable royal and clerical regulations concerning property, inheritance, and trade, as well as commendable individual conduct and decent opinions. This roster of regulations pertained equally, even if differently, to all men, whether aristocrats, gentlemen, merchants, artisans, peasants, cottagers, or servants.[119] The main rule was simple: Whatever was not explicitly permitted remained prohibited. Seventeenth-century political absolutism has sometimes been characterized as nothing but a fully secularized version of this, presumably divinely recommended, universal model of human society.[120]

Contrary to this whole mode of thought, Jefferson argued that in France, as elsewhere, the liberation of internal and international commerce, reform of criminal law, and establishment of nationwide popular elections would constitute "a great mass of improvement in the condition of the people."[121] Similarly, his advocacy of religious freedom and his role in banning restrictions on free inheritance in Virginia appear to support the image of Jefferson as an Adam Smith–inspired liberal. Jefferson wholeheartedly embraced the blessings of the nascent industrial revolution, even if he never fully realized it was about something more than a gradual development of time-saving gadgets for husbandry. He took pride in his slave-run nail factory at the Monticello plantation, hailed the invention of the cotton gin as well as the construction of the Erie Canal, and showed keen interest in patent legislation. Perhaps the most characteristic example of his economic concerns was his commitment to acquire reliable statistics about population growth and gross national production in order to determine taxation and the proper amount of currency to circulate.[122]

But does Jefferson's famous agrarian vision of the free yeoman as the backbone of American freedom fit into this picture?[123] The divergence is apparent, not real, if one is careful not to confuse principles with policies. Jefferson's preference for the yeoman over the manufacturing man derived from the historical evidence that the "mobs of great cities add just so much to the support of pure government as sores do to the strength of body."[124] The logical solution was to let the Europeans produce the manufactured goods for the American husbandmen. In fact, this tenet drew on the simple presumption that as one nation among other civilized nations, Americans would be better off remaining agricultural and civilized rather than becoming industrial and urban.

This was not to question commerce as a prerequisite of civilization itself. Well before the Revolution, Jefferson had argued that access to "international free trade with all parts of the world" was "possessed by the American colonists, as of natural right."[125] Once the Napoleonic wars halted Atlantic trade altogether, Jefferson changed his opinion about domestic manufacturing. He had never denied the American need for the manufactured "comforts." The interruption of international trade called for a change in national policy, not in principles. "He, therefore," Jefferson averred in the midst of the Napoleonic Wars, "who is now against domestic manufacture, must be reducing us either to dependence" on that European power struggle "or to be clothed in skins."[126]

In sum, there is little evidence for any utopian leanings in Jefferson's statecraft.[127] He aspired to achieve control of all kinds of contemporary social developments. Control over socioeconomic developments is political power. Control over the improvement of "the human mind, in science, in ethics, in government" is even more so.[128] And if anything, Jefferson was a politician to the bone.

The Jeffersonian ideal of self-government rested on the extension of democratic rights to all free men and on their active participation in directing – and gaining control over – all kinds of social developments in their own community. Yet, against Jefferson's constant calls from 1776 on to adopt universal male suffrage, even in his home state, approximately half of white, free male Virginians remained excluded from the ballot well after his death in 1826.[129]

ANTI-UTOPIAN NOTION OF POLITICS

Jefferson's much discussed loss of optimism, which some scholars date to his retirement years, appears rather an omnipresent trait of his intellectual outlook.[130] Moreover, it is worth asking to what extent he relied on any given progress of history itself. In the immediate aftermath of the Revolution he already concerned himself with the threat of the people's loss of control of their government as the result of their sole concentration on making money.[131] Only a couple of months after the inaugural of George Washington's first presidential term in 1789, Jefferson asserted that "no society can make a perpetual constitution, or even a permanent law."[132]

Achieving political control of general social developments could realize the human potential for progress. Losing control would result in degeneration and eventual chaos. This perception underlies Jefferson's sometimes desperate advocacy of the French Revolution. In the so-called Adam and Eve letter of 1793 he defended the early phase of Jacobin terror by holding that "the liberty of the whole earth was depending" on the developments in France. Hyperbolically, he went on to proclaim that were "there but an Adam & an Eve left in every country, & left free," the world "would be better than it now is."[133]

During the 1790s, Jefferson spent most his energies in defending the idea of free government against both real and imagined threats on the part of the Federalist "barbarians." He resigned from Washington's cabinet in 1794 in a fit of moral fury. Even as vice-president he opposed the John Adams administration's infamous Alien and Sedition acts, which appeared to nullify the very idea that a free citizenry could criticize its own government.

The Revolution of 1800 itself turned out to be but a brief catching of breath. Only five years after assuming the presidency, Jefferson again called for a thorough recommitment to the fundamentals of American freedom. "Convinced that the people are the only safe depositories of their own liberty, & that they are not safe unless enlightened to a certain degree," Jefferson reflected, "I have looked on our present state of liberty *as a short-lived possession* unless the mass of the people could be informed."[134] Obviously, along with the basics of modern natural and moral sciences, people needed to be informed that "Human nature is the same on every side of the Atlantic."[135]

Again, during the war of 1812, history manifested itself in sheer "acts of barbarism which do not belong to a civilized age," when British "Vandalism" culminated in the burning of the nation's capital.[136] At the end of the decade Jefferson was appalled by the Missouri crisis. At that time, Northern hardcore abolitionists appeared ready to dissolve the Union, thus leaving the sage of Monticello to "die in the belief" of the ultimate uselessness of the sacrifices made by "the generation of 1776, to acquire self-government and happiness to their country."[137]

Only a year before his death, Jefferson still called for perseverance in pursuing the American "great experiment which shall prove that man is capable of living in society, governing itself by laws self-imposed, and securing its members the enjoyment of life, liberty, property, and peace."[138] He felt it necessary to add that "even when the government of its [people's] choice shall manifest a tendency to degeneracy," one should not despair, but "recall it to original and legitimate principles, and restrain it with the rightful limits of self-government."[139] Hence, the commitment to mere popular sovereignty could protect neither public opinion nor the government dependent on that opinion from moral erosion. As late as 1820, even free Virginians were to be saved "from the degradation of becoming the Barbary of the Union." They appeared to be "sinking into the barbarism of our Indian aborigines," if not "falling into the ranks of our own negroes."[140]

In the final analysis, Jefferson's belief in any evidently progressive history appears to fall apart. His famous principle of generational independence – notably first argued in reference to free Virginians – held that "Each generation is as independent as the one preceding." As in Virginia, so in its "sister states," each generation possessed "a right to choose for itself the form of government it believes most promotive of its own happiness."[141] This principle remained valid in regard to not only the "progressive advances of the human mind," but all kinds of "changes in human affairs."[142]

History could still bring about backward development in the civilized world as in the case of the Napoleonic Wars. Until the end of his life, Jefferson remained uncertain about Americans' capacity for maintaining their still rudimentary democracy. Were the goals of general education and the extension of democracy sacrificed, Jefferson predicted, "we shall go on, as other nations are doing, in the endless circle of oppression, rebellion, reformation; and oppression, rebellion, reformation again."[143]

Indeed, taking Jefferson at his word about the "endless circle of oppression," one must ask anew: Did he embrace a progressive or a cyclical understanding of history? Or was he simply concurring with the old quip that every time history repeats itself, the price gets higher? What Jefferson thought was that free, representative government could tame this endless, circular revolution into a political phenomenon.

To avert the sorry repetition, all that was required from an individual was to compromise with current majority opinion, even if only to change it. Within Jefferson's conflict-ridden view of humanity, civil society under government was a simple necessity for securing the essentially imperfect rights of man and for extending such rights to those still devoid of them. American society was only one among many political experiments in human morality. Its morality rested on the maxim that the national constituency and its representatives owed justice to their equals and benevolence to all other, more or less subordinated social groups, whether slaves, women, or children. And, even within the most democratic society, each generation would assume the same moral responsibility for promoting equality among the living.

Jefferson did not pretend to be a philosopher of history. Nor did he claim that history manifests itself solely in human progress. As to whether man could truly be "trusted with the government of himself," Jefferson thought it evident that even Americans needed to "Let history answer this question."[144] But history could provide the answer only in retrospect. As Jefferson lamented in 1810 about "the hurricane" of the Napoleonic Wars blasting both the physical and the moral world, history could still bring about either the elevation or the degeneration of humankind, collectively and individually, in time and place, generation by generation.[145] Only in this sense may any grand concept of history stay open-ended.

By and large, the open-ended notion of history draws on the simple epistemological point that the script of the grand narrative remains hidden from any individual living in its midst. It remains equally impossible to prove or disprove, for example, the Christian view of meaningful time as consisting of the rotary motion from the fall of man back to his redemption, a movement comprising only one, nonrecurrent cycle on the linear, historical timeline. Finally, insofar as it is impossible to foresee the end of all history, it is impossible to claim that history as a whole has a meaningful direction.[146]

To be sure, Jefferson's position differed slightly from this set of claims. He believed that something genuinely novel would unfold in the future. Yet, the direction of history remained open-ended, for Jefferson clearly held that the nature of such novelties was unforeseeable. Above all, he believed that the achievement and maintenance of free government, resting on enlightened majority opinion, was requisite for the narrative to retain its openendedness – in opposition to all kinds of short- and long-term prophecies of success or of failure.

At this point the figure of Jefferson ceases to appear as an eighteenth-century (meta-)historian and needs to be viewed as a politician with his own convictions about the desirable future. And regarding the desirable future, Jefferson's position was no more time-bound than ours is, whether thought of in terms of a utopian or a progressive vision. Professedly progressive political thought does not necessarily arise from utopianism. Consider, for example, Jefferson's comment on Mercier's renowned utopian writings: "Mercier has given us a vision of the year 2440, but prophecy is one thing, history another."[147] Jefferson kept utopian thought distinguishable from retrospective historical knowledge as well as from the politics related to the future.

A political progressive and a utopian differ not in their future orientation but in their attitude to the present. A utopian characteristically draws on ahistorical, abstract ideals and thus treats the past as insignificant to the future. A progressive politician, such as Jefferson claimed to be, sees the present as intimately related to the past, meaning that the so-called burden of history is precisely that with which a politician deals in his orientation to the future. For example, the eighteenth-century legal institution of slavery had to be dealt with as a legal problem of the present. Insofar as one was not suggesting a wholesale, perhaps violent denial of the contemporary legal order, the only way open was political action for change of the laws. In contrast to Jefferson's outspoken desire, there were many Americans who did not believe in equal justice enough to support the abolition of slavery – even in principle.

JEFFERSON'S ANTISLAVERY STANCE

Jefferson not only condemned slavery as an institution; he even subscribed to the slave's right to armed resistance under the moral law of nature. During the political upheaval that brought Jefferson to power in the elections of 1800, another "Revolution of 1800" was in the making. Gabriel Prosser, a literate slave blacksmith, devised a widespread slave conspiracy in Richmond and the surrounding Virginia counties in order to end slavery there and perhaps to found a separate black state within Virginia boundaries. Most of the leading figures of the conspiracy were skilled slaves and free blacks from Richmond and smaller towns nearby. The conspiracy, which had been in preparation for several months, was revealed in August 1800, and the whole scheme fell apart without a battle.

By late October, practically all those involved had been tried in the county courts, and Prosser and twenty-six of his followers were hanged. In the midst of the hangings and continuing trials, the white establishment tired of the process and realized that the executions cost too much. The state had to pay the owners considerable sums for their loss of property in executed and imprisoned slaves. The remnants of the black "army" – eight men and one woman in jail – were finally sold as slaves outside Virginia.[148]

The most striking aspect of Jefferson's attitude to the Gabriel conspiracy was his unwillingness to hold the insurgents' action as properly speaking criminal. Jefferson was no doubt consciously ambiguous when lecturing Governor Monroe on how the insurgents' action, while "deemed criminal by us," would appear "meritorious" in the eyes of the black government in St. Domingo.[149] He held the rebels "not of the character of common felons, but guilty of insurgency only," and talked of sending them to Sierra Leone "as free persons."[150] Under the law of nature, slaves were entitled to liberty, even if not in the United States.

Jefferson's view of the Gabriel conspiracy was consistent with his larger position on slavery. He opposed slavery, and his position remained essentially the same throughout his life. It should be considered separately from his self-confessed racist prejudices. To grasp Jefferson's problem right side up, it is important to see that his antislavery stance was primarily intended to protect the "physical and moral characters" of white Americans.[151] Neither did his position derive from the kind of moral individualism one may find in John Locke's political writings concerning religious freedom. In his *Carolina constitutions*, authored with the Earl of Shaftesbury, Locke stated that "it shall be lawful for slaves, as well as others, to enter themselves, and be of what church or profession any of them shall think best."[152] Jefferson went a good deal beyond urging religious freedom for slaves.

In Jefferson's *Notes on the State of Virginia*, reprinted many times during his life, he held that "the whole commerce between the master and slave is a perpetual exercise of the most boisterous passions, the most unremitting despotism on the one part, and degrading submissions on the other."[153] His principle was that, even if black people were inferior to white, it was contrary to human morality to hold them in bondage. Slavery prevented its victims from ever acquiring moral accountability as individuals. As human beings, they had to be given freedom to take their destiny in their own hands – even if outside white America.

In his uncompleted autobiography from 1821, Jefferson famously noted of enslaved African Americans that "nothing is more certainly written in the book of fate than that these people are to be free" – albeit with a crucial provision: "Nor is it less certain that the two races, equally free, cannot live in the same government."[154] Black people were to become "equally free" as whites, but not under the American government. Jefferson's solution was a nationwide program to gradually send the entire African-American population out of the United States. He never dreamed of America becoming an ethnically equal society. Nor did he dream of it remaining multiethnic – with or without slavery.[155]

In Jefferson's imagination, African Americans should live in the Caribbean, not the United States. His sole claim about the problem of slavery was that he had a feasible, even if dreadfully expensive solution to it. Abolition, as Jefferson argued from at least the early 1780s onward, was to be achieved not by emancipating all slaves, but by emancipating all newborn slave children. These children "should continue with their parents to a certain age, then be brought up, at the public expence [sic], to tillage, arts or sciences, according to their geniusses, till the females should be eighteen, and the males twenty-one years of age." Once the children, generation by generation, had thus been schooled by the whites and reached adulthood, they were to be "colonized to such place as the circumstances of the time should render most proper, sending them out with arms, implements of houshold [sic] and of the handicraft arts, feeds, pairs of the useful domestic animals, &c," so as to be declared "a free and independent people."[156] As late as 1817, Jefferson proclaimed that "Personally I am ready and desirous to make any sacrifice which shall ensure their gradual but complete retirement from the State, and effectually, at the same time, establish them elsewhere in freedom and safety."[157]

Neither was the abolition program put forward in the *Notes on the State of Virginia* Jefferson's first public attack on the institution. The Continental Congress had made a resolution against the slave trade in 1774.[158] In his *Summary View of the Rights of British America*, from the same year, Jefferson had already publicly suggested restricting the slave trade as the precondition for the "abolition of domestic slavery." This he argued to be "the great object of desire in those colonies."[159] Even his original draft of the Declaration of Independence included a section condemning slavery, which the Continental Congress censored from the final version. There he accused the king of neglecting to confirm even the moderate legal restrictions of the African slave trade recently suggested in the colonies. From Jefferson's point of view, the incorporation of the slavery issue into the Declaration of Independence would have afterwards provided him with a strong argument for his political program of gradual abolition in the name of the universal rights of man.[160]

According to Jefferson's own testimony, the Revolutionary-era emancipation program was initially devised as part of the general revision of the Virginia slave codes, although it was deemed useless to be presented to the still overwhelmingly pro-slavery state legislature.[161] In Jefferson's 1784 draft of the famous 1787 Northwest Ordinance, slavery was to be banned in the new territories.[162] In 1807, during his presidency, the Congress enacted the national prohibition of the international slave trade, as suggested in the Constitution of 1787.

The aspect of Jefferson's stance on slavery most often mistaken is his eagerness to restrict rather than loosen the legal basis of "the peculiar institution." In order to free white Americans from the moral evil of being a slaveholding nation, Jefferson insisted on strict color-line legislation so that abolition and deportation could be achieved by a single program. Thus, even his early revision of the Virginia slave codes strengthened the institutional basis of slavery.[163] Neither does he appear to have had any objections to restricting slaves' rights later on.

During his presidency, from 1801 to 1809, Jefferson preferred not to be too open about his wish to end slavery. That is hardly surprising given his reputation as a French-minded radical and his obvious need to keep the southern slaveholders loyal to the still fragile federal government. After retirement, he turned into an advocate for the extension of slavery to the western territories. Regarding this so-called diffusion argument, Jefferson's rationale was that spreading the institution to the West would increase the number of taxpayers, who would cover the cost of the deportation. The goal of abolition and removal did not change. In 1824, only two years before his death, Jefferson still insisted that the African-American population must be deported, generation by generation, to "some country and climate friendly to human life and happiness" where they could establish themselves "as a separate, free and independent people."[164]

As to the moral repercussions of Jefferson's abolition program, it did not entail asking the wishes of the slave parents or the children. Jefferson readily admitted that most slaves were unlikely to "voluntarily consent" to deportation. By the same token, he argued that only a "few of those advanced to a certain age in habits of slavery, would be capable of self-government," thus indicating his rationale for expatriating the children, not the adults.[165] Neither was Jefferson alone in his opinions.[166] As James Madison once phrased the fundamental problem: "[I]f the blacks [are] retained among the whites, under the degrading privation of equal rights, political and social, they must be … always secretly confederated against the ruling and privileged class."[167]

That his position was political, Jefferson made exceptionally clear in his famous 1814 letter to Edward Coles. Coles was a Virginia abolitionist who wished to carry his slaves out of the state in order to free them. Jefferson urged him not to leave Virginia and thus lessen "its stock of sound disposition." With Jefferson, Madison, and other antislavery slaveholders, Coles could "come forward in the public councils" and "insinuate & inculcate" emancipation "softly but steadily" in order to change public opinion. The ultimate goal was still the "emancipation of those born after a given day, and of their education and expatriation after a given age."[168]

Much confusion has arisen from the lip service Jefferson paid to the idea of slaves' voluntary migration to Africa. It is unlikely that Jefferson ever thought it possible to carry the whole slave population to a distant Africa.[169] Moreover, he spoke of the deportation scheme without any suggestion that individual manumissions could help solve the problem. Rather, these would only entangle the legislators with the further problem of coping with a larger, free black population. Such a development was an obvious threat to Jefferson's fifty-year-long program of gradually sending all African-American children out of the country – against their will, if necessary. A politician to the bone, he carefully avoided going into details, but hoped, among other things, that the slave states would bring German immigrants to replace the slaves, and even that "at the general expense."[170]

Jefferson's personal compromises regarding this stance are astoundingly few. He let a couple of Hemings-family slaves escape from Monticello to the free States, probably because they were his relatives and white enough to assimilate to white society.[171] In his will he freed a couple of more slaves, who were too old to do more than enjoy a few retirement years – albeit it is not known on what assets. As to the famous Sally Hemings, Jefferson never acknowledged his very probable, perhaps decades-long liaison with her. Neither did he change his openly racist public views because of the relationship.[172] The still-continuing debates about their feelings toward each other, and toward their possible common slave children, carry such ethically charged dimensions of their own that Jefferson's outspoken racist convictions often seem the least of his sins.[173]

Nevertheless, a number of scholars still confuse Jefferson's position on slavery with his racist attitudes, making belittling remarks about his "antislavery moments."[174] How stubbornly must a politician cling to one position, over a period of fifty years, so as to appear consistent enough? The slavery question was far from the only one on which Jefferson failed to make the nation agree with him. In Virginia, as in many other states, many free men were still excluded from the ballot after Jefferson's death. Neither did the states all offer legal guarantees of religious freedom during his life.

It is important to distinguish Jefferson's hopes for a democratic America without slavery from other hopes of his day. Jefferson's vision was not that of the famous "Celadon" pamphlet of 1785, often considered the summary of the Revolutionary War generation's multicultural convictions. The document dreamed of America as divided into "Nigrania," "Savagenia," "a French, a Spanish, a Dutch, an Irish, an English, &c. yea, a Jewish state here in process of time" with "all of them united in brotherly affection" and thus eventually forming "the most potent empire on the face of earth."[175] That was not Jefferson's dream. He wanted to expel the entire African-American population from the Union. They were to enjoy democratic self-government somewhere else.

Providing all future generations of African Americans with such an opportunity was what Jefferson asked of the free Americans still living in the midst of their own attempt to achieve mass democracy. In this fundamental sense, Jefferson's solution to the problem of slavery was subordinate to his preoccupation with preventing America from becoming a new kind of society of orders, even if only political ones. His fears were warranted. Even the America of 1963 – at which time the color of skin could still function as a voting qualification – was just such a society. That is why Martin Luther King, Jr. held his "I Have a Dream" speech on behalf of the African-Americans' political rights, still only dreaming that "one day this nation will rise up and live out the true meaning of its creed" that "all men are created equal."

In purely historical terms, Jefferson's problem was twofold. First, he opposed the idea of a multiethnic America, with or without slavery. Second, throughout his life, and particularly during the Missouri crisis of 1819,

Jefferson was afraid of the situation that Lincoln faced in 1861: A war over the *political meaning of natural rights* – which, if the slaveholders were to win, would destroy the American political system without even destroying slavery. Jefferson's progressive vision was inclusive enough to embrace an evidently multiethnic image of humankind, although he never envisioned any genuinely multiethnic or multicultural America. Again, none of this is to suggest that even someone clinging to the so-called Jeffersonian tradition today could agree with Jefferson's eighteenth-century views on such issues.[176]

To sum up the findings from the Jefferson archive thus far, progress meant something people could attain only in common. In isolation from others, anyone could harbor goodwill to all humankind. Progress, however, was about material and educational improvements as well as about, hopefully, unprecedented positive changes in actual human conduct. Such innovations of the future were not to be looked for in the history books, but in political discourse, which by definition is discourse over the future. That is why Jefferson's ideal of progress also called for a genuine commitment to free, democratic government. Chapter 2 will consider to what extent Jefferson's image of man as "an animal destined to live in society" determined his Baconian commitment to increasing knowledge, both in natural and moral sciences.

2

Progress in Natural and Moral Sciences

SCIENTIFIC "SUPERSTRUCTURES" AND DEISTIC BELIEFS

As a man of the Enlightenment, Jefferson never ceased praising the value of the sciences for human progress. He was an early advocate of Edward Jenner's famous smallpox vaccination, and gained certain renown as a part-time scientist himself. The endless lists of various animate and inanimate forms of nature in the *Notes on the State of Virginia* reflect his characteristically encyclopedic interest in data collecting. His perseverance in making weather observations, the number of which exceeded 3,000 as early as 1777, bespeaks the same attitude.[1] So does his purchase of a telescope in order to measure the exact longitudes of Virginia, and his slightly amusing experiment to prove that the number of garden peas making a pint is 2,500.[2]

Jefferson's emphasis on the usefulness of science made him sometimes impatient about more complicated scientific topics. In his opinion, the most renowned astronomer of the time, William Herschel, was a "good optician only."[3] Herschel's speculations about life on the moon provided a solid rationale for Jefferson's claim. But even in addressing Herschel's discovery of the planet Uranus, Jefferson noted only that the star had been observed earlier.[4] In the most important debate in contemporary chemistry, leading to the end of Phlogiston chemistry, Jefferson initially sided with Joseph Priestley against Antoine Laurent Lavoisier. As it turned out, Lavoisier rightly insisted that the experiment both he and Priestley had performed proved the existence of an unknown element in the air, which Lavoisier called oxygen.[5]

Most tellingly, even though Jefferson frequently complained of bad English translations of Latin classics and did some translations from French himself, he rarely found time to probe contemporary philosophy in depth. He hailed Destutt de Tracy's treatise on "ideology" as one of the cornerstones of the post-Lockean investigation of the human mind, but probably never read the book entirely. The explanation was that "I am not fond of reading what is merely abstract, and unapplied immediately to some useful science."[6] Useful sciences could clearly contribute to Jefferson's conception of progress as the general commitment to improve the material, educational, and moral conditions of mankind. Still, there is not much reason to view Jefferson as a scientific theorist rather than an exceptionally well-informed intellectual, whose philosophy of science is well summarized in his phrase that "[i]gnorance is preferable to error."[7] What this chapter seeks to define is how *little*, in fact, the latest eighteenth-century natural and moral sciences shaped Jefferson's image of man, and, consequently, his fundamental premises of human progress.

To grasp the characteristics of Jefferson's commitment to increasing scientific knowledge, it is useful, first of all, to distinguish his progressive beliefs from his deistic convictions. Jefferson was in no sense an exceptional eighteenth-century thinker in presuming that the ultimately divine ordering of the universe was of natural as well as moral character. Providential naturalism – often associated with such contemporary moralists as Joseph Butler, Lord Kames, Thomas Reid, and George Turnbull – presumed the same.[8] Still, Jefferson's deistic beliefs were not scientific views even in his eyes. Although he saw nature as permeated by some higher rationality, and therefore could consider "moral facts as important as physical ones," he definitely distinguished the study of facts from that of values.[9]

Jefferson's scientific views did not rest on his philosophical stance, but on a new approach to the very concept of knowledge. As he declared, Francis Bacon, John Locke, and Isaac Newton had fundamentally altered the "foundation of those superstructures which have been raised in the Physical and Moral sciences."[10] This new "foundation" of scientific "superstructures" concerned solely the methodology of acquiring reliable knowledge. It was not about challenging purely religious beliefs, but about excluding the deductive method from the field of sciences, now supposed to rest only on experience and induction.

As for Jefferson's actual philosophical position, it was that of "the material deist who believes that matter alone can operate on matter." This commitment to an ontologically material universe led him on occasion to somewhat awkward ponderings about God as "light and thin indeed, an etherial [sic] gas; but still matter."[11] But these musings were hardly aimed at persuading others about the true character of divinity. They certainly did not rest on any interpersonally valid scientific criteria. In fact, Jefferson considered philosophy itself as little more than a personally rationalized metaphysics, which should not prevent one from suspending judgment in the face of the unknown.

When John Adams confronted Jefferson with the question of how "certain forms of matter" had become endowed "with the faculty of thought," Jefferson considered it simply irresolvable. Adams's question suggested that one should either presume spirit to be capable of providing matter with thought or vice versa.[12] Were it "necessary to form an opinion," Jefferson answered, he would opt for the position he assigned to John Locke and hold that certain forms of matter are capable of thought within the ontologically material universe.[13]

But choosing between these opinions brought the whole dilemma down to a decidedly lower epistemological level. One would be giving an explanation of something that remained essentially unknown. Hence, Jefferson chose the "single incomprehensibility of matter endowed with thought."[14] This is why he asserted that "ignorance, in these cases, is truly the softest pillow on which I can lay my head."[15] This notion of *swallowing incomprehensibilities* is the seminal aspect of Jefferson's intellectual outlook. Neither should his philosophical position as a material deist be confused with his making truth claims.

Jefferson's reliance on empiricist methodology did not rest solely on John Locke's philosophy. Consider Jefferson's much discussed maxim, "I feel: therefore I exist," in its philosophical (or metaphysical) rather than in any clear-cut epistemological meaning. The maxim, which he offered as his "habitual anodyne" – primarily a medicine for skepticism – represents a more or less sensationist version of the Cartesian paradigm, "I think, therefore I am."

This is Jefferson's formulation of the maxim and its consequences:

> 'I feel: therefore I exist.' I feel bodies which are not myself: there are other existences then. I call them *matter*. I feel them changing place. This gives me *motion*. Where there is an absence of matter, I call it *void*, or *nothing*, or *immaterial space*. On the basis of sensation, of matter and motion, we may erect the fabric of all the certainties we can have or need.[16]

In his embrace of subjective sensations, Jefferson did not here address, for example, the Lockean distinction between simple and complex ideas. He wrote the paragraph in response to John Adams's disturbing letter, which concerned the post-Lockean skepticism stemming from George Berkeley's idealism. Whereas Locke thought that true knowledge is knowledge of our ideas and held the ideas to be particular things occurring solely in the mind, Berkeley's central contention was that nothing but ideas can be proven to exist. In the popular eighteenth-century reading of Berkeley, existence itself became reduced to the notion of being perceived.[17] Perhaps Jefferson's anodyne was also aimed against Hume's famous suggestion that it is precisely one's "self" that tends to dissolve once the transience of each idea passing through the mind is fully recognized.

One probable source for Jefferson's "anodyne" is D'Alembert's preface to the French *Encyclopedia*.[18] There one finds the argument that the first thing suggested by an animate creature's sensations must be its own existence, whereupon the first reflective idea is the existence of its own mind. After that, bodily sensations and consciousness of one's own body as separate from other bodies would just as naturally follow. For the French Enlightenment,

Locke's greatness stemmed from his reducing metaphysics to its proper field, namely "la Physique expérimentale de l'ame," experimental physics of the soul (or the mind).[19] It appears to have been this Condillac-inspired sensationism – arising from the sense of touch – that lurks behind Jefferson's overall conception of human understanding.

It is unlikely that Jefferson's "habitual anodyne" aimed at disproving philosophical idealism. Rather, its purpose seems to have been to dismiss any such a position as generally unnecessary. He argued against confusing even the most philosophically coherent metaphysics with epistemologically coherent natural science arising solely from the inductive, empirical method. To Jefferson, philosophical claims about the ontological character of the universe as either material or immaterial counted for mere "hyperphysical and antiphysical" speculations. They could be freely dismissed because "once we quit the basis of sensation, all is in the wind." As opposed to such speculations, there were enough "realities" for "all the purposes of life."[20] About these essentially physical and particular realities, the human "senses" comprised the only "organs of information." Even if a single organ could not always be relied on, all bits of information could be compared and combined with the "faculty of reasoning" and turned into a "fabric of all certainties we can have or need."[21] None of this was to deny that some aspects of reality remain beyond human certainties, for other "things ... may indeed be."[22] And regarding the human "fabric of certainties," Jefferson proclaimed that "truth can stand by itself."

As this chapter will demonstrate, Jefferson's belief in accumulative scientific knowledge was in fundamental opposition to the assumption of fixed views of the cosmos, nature, or man. Consider, for example, his notoriously outspoken racial prejudices. In a letter to the Marquis de Chastellux from 1785, Jefferson wrote that the American Indian was intellectually equal to any uneducated white man, and proceeded to opine that "the black man, in his present state, might not be so," whereas "it would be hazardous to affirm, that, equally cultivated for a few generations, he would not become so."[23] This notion of the conscious cultivation of all human faculties is essential to the comprehension of both Jefferson's naturalistic and moral beliefs about human progress. To see African Americans as presently inferior was not to claim that they will always remain so.[24]

This does not at all clear Jefferson's bill on the issue of race. The point is to distinguish between what he took as demonstrated knowledge and what he did not. As this chapter shows, Jefferson's problem with the concept of race arose from the general notion that not only the Africans, but also the Europeans of the New World appeared to have been misplaced from their original "culture and place," as Carolus Linnaeus (Carl von Linné) had once defined the natural varieties of humankind.[25] By the same token, it is worth considering what the contemporary moral sciences had actually proven about the possibilities of human improvement in Jefferson's eyes.

For example, he believed in the existence of the moral sense of man, but not as a scientific fact. But let us begin by taking a closer look at Jefferson's naturalistic beliefs.

THE COSMOS AND NATURE IN CONSTANT CHANGE

Jefferson believed in Francis Bacon's conception of progressive knowledge. The fundamental premise of progressive knowledge is that insofar as knowledge increases, something potentially knowable remains unknown. This is why Jefferson's deistic, ontological convictions must be distinguished from what he thought had been proven true about the overall ordering of the universe.

In the simplest terms, Jefferson viewed the universe as comprised of atoms in different compositions, while holding that the principle according to which these compositions occur in time was unknown. He was hesitant even about the ramifications of the Newtonian "movements of the heavenly bodies, so exactly held in their course by the balance of centrifugal and centripetal forces."[26] In 1819, he learned about the mathematician Daniel Bowditch, who was then translating Pierre Simon Laplace's famous astronomical works into English. One of Bowditch's "very learned mathematical papers" shattered Jefferson's understanding of the solar system. This is how Jefferson explained the case:

> One of them impairs the confidence I had reposed in La Place's demonstration that the excentricities [sic] of the planets of our system could oscillate only within narrow limits, and therefore could authorise no inference that the system must, by it's own laws, come one day to an end. This would have left the question of infinitude, at both ends of the line of time, clear of physical authority. [27]

What can be inferred from this somewhat confusing statement? At least one may conclude that Jefferson was still, in his retirement years, uncertain even about the stability of the solar system. As he here confirmed, for the better part of his life he had relied on Laplace's famous calculations, according to which the planetary system was not in need of even occasional divine adjustments, unlike Newton's solar system. This feature of Newton's astronomy had been one of the reasons for Leibniz's famous accusation that Newton's god was an incompetent watchmaker.[28]

Jefferson's remark, that the infinitude was "clear of physical authority," referred to Laplace's famous assertion that there was no scientific need for an active, divine superintendent of the physical universe. At least the solar-system-related conception of time, that Jefferson spoke of here, could denote the notion of time having neither a beginning nor an end.[29] This kind of problem about time arose simply from what Jefferson thought all scientists already agreed on – namely, the constant circulation of matter in various forms within the universe.[30] In Jefferson's statements, the deistic and atheistic views of this ordering differed mainly on the question of whether or not the self-regenerating universe had a beginning in time. They still could agree on the general Newtonian ordering of the universe, although such an ordering did not appear purposeful in the sense of explaining why the laws of nature work as they do.[31] A man of science would ask only how they work.

Laplace's philosophical position rested on the human inability to calculate all the probabilities involved in the causal relations of the ultimately determinist universe. Rather than contingency or pure chance, it was probably the inherent determinism that Jefferson found most problematic in the so-called atheist view. The general contemporary conception of atheist "fatality," present even in Montesquieu's *Spirit of Laws,* may explain Jefferson's accusation that the Calvinist doctrine of predestination amounted to atheism.[32] To be sure, one may find quite a different – but equally problematic – view of determinism in the works of Jefferson's favorite Scottish thinker, Lord Kames. Jefferson not only read Kames in his early years, but also kept recommending his works to others, be the subject religion, morality, law, or literary criticism.[33]

In his *The Principles of Morality and Natural Religion* (1751), Kames explained the existence of "the meanest plant" up to the "moral world" as "happily adjusted" to the "glorious purposes" of the creator of the universe. Eventually there appeared "the great chain of causes and effects, which renders the whole order of both the natural and moral world unalterably determined in every article."[34] Kames encountered fierce opposition to his quite logical conclusion that, within such a divinely ordered, determinist universe, the concept of free will must be illusory, although Kames insisted on distinguishing such an ordering from the human realm of moral choices.[35] Be that as it may, Jefferson never claimed that the current stage of natural and moral sciences amounted to a fixed worldview. Rather, he was interested in the human possibilities of adaptation to a nature, which appeared to be under constant change itself.

Indeed, Jefferson's problems in defining the category of "natural" arose from his seeing nature in permanent change. In a late statement from 1823, one finds the whole Jeffersonian cosmos in constant tumult with not only some races of animals, but even stars disappearing:

> Stars, well known, have disappeared, new ones come into view, comets, in their incalculable courses, may run foul of suns and planets and require renovation under other laws; certain races of animals are become extinct; and, were there no restoring power, all existences might extinguish successively, one by one, until all should be reduced to a shapeless chaos.[36]

Jefferson's appeal to the "restoring power" that kept "all existences" from falling into chaos may refer to an extra-natural divine power. But more often, he has been viewed as a deist who believed in some kind of an intelligent creator of the universe as a self-regenerating consistent whole – a conception known as the great chain of being.[37]

The prevalent, self-regenerating notion of *scala naturae* had little to do with, say, Carolus Linnaeus's catalogues of animate and inanimate nature. Instead, *scala naturae* comprised all modes of being, ranging from stones to angels as well as to the essences of all things that exist, have existed, or are only coming into being.[38] In this temporalized sense, nature figured as a kind of great treadmill out of which particular beings emerge in time only to disappear again. One could, hence, discern constant recurrences in natural time, such as the cyclical appearance of human generations as more or less similar to one another. The naturalists' central problem lay in defining the presumably permanent units or forms of existence within such a cyclical notion of natural time. As for even such permanent units, Jefferson thought it fully possible that "certain races of animals" might become extinct and that even some stars might vanish.

This is why Jefferson's conviction that the ultimate ordering of all nature was essentially immutable should not be confused with a belief that the current orders of animals, plants, and minerals must be equally so. This confusion easily follows from Jefferson's 1787 assertion, made in the *Notes on the State of Virginia*, that such "is oeconomy [sic] of nature that no instance can be produced of her having formed any link in her great work so weak as to be broken."[39] In 1797, as president of the American Philosophical Society, he treated nature's chain in clear-cut cyclical terms: "The movements of nature are in a never ending circle. The animal species which has once been put into a train of motion, is still probably moving in that train. For if one link in nature's chain might be lost, another and another might be lost, till this whole system of things should evanish [sic] by piece-meal."[40]

One may speculate that Jefferson was speaking of nature's chain as comprising a stable number of ecological niches, but he does not appear to have been convinced that each niche must remain filled with the same species. For Jefferson, who saw Europe primarily as an overpopulated continent lacking uncultivated land and dreamed of putting the American West under cultivation, it must have been evident that nature, as a worldwide ecosystem, was undergoing profound change.[41] For example, in the *Notes on the State of Virginia*, he pointed out that the Virginia climate had probably warmed considerably during the past few decades, and his lifelong records of weather observations eventually served to track long-range climatic changes there.[42] As historian Alexander O. Boulton has noted, Jefferson's suggestion that rocks perhaps grow bespeaks his belief that the constant regeneration of nature concerned not only animal species, but also the landscape.[43]

In fact, Jefferson's 1787 claim that nature had not "formed any link in her great work so weak as to be broken," is considerably more qualified than it may first appear. This statement concerned the possibility that Indians had hunted the mammoth into extinction. Jefferson regarded the mammoth's "early retirement" possible, even if unlikely. He actually wrestled with the issue of the perhaps dangerous human impact on nature.[44] According to the 1797 testimony, the mammoth still lived on earth, but even this claim Jefferson qualified with the term "probably."[45]

Given that whole races of animals could disappear and even stars could vanish, what were the permanent units that recurred in the great chain of nature? Jefferson's naturalistic views were linked to those of the Count de Buffon, with whom he entered a lengthy debate in the *Notes on the State of Virginia*. Buffon's major claim was that the proper object of natural science lay in exposing the innumerable gradations of natural beings, some of which could become extinct, whereas others could be genuinely new. In essence, the yet unknown ordering of nature's chain was not understood as something that keeps nature essentially immutable, but as something that keeps it from falling into chaos.

Subscribing to the notion of constant regeneration of nature did not entail making truth claims about the mechanism of the regeneration. In Holbach's *System de la Nature* (1770), Jefferson found a consistent atheist naturalism, which in his words "agreed in the order of the existing system" with that of any deist or theist. In Jefferson's words, this "order" consisted of nothing less than "the unceasing motion and circulation of matter thro' the animal, vegetable and mineral kingdoms, never resting, never annihilated, always changing form, and under all forms gifted with the power of reproduction."[46] Holbach had already asked the crucial question – namely, whether animate nature could "give rise to wholly new generations," such that "will have nothing in common with the species at present existing."[47]

The epistemological point on which Jefferson agreed with the "atheists" was that contemporary science provided no reliable explanation of the "forms" in which matter circulated through the universe. Concurring with this prevalent view, Jefferson held simply that "Nature has hidden from us her modus agendi."[48] Hence, historians encounter a host of eighteenth-century intellectuals, Jefferson included, entangled with such – to us oddly ridiculous – problems as whether nature's apparent self-regeneration applied to the mineral world, whether anthropoids preferred reproducing with human beings, and to what extent the physical mixture of human races was natural.

Nevertheless, with regard to the "forms gifted with the power of reproduction,"[49] Jefferson held that contemporary natural science had no objective criteria for discerning the real "units" of nature. Ultimately, the "unceasing motion and circulation of matter thro' the animal, vegetable and mineral kingdoms" could well take place in a universe consisting of nothing but atoms. There appeared to be an "indefinite power in every atom" to reappear as a particle of a new unit in the great chain of being.[50] Nature's "creation is of individuals," Jefferson insisted, and this view could amount to the presumption that "no two particles of matter are of exact resemblance."[51]

To conclude, Jefferson's cosmology included speculations about the ultimate meaning of the Newtonian laws of gravitation as well as about the permanence of animate modes of life within the *scala naturae*. With the Baconian revolution in progressive physical sciences, the microscope and the telescope could now serve as equal means of human refinement, allowing mankind gradually to discern the universe in its whole diversity. Perhaps, indeed, nature had a history of its own – including irreversible changes in nature herself.

THE NATURALISTIC VIEW OF MAN

Within Jefferson's cosmos – comprised of matter and motion as physical "realities" – the human being, too, could be viewed as a composition of matter.[52] This is why Jefferson considered John Locke, first and foremost, as a predecessor to such later "Investigators of the thinking faculty of man" as Dugald Stewart, Destutt de Tracy, and Pierre-Jean-Georges Cabanis.[53] Stewart, according to Jefferson, gave the human mind its "natural history" in studying how the child's thinking develops into that of an adult.[54] De Tracy, as Jefferson explained, examined the subject in its "modes of action and deduction" called "Logic, and Ideology." In the simplest terms, de Tracy held that "all our thoughts are things felt" because sensibility "constitutes and comprehends the whole existence of an animated being."[55] Finally, there was Cabanis, who had put under anatomical investigation those "particular organs in the human structure which may most possibly exercise" thinking.[56]

Jefferson could thus conceive of the thinking faculty of man as a physical quality of the particular composition of matter called the human being. Such a quality was analogous to what magnetism was to a lodestone, which "nobody supposes to retire to hold a substantive and distinct existence" once the lodestone has vanished.[57] In Jefferson's view, human understanding arose from the same source as that of other animals – some specific logic of animate sensibility, more or less consistently divisible into sensations, reflection, and reasoning. With equal ease he held that the notion of "justice" results from "the construction of man" and is "instinct, and innate" for the human being as "an animal destined to live in society."[58]

What this half-naturalistic definition of man – as an animal destined to live in society – suggested was that, even in naturalistic sciences, human capacities (potentially comparable as they were to those of other social animals) were to be examined primarily as cultural characteristics. In comparison to such an anthropological approach, the contemporary speculations about the genetic differences between peoples and human races were of secondary importance.

In order to see how little Jefferson claimed to know about the genetic characteristics of humans, it is useful to examine his famous attack on Buffon's claims about the New World in the *Notes on the State of Virginia*. There he set out to question Buffon's assumption that the American continent was an unfavorable environment for animate life. This challenge had to be faced owing to Abbé Raynal's quite logical conclusion that, if Buffon was right, not only the Indians and African Americans, but also the European migrants to America were facing inevitable degeneration in such an environment. The question concerned "the man of America, whether aboriginal or transplanted."[59] Conspicuously, the central formulation of this refutable hypothesis Jefferson found in Raynal's remark that "America has not yet produced one good poet."[60]

Jefferson's attack against European natural scientists' too-broad assumptions about the central characteristics of the distant American continents included considerations of geology, climate, and biology, as well as of cultural traits of different Americans – Indians, blacks, and whites. Jefferson began by considering geological developments. In the *Notes on the State of Virginia*, Query VI, he brought up the issue of seashells found high in the Andes. For explanations of such findings, Jefferson listed three hypotheses: First, the theory of general deluge; second, the suggestion that all mountain ranges had been formed by geological upheavals; and third, some yet unexplainable phenomenon within the mineral kingdom, such as the growth of shells. In fact, he found all three hypotheses unsatisfactory at the time.[61]

After these speculations, Jefferson launched a lengthy attack against Buffon about the size, characteristics, and the frequency of different animal species in North America. He particularly sought to refute Buffon's conclusion that the mammoth, the extinction of which Jefferson still doubted, was a degenerated American variety of the elephant.[62] Then he proceeded to question Buffon's unfavorable view of the American Indians as less fertile, physically weaker, and less capable of cultural development than the Europeans.

Given that Jefferson's ultimate goal was to challenge Abbé Raynal's suggestion that the American environment would degenerate white Americans, it is no wonder that his own conclusions remained tentative. First, he left the problem of the shells unsolved as all three hypotheses were "equally unsatisfactory." Ignorance, after all, remained "preferable to error."[63] Similarly, he cast doubt on Buffon's assertion that the American climate was more humid than the European because "we are not furnished with observations sufficient to decide" the question. The very notion that moisture was "unfriendly to animal growth" in general was a "hypothesis" itself.[64] Probability characterizes Jefferson's entire attitude to contemporary natural sciences.

How fixed, then, were Jefferson's racist convictions? In his now notorious Query XIV in the *Notes on the State of Virginia* on African Americans, Jefferson held that "the improvement of the blacks in body and mind, in the first instance of their mixture with the whites, has been observed by every one, and proves that their inferiority is not the effect merely of their condition of life."[65] Given that this reference to racial mixture did not necessarily denote genetic (rather than only cultural) mixture, one may ask whether the observed improvement among black people was of more crucial importance than their presumed inferiority to whites.

In the *Notes on the State of Virginia*, Jefferson famously lamented the fact that Native Americans and African Americans "have never yet been viewed by us as subjects of natural history." As for a fruitful research hypothesis, he held that it "is not against experience to suppose, that different species of the same genus, or varieties of the same species, may possess different qualifications." In this sense Jefferson well deserves his notoriety as a predecessor of the late-nineteenth-century racial sciences. But his hypothesis drew on his own life experience as a slaveholder, not on experimental research of the issue, which was nonexistent at the time. Neither did he say anything about the possible methodology of such a research.[66]

There is no question that Jefferson personally embraced clear-cut racist assumptions. He considered the inferiority of black skin color as a matter of simple, apparently objective, aesthetic judgment, just as he held African Americans less elegant in the "symmetry of form" and found even their "odour" disagreeable.[67] This argument for the aesthetic superiority of whites was grounded on black people's alleged preference for whiter skin. Moreover, Jefferson regarded this inclination as analogous to the "preference of the Oranootan for the black women over those of his own species."[68] Speculation about anthropoids' sexual preference for human beings over their own species was a common theme among thinkers of the period. Both Rousseau and Buffon mentioned it.[69] Jefferson's reliance on Carolus Linnaeus's (Carl von Linné's) famous *Systema Naturae* did not offer much help in refuting this oddly persistent legend.[70]

The categories of animate life that Linnaeus related to human beings were the following: The class of mammals, the order of primates, and the genus *Homo* divided into two species – although confusingly under the common term *Homo nosce Te ipsum* (know thy self, or *Homo sapiens*). The species were: *Homo diurnus* (what we would today call *Homo sapiens sapiens*) and *Homo nocturnus* (the orangutang or anthropoids generally).[71] The human species itself was divided into six "varieties": *Ferus*, *Americanus* (American), *Europaeus* (European), *Asiaticus* (Asian), *Afer* (African), and *Monstrosus*. The *Ferus* denoted "mute and hairy" people (probably alluding to humans degenerated to the level of animals), whereas the *Monstrosus* covered various minor physical exceptions within the other four varieties.[72] The four remaining varieties – the American, European, Asian, and African – comprised the main human races, determined "by culture and place."[73]

Before discussing Linnaeus's definitions of races by culture and place, it is worth considering some ramifications of his dramatic suggestion that anthropoids belong to the same genus of *Homo* as the humans, if not to the same species. His assumption did not initiate, but was certainly linked to the growing enthusiasm for discovering the missing links of the great chain of nature. Such links were sought between man and ape as well as between plants and stones.[74] It is not surprising, then, to find Jefferson using such terms as "gradations," "race," and "species" just as equivocally as did the most prominent natural scientists of the time.[75] This is how Jefferson ended his own speculations about the specific characteristics of the non-European Americans:

> To our reproach it must be said, that though for a century and a half we have had under our eyes the races of black and of red men, they have never yet been viewed by us as subjects of natural history. I advance it therefore as a suspicion only, that the blacks, whether originally a distinct race, or made distinct by time and circumstances, are inferior to the whites in the endowments both of body and mind. It is not against experience to suppose, that different species of the same genus, or varieties of the same species, may possess different qualifications.[76]

In sum, Jefferson here neither dismissed nor fully endorsed the possibility that Africans could prove to be an originally distinct human species by future research.[77]

However, as has been shown, Jefferson's beliefs about the *scala naturae* did not amount to any fixed Linnaean or other categorical ordering of animate nature. On the contrary, he proclaimed that "Nature has, in truth, produced units only through all her works. Classes, orders, genera, species, are not of her work."[78] Jefferson does not appear to have ever claimed that the black race – any more than "orders, genera, and species" – was a known "unit" in contemporary natural sciences. Instead, he frequently insisted that his mere "opinion that they [African Americans] are inferior in the faculties of reason and imagination must be hazarded with great diffidence."[79] It is also worth noting that Jefferson probably never took any notice of Buffon's later idea that the defining characteristic of an animate species was the capacity of its offspring to reproduce.[80] Most importantly, Jefferson's "conjecture" or "suspicion only" about there being a difference "perhaps of faculty"[81] between white and black people did not warrant the conclusion that blacks were less capable of improvement than whites.

Jefferson's consistently loose formulations of the issue stemmed from the prevailing perplexity over the best explanation of apparent racial differences. In retrospect, the most notorious eighteenth-century explanation of the topic was the theory of polygenesis of the human species. Its basic premise of distinct creations of the human races amounted to the view that genetically different races – in fact, different human species – could exist. Lord Kames, along with David Hume, was one of the adherents of this theory.[82] Jefferson did not need to reject this hypothesis in order to resist slavery. His argument was that even if Africans had been "*originally* a distinct race," namely, a "different species of the same genus" as all other humans, their enslavement would "degrade a whole race of men from the rank in the scale of beings which their Creator may perhaps have given them."[83]

Still, the underlying assumption was that there is a "scale of beings" within animate life and that it is discernible in "the gradations in all the races of animals." To be sure, nature herself permitted the genetic mixing of some such gradations, as when the slave, in Jefferson's formulation, was "staining the blood of his master."[84] But the idea of the ranking between the "gradations" being natural remained problematic because of the pending question about the origins of the gradations themselves. The theory of polygenesis provided one answer, but did not explicitly explain the ranking of gradations. Neither did the more prevalent explanation, the so-called environmentalist argument. According to it, when a geographically isolated portion of a species adapts to its natural environment over a long enough period of time, it eventually constitutes a more or less permanent *variety* (or race) of the original species. The argument devolved from what is today called soft inheritance, namely the notion that even some acquired features might be genetically inheritable. The darker skin of the Africans was thus imagined to result from generations-long exposure to tropical sunlight, meaning that dark skin color was essentially genetically inherited tanning.[85] But in itself, even soft inheritance did not offer a criterion for the actual ranking of the human races regarding their emotional and rational capacities.

As implied by Jefferson's argument, any variety (or race) of a given species could also be considered as "a gradation" within that species, just as every species could supposedly be "graded" or ranked with reference to all other species. The underlying presumption was that there was an inherent ranking in nature's chain from simple to more complex modes of being. Such a ranking could range from inanimate up to different grades of animate nature. Charles Darwin's seminal finding was that evolution accounts for such differences throughout animate life. But contrary to what most of Darwin's readers (half a century after Jefferson's death) thought, Darwinian evolution did not prefer complicated "gradations" of beings to simpler ones. Evolution had no intentions whatsoever. In this fundamental sense, Holbach – to whom Jefferson referred as an exemplary natural scientist of the atheist camp – had been on the right track, asking why nature would suffer or profit from the degeneration, if not the disappearance, of the whole human species.[86]

Given all the pending problems of natural history – for example, the possibility that Indians had hunted a whole natural species, the mammoth, into extinction – it is no wonder that Jefferson's statements about more explicit racial issues were replete with conjectures. His conclusion about the genetic mixture of black and white people remained in the form of a question: "Will not a lover of natural history," he asked, "excuse an effort to keep" them "as distinct as nature has formed them?"

Jefferson's excuse rested mainly on the situation created in America by the Atlantic slave trade. In view of Buffon's grim characterization of the

Americas as inappropriate for higher cultural life, the misplaced Europeans in America should avoid further risking their own survival by mixing with the equally misplaced people from the even less-known African continent. On a yet larger scale, Jefferson here embraced a simple precautionary principle when dealing with the possibly harmful human impact on nature's entire – perhaps functionally graded – scale of beings.

This precaution was not grounded in a fixed racial theory. What Jefferson wrote about Native Americans was that "we shall *probably* find that they are formed in mind as well as in body, on the same module" with the Europeans.[87] Similarly, when embracing the idea that African Americans shared the same, affectionate moral instinct with Euro-Americans, he spoke of mere probability, not fact. "Whether further observation will or will not verify the conjecture, that nature has been less bountiful to them in the endowments of the head," he mused, "I *believe* that in those of the heart she *will be found* to have done them justice."[88] Finally, Jefferson left it entirely open whether these people were originally a distinct "species of the same genus" or had become a distinct race "by time and circumstances." Clearly, his use of "gradations" and "races" carried connotations of a rudimentary historical view of genetic changes, whether deemed positive or negative in character.

What options did Jefferson have in attacking Raynal's thesis of the degenerating American man? In fact, he resorted to a comparison of progressive cultural capacities between the Americans and Europeans. Given the limited number of only 3 million Americans and their short national history, Jefferson noted, the Americans had proven themselves fully competitive with "the genius" of 20 million Frenchmen. In comparison to Buffon, Voltaire, and other prominent French intellectuals, the Americans could offer such specimens in human excellence as Washington in the art of war, Franklin in physics, and Rittenhouse in astronomy.[89] After all, Jefferson held that "numbers produce emulation, and multiply the chances of improvement, and one improvement begets another."[90]

IMPROVEMENT OF HUMAN CAPACITIES

To fully grasp the central role of cultural criteria in Jefferson's view of man, it is worth taking another look at his statement on the evident improvement of African Americans once situated among whites. In the *Notes on the State of Virginia,* he offered a list of "political," "physical," and "moral" reasons for his segregationist position.[91] The political objections involved "deep rooted prejudices entertained by the whites" and "ten thousand recollections, by the blacks, of the injuries they have sustained," as well as "new provocations."[92] The physical reasons, or differences "fixed in nature," consisted of African Americans' overall physical complexion, skin color, and odor.[93]

But when turning to discuss the moral reasons for perpetuating the separation of the two races, Jefferson took up such issues as bravery, sexual behavior, and the patterns of grief among the African Americans:

> They are at least as brave, and more adventuresome. But this may perhaps proceed from a want of forethought, which prevents their seeing a danger till it be present. When present, they do not go through it with more coolness or steadiness than the whites. They are more ardent after their female: but love seems with them to be more an eager desire, than a delicate mixture of sentiment and sensation. Their griefs are transient [sic].... In general, their existence appears to participate more of sensation than reflection.[94]

In other words, Jefferson's so-called "moral reasons" consisted in what might be characterized as anthropologically observable, fixed patterns of behavior among African Americans. The notion of "bravery" stood in contrast with "forethought." Sheer desires or sensations Jefferson here distinguished from "sentiment" and "reflection." He viewed not only such simple character traits as courage, but the whole category of sensations as preceding reflection and sentiment. Finally, simple sensations and more reflected sentiments were to be followed by reasoning or "forethought."

In fact, Jefferson grounded his apparently genetic claims about the mental inferiority of black Virginians on his assessments of contemporary African-American cultural achievements. The works of Phyllis Wheatley and Ignatius Sancho, the two literate figures Jefferson mentioned, proved that the African-American conception of "love is ardent, but it kindles the senses only," and thus appeared to prefer "sentiment for demonstration." All in all, African Americans honored "more the heart than the head." Natural sensations rarely arose to sentiments of humanity among them, not to speak of their sentiments ever arising to the "restraint of reason and taste"; that is, to any elevated scientific or aesthetic value.[95] Clearly, even if, as Destutt de Tracy held, every thought of an animate being was first felt, all human sensations and sentiments could also be subjected to reasoning according to scientific, moral, or aesthetic criteria.

In striking opposition to the African Americans' deficiencies in reason, sentiment, and imagination, Jefferson suggested that the Indian race was probably formed "on the same module with the 'Homo sapiens Europaeus'."[96] Yet he discussed the apparently genetic characteristics of the Indian race only in terms of "genius," just as he did when comparing American and French cultural achievements.[97] His own experience did not warrant the assumption that the American Indian possessed a weaker capacity for cultural progress than the European. The Indians, Jefferson observed,

> often carve figures on their pipes not destitute of design and merit. They will crayon out an animal, a plant, or a country, so as to prove the existence of a germ in their minds which only wants cultivation. They astonish you with strokes of the most sublime oratory; such as to prove their reason and sentiment strong; their

imagination glowing and elevated. But never yet could I find that a black had uttered a thought above the level of plain narration; never see even an elementary trait of painting or sculpture.[98]

This comparison of the Indian and the African is strikingly unfavorable to the latter. However, Jefferson was hardly claiming that even Native Americans were therefore equal to Euro-Americans. He spoke here of "a germ in their minds which only wants cultivation," namely their apparent capacity for development in reason, sentiment, and imagination. Jefferson's commitment to the constant cultivation of the human mind in the respective disciplinary fields of sciences, morals, and arts is the key to his essentially cultural conception of man. His lifelong advocacy of general elementary education resulted from the simple conviction that the nation must "avail the state of those talents which nature has sown as liberally among the poor as the rich, but which perish without use, if not sought for and cultivated."[99]

For Jefferson, man was an animal with specific mental capacities, just as apt to development as to degeneration. Consider this in light of his view about the European monarchs, such as Louis XVI, George III, Joseph of Austria, or Gustavus III of Sweden: "Now, take any race of animals," Jefferson wrote, "confine them in idleness and inaction, whether in a stye, a stable, or a state-room ... gratify all their sexual appetites, immerse them in sensualities, nourish their passions, ... and banish whatever might lead them to think, and in a few generations they become all body and no mind."[100] This is why Jefferson was so interested in French physiologists' experiments with animal brains, which appeared to prove that "the cerebrum is the thinking organ," without which vertebrate animals could be kept alive by feeding them in their state of "absolute stupidity."[101]

Despite the slaves' perhaps inferior intellectual capacities, Jefferson's accusation against slavery was that it kept human beings from developing their capacities. As he lamented, the slave by definition "must lock up the faculties of his nature."[102] His memorandum on Condorcet's views on slavery serves well to clarify the issue:

In fact the slave is despoiled not only of all property moveable and immoveable but of the faculties of acquiring it, of property in his time, in his strength, of whatever nature had endowed him with to preserve his life or to satisfy his wants. To this wrong is added that of taking from the slave the right to dispose of his person.[103]

In other words, individual responsibility, from satisfying one's natural needs to self-determination, was what truly made man an individual. Purposefully held in an arbitrary state of childhood, the slave was not allowed to attain such individuality. The practice of slavery was against the very notion of man as a social animal. It was unnatural.

When one shifts the focus from Jefferson's naturalist view of man as a social animal to man as a moral being, it begins to unfold that the notion of cultivation of one's natural capacities was no less a seminal notion in his moral outlook. As noted, even if "nature has been less bountiful to" the Africans "in the endowments of the head," Jefferson believed that "in those of the heart she will be found to have done them justice." One of the endowments of the heart was "the moral sense," which every African American apparently shared with every Euro-American.[104]

THE CONCEPT OF THE MORAL SENSE

Jefferson's belief in the necessity of cultivating one's inborn capacities was as important to his moral thought as to his naturalistic views of man. This was so even regarding his much-discussed commitment to the doctrine of an inborn moral sense of man. His letter to Peter Carr sent from Paris in 1787 serves well to illuminate the topic: Jefferson stated first that man "was destined for society. His morality therefore was to be formed to this object. He was endowed with a sense of right and wrong merely relative to this." Eventually, Jefferson summarized the issue thus:

> The moral sense, or conscience, is as much a part of man as his leg or arm. It is given to all human beings in a stronger or weaker degree, as force of members is given them in greater or weaker degree. It may be strengthened by exercise, as may any particular limb of the body.[105]

Here one has the core notion of the Jeffersonian moral sense as something inborn to be "strengthened by exercise."

Jefferson's belief in the existence of the moral sense is so forcefully present in his numerous letters that, in order to understand its limitations, one must focus on the terms in which it was expressed. He understood this inborn sense to be disseminated "in a stronger or weaker degree" among men. Similarly, his argument that the moral sense could be strengthened by exercise certainly contradicts any fixed moral equality of all men in Jefferson's intellectual outlook.[106] Most importantly, the existence of the moral sense was not a scientific fact in Jefferson's eyes. In determining Jefferson's precise understanding of the concept, the difficulty is that he never made it quite clear which claims of contemporary moral philosophy he embraced and which he opposed.

The concept of the moral sense was introduced by the Earl of Shaftesbury (Anthony Ashley Cooper) and established as one of the key terms in moral philosophy by Francis Hutcheson in his *Inquiry into the Original of Our Ideas of Beauty and Virtue* (1725).[107] Moral theories centering on human sentiments rather than rationality had thus become the prevalent version of moral philosophy shortly before the American Revolution. Reason, in Adam Smith's characteristic formulation, "cannot render any particular object either agreeable or disagreeable to the mind for its own sake."[108] What Scottish moralists, however, shared with such natural-law writers as Grotius, Pufendorf, and Vattel was that an individual's religious convictions were the final stage of moral understanding rather than its starting point.[109] As even Shaftesbury contended, in order to conceive of the laws of nature as expressions of God's ultimate benevolence, human beings must first possess an instinctive sense of good and bad.[110]

In the common contemporary reading, the Hutchesonian moral sense functions as a two-stage mental operation separate from rational capacities. First, the moral sense procures simple perceptions of approbation and disapprobation of the qualities of human affections involved in a given action. Second, the same faculty would perform an immediate "reflection act," providing the agent or the spectator with a feeling (or a moral sentiment) of the actual approval or disapproval of the perceived affections. The criterion for the approval was whether or not the affections manifested disinterested benevolence.[111]

In sum, benevolence was the fundamental – independently existing – natural quality perceived by the moral sense. Natural law itself rested on such a prevalent benevolent disposition, although as a "natural" quality it ultimately was guaranteed by divine benevolence.[112] Hutcheson could thus also bring the concept of virtue again to the center of moral philosophy, for all true virtues (as individual moral qualities) could only flow from disinterested, universal benevolence – from genuine, Christian charity toward all mankind.[113]

Adam Smith held to the Hutcheson-inspired conception of moral approval and disapproval evolving from genuinely varying sentiments in different situations. But Smith rejected the existence of a distinct, moral sense as distinguishable from reason and sentiment.[114] Add to this Thomas Reid's commonsense view of the moral sense as a faculty of intuitive judgment of principles rather than of emotions, and one gains a rich enough picture of the prevailing intellectual confusion about the concept as Jefferson became acquainted with it. Reid took the moral sense to be a distinct natural faculty that provides one with certain self-evident moral principles as intuitive judgments that cause moral feelings, rather than be caused by them. The tenet was in obvious contrast to the moral sentimentalism contemporaries saw in Hutcheson's philosophy.[115]

Jefferson never made it entirely clear to what extent he was aware of the disagreements between these authorities, to all of whom he referred every now and then.[116] It is notable, for example, that Hutcheson's doctrine distinguished natural human affections as the sufficient basis for justice from the properly moral sentiments that needed to arise from disinterested benevolence.[117] By contrast, Jefferson often spoke of the moral sense as arising from a sense of justice that was "instinct, and innate" and "as much a part of our construction as *necessary* in an animal destined to live in society."[118] This innate, instinctive sense of justice could be expressed in terms of simple "reciprocation of rights."[119]

Reid's stand is perhaps not so far from Jefferson's treatment of the moral sense as a distinct faculty for judging behavior rather than only affections.

Jefferson frequently associated his own thought with the views of Reid's close associates, Lord Kames and Dugald Stewart. But he never explicitly embraced Reid's doctrines. Nor did he ever comment on Reid's outspoken opposition to the Lockean conception of simple ideas.[120] He even claimed to share Thomas Law's defense of the Hutchesonian, sentimentalist conception of the moral sense, which ran counter to Reid's use of the term.[121]

Linking Jefferson's moral-sense beliefs to any clear-cut Lockean position is equally difficult. A telling example can be found in his correspondence with Richard Price. Price thought it evident that Hutcheson's moral-sense theory was irreconcilable with the Lockean view of the human mind. In Price's reading, Locke's concept of human experience provided all reliable information and comprised only two elements: First, the simple ideas of secondary qualities imposed on the mind by sense experience; and second, the ideas pertaining to the mind itself – such as pain and pleasure, thinking, and doubting – all of them evolving from reflection. Neither ingredient of experience – sensation or reflection – attained to moral ideas. Only abstract reasoning combined the ideas of sensations into complex, moral ideas. From the tenet that moral ideas are complex ideas, in turn, evolved the Lockean tripartite conception of law as the rational rather than emotional basis of all morality, divisible into the law of God, civil law, and the law of opinion.[122]

When Price confronted Jefferson with this problem of the sentimentalist moral-sense theory, Jefferson's response was far from unequivocal. He stated merely that "we may well admit morality to be the child of understanding rather than of the senses, when we observe that it becomes dearer to us as the latter weaken, & as the former grows stronger by time & experience till the hour arrives in which all other objects lose all their value."[123] In other words, Jefferson chose to circumvent the whole problem of what, in contemporary moral pneumatology should – strictly speaking – count for sense experience as distinct from reflection, and reflection as distinct from pure intellect. Rather, one finds Jefferson frequently referring to sensations, sentiments, and forethought as interrelated aspects of moral understanding, and all of them related to actual social circumstances.

Had Jefferson viewed the moral sense as a metaphysical kind of guarantee of some essential goodness of man, he never could have made the claim that a "man's moral sense must be unusually strong if slavery does not make him a thief."[124] In fact, the Jeffersonian moral sense represented only an instinctive human capacity for moral distinctions. These distinctions were supposed to arise to the level of personal, cognitive recognition as sentiments, eventually reflecting the abstract concept of universal benevolence as more or less compatible with human sociability itself.

To cast light on this view, it is necessary first to establish that Jefferson's understanding of the moral sense was not radically at odds with Helvétius's moral egoism. The assertion of its existence answered the apparently empiricist fact that people often act benevolently. Second, it is necessary to examine

Jefferson's use of the moral sense in the context of historically variable morals, manners, and the general feeling of justice. Third, as will become clear, his moral thought rested on what he called "a sound system of morals" rather than on any given moral pneumatology. Most importantly, Jefferson's belief in moral progress stemmed from the vision of a gradually more widely shared standard of universal justice, a view calling for political action rather than adherence to any particular theory of moral perfectionism.

THE THOMAS LAW LETTER

Jefferson's 1814 letter to Thomas Law is his most comprehensive account of contemporary moral philosophy. Law had sent Jefferson his long essay on Hutcheson, Reid, and other renowned contemporary moralists, titled *Second Thoughts on Instinctive Impulses*. Jefferson began his response with a complimentary remark that Law's work "contained exactly my own creed on the foundation of morality in man."[125] Jefferson's several-page-long account of the issue began with his wondering what made that foundation so problematic for moral theorists:

> It is really curious that, on a question so fundamental, such a variety of opinions should have prevailed among men; and those too of the most exemplary virtue and first order of understanding. It shews [sic] how necessary was the care of the Creator in making the moral principle so much a part of our constitution as that no errors of reasoning or of speculation might lead us astray from it's observance in practice.

Jefferson here asserted that there was a moral principle, which the creator had set in the human mind. People, in general, obeyed the principle regardless of theorists' persistent disagreements about its origins and central characteristics.

Regarding "the theories on this question," Jefferson first rejected Wollaston's speculations about the concept of truth as the proper foundation for examining the issue.[126] Then he refused "the love of god" as the universal motive for benevolent action because there were exemplary atheists "among the most virtuous men." He also pointed out that as "a faculty," the moral sense was "entirely distinct" from the taste for beauty. He further objected to self-love as the central motive for moral action on the grounds that "our relations with others" comprise "the boundaries of morality," for to "ourselves, in strict language, we can owe no duties." Clearly, the Jeffersonian moral sense could not be equated with instrumental reasoning of merely selfish interests.[127]

But Jefferson went on to distinguish sheer self-love from the subjective feeling of pleasure that benevolent action appeared to provide. In reference to Helvétius, he noted that "Egoism, in a broader sense has been thus presented as the source of moral action." Jefferson could fully concur with Helvétius's central idea that a humane man is one who naturally finds other people's suffering emotionally so intolerable that he is "forced to relieve the wretched," even if only for his own sake.[128]

Even this explanation, Jefferson asserted, fell short of fully clarifying why "good acts give us pleasure." And Jefferson's claim was that they do so because "nature hath implanted in our breasts a love of others, a sense of duty to them, a moral instinct in short, which prompts us irresistibly to feel and to succor their distresses."[129] The moral sense thus consisted of two ingredients: First, an involuntary propensity to be emotionally pained by others' distress; and second, an equally involuntary inclination to help them. This account suggests that Jefferson's moral sense was a given natural desire, the satisfaction of which, via benevolent action, was subjectively pleasurable. Hence, it also appeared compatible with some unspecific human inclination toward moral self-betterment.

Jefferson's records provide ample evidence for this kind of summary interpretation of his view of the moral sense. As early as 1771, he argued that morally commendable action pleases the individual subjectively wherever one perceives it. Such pleasure could occur when reading fictional descriptions of virtuous action. As the young Jefferson explained the case to his close friend, when "any signal [sic] act of charity or of gratitude, for instance, is presented either to our sight or imagination, we are deeply impressed with it's beauty and feel a strong desire in ourselves of doing charitable and grateful acts also."[130] Even as spectators, people could experience benevolent action as subjectively pleasurable. In his retirement years' correspondence with John Adams, Jefferson still asserted his belief "that every human mind feels pleasure in doing good to another."[131]

But in all this Jefferson does not appear to have gone much beyond Helvétius's egoism. In essence, the Jeffersonian notion of the moral sense is an individual capacity, which may or may not develop into reflected, self-conscious sentiments of morally commendable behavior. Consider how lightly he circumvented the famous tenet of the Frenchman that it is equally impossible to "love what is good for the sake of good, as to love evil for the sake of evil": Jefferson's counterargument was that the "creator would indeed have been a bungling artist, had he intended man for a social animal, without planting in him social dispositions."[132] Here, as elsewhere, Jefferson simply identified social dispositions with the moral ones.

It is, hence, important not to lose sight of the principal question to which the theory of the moral sense provided an answer in Jefferson's thought. As noted at the very beginning of the Law letter, the doctrine helped explain the apparent fact that people, more or less everywhere, obey "the moral principle." Neither was Jefferson alone in his awe at this phenomenon, for even Hutcheson assumed that genuinely disinterested behavior was an empirical fact.[133] Adam Smith began his renowned study of moral sentiments by noting how "selfish soever man may be supposed, there are evidently some principles in his nature, which interest him in the fortune of others ... That we often derive sorrow from the sorrow of others, is a matter of fact too obvious to require any instances to prove it."[134] For his part, Jefferson settled on the simple idea that people generally follow the principle of justice, and occasionally even that of benevolence, because they are naturally endowed with an innate capacity for grasping them, a capacity worth the title of moral sense.

At the end of the Law letter, Jefferson referred to Lord Kames as "one of the ablest advocates" of the moral-sense doctrine, although he admitted to not having reread Kames's *Essays on the Principles of Morality and Natural Religion* (1751) for almost 50 years. Given Jefferson's frequent references to Lord Kames over the years, the 1751 edition of the book had probably been the young Jefferson's main inspiration in adopting the concept of the moral sense.

In brief, Kames argued that the Hutchesonian distinction between the moral sense and the sense of justice amounted to turning the human moral orientation into absolute obligation to universal benevolence, hence leaving justice out of the equation. This left the door open for David Hume's apparently skeptical insistence that the human sense of justice, even if not arbitrary, was, morally speaking, artificial – a self-interested human propensity for peaceful social life. All in all, Kames fought to prove the naturalness of the human sense of justice and claimed that, just as Hutcheson and others failed to see any selective, "partial benevolence" as genuinely moral, so David Hume failed in resolving "the moral sense into pure sympathy."[135]

Instead of linking the moral sense to either the obligatory notion of universal benevolence or to mere sympathy, Kames appears to have held the sense to be simply an instinctive capacity for distinguishing just, morally acceptable, and effective action from unethical or erroneous behavior.[136] Kames further insisted that this instinctive capacity (for both just and benevolent action) can generally develop in the course of history into a richer, more nuanced – and more abstract – comprehension of people's initially crude patterns of behavior. Kames's example of this development in morals – or the principles of action, as he also called them – was the ancient practice of slaughtering war captives regardless of age or sex. Some contemporary savage peoples, even though sharing the human, instinctive capacity for moral distinctions with all others, still failed to see this practice as immoral.[137]

Yet, how can one reconcile Jefferson's view of the moral sense – as an instinctive capacity for moral distinctions that needed to rise to the level of personal, cognitive moral sentiments – with his claims about how easily people lose sight of universal justice and benevolence, as when slavery turns an individual into a thief?[138] In the end of the Thomas Law letter, Jefferson resorted to the following formulation of Lord Kames's moral-sense doctrine: "[A] man owes no duty to which he is not urged by some impulsive feeling. This is correct, if referred to the standard of general feeling in the given case, and not to the feeling of a single individual."[139] No matter how unerring the moral sense might be, some interpersonally valid interpretation of its dictates was needed. Only a couple of lines earlier, Jefferson stated that "nature has constituted *utility* to man the standard and test of virtue," and even that "different utilities" can be found "under different circumstances."[140] As to the coherent rationale behind such utilities, he once noted that Jesus's attempt to reform the Jewish religion was intended to bring it to "the standard of reason, justice & philanthropy."[141]

MANNERS, MORALS, AND THE STANDARD OF JUSTICE

In elaborating the meaning of the standard of general feeling, it is useful to turn to Query XVIII in the *Notes on the State of Virginia*. This exceptionally brief and extraordinarily gloomy chapter was dedicated to examining the "particular customs and manners" of Virginians themselves. The pessimistic tone emanated from the central theme that white slaveholders had learned customarily to "trample on the rights" of black Virginians. The chapter begins with an interesting remark that it is conspicuously "difficult to determine on the standard by which the manners of a nation may be tried, whether *catholic*, or *particular*."

Whether seen in terms of divine or secular justice, the "whole commerce between master and slave," Jefferson insisted, "is a perpetual exercise of the most boisterous passions, the most unremitting despotism on the one part, and degrading submissions on the other." The larger argument was that there was a standard feeling, and that it was, hypothetically speaking, easier for a foreigner than for a native "to bring to that standard the manners of his nation."[142] Not coincidentally, this Query also includes Jefferson's famous acknowledgment of the ultimate implications of such a standard: "I tremble for my country when I reflect that God is just." The standard stood in direct opposition to the then-legal practice of slaveholding. In sum, the standard of equal justice was available to any slaveholder who did not deliberately choose to subordinate it to the mere written law.

However, Jefferson's primary concern here was the psychological impact of slavery on white children who became accustomed to the "most unremitting despotism" by merely witnessing the practice as innocent bystanders. White children were constantly exposed to the scenes where the "parent storms, the child looks on, [and] catches the lineaments of wrath" toward the slave member of the family. All over the state, generation after generation, its free population was "nursed, educated, and daily exercised in tyranny."

On the moral repercussions of this intergenerational process of simple emulation, Jefferson offered this key line: "The man must be a prodigy who can retain his manners and morals undepraved [sic] by such circumstances."[143] Manners and morals were two different things. What Jefferson maintained was that it was impossible to retain either of them "undepraved" under the contemporary socio-moral conditions of slaveholding Virginia. To be sure, any clear-cut distinction between manners and morals was hardly self-evident, even to contemporary readers. As Mary Wollstonecraft felt it necessary to explain, "manners and morals are so nearly allied that they have often been confounded," whereas, in fact, manners are but "the natural reflection" of morals.[144] Similarly, Adam Smith spoke of the "different manners which custom teaches us to approve," and noted that custom could occasionally lead people into practices alien to ordinary humanity.[145]

Jefferson's Query XVIII sought to establish a link between the simple standard of equal rights, morals, and manners. To grasp the linkage, it is best to begin with what Jefferson stated about the "manners of a nation" as they pertained to an individual: Everyone became familiarized with national manners "by habit."[146] The human being was an "imitative animal" to the extent that from "his cradle to his grave he is learning to do what he sees others do."[147] This was not to suggest that the individual would be a mere machine habitually internalizing communal manners. By "the morals of the people," Jefferson clearly denoted some more or less shared sentiments informing and upholding the manners. Finally, there was the simple standard of equal rights. Even if the exact repercussions of the standard were difficult to discern in daily life, it remained possible for every man to compare any given set of national morals and manners to that standard. The immoral "particular customs and manners" of Virginia slaveholders resulted from retrograde historical developments that called for thorough reforms. In Jefferson's view, even the historical Jesus had mainly aimed "to reform" a set of old-fashioned "moral doctrines to the standard of reason, justice & philanthropy."[148]

Jefferson's 1813 letter to John Adams on the history of philosophy serves well to illustrate how he saw the notion of public morals embodied in historical developments. Drawing on Jacob Brucker's writings in the field, Jefferson argued that the Jewish "books of Morals chiefly consisted in a minute enumeration of [hundreds of] duties." Of all these, the fulfillment of a single one, such as a deathbed confession, could suffice for one's salvation. The Talmud, therefore, served only to evince "the low state of moral philosophy" among the Jews. Most interestingly, Jefferson concurred with Brucker that "a wretched depravity of sentiment and manners must have prevailed before such corrupt maxims could have obtained credit."[149]

Methodologically speaking, study of "the morals" of Old-Testament Jews required, first, seeking out the "precepts" in their literate culture and, second, exploring the "history for it's practices and the principles they prove."[150] In sum, Jefferson suggested that examining the morals of a given nation should start with consideration of the culture's religious precepts and then proceed to exploration of the extent to which these precepts were practiced. According to this method, a nation's morals comprised its principles only as they manifested themselves in national manners.

This general epistemological approach figures in Jefferson's other statements as well. Regarding Native-American cultures, Jefferson talked of investigating "their religion, their morals, their manners, customs, habits, and physical form."[151] This particular formulation may have aimed at a kind of primitive emic-etic distinction between the concepts in question. The first three concepts – religion, morals, and manners – would reflect the insider's point of view that can be observed by an outsider via customs, habits, and physical expressions. Religion thus serves as the rationale for objectively observable customs, morals similarly account for habits, and manners eventually affect even the physical characteristics of a people. As Jefferson elsewhere noted, Indian braves appeared to be generally less muscular than white men as a result of their common practice of leaving all manual work to women.[152]

Be that as it may, on other occasions Jefferson referred to a blend of "morals, manners, and habits" that the Americans historically shared with the British. Or he could speak of an individual possessing "sober and correct morals & habits."[153] Dugald Stewart thought it evident that whenever moral approbation and affections are distracted from the universal end of private happiness, one is dealing with something "properly called [mere] *habits*."[154] All in all, it was clear to Jefferson that "habit alone confounds what is civil practice with natural right."[155]

In this context one can readily understand the limitations of Jefferson's famous assertion that even African Americans were endowed with the moral sense. Jefferson's formulation of the issue was, typically for him, problem-oriented: "Their disposition to theft with which they have been branded, must be ascribed to their situation, and not to any depravity of the moral sense."[156] Hence, his endorsement of the black man's moral equality with the white man became qualified by black people's objectively observable inclination to theft. In striking contrast to this deficiency of character, Jefferson hastened to remark that "we find among them numerous instances of the most rigid integrity, as many as among their better instructed masters, of benevolence, gratitude and unshaken fidelity."

Jefferson's explanation for this apparent contradiction was that the general disposition to thievery among the blacks stemmed from the condition of slavery. The universal grounds of the case, in his eyes, resulted from the fact that for any individual deprived of the "reciprocation of rights," such "rules of conduct" as respecting private property would never be found "in conscience," but would remain "arbitrary."[157] In such conditions, the individual's moral instinct, even if it absorbed raw sensations of justice, did not turn into a conscious moral sentiment of just reciprocity. That was why a "man's moral sense must be unusually strong if slavery does not make him a thief."[158] Again, one encounters the notion of the moral sense as a mere individual capacity, which may or may not develop into reflected, self-conscious sentiments of morally commendable behavior.

Slavery was the initial problem because it deprived black people of the right to cultivate their inborn capacities as human beings. This was Jefferson's explanation for the origins of their "deteriorated state":

> For men probably of any color, but of this color we know, brought from their infancy without necessity for thought and forecast, are by their habits rendered as incapable as children of taking care of themselves, and are extinguished promptly wherever industry is necessary for raising young.[159]

The general underdevelopment of "thought and forecast" among the African Americans undoubtedly pertained to both intellectual and moral capacities. Jefferson clearly associated this underdevelopment with the neglect in the training of their natural capacities, and eventually with the corrupt "habits" with which this negligence had left them. Most tragically, he here contended, black people's capacity for raising their own children as free people had been as permanently damaged as their personal intellectual and moral capacities. In conclusion, African Americans' actual conduct appeared to convey psychological underdevelopment among them, analogous to the typically impulsive behavior of children.[160]

Because of such an intergenerational underdevelopment, Jefferson thought that even the freed Virginia blacks were, in their current state, nothing but "pests in society by their idleness, and the depredations to which this leads them."[161] This intergenerational underdevelopment among African Americans is an omnipresent theme in the Jefferson archive. According to him, Quakers' early attempts to turn slaves into free tenants regularly failed because former masters had to "watch them daily" in order to keep them working instead of stealing from their neighbors. In most cases, Jefferson related, they were eventually reduced again to slavery.[162] Similarly, he argued, the freedmen's colony in British Sierra Leone remained in constant danger of collapsing as a result of the general "idleness and turbulence" of the population, which consisted of former American slaves.[163]

Nevertheless, the subject received so much of Jefferson's attention because white slaveholders were equally victims of mere habits, and "habit alone confounds what is civil practice with natural right."[164] General elementary education was the key to all human progress. Even Jefferson's abolition plan included the provision that slave children would be trained and educated prior to their compulsory expatriation. From early on, he held that they should be "brought up at the public expense, to tillage, arts or sciences," most notably, "according to their geniusses."[165] In 1814 he spoke of "their education and expatriation after a given age."[166] As late as 1820, he made a brief remark about setting the slave children "under guardianship of states."[167] By the same token, the Liberian colony of freed slaves could "introduce the arts of cultivated life, and the blessings of civilization and sciences" to the whole African continent.[168]

In essence, Jefferson's problem with slavery resulted from the corrupt habits of Virginia slaveholders. In light of his account of national morals, manners, and the standard of justice, it was evident that neither slaveholders' philanthropic sentiments toward the slaves, nor their proper "self-love" regarding their children's best interests, had proved strong enough to put a stop to the unjust and harmful practice of slavery in Virginia. To sum up Jefferson's thinking, manners were nothing but a reflection of morals, and morals guided human behavior. Any given individual's morals, however, inevitably comprised his *own reasoning* about the whole set of principles guiding his conduct. That reasoning could always be measured against the standards of equal justice and universal benevolence.

A SOUND SYSTEM OF MORALS

From this notion of individual morals arose the crucial epistemological question in Jefferson's Law letter: "If we did a good act merely from the love of god, and a belief that it is pleasing to him, whence arises the morality of the Atheist?" The question stemmed from Thomas Law's failure to address the fact that "Diderot, D'Alembert, D'Holbach, and Condorcet are known to have been among the most virtuous men. Their virtue, then, must have had some other foundation than the love of God." Similarly, Helvétius, with his egoistic account of morality, was to be regarded as "one of the best men on earth."[169]

Given that Jefferson in this same letter subscribed to the doctrine of the moral sense, he could have resolved the question on purely theoretical grounds – namely by arguing that, if not God, "nature hath implanted in our breasts a love of others, a sense of duty to them, a moral instinct in short." But instead, Jefferson hastened to assert of the atheist: "It is idle to say as some do, that no such being exists. We have the same evidence of the fact as of most of those we act on, to wit, their own affirmations, and their own reasonings to support them." Jefferson's point here was that we "have the same evidence of the fact" that an atheist is truly an atheist, as we have of all other individuals being something else. And evidence in this case consisted merely of "their own affirmations, and reasonings to support" their position.[170]

What, in fact, is the Jeffersonian claim about the moral relevance of individually variable human beliefs, if they are dependent on personal reasoning? Philosopher Morton White finds the key to this question in Jefferson's statute of religious freedom in Virginia, according to which, "the opinions and belief of men depend not on their own will, but follow involuntarily the evidence proposed to their minds."[171] The passage clearly suggests that people cannot simply choose what they actually believe. Indeed, the classic Lockean conception of a man being free is distinguishable from the notion of free will. Or consider Destutt de Tracy's phrase that "we will or we do not will, but we cannot will to will."[172] The statute, in sum, appears to hold that an individual's worldview is not a result of free choice. Rather, one's capacity to judge between true and false and between good and evil is dependent on the evidential support one sees as valid in regard to any given proposition. White captures the core point with the maxim that, "one man, A, has a duty not to try to get another man, B, to try to form his opinions by appealing to anything but the evidence as B sees it."[173]

It is not so surprising, then, to find Jefferson arguing that even a religious belief was only "the assent of the mind to an intelligible proposition."[174] Moreover, as an empiricist, Jefferson readily agreed with any atheist that "no sense informs us" of the existence of a supreme being.[175] In fact, some of "the best men on earth" refuted not only the existence of god, but also the tenet of the inborn moral sense of man. Destutt de Tracy was the theorist Jefferson most often acclaimed when it came to the questions of how the human mind is constructed and how knowledge is attained. But the Frenchman made no appeal to divinity of any kind and positively rejected the existence of the moral sense.

According to Jefferson, Destutt de Tracy agreed with the Hobbesian view of justice as a matter of a contract rather than a result of "the construction of man." What Jefferson had to say about all this was: "Yet, however we may differ as to the foundation of morals, (and as many foundations have been assumed as there are writers on the subject nearly) so correct a thinker as Tracy will give us a sound system of morals."[176] Clearly, Jefferson did not subscribe to any doctrinaire view of the actual foundation of morals.

Consider Jefferson's advice to young Peter Carr: "Moral philosophy. I think it lost time to attend lectures in this branch." Instead of attending lectures, Jefferson recommended to Peter a list of moral readings beginning with Sterne's *Sermons,* and including Socrates, Cicero, Lord Kames, Helvétius, Locke, Lucretius, and Jean Zacharie Paradis de Raymondis's *Traité de Morale et de Bonheur*.[177] Poring over such different moral doctrines was unlikely to convince the young student of any theoretical agreement on the issue. On this occasion Jefferson went even further, insisting that "the rules of our moral conduct" should not be viewed as "a matter of science."[178] This was not to argue that there was no valid set of minimal rules, but only that no scientifically reliable explanation of their true character, as natural or divine or wholly man-made, had yet been attained. Jefferson could certainly have concurred with Reid's famous insistence that within moral sciences, "the practical rules ought to be the standard by which the theory is to be corrected."[179]

This is why Jefferson's theoretical view relied on the Helvétius-inspired natural sociability argument that a humane man tends to find other peoples' sufferings so intolerable that he is emotionally compelled to help them, even if only for his own peace of mind. There is little evidence that Jefferson disagreed with Helvétius's further insistence that an individual's moral judgments about others rarely apply to their true intentions, which may remain obscure even to themselves.[180] The reason was simple: No human being could gain entrance to another person's true motives. Only an individual's actual behavior could prove his virtuousness or viciousness.[181] For his part, Jefferson claimed to have always judged even "the religion of others by their lives" and insisted that by this "same test" the world must judge him.[182]

All in all, Jefferson thought it "remarkable that so many writers, setting out from so many different premises, yet meet, all, in the same conclusion," namely in some general "system of morals."[183] The most obvious "system" available was traditional natural jurisprudence, resting on a few rational principles about reciprocal justice. Adam Smith famously suggested that once the complexities of moral sentiments were fully revealed (as he had managed to do), the further development of moral philosophy should occur mainly in the field of natural jurisprudence.[184] There were, of course, theoretical disagreements even between natural lawyers, such as Grotius, Pufendorf, and Vattel. However, Jefferson was not any more interested in their disagreements than in those of Hume, Hutcheson, Kames, Reid, and Smith. What he said of natural lawyers was that, because these "wise & honest" experts in the field of justice often differed on practical details, "we must appeal to our own feelings and reason to decide between them."[185] In sum, Jefferson submitted to a "sound system of morals," and whether he ever subscribed to any more elaborate notion of morality remains questionable.[186]

This sound system of morals consisted of two elements. First, there was natural jurisprudence under which all rules of conduct were studied in terms of reciprocal rights. Second, there was the principle of universal benevolence, with which the historical Jesus had "supplemented" the tenets of ancient virtue ethicists. Jefferson offered only few practical rules of benevolence, all of them in the language of virtue. He believed that the "essence of virtue is in doing good to others" and, further, that "virtue does not consist in the act we do, but in the end it is to effect" – the end being "the happiness of him to whom it is directed."[187] The "others" – to whom we "strictly speaking owe" all duties – remained definable as any group of people to whose happiness our action might contribute.[188] The underlying rule was simple: The action directed to enhance the situation of one group of people must not worsen the situation of any other group or individual. The principle of justice needed to remain untouched by actions resting on merely selective, "partial benevolence" – as one could find the term in the teachings of Lord Kames.[189]

But how were Jefferson's personal morals related to the morals of the nation? His extraordinarily pessimistic Query XVIII in the *Notes on the State of Virginia*, about the degenerating impact of slavery on both the slaves and their masters, ended with the hopeful remark that, in the aftermath of the still recent Revolution, "the spirit of the master" must be "abating."[190] It is public opinion that provides the crucial, historically reliable standard for Jefferson's progressive moral outlook. All genuinely effective changes for the better rested on that opinion. As Jefferson observed of the Native Americans, among them "public opinion is in the place of law, & restrains morals as powerfully as law ever did."[191] Human "laws and institutions must go hand in hand with the progress of the human mind," Jefferson maintained.[192] It was equally evident that the most respected "men of learning" were those academics whose "manners, morals and habits, are perfectly harmonious with those of the country."[193] Therefore, with "our government," Jefferson hoped, "we shall be able by degrees to introduce sound principles and make them habitual" among the people. In similar terms, it would take "a great man, thoroughly knowing the habits of France," to "accommodate to them the principles of free government."[194]

Jefferson's often-quoted ethical maxim about practice overcoming theory was a maxim of statecraft only. It held that what "is practicable must often controul [sic] what is pure theory; and the habits of the governed determine in great degree what is practicable." Eventually, it was owing to "the different circumstances, prejudices, and habits of different nations" that "the constitution of no one would be reconcilable to any other in every point."[195] This understanding lay behind Jefferson's most central contention about moral progress: It did not require a commitment to one or another theoretically disputed foundation of morality, but a commitment to developing generally shared standards of equal justice to all and benevolence toward those in need of help.

SCIENTIFICALLY CONSISTENT BELIEFS

Individuals living in the Jeffersonian world of imperfect knowledge could hold to different worldviews with personal constancy and moral rectitude. Doing so, any man of Enlightenment first acknowledged the limits of his own cosmological assumptions. Describing his personal views about the ultimate ordering of the universe, Jefferson wrote that "it is impossible, I say, for the human mind not to believe that there is, in all this, design." What he thought even atheists could agree with him on was that empirically verifiable "realities" consisted of matter, motion, and of the yet inexplicable "principle of reproduction" that turned matter "into new and other forms." All this Jefferson could constantly "see and witness" in full agreement with an atheist, just as he held that, in strictly empiricist terms, "no sense informs us" of the existence of "an ulterior cause, or Creator of the world."[196] Similarly, the currently incalculable routes of comets could "require renovation under some other laws" than the familiar Newtonian ones, and the mammoth "probably" still was a living species.[197]

Insofar as people lack interpersonally demonstrable knowledge of the providential ordering of the universe, one could leave the majority to determine the contemporary common understanding of such questions – without letting it dictate what an individual citizen should think of them. After all,

Jefferson never claimed to know what the result of human progress would look like at the end of days. That is why freedom of conscience remained a terminal value in his professedly progressive worldview.

In the field of ethics, Jefferson adhered to the notions that human sociability arises from given, natural emotions of man as "an animal destined to live in society" and that these emotions are expressible in genuinely moral terms as individual sensations and sentiments only when considered together with such abstract concepts as universal justice and benevolence. Thus, Jefferson could concur with Hutcheson's tenet that natural human affections serve as a sufficient basis for the sense of justice needed to keep society together. Nevertheless, Jefferson did not consider such affections as evidently distinguishable from disinterested benevolence as Hutcheson appeared to do. In the case of parenthood, for example, Jefferson acknowledged that the compulsory deportation of slave children and the "separation of infants from their mothers, too, would produce some scruples of humanity" – even if, as he held, that "would be straining at a gnat, and swallowing a camel."[198]

Jefferson's central accusation against slavery was that it kept human beings from developing their natural capacities – regardless of their perhaps different genetic character. The slave by definition had to "lock up the faculties of his nature" in his lifelong compulsory state of irresponsible childhood.[199] Slavery was just as apparently morally wrong as it was unnatural for its victims. The inborn human capacities for moral and intellectual improvement did nothing by themselves. Only when an individual began reflecting his own social surroundings could his personal capacities gradually begin to provide him with intellectual and moral virtues.

One may argue that it is dangerously close to confusing facts with value statements to insist, as Jefferson did, that moral concepts can be approached from the notion of human sociability. Yet there is no need to over-interpret the significance of the Humean guillotine distinguishing between "is" and "ought" as if no distinction between facts and values had ever occurred before Hume. The assessment of animal behavior as morally irrelevant was clear to such early natural lawyers as Francis Suarez and Samuel Pufendorf, for example.[200] It was equally clear to Emer de Vattel that the "Romans often confounded the law of nations with the law of nature," thus erroneously equating jus gentium with the moral natural law. Even the famous Justinian codification of ancient Roman laws appeared to speak of the law of nature as pertaining to all animate life rather than only "that natural law which is peculiar to man."[201] By the same token, when probing the moralities of Helvétius, Hume, Hutcheson, Kames, Reid, and Smith, one could find them simply pitying a man who cannot distinguish between right and wrong.[202] In this they shared the ancient paradigm that some personal propensity to self-betterment was a precondition rather than a consequence of theoretical moral studies.

Jefferson's position that the safest epistemological approach to morality begins with the notion of human sociability may appear reconcilable with the modern, evolutionary notion of altruism. Even such a position does not necessarily preempt acknowledgment of hugely complicated, varying human patterns of behavior as qualitatively distinct from those of the rest of animate nature. None of the aforesaid is to question Jefferson's personal belief that "the moral sense or conscience" provides us information about somehow objectively existent moral qualities or relations emanating from the twofold – physical and moral – divine ordering of the world.[203] However, Jefferson's records give us no insight into what such qualities and relations could objectively be. In the case of qualities, his metaphysics did not go further than subscribing to the magnetism of a lodestone, which "nobody supposes to retire to hold a substantive and distinct existence" once the lodestone ceases to exist.[204] In addressing moral relations, Jefferson frequently treated them as simply juridical relations between equal, free moral agents under the law of nature. Moral qualities he equated with virtues as morally desirable individual character traits. Such character traits were observable only in the actual conduct of men and in their own utterances about the morals that supposedly underlay their conduct.

Politically, Jefferson sought for such an epistemologically circumspect image of man as a moral agent that it could shape the morals of the nation and lead to peaceful changes in law more compatible with universal justice and benevolence. At the end of his life he lamented that, even regarding the abolition of slavery, the necessary "revolution in public opinion" was not in sight.[205] Nevertheless, Jefferson's morality did not remain a captive of mere political expediency. To understand why not, one needs to consider his Stoic-inspired ideal of the man of virtue and wisdom.

3

Progress and the Wise Man's Virtue

VIRTUES OF THE HEAD AND HEART

Jefferson's conviction that "death alone can seal the title of any man to his honor" drew on the ancient, eudaemonistic notion of the man of virtue leading an individually satisfying and morally good life.[1] It is from this twofold notion of purposeful life that the most crucial concepts of Jefferson's ethics – virtue and wisdom – arise. Indeed, the Jefferson archive teems with remarks about praiseworthy individuals of "talents and virtue" or of "virtue and wisdom." Such men appeared to form a natural aristocracy of the genuinely "good and able," a conception that Jefferson readily contrasted to an "artificial" aristocracy of "wealth and birth."[2] Most tellingly, Jefferson regarded the historical Jesus as the personification of the "best qualities of the human head and heart" – combining at once the "wisdom" of the head and "justice and goodness" of the heart.[3]

The ancient image of the wise and virtuous man could relate to a man leading a good life, as defined in Aristotelian ethics, or a self-sufficient, Stoic figure partaking of the divine universal reason of nature, or an Epicurean enjoying true tranquility of the soul, freed even from the fear of death. In Jefferson's parlance, the image denoted a man of the Enlightenment seeking wisdom and virtue, within the limits of his inborn talents and inclinations. As this chapter shows, seeking moral and intellectual self-betterment appeared an apparently natural imperative in Jefferson's imagination.

As for the ancients, so for Jefferson; virtues were morally desirable character traits. He could thus equate "the practice of virtue" with "the practice of morality."[4] It is worth remarking first of all that Jefferson's stated Epicurean convictions coexisted with his embrace of the much more common eighteenth-century use of the Stoic conception of honesty as the sum of all virtue.[5] Jefferson's letters and memoranda teem with such personal assessments as the claim that Aaron Burr had never been "an honest, frank-dealing man."[6] One Dr. Mason's "character" he knew equally well, for his "lying and slandering."[7] When it came to the "virtues" of the French General Dumouriez, Jefferson was convinced that he "has none."[8] The most telling example is Jefferson's comparison of John Adams and Alexander Hamilton. Adams "was honest as a politician, as well as man," whereas Hamilton was "honest as a man, but as a politician" less so because of his belief "in the necessity of force or corruption to govern men."[9] Ironically or not, Jefferson also thought it "fortunate for those in public trust that posterity will judge them by their works" and not by the opinions of their opponents.[10]

Honesty was not equivalent to its social appearance: honorable reputation. To be sure, in the commonplace parlance of the eighteenth century, a gentleman's honor could well comprise both his moral and intellectual worth – at least among those considered his equals.[11] Alexander Hamilton died defending his honor in a duel with Aaron Burr. Jefferson, who never appears to have been challenged to a duel, preached against this "barbarious [sic] custom" as incompatible with the dignity of a civilized man.[12] His implicit distinction between true honesty and its mere appearance also figures in his political statements. He famously mocked British bicameralism for resting "on the house of commons for honesty, and the lords for wisdom" as "if honesty were to be bought with money" and "wisdom were hereditary."[13] At least after the "revolution of 1800," the American people could rely on the "wisdom and integrity" of their national leaders.[14]

For Jefferson's understanding of the concept of virtue itself, the difference between inborn abilities and good qualities is of fundamental importance. Even if the aspiration to virtue and wisdom appeared natural, the qualities themselves were not inborn. Rather, the initial stage of all education was aimed at a gradual awakening of a child's inborn intellectual and moral capacities for virtue. This is why one finds Jefferson summing up the purpose of all education as twofold – an "honest heart being the first blessing," while the second was "a knowing head."[15] He frequently encouraged his daughters, grandchildren, and numerous other youngsters to the constant exercise of virtue. In a typical passage, Jefferson warned his favorite nephew, Peter Carr, not to presume that "under any circumstances, it is best for you to do a dishonorable thing." Even in secrecy, away from the eyes of others, one should inquire of oneself "how you would act were all the world looking at you." "Encourage all your virtuous dispositions," Jefferson lectured, "and exercise them whenever an opportunity arises."[16] Jefferson's daughter, Martha, was similarly counseled to develop "daily those principles of virtue and goodness which will make you valuable to others and happy in yourself." She also was to acquire "those talents and that degree of science, which will guard you at all times against ennui, the most dangerous poison of life."[17]

Intellectual virtues of the head carried definite ethical significance of their own in Jefferson's thought. In addition to lecturing Peter Carr about the blessings of true honesty, Jefferson sent his young disciple long reading lists in history, philosophy, mathematics, and poetry. But it was only when Peter reached the age of seventeen that Jefferson urged him to begin religious studies. Were Peter, in the course of his critical scrutiny of the scriptures to lose his faith in them, he was answerable not for the "rightness, but uprightness" of his mature convictions. Even so, Peter could "find incitements to virtue in the comfort and pleasantness" people naturally felt "in it's exercise."[18] Honesty included the intellectual constancy owed to oneself.

The development of one's intellectual and moral capacities remained a lifelong task. As the young Jefferson quoted Lord Bolingbroke in his Literary Commonplace Book, there was a "perpetual conflict in the breast of every man" between virtue and vice.[19] Even "the virtues of the heart" or "its good dispositions" could weaken, as Jefferson made clear to Peter Carr when warning him of the allure of excessive traveling. Losing touch with one's own country and cultural background could undermine Peter's chance of becoming "precious to your country, dear to your friends, happy within yourself."[20] Failure to maintain virtuous character traits was certain to erode one's sensitivity to the moral aspects of everyday life. The active mind, Jefferson emphasized, was "the grand recipe for felicity" because intellectual idleness alone could drive people to such "miserable" pastimes as "gaming, which corrupts our dispositions, and teaches us a habit of hostility against all mankind."[21]

In order to establish that Jefferson's ethics were based on moral rather than any strictly religious faith, this chapter will first deal with the question of how Jefferson's religious convictions related to his ethics of wisdom and virtue. Second, it is necessary to distinguish his embrace of natural, human affections from his moral sentimentalism. Only then may one ask in what sense virtues were individually acquirable qualities and how Jefferson's Epicurean notion of virtue was tied to the idea of universal benevolence. In his famous 1786 "Head and Heart" letter to Maria Cosway, the whole domain of morals was left to "the mechanism of the Heart." Once the role of this mechanism in moral judgments is properly understood, Jefferson's definitions of virtue and virtuous action can be related to the concept of utility and, eventually, to the role of virtue in politics.

MORAL FAITH

Just as Jefferson customarily distinguished his deistic beliefs from scientific facts, so he kept his personal religious opinions separate from his moral faith. There is no question that he regarded the historical Jesus of Nazareth as the greatest moral teacher in history. Whereas the ancients had taught justice "toward our neighbors & countrymen," only the historical Jesus had introduced the doctrine that one should "embrace with benevolence the whole family of mankind."[22] Jefferson thus fully agreed with John Adams's lifelong "religious reading" resulting in the simple command to "be just and good." With this command, Jefferson further exclaimed, "all our enquiries must end."[23] The point was to keep the moral faith in universal justice and benevolence separate from any particular religious or nonreligious doctrines.

Jefferson famously questioned a number of conventional Christian tenets, beginning with the trinity.[24] As to the so-called biblical truths, he was convinced that "the day will come when the mystical generation of Jesus, by the supreme being as his father in the womb of a virgin will be classed with the fable of the generation of Minerva in the brain of Jupiter."[25] Even though Jefferson considered Jesus a "Great Reformer of the Hebrew code of religion, it is not to be understood that I am with him in all his doctrines. I am a Materialist."[26] Even the ethical teachings of Jesus he read just as he read "those of other antient [sic] and modern moralists, with a mixture of approbation and dissent."[27] In explicating the differences between their moral codes, he noted that, although Jesus "preaches the efficacy of repentance towards forgiveness of sin, I require a counterpoise of good works to redeem it."[28]

The underlying rationale for Jefferson's position is well captured in a statement from 1789:

> I never submitted the whole system of my opinions to the creed of any party of men whatever in religion, in philosophy, in politics, or in anything else where I was capable of thinking for myself. Such an addiction is the last degradation of a free and moral agent. *If I could not go to heaven but with a party, I would not go there at all.*[29]

Jefferson thought of himself as a moral agent responsible for thinking for himself and believing only what he could personally grasp. Were God to demand more, he would prefer not go to heaven.[30] But contrary to widespread Federalist accusations that Jefferson was an atheist, he definitely considered himself a religious man. There is no evidence that he ever resigned from the Virginia Episcopal Church, but there is evidence that he occasionally donated money to the Episcopal as well as other churches.[31] As Jefferson fully agreed with the central tenet of universal benevolence as preached by the historical Jesus, he proclaimed himself "a Christian in the only sense in which we wish anyone to be; sincerely attached to his doctrines, in preference to others; ascribing to himself every *human* excellence, and believing he never claimed any other."[32]

Jefferson's stated hope that Unitarianism would eventually become a national American religion hardly provides the key to his moral faith as compatible with his open-ended notion of human progress. His ethics did not assume that all mankind must eventually agree with his religious opinions. In fact, it is next to impossible to determine what strand of Unitarianism would have been truly compatible with Jefferson's central moral tenet of never giving "up morals for mysteries."[33]

Jefferson's famous attempt to draft a reliable summary of the New Testament at the beginning of his second presidential term reveals the difficulties of reconciling his views with any known version of Christianity. It took only a couple of evenings in 1804 for Jefferson to extract what he considered to be the reliable parts of the Gospels and to compile his own only forty-six-page summary of them. He titled the outcome *The Philosophy of Jesus of Nazareth Extracted from the Accounts of His Life and Doctrines as Given by Mathew, Mark, Luke, & John*. The compilation became known as the "Jefferson Bible" only in the twentieth century, for Jefferson never published it.[34]

The most probable reason why the compilation remained unpublished was the instant opposition he encountered concerning the very premises of the alleged "philosophy of Jesus." Both his most respected authorities in religious matters, Benjamin Rush and Jefferson's hand-picked high priest of Unitarianism, Joseph Priestley, disagreed with his Unitarianism. In his memoranda related to the project, Jefferson subscribed neither to Jesus's divinity nor to the idea that Jesus viewed his mission as divine. The latter rejection was too much even for Jefferson's friends. When, years later, he admitted that Jesus perhaps did believe his mission to be divine, he still held the point ethically irrelevant.[35] Be that as it may, publication of any part of the "Jefferson Bible," particularly during his presidency, would have ignited a furious public debate about his Christianity.

Jefferson's "Philosophy of Jesus of Nazareth" was dedicated to the American Indians, and it was meant to disseminate the ethics of universal benevolence, not to settle any theological issues. Neither do Jefferson's later comparisons of the translations of the New Testament prove that he ever took the Bible as the word of God. In 1825, he strongly advised one Alexander Smyth against expending energy in interpreting the Apocalypse: "What has no meaning admits no explanation. And pardon me if I say, with the candor of friendship, that I think your time too valuable and your understanding of too high an order, to be wasted in these paralogisms [sic]."[36] To the Reverend Isaac Story, interested in the "transmigration of souls," the president calmly responded that he was relieved that "these speculations" had been "only the amusement" of the Reverend's "leisure hours." Ever since his early youth, Jefferson had "ceased to read or think" anything that dealt with "knowledge of the country of spirits."[37]

Despite both contemporary and later speculations that Jefferson matured into a more religious person over the years, it seems that his "true religion" remained very close to his early characterization of the subject in the *Notes on the State of Virginia*. His commitment was, first and foremost, against error. It barred confusing theological tenets with the accumulating knowledge in natural and moral sciences. In 1817, his religion consisted of two notions: First, "the moral precepts, innate in man, and made part of his physical constitution, as necessary for a social being"; and second, "the sublime doctrines of philanthropism [sic], and deism taught us by Jesus of Nazareth." Even on this occasion he qualified both doctrines, considering them true only to the extent "which all agree."[38]

Jefferson's personal faith in a benevolent supreme being as the ultimate source of justice and benevolence never superseded his commitment to the interpersonally valid precept of individual freedom of conscience. Whomever he might have considered the "saviour" of mankind, he maintained that even his syllabus of the teachings of Jesus was "of his doctrines, not all of mine."[39] When the University of Virginia was founded on Jefferson's initiative in the early 1820s, he caused nothing short of a cultural shock by excluding theology from its curriculum. The "general religion" of "peace, reason, and morality" would best be advanced by letting students practice religion elsewhere and keeping priests out of the grounds.[40]

In the face of a legion of "true" Christians concerned about the state of the president's soul, the elder Jefferson, time and again, asserted his "right to believe in one god, if so my reason tells me." This was not to deny the right of others to believe in the trinity. Both religions could "make honest men."[41] On another occasion, Jefferson insisted that he had always "judged of the religion of others by their lives," which was the very "same test [by which] the world must judge me."[42] In essence, he considered any "religion substantially good which produces an honest life."[43] In famously proclaiming that "my religion ... is known to my god and myself alone," Jefferson treated his religious beliefs as essentially incommunicable. They fell beyond any interpersonal criteria of truth.[44] To assess such a religion in moral terms, it thus followed that its "evidence before the world is to be sought in my life. If that has been *honest and dutiful to society*, the religion which has regulated it cannot be a bad one."[45]

Committed to a religion that may produce an honest life, Jefferson's moral faith had little concern with the afterlife. Rather, it was supposed to rest on a minimum set of moral tenets on which all could agree. Although the historical Jesus, more than any other man, personified genuine "justice and goodness," his teachings about the afterlife could be considered as merely "supplementary to the other motives to moral conduct."[46] Even an atheist could consent to the idea that human morality should rest on equal justice and universal benevolence. Consequently, in Jefferson's account, the historical Jesus, rather than introducing a divine love commandment, needed only extend the scope of moral study by pushing "his scrutinies [sic] into the heart of man."[47] Jefferson's moral sentimentalism amounted to little more than a belief in an innate human inclination to keep good faith with all human beings.

Interestingly, it is in Jefferson's numerous memoranda on the law of nature and nations that one finds him most forcefully arguing that every man, "savage or civilized," could find the general precepts of justice and benevolence as "written in the heart of man."[48] That faith one was to keep equally with all human beings. In his early memorandum on religious toleration, Jefferson noted that John Locke

> denies toleration to those who entertain opns. contrary to those moral rules necessary for the preservation of society; as for instance, that faith is not kept with those ... who deny the existence of a god. [It was a great thing to go so far (as he himself sais of the parl. who framed the act of tolern.) but where he stopped short, we may go on.][49]

In light of this quotation, it is clear that Locke's religious toleration ruled out nonbelievers, whereas Jefferson advocated freedom of conscience. In his autobiography from 1821, he insisted that the Virginia statute for religious freedom from 1786 was intended to apply not only to the Christian, the Jew, the Muslim, and the Hindu, but also to "the Gentile" and the "infidel of every denomination."[50]

Whether or not inscribed in the heavens, universal benevolence – and notably, even some of its juridical applications – could be taught to innocent children, to ignorant savages, and to degenerate barbarians alike. The teacher needed only appeal to something they all would find in their hearts. Such an endeavor appeared both natural and moral within Jefferson's progressive historical outlook. To be sure, Jefferson occasionally appealed to "the head & heart of every rational and honest man" as a twofold site where "[n]ature has written her moral laws and where every man may read them for himself."[51] While rational head was often requisite for grasping the fine points of natural law, "the preservation of good faith" remained the ultimate end.[52]

As to purely jurisprudential concerns, Jefferson fully concurred with Emer de Vattel's maxim that all "the tranquillity, the happiness & security of mankind rest on justice, on the obligation to respect the rights of others." Respect for "our actual possession" of mental and material rights was the first aspect of justice; the second consisted of promises concerning "the things that cannot be delivered or executed on the spot." Commitment to "the faith of promises" sufficed for justice.[53] To formulate this maxim in more universal terms, one should keep faith in other people's sense of honor – with or without specific contracts. This fulfilled the Jeffersonian, tacit obligation of respect for the rights of man. A man who breaches his promises "violates his faith" in simple honesty, Jefferson thought. Honesty signified the human obligation to reciprocal justice on a global scale as well.[54] In international politics, Jefferson often referred to Americans' "good faith towards other nations."[55] Similarly, he considered it a crude abuse of his faith for European leaders to act as if it were mere "folly for an honest man to suppose that others could be honest also."[56]

THE LIMITS OF LOVE

Jefferson's outspoken conviction that human morality evolves from sentiments rather than from reason is reconcilable with his use of the language of virtue. Yet, as the young Jefferson could have learned from Bolingbroke, there was a perpetual conflict "between virtue and vice" in "the breast of every man," and to manage that conflict man had "to restrain his appetites, to govern his passions, and to make reason the law of life."[57] As Jefferson saw it, the teachings of ancient Stoics and Epicureans were, in essence, about "the government of those passions which, unrestrained would disturb our tranquillity of mind."[58]

Generically speaking, then, virtue was about getting the usual roster of emotions, desires, affections, and passions under self-control. Each emotion was to be deemed either proper or improper in relation to the situation where it arose. In Jefferson's words, the "perfection of the moral character" resided in "a just equilibrium of all the passions."[59] Even his draft of the Virginia criminal codes began with the simple presumption that people, whenever under the "dominion of inordinate passions, commit violations of the lives, liberties and property of others."[60] By the same token, Jefferson's occasional puzzlement about "the many useless miseries to which Providence seems to expose us" resulted from the conviction that every "passion" was hypothetically useful "within proper bounds."[61]

Love itself could appear as a mere natural affection, neutral in moral terms – and, if escaping all self-control, a depraved passion. In response to Helvétius's classic claim that one may fall in love with vice as easily as with virtue, Jefferson invoked the simple notion that the creator had planted a moral instinct in all men as essentially "social" beings. Whether or not sociability provides a solid basis for properly moral, disinterested motivation, for Jefferson all human affections appeared measurable in relationship to sociability. In this sense, they also were conceivable in terms of respect for others, given that self-love was "no part of morality."[62]

Jefferson's implicit concern with the proper use of the term "love" recurs in the letters to his daughter Martha. She was encouraged to "be good and industrious" so as to become what her father would "most love in the world."[63] In one letter, Jefferson provided Martha with an astonishingly detailed schedule for the practice of music, dance, letter writing, and the study of French and English from early morning to bedtime. He supplemented these remarks with the suggestion that she should strive to become more worthy of her father's affections:

> The acquirements which I hope you will make under the tutors I have provided for you will render you more worthy of my love, and if they cannot increase it, they will prevent it's diminution ... If you love me then, strive to be good under every situation and to all living creatures, and to acquire those accomplishments which I have put in your power... [64]

The suggestion that a father's love could increase or weaken according to his daughter's accomplishments may strike the modern reader as stunningly insensitive.[65] However, Jefferson did not here refer to fatherly love in the conventional sense of the word. Martha's whole education was about developing her given abilities to attain "what is right or what is clever."[66] Jefferson's natural, parental affection was meant to be elevated into a more noble feeling of compassion by her gradual refinement of character – that is, her personal growth in moral and intellectual virtues. Similarly, the young Peter Carr was instructed not to lose any occasion to "increase" his "worth" by constant exercise of his "will."[67]

Neither was sexual love a simple desire in the Jeffersonian imagination, but something meant to reach "a delicate mixture of sentiment and sensation."[68] By the same token, Jefferson thought that excessive reading of romantic novels turned youngsters into sentimentalists with "sickly judgment."[69] He specifically lamented about African Americans that their "love is ardent, but kindles the senses only, not the imagination." As their imagination generally appeared to escape "every restraint of reason and taste," even their poetry did "more honour to the heart than the head."[70]

Ethics arising from sentiments could well include tragic choices. In the famous "Adam and Eve" letter Jefferson warned his private secretary, William Short, not to fall victim to too much sensibility when assessing the radical phases of the French Revolution:

> The liberty of the whole earth was depending of the issue of the contest, and was ever such a prize won with so little of innocent blood? My own affections have been deeply wounded by some martyrs to this cause, but rather than it should have failed, I would have seen half the earth desolated. Were there but an Adam & an Eve left in every country, & left free, it would be better than as it now is.[71]

Jefferson's "deeply wounded" affections provided him little guidance in assessing the overall significance of the French Revolution. On another occasion, he described it as highly "painful" that he could not actively promote slave emancipation from the president's office.[72] In the midst of the Haitian revolution, then Secretary of State Jefferson denied financial help to the white fugitives from Santo Domingo "with a bleeding heart."[73] By the same token, Jefferson readily admitted that his emancipation plan, separating slave children from their parents, would cause "some scruples of humanity," although, in fact, "this would be straining at a knat and swallowing a camel."[74]

Although Edward Coles's benevolent motives in promoting immediate slave emancipation certainly honored "both the head and heart," Jefferson severely warned him of too much sensibility. As he viewed it, "no lover of excellence in the human character can innocently consent" to the black population's "amalgamation with the other color" and to the general degradation that was certain to follow. In 1820, northern abolitionists with their "unwise and unworthy passions," appeared ready to dissolve the Union and leave the old Jefferson to die in the belief that all the sacrifices of "the generation of 1776, to acquire self-government and happiness to their country," had been useless.[75] On a more general level, Jefferson could argue that the most dangerous enemies of Latin Americans were ignorance and superstition residing "in their own breasts," a fact that first and foremost called for "emancipation from their priests." After all, he insisted, "ignorance and bigotry, like other insanities, are incapable of self-government."[76]

ARTIFICIALITY IN LEARNING VIRTUE

The central role of emulation as the method of learning moral virtue is a notion that Jefferson shared with the ancients. Moral virtue, being in essence a fully internalized, fixed disposition to act, could not be acquired by mere theoretical study of moral philosophy.[77] As Jefferson mused in a letter to his friend Robert Skipwith, "dispositions of the mind, like limbs of body, acquire strength by exercise. But exercise produces habit; and in the instance we speak, the exercise being of the moral feelings, produces a habit of thinking and acting virtuously."[78] As the ancients held, moral deficiency in conduct manifested the weakness of will – the human tendency to occasionally act against one's better knowledge. Virtues were achievable via virtuous action, and if left unpracticed, they could fade away.[79]

Jefferson's grandson, Thomas Jefferson Randolph, recalled riding with his grandfather when an African American passed them on the road and bowed to them. Unlike Jefferson himself, his grandson did not care to respond. Jefferson afterward lectured him on the importance of good manners, asking, as Randolph later reminisced, "Do you permit a negro to be more of a gentleman than yourself?"[80] Given the racist aspect of the lesson, Jefferson was hardly suggesting that the young Randolph should fall into considerations about whether an African American was his moral equal. Instead, Jefferson counseled his grandson about habitual good behavior as the first step in internalizing virtue. One needed to act like a gentleman in order to become one.

Similarly, Jefferson told the young Peter Carr to encourage his "virtuous dispositions, and exercise them whenever an opportunity arises; being assured that they will gain strength by exercise, as a limb of the body does, and that exercise will make them habitual."[81] In sum, virtues were individual character traits constructed on the foundation of the person's inborn talents and inclinations by means of constant practice. Even on a national level, Jefferson thought that "numbers produce emulation, and multiply the chances of improvement, and one improvement begets another."[82]

Jefferson's attachment to Scottish sentimentalist tenets did not alter this fundamental aspect of his virtue ethics. For Adam Smith, virtue required habit, resolution, and delicacy of sentiment.[83] In order to achieve such delicacy, Smith insisted that the art of distinguishing between a pleasing and displeasing "tenor of conduct" required learning from "a vast variety of instances."[84] Francis Hutcheson's passing remark that, at an individual level, the "origins" of virtue lay in "instruction and habit" was certainly not intended to refute his own tenet of the natural moral sense of man.[85]

Another of Jefferson's favorite Scottish moralists, Lord Kames, made an interesting distinction among natural, primary, and secondary virtues. Natural virtue referred to the inborn human sense of justice, which, when manifested in the action of a voluntary agent, was called a primary virtue.[86] The distinction between primary and secondary virtues was more genuinely individualistic. Kames argued that "friendship, generosity, [and] softness of manners, form particular characters, and serve to distinguish one man from another."[87] Secondary virtues assumed the presence of primary virtues in a person seeking self-betterment. In Kames's words, "refinement in taste and manners, operating by communication upon the moral sense, occasions a stronger feeling of immorality in every vicious action, than what would arise before such refinement." Eventually, even "the moral sense improves in its delicacy, as well as other senses."[88]

David Hume famously claimed that the sense of justice is morally speaking "artificial," but not "arbitrary," as if at odds with human nature.[89] Jefferson tended to use the terms "arbitrary" and "artificial" as synonyms, but that does not mean that he did not distinguish between a moral error and an artificial, conventional approximation of justice and morality.[90] As he insisted, once deprived of the basis of "reciprocation of rights," even such elementary "rules of conduct" as respect for private property could never be found "in conscience," but would remain "arbitrary."[91] The conception of arbitrary morality underlies Jefferson's argument that the "want or imperfection of the moral sense in some men, like the want or imperfection of the senses of sight and hearing in others, is no proof that it is not a general characteristic of the species." For those suffering from severe imperfection of the moral sense, he mused, "we endeavor to supply the defect by education, by appeals to reason and calculation." This task Jefferson attributed to a tripartite class of moral educators. Priests were to lecture about "the prospects of a future state of retribution for the evil as well as good done while here." Legislators' "corrective measures" consisted of "rewards and penalties established by law." The moralists' role was confined to demonstrations of how "honesty promotes interest in the long run."[92] Although the list of corrective measures corresponded to the traditional division of duties into those owed to God, to others, and to oneself, they all appealed to the selfish maxim that right conduct pays off.

As for the distinction between arbitrary and artificial in Jefferson's parlance, it is worth emphasizing that the orientation toward virtuous behavior was, in a sense, necessarily artificial until the process of learning virtue began to modify one's character. When initiating the young, Jefferson offered his disciples conspicuously artificial, self-serving reasons to learn virtue. "From the practice of the purest virtue," he lectured the fifteen-year-old Peter Carr, "you may be assured you will derive the most sublime comforts in every moment of your life, and in the moment of death."[93] The young Thomas Jefferson Randolph was to study virtue for such a self-interested reason that the "determination never to do what is wrong, prudence, and good humor, will go far towards securing you the estimation of the world."[94]

Jefferson never let go of his belief that moral conceptions needed to apply to the assumption of human sociability. As a morally desirable character trait of an individual social being, genuine virtue could not be unsocial. In Jefferson's use of terms, virtue was artificial insofar as it was not yet fully internalized so as to qualify as a permanent, personal disposition to act. This is why the Jeffersonian refinement in taste and manners was never impersonal, nor ultimately artificial. This feature of Jefferson's moral faith is in tension with the much-discussed notion of politeness as a new social, rather than moral, virtue in the eighteenth-century discourse on human refinement.[95]

Jefferson's letter to Charles Bellini from 1785 provides a telling example of his indifference to politeness as a value in itself. When it came to "what is called polite manners," Jefferson fully acknowledged that the Europeans were well ahead of the crude Americans in habitual table manners. He also remarked that the American literary elite remained approximately half a dozen years behind their French counterparts. The somewhat ironical explanation for this was that it took an average of six years for a significant book to reach the New World. But it was just as evident to Jefferson that the American "mass of the people" was two centuries ahead of the French.[96] Post-revolutionary America had simply reached a general level of civilization a good deal more ethically advanced than that of pre-revolutionary France.

Another, even more pertinent reference to the concept of politeness occurs in Jefferson's 1808 letter to his grandson Randolph. Jefferson counseled the young man against getting into useless arguments in social life, while he carefully pointed out that politeness was not a real virtue, albeit very close to good humor as a character trait:

> I have mentioned good humor as one of the preservatives of our peace and tranquillity. It is among the most effectual and it's effect is so well imitated and aided artificially by politeness, that this also becomes an acquisition of first rate value.... In truth, politeness is artificial good humor, it covers the natural want of it, and ends by rendering habitual a substitute nearly equivalent to the real virtue.[97]

In light of this crucial passage, Jefferson's politeness was simply an artificial mode of the virtue of good humor. The grandson needed to grasp the difference on his own. This is why the grandfather offered only advice on how to begin developing the virtue in question. Without exhibiting politeness the grandson was unlikely ever to acquire genuine "good humour," for only when internalized as a permanent disposition to act, it counted as a virtue.

Conspicuously, the method for learning virtue appears wholly artificial throughout this letter. Jefferson reminisced about how he had learned to "direct himself" as a youngster and pointed out that, unlike many of his early friends, he had avoided becoming "as worthless to society as they were." The young Jefferson had acquainted himself with such remarkable men of virtue and of general approbation as Dr. Small, Mr. Wythe, and Peyton Randolph. "Knowing the even and dignified line they pursued," he had been able to opt for the proper line of conduct by emulating these "characters of very high standing." For a youth in his formative years, like Jefferson in Williamsburg, the method for discerning the secrets of right conduct was emulation of his betters, "whereas seeking the same object through a process of moral reasoning, and with the jaundiced eye of youth, I should often have erred."[98]

Insofar as virtues were initially artificial, so were vices. Telling a lie once only made it easier the second time, Jefferson lectured, until lying "becomes habitual."[99] The habitual basis of learning both virtues and vices could prove decisive in the earliest phases of one's moral orientation. According to Jefferson, man is but "an imitative animal," and from "his cradle to his grave he is learning to do what he sees others do."[100] As Jefferson noted about the current situation among Virginia slaveholders, if "nursed, educated, and daily exercised in tyranny," only a prodigy could "retain his manners and morals undepraved [sic] by such circumstances."[101] Putting aside Jefferson's deep-rooted racism, his ethics can be seen as concurring with the quip of C.L.R. James (the first black biographer of Toussaint L'Ouverture) that "blacks, like horses, dogs, cats and some wild animals, judged a man not by the color of his skin but by the way he behaved."[102]

As social environment had such a crucial impact on character formation, political promotion of equal justice remained an intrinsic aspect of Jefferson's moral faith. It appeared equally evident to Jefferson that although science "has liberated the ideas of those men who read and reflect," the corrupt "mobs of the cities," being "debased by ignorance, poverty and vice, could not be restrained to rational action."[103] All in all, Jefferson's moral sentimentalism was grounded in the idea that natural passions and affections only gradually turn into personal moral sentiments via individual reflection. All moral judgments, in turn, involved active deliberation about the different means of promoting justice and benevolence. Even the best educated could "be led astray by artificial rules."[104] Thus, practical reasoning, or deliberation, seems a crucially important element in Jefferson's virtue ethics – also highlighting the central role of prudence in his Epicureanism.

THE EPICUREAN VIRTUES

For both Stoics and Epicureans, moral philosophy amounted to the study of the "art of life," as the discipline was still characterized by such eighteenth-century authorities as Francis Hutcheson and Lord Kames – and occasionally by Jefferson himself.[105] In addition to the questions of justice and benevolence, moral philosophy included what Jefferson called the ethics of "ourselves," concerned with "the government of those passions which, unrestrained would disturb our tranquillity of mind." In Jefferson's view, the masters of this special branch of ethics were such ancient philosophers as Socrates, Epicurus, Cicero, and Aurelius.[106]

Only four years after his final retirement from public duties, Jefferson proclaimed that the greatest good, the "*summum bonum* with me is now truly Epicurean, ease of body and tranquillity of mind, and to these I wish to consign my remaining days."[107] Unlike the young man he had been, the sage of Monticello now saw his happiness mainly as the consolation drawn from a "sound philosophy, equally indifferent to hope and fear."[108]

This did not mean that Jefferson's view of the virtuous life had drastically changed from active exercise of moral virtues to "Stoical apathy."[109] Neither had his Epicureanism anything to do with hedonistic sensual pleasures, which would eventually turn a man "into all body and no mind."[110] An active mind itself, he counseled the young Martha, was a grand recipe against "ennui." Intellectual boredom, he thought, "corrupts our dispositions, and teaches us ... hostility against all mankind."[111] Even at age seventy-six, Jefferson could not afford "a suspension of healthy exercise, a relaxation of mind, an indifference to everything around" him without falling into "debility of body, and hebetude of mind, the farthest of all things from the happiness which the well-regulated indulgences of Epicurus ensure."[112]

In his 1819 letter to William Short, Jefferson declared that "I too am an Epicurean." In moral terms, his Epicureanism needs to be viewed in the context of his commitment to the principle of universal benevolence. In the letter, he made it explicit that "Epictetus and Epicurus give laws for governing ourselves, Jesus a supplement of the duties and charities we owe to others."[113] Jefferson's famous one-page summary, "*Syllabus of the Doctrines of Epicurus*," which he enclosed with the Short letter, was divided into sections of physical and moral assumptions.

The section on physical assumptions includes an interesting set of ontological claims, which Jefferson apparently could share with the heathen ancients as well as with contemporary atheists. The atomistic, Epicurean universe was in a state of "eternal circulation of the elements of bodies" – with all its "parts, great and small" being "interchangeable." This universal ordering of things was defined as "eternal" instead of created. Whereas the set of physical assumptions acknowledged the Epicurean belief in "gods," they were defined as an order above human beings, "not meddling with" human concerns.

The Epicurean "Moral" doctrines followed these ontological precepts. The first line of the moral section reads: "Happiness the aim of life." The next line identifies "Virtue" as "the foundation of happiness." The third line, "Utility the test of virtue," suggests that, as specific character traits, virtues are instrumental to true happiness. Even if only "utile" for attaining the aim of life, virtuous dispositions are still necessary for a man aspiring to genuine happiness. Given the apparently subjective notions of summum bonum as "not to be pained in body, nor troubled in mind," and man as "a free agent," it seems clear that the notion of "happiness as the aim of life" borders on what is today called individual self-determination. But it does not follow from this – or from Jefferson's earlier remark about Jesus's supplementary role – that his Epicureanism would have rested only on subjective pleasures. The syllabus concludes with the fourfold notion of virtuous dispositions as the principal means by which an individual may attain happiness: "Virtue," Jefferson stated, "consist in 1. Prudence. 2. Temperance. 3. Fortitude. 4. Justice." The opposites of these he listed as "1. Folly. 2. Desire. 3. Fear. 4. Deceit."[114]

Functionally, the four virtues divide into two groups: First, the self-serving virtues of temperance and fortitude and, second, the morally charged virtues of prudence and justice, concerned with respect for others. Regarding the self-serving functions, the syllabus contended that "the principal diseases of the mind" are "desire and fear." Fortitude counters even the fear of death. Temperance arises from the notion that "the indulgence which prevents a greater pleasure, or produces a greater pain, is to be avoided."[115] When, on another occasion, Jefferson posed the tranquility of mind as "the greatest good of life," he also remarked that his strongest desire was "that of dying in the good will of all mankind."[116] Even temperance could not achieve such a self-gratifying goal as this. "After all," as Jefferson consoled himself in the spirit of ancient self-sufficiency, "men of energy of character must have enemies" as well.[117]

Unlike temperance and fortitude, the Syllabus's second group of virtues – prudence and justice – carry clear-cut social connotations. The opposite of justice is deceit instead of injustice. Such an internalized sense of justice is not far from the classical Stoic notion of honesty as the sum of all virtue. This is all the more important, given that universal benevolence is omitted from the list. Eventually, it is for prudence to keep the wise man from falling into folly in his pursuit of justice, truth, and peace of mind. The opposite vice – folly – does not appear directly antagonistic to justice or even to benevolence, whereas prudence certainly cannot generate them. This is why prudence is usually regarded as an intellectual, rather than a moral, virtue.

It is important, however, not to dismiss the link between prudence and justice. Prudence is not merely self-serving intellectual virtue, for if it were, it would all too easily merge with the temperance regulating self-indulgence. As Adam Smith noted, Epicurean temperance could be viewed as "nothing but prudence with regard to pleasure."[118] Jefferson undoubtedly grasped the difference, although he sometimes failed to explicate it. In a sense, losing sight of this distinction is precisely what happens in Jefferson's most often quoted letter speaking to his moral sentimentalism, the famous "Head and Heart" letter to Maria Cosway. As the distinction between temperance and prudence is easily lost, the letter deserves a closer look, particularly as it can also help one understand the relationship between the classical cardinal virtues and the principle of universal benevolence.

TWO KINDS OF PRUDENCE

In the 1786 Head and Heart letter to an English lady, Maria Cosway, Jefferson most closely associated moral considerations with the broader notion of ethics as the "art of life."[119] The letter is the most often quoted source for Jefferson's love affairs after his wife's early death in 1782.[120] It was written to a married woman, whom Jefferson wished to bring to Virginia from Paris, albeit he implicitly welcomed Lady Cosway's husband as well. However, the letter also reveals a good deal about Jefferson's deepest ethical convictions. Most importantly, he there used the concept of "prudence" in two ways – as equivalent to self-regarding temperance and as a morally charged virtue of its own.

The actual problem that Head and Heart embarked on solving at the beginning of the letter was Jefferson's overwhelming grief after departing from the charming Lady Cosway. When sitting "solitary & sad" at his fireplace after escorting the lady to her carriage, Jefferson let his head and heart enter a several-page-long dialogue deliberating the best means for restoring his peace of mind:

> Seated by the fireside, solitary & sad, the following dialogue took place between my Head & my Heart:
>
> *Head.* Well, friend, you seem to be in a pretty trim.
>
> *Heart.* I am indeed the most wretched of all earthly beings. Overwhelmed by grief, … I would willingly meet whatever catastrophe should leave me no more to feel or to fear.
>
> *Head.* These are the consequences of your warmth & precipitation…. You confess your follies indeed; but still you hug & cherish them; & no reformation can be hoped, where there is no repentance.

The Head thus begins the dialogue by blaming the Heart's warm affections for the fact that their common "empire" – Jefferson's mind – had fallen into the apparently insurmountable feeling of grief. In the course of the dialogue, the Head also preaches "prudence"[121] and accuses the Heart of "imprudently engaging your affections."[122] The Heart's argument, in turn, centers on Lady Cosway's praiseworthy virtues. In addition to her briefly mentioned beauty, these qualities include good sense, good humor, honesty, musicality, modesty, and, as she painted miniatures, her "eminence" in art as well.[123]

Given that the sentimental Heart eventually wins the argument over the intellectual Head, the letter seems to bespeak only Jefferson's sentimentalism.[124] Still, the Head's and Heart's common concern is nothing less than Jefferson's "felicity" – genuine happiness. At the culminating point of the dialogue, the Head argues that "the most effectual means of being secure against pain is to retire within ourselves, & to suffice for our own happiness" by embracing the solitary pleasures of an intellectual life. In other words, contemplative action provides "the only pleasures of a wise man."

The rest of the letter consists of the Heart's eventually successful attack on this position.

The Head is urged to reverse its erroneous favoring of monkish isolation over social pleasures and to give up "the mantle of self-sufficiency." The Heart briefly appeals to the Head's prudential utilitarianism by pointing out that "assuredly nobody will care for him who cares for nobody." But the core point of the Heart's winning argument is that the Head mistakes happiness to be "the mere absence of pain."[125] The question is whether the Head's self-centered, purely intellectual prudence truly counts for wisdom and thus contributes to Jefferson's happiness.

The Heart's crucial move is to point out that sheer grief may be an expression of a genuinely sublime feeling behind it. The Heart argues that there is intrinsic value in true friendship, no matter how brief an enjoyment it offers:

> *Heart* ... This world abounds indeed with misery: to lighten it's burthen [sic] we must divide it with one another.... You confess that in the present case I could not have made a worthier choice. You only object that I was so soon to lose them. We are not immortal ourselves, my friend; how can we expect our enjoyments to be so?

As indicated in this passage, even the Head admits that the Heart's choice of Lady Cosway's friendship is genuinely worthy. Jefferson's feelings of friendship appear to emanate from pure respect for his friend's genuinely virtuous dispositions. The Heart here defends the classical Epicurean joy of human companionship.

All the Jeffersonian constituents of the "art of life" are described in the language of eudaemonistic ethics throughout the letter. The dialogue abounds with references to "worthy choices" and "happiness" from which only momentary "enjoyments" would follow. The end result, supposedly acceptable to the wisest man, is that as "mere mortals," people would be wise to accept momentary happiness as well as the momentary grief that follows it. Happiness, as promoted by the Heart, approaches the purely mundane notion of the individual enjoyment of life. In this sense, the Head and Heart letter is an exercise in mere Epicurean temperance, which could be presented as prudence, although only regarding subjective pleasures.[126]

Yet, the classical notion of prudence as distinguishable from both temperance and mere instrumental reason also appears in the dialogue. To be sure, it creeps in there alongside the calculating prudence that the Heart explicitly excludes from the field of "morals." Moreover, this notion of prudence as the virtue of practical reasoning enters the dialogue precisely at the point where commentators usually find Jefferson arguing that morality results solely from affectionate sentiments. This is what the Heart argues:

> *Heart* ... When nature assigned us the same habitation, she gave us over it a divided empire. To you she allotted the field of science; to me that of morals ... [I]n denying to you the feelings of sympathy, of benevolence, of gratitude, of justice, of love,

of friendship, she has excluded you from their controul. To these she has adapted the mechanism of the heart. Morals were too essential to the happiness of man to be risked on the incertain [sic] combinations of the head. She laid their foundation therefore in sentiment, not in science.

There is a special "mechanism of the heart" to control Jefferson's personal morals. The Heart houses all sentiments (or feelings) of sympathy, benevolence, gratitude, justice, love, and friendship, which provide the foundation of his morals. But the use of terms is worth attention at this point. What Jefferson elsewhere called "honesty" of the heart and knowledge of the head are here called only "sentiments" and "science." In this passage, the functions of the "head" refer exclusively to the faculty of scientific reasoning, that is, to human rationality in the Baconian and Pascalian sense of theoretical reasoning, or in its ancient meaning as contemplative capacity. This commonplace distinction between the moral and contemplative powers of man is omnipresent in the teachings of such Scottish philosophers as Francis Hutcheson, Thomas Reid, and Dugald Stewart.

Yet in this crucial passage of the Head and Heart letter, the argument goes beyond the division between sentiments and scientific reasoning. The Head is declared incapable not only of benevolent and just feelings, but also of any "controul" over them. This is in obvious contradiction to Jefferson's more traditional description of prudence, as in George Washington's disposition never to act "until every circumstance, every consideration, was maturely weighed; refraining if he saw a doubt."[127] In the Head and Heart letter, however, the Head is "not organized for our moral direction." Instead, the whole function of moral direction is left to a particular "mechanism of the heart."[128]

What is this mechanism of the Heart like? Were the sentiments themselves the criteria here, no such mechanism would be necessary. But even the rational Head admits that the Heart tends to esteem only people of "the greatest merit, possessing good sense, good humour, [and] honest hearts," suggesting that the heart does more than feel. The Heart, therefore, has good grounds to insist that the Head should leave the Heart "to decide when & where friendships are to be contracted."[129] The function of the Heart's mechanism is that of making judgments. It thus appears fully compatible with Thomas Reid's remark that "there is no judgment of the heart of man more clear, more irresistible, than this, that esteem and regard are really due to good conduct."[130] With its particular mechanism, the Heart represents not only the sentimental basis of morality, but the entire human faculty of both apprehending the good and making practical moral judgments.

The ancient conception of practical reasoning remained an essential ingredient of Jefferson's moral outlook. Given that the virtue of justice was the opposite of deceit (according to Jefferson's Syllabus of Epicureanism), it obviously fell on prudence alone to counter folly. In this sense, the argumentative construction of the Head and Heart letter as a struggle between a rational head and a moral heart appears imbalanced. Consider, for example, Jefferson's language when describing George Washington as the embodiment of prudence. The first president's "heart was not warm in its affections," but Washington still "exactly calculated every man's value, and gave him a solid esteem proportioned to it."[131] Washington's moral judgments of other men emanated from calculations, be their source his affectionate (although not warm) heart or simply the rational head.[132]

How did this wavering view of the role of reason and sentiment in moral judgment reflect Jefferson's outspoken belief in the inborn moral sense of man? As noted, the Hutchesonian moral sense functioned totally separate from rationality: First, it provided a simple sense-experience of approbation and second, a "reflection act" providing the sentiment of approval.[133] Similarly, Lord Kames talked of "the moral sense, both in the direct feeling, and in the act of reflection."[134] As for the Hutchesonian use of "approbation," Jefferson occasionally employed the term in at least approximately the same sense. His personal attitudes to moral theorists varied between more or less instant "approbation and dissent."[135] On another occasion, he argued that the ancient Saxons' "semi-barbarous" constitution could be inferred from "whatever their history and laws shew to have been practiced with approbation."[136]

Yet, even the Jeffersonian moral sense was in need of the guidance of reason, albeit to a very limited extent: "This sense is submitted indeed in some degree to the guidance of reason; but it is a small stock which is required for this: even a less one than what we call Common sense."[137] The needed stock was low precisely because the sense itself functioned as an instinctive, if not simply intuitive, basis for moral distinctions.[138] In fact, there is little in Jefferson's records that would counter Thomas Reid's two self-evident, common-sense principles of morality – first, the conception of prudence as arising from the notion of "our good upon the whole" and, second, the intuitive conception of moral obligation without which the notion of the moral sphere could not be apprehended.[139]

Perhaps, however, Jefferson's concept of moral sense is closest to that of Jean Jacques Burlamaqui, one of his favorite authorities in legal studies. By the moral instinct, Burlamaqui meant a kind of "momentary approbation," which he equated with "a kind of deliberation."[140] Once momentary approbation is thus linked to deliberation, one appears to be dealing with a kind of initial perception of the relation of ends and means, approaching the traditional virtue of prudence as the key to practical, moral reasoning.[141]

After positing the heart's mechanism as the proper director of Jefferson's morals, the Head and Heart letter turns into a series of personal reminiscences of at least apparently true events from Jefferson's life. In all these examples, Jefferson's head betrays him as a guide to right conduct. In the first example, Jefferson's head guided him not to take a weary soldier into his carriage, because he could not treat all the other soldiers marching on the road with equal benevolence. Eventually his heart persuaded him to turn back to find the soldier. The second instance took place in Philadelphia, where a "poor woman came to ask a charity," and Jefferson's head "whispered that she looked like a drunkard, & that half a dollar was enough to give her for the ale-house." Again, Jefferson's heart got the better of him, and it turned out that the money went to the education of the woman's son. In the third example, it was Jefferson's heart that pointed out how mere rational calculations of the comparative strengths of the American patriots and the British armies could never have led him to join the noble cause of the War of Independence.[142]

The reminiscences were not examples of Jefferson's failure to follow the rules of justice. In the case of the weary soldier, Jefferson's rational prudence suggested that he could not treat all the soldiers alike if he gave the one a ride. The error lay solely in not viewing this particular action – embodying selective, partial benevolence – as worth the trouble. In all these examples, the purely instrumental rationality of the head failed Jefferson as a moral agent, whereas "the mechanism of the Heart" did not. The mechanism appears to function like Burlamaqui's notion of momentary approbation, and thus to embody the initial stage of moral deliberation in itself.

In its most classical meaning, prudence alone represented this ability to deliberate about real life situations in which only the means were compared to one another in their relation to the end of genuine eudaemonia. All three examples can thus be viewed as occasions of classical moral reasoning. Such reasoning was needed in practical, moral considerations as distinct from the contemplative, demonstrative reasoning in search of truth. The classic example of such prudence is Aristotelian *phronesis*, referring to action according to right reason in particular cases.[143] Aristotelian moral virtue consisted in achieving "the mean" (the middle ground) between various, inborn emotional dispositions. Virtue actualized as the constant choice of the best in the constantly varying particular situations. Courage, for example, called for a balance between rashness and cowardice (without falling into either of them) and was thus displayed quite differently in different situations.[144]

For Cicero, the cardinal virtues of prudence, justice, courage, and temperance were middle (*medium*) in the sense of being imperfect dispositions regarding what was absolutely right or just (*rectum*). This view derived from the assumption that most people do not possess true wisdom. Wisdom alone yielded proper understanding of all the complexities of man's proper place in nature and, consequently, of naturally commendable human behavior. The well-known Ciceronian division of duties into perfect and medium duties ("offices") thus evolved from the societal presumption that true honesty was "found in wise men only," whereas the "middle" virtues were "shared, and widely accessible."[145]

In light of Jefferson's reminiscences, the dialogue of the Head and Heart letter no longer hinges on a choice between sentiments and reason. At that point, the argument turns into an exercise in practical moral reasoning. The Heart triumphs only because it represents the entire moral faculty as capable of both initial approbation and practical judgment on right conduct.

UTILITY AND JEFFERSONIAN VIRTUE

To reconcile Jefferson's conception of virtue with his subscription to benevolence and with his understanding of the concepts of rights, morals, and the moral sense, it is necessary to keep in mind the three key features of virtue. First, Jefferson insisted that virtue was a natural, genuinely moral human character trait. Second, virtuous character traits were never given, but individually acquired by instruction and habit. Third, as he proclaimed in the Thomas Law letter and elsewhere, "nature has constituted utility to man as the standard and test of virtue."[146]

In Jefferson's moral faith, all the moral virtues of the heart were built on the natural moral sense, whereas all the intellectual virtues of the head were built on one's inborn rational capacities. Jefferson thought that there were individuals who lacked the moral instinct altogether, just as there were blind people. Yet, neither fact altered his general definition of man.[147] Helvétius made it simpler still when remarking that the one "who to be virtuous must always conquer his inclinations, must necessarily be a wicked man."[148]

"The essence of virtue is in doing good to others" Jefferson once insisted to John Adams.[149] In other words, virtue denoted benevolent action beyond mere justice. Yet on another occasion, he spoke of "the social utilities which constitute the essence of virtue."[150] Which one was it? There is a definite utilitarian aspect to Jefferson's ethics. Still, viewing "social utilities" as the essence of virtue seems an overstatement on Jefferson's part. It is important to distinguish between genuinely virtuous action and the social utilities that such action would accomplish.

Twice, in 1814 and 1819, Jefferson described "utility" as the "test of virtue."[151] The utility test did not need to apply to the end of the action. Rather, it was about assessing particular acts as means to an end. By definition the Jeffersonian "social utilities" could exclude antisocial, purely selfish considerations. Neither is there any reason to equate these utilities to some particular short-term majority interest or public opinion. For example, Jefferson obviously thought that his grand plan of deporting all African Americans was socially desirable. He just never found a white majority in Virginia to act on it. Finally, given his insistence on virtue as intrinsically moral, the utility of a given policy should be viewed as a necessary but not yet sufficient feature to prove its virtuousness.

To be sure, Jefferson's understanding of virtuous action occasionally borders on the most problematic version of utilitarianism, often called consequentialism. He proclaimed that "virtue does not consist in the act we do, but in the end it is to effect." However, contrary to any outright utilitarian view, which would prefer majority over minority interests, he furthermore asserted that if "it is to effect the happiness of him to whom it is directed, it is virtuous."[152] Thus, "the effect" should not touch others – those not targeted by the action. There was nothing extraordinary in this view. Even Francis Hutcheson considered acts meeting such a test fully just and lawful – as well as morally right.[153] Nevertheless, the concept of effectiveness can be distinguished from Jeffersonian virtue as something that characteristically emanates from the human pursuit of justice and benevolence.

Insofar as one can find the notion of moral obligation in the Jefferson archive, it appears to consist of an individual's constant effort toward self-betterment via the exercise of both intellectual and moral virtues. Which inclination but that toward self-betterment could motivate a man of the Enlightenment to the study of ethics in the first place? As even Aristotle held, a man's character "must somehow be there already with a kinship to virtue" before entering theoretical studies of virtue, for "to the incontinent, knowledge brings no profit."[154]

There is no question that the Jeffersonian individual sought happiness. Yet like a modern-day liberal, Jefferson consistently suspended judgment of what individual happiness truly is like. Such a provision is in opposition to any strictly communitarian interpretation of the ancient ideal of a good life. Jefferson's ethics emanated from the simple tenet that a good life cannot be precisely the same for each and every individual – even under identical circumstances.[155] His view was fully consistent with the argument that individuals are different in their inborn talents and inclinations, out of which they are supposed to develop their personal virtues.

The epistemologically safest presumption about true human happiness was that it should allow individual variation. Indeed, Jefferson's definition of the rightful powers of government arose solely from the conception of "the happiness of the individuals who compose" a nation under a government.[156] Individualism in Jeffersonian thought arose from the image of a human being as born with given capacities, which every individual develops into moral and intellectual qualities and in fact exercises "from his cradle to his grave." As in ancient eudaemonistic ethics, judging one's life a good life was thus possible only postmortem.

Jefferson's ethics definitely included tragic situations in which the primary ends – justice and benevolence – appeared to compete against each other. He saw his own antislavery stance as the exact opposite of the contemporary pro-slavery position, which amounted to inaction. At the same time, he held that one could not "innocently consent" to immediate abolition, which was certain to lead to permanent racial "amalgamation" in the country. Still, African Americans were entitled to freedom. "As to the method by which this difficult task is to be effected," Jefferson's plan was the gradual expatriation of all slave children.[157] The plan was not in inherent opposition to viewing all races as equal on a global scale. Simply put, Jefferson argued that the "[m]oral duties which exist between individual and individual in a state of nature, accompany them into a state of society."[158] When entering such a state individuals also distinguished themselves from the rest of mankind. Henceforward, their universal respect for all mankind was supposed to turn into a matter of international law as derivable from contemporary jurisprudence on the law of nature and nations.

From this perspective of global, international equity, Jefferson's commitment to prudence as the opposite of "folly" begins to make sense. Nothing in his characterization of himself as one "among those who think well of the human character generally" was meant to ignore human weakness in either reason or morality.[159] The French radicals, being "closet politicians merely, unpracticed in the knowledge of men," had lost their good cause to Robespierre's tyranny owing to "the imprudence of giving up the certainty of such a degree of liberty" as the constitutional monarchy of 1791 would have provided the nation.[160]

Prudence, in sum, referred to a permanent disposition to scrutinize carefully the available means in relationship to their expected effects. Assessment of the means resulted from an analysis of their potential efficacy in a given situation. Prudence, however, could hardly offer guidance about the moral ends. And benevolence and justice were no less primary obligations of a statesman than of a private person. Yet particularly in politics, the moral and intellectual qualities of a man rested on long experience in that particular practice. This is why Aristotle, for example, thought it useless to teach politics to the young.[161]

THE VIRTUE OF A POLITICIAN

Nothing in the wise man's prudence prevented cunning when seizing power. "The prudent man," Adam Smith noted, "though always sincere ... is not always frank and open."[162] Jefferson never claimed otherwise. Still, political virtue did not essentially differ from other worthy human qualities. Jefferson rarely saw more than two possible main lines of decent political action in the pursuit of benevolence and justice: There were the politics of timid, natural Tories and the politics of courageous, natural Whigs. The latter believed in human progress enough to attempt innovations not validated as practicable by previous historical experience. Jefferson no doubt deemed many of his own ideas to be just such innovations. His program for the compulsory expatriation of the entire African-American population required an unprecedented scale of political coordination. Such were also both his commitment to universal male suffrage and his advocacy of a comprehensive system of public education.

Both intellectual and moral character traits manifested themselves in politics. In his evaluations of the characters of John Adams and Alexander Hamilton, Jefferson carefully acknowledged their personal virtues while attacking their political tenets. Jefferson condemned Hamilton's secretive advocacy of the so-called monied interest, because it necessitated the "force or corruption" in governing the rest of the people. Still, he could deem Hamilton an honest individual. Hamilton's error lay in regarding strong national government as an end in itself.

Adams, according to Jefferson, was honest both as a man and as a politician.[163] His weakness was solely intellectual, for it resulted from his one-sided erudition in political history. This situation was analogous to that of a university professor being "led astray by artificial rules."[164] Relying only on historical precedents, Adams ended up advocating traditional bicameralism – the doctrine that, if not the traditional aristocracy, at least the wealthy must be assigned a separate chamber of representation so as to stabilize the nascent American mass democracy. Contrary to Hamilton, who appeared to advocate corruption of the masses in order to achieve a strong government, Adams sought a government that would keep the masses under the control of their social betters.[165]

In the simplest terms, classical republican virtue referred to the free man's ability to put the public good ahead of his self-interests. Rather than associating the concept of political virtue with, say the Aristotelian notion of man as a political animal, one should think of it as derivable from its primary purpose to conduct politics successfully. The classic summary of all the elements of political virtue could be found in the famous Pericles's Funeral Oration in Thucydides's *Peloponnesian Wars*. There Athenian politics was characterized as follows:

> We cultivate refinement without extravagance and knowledge without effeminacy; wealth we employ more for use than for show, and place the real disgrace of poverty not in owning to the fact but in declining struggle against it. Our public men have, besides politics, their private affairs to attend to, and our ordinary citizens, though occupied with the pursuits of industry, are still fair judges of public matters; for unlike any other nation, we regard the citizen who takes no part in these duties not as unambitious but as useless ...[166]

If one wishes to associate classical republicanism with Jefferson's democratic faith, here are enumerated all its key ingredients: Refinement without effeminacy, active concern about poverty, and the belief in the common man's ability to judge between statesmen's policies. Most importantly, even ancient politics consisted of problem solving through open discussion. The passage continues with this concluding note: "And instead of looking on discussion as a stumbling block in the way of action, we think it an indispensable preliminary to any wise action at all."

Discourse was the key to the formation of respectable policies as well as to the concept of politics itself. Additionally, as implied even in Adam Smith's conception of prudence, the politics of virtue could entail devious play behind the curtains as well as open conflict at the negotiation table.[167]

Yet most of the time it consisted of persuasion – the intellectual effort to change the minds of one's opponents.

Politics thus called for the skills of politeness and of circumspection. The statesman was not supposed to attempt to push his whole program through at once. When proceeding with one compromise at a time, he did not need to inform his opponents about what the next issue to be put on the negotiating table would logically be. As Jefferson summed up the essentials of the game, "the ground for liberty is to be gained by inches," meaning that "we must be contented to rescue what we can get from time to time, and eternally press forward for what is yet to get."[168] This was not a game for innocent youths, whom Jefferson so willingly guided toward truth, justice, and "plain dealing."[169]

Jefferson's political temper was about perseverance in gradually putting forward and winning assent for his views. This was very far from any naïve notion of speaking one's mind, as his 1798 letter to John Taylor well illustrates. In this remarkable document, Jefferson defended the federal government to Taylor, who speculated about southern secession from the Union in reaction to the Federalists' apparently unbearable policies. In his response Jefferson argued that, were the southern states to secede, they would soon enter political schisms among themselves. Historical experience showed that "an association of men who will not quarrel with one another is a thing which never yet existed, from the greatest confederacy of nations down to a town meeting or a vestry." Jefferson went on to point out that, with "a little patience," one was bound to see the Federalist "reign of witches pass over, their spells dissolve, and the people, recovering their true sight, restore the government to it's true principles."[170]

Jefferson's early emphasis on perseverance as the key to political success is similarly present in his 1814 advice to Edward Coles. In order to accomplish abolition and deportation of the slave population, one needed to "come forward in the public councils, become the missionary of this doctrine truly christian; insinuate & inculcate it softly but steadily, through the medium of writing and conversation; associate others in your labors, and when the phalanx is formed, bring on and press the proposition perseveringly until its accomplishment."[171]

Against such a formidable enemy as Hamilton, the game was even more clearly to be played in the mundane, temporal world: "If the game runs sometimes against us at home we must have patience till luck turns, & then we shall have an opportunity of winning back the principles we have lost, for this is a game where principles are the stake." Making it clear that, even with such high stakes, the game was about seizing power, the politician Jefferson – only two years prior to his presidency – reminded his correspondent, Taylor, not to let this statement "get before the public."[172]

If open political sectionalism was needed, Jefferson could consent to that, as his eventual rise into national leadership well demonstrated. All in all, he was not half as thin-skinned and touchy a politician as scholars often portray him as being – in the face of all the accusations against him as a cowardly Governor of Virginia during the War of Independence or as an effeminate "theorist, holding French principles of government," in favor of "licentiousness and anarchy" over law and order.[173]

Well before the Federalists had erected their "reign of witches," Jefferson had noticed that it "takes time to persuade men to do even what is for their own good."[174] The maxim pertained to all groups of people, American and non-American alike. Devious action could be employed to eradicate ignorant Native-American cultures so as to let these people share the blessings of progress, which they could not yet even imagine.[175] Although it was against Jefferson's morality to strip the ignorant savages of their homelands openly, he felt it "consistent with pure morality" to manipulate them to voluntarily sell the lands or even to secretly run them to such debts that they would be compelled to sell them to their white creditors.[176]

Even after the Latin American revolutions, Jefferson recommended that these peoples should remain under nominal submission to Spain, for they still lingered under the sway of ignorance and superstition and could "obtain freedom by degrees only."[177] For the Spanish themselves, Jefferson showed little more respect. Once the Louisiana Territory was shifted from Spain to France in 1800, he had no scruples about purchasing the area from its new owner in 1803 – no matter that Napoleon's ownership of the lands (and his rule over the Native Americans living there) was questionable even by the standards of the time. In order to later capture Florida and parts of Texas from the backward-looking Spanish, Jefferson advised his administration to wait patiently for the Spanish to become entangled in one or another international crisis and then "push them strongly with one hand, holding out a price in the other."[178]

The secret to all progressive politics was persuasion. As Jefferson argued, it was wrong "to subject the Indians to our laws without their consent," particularly as "a little patience and a little money are so rapidly producing their voluntary removal across the Mississippi, that I hope this immorality will not be permitted to stain our history."[179] Jefferson refused to believe, even in retrospect, "that in the four administrations which have taken place, there has been a single instance of departure from good faith towards other nations. We may sometimes have mistaken our rights, or made an erroneous estimate of the actions of others, but no voluntary wrong can be imputed to us."[180]

To an extent, secretiveness characterized Jefferson's entire career as a politician. It is illuminating to consider how rarely he thought it wise to speak his mind, when for example, politicking for a comprehensive elementary education system in Virginia. Neither was he in this effort true to his reputation as the foremost opponent of public spending.[181] From 1778 onward, his plan laid the burden of building and maintaining the elementary schoolhouses on local communities, called hundreds or townships. As he explained the idea, increases in taxes would necessarily follow, although so as to "throw on wealth the education of the poor."[182] Jefferson's idea of dividing counties into school wards was not realized.

By 1816, Jefferson, therefore, came to consider the possibility of introducing the still non-existent school districts on the existing militia wards, thereby integrating such townships as "ward-republics" into the official state administration. He also had come to insist that counties could contribute such a "trifling" sum of money as was needed for building a schoolhouse for exceptionally poor townships. Regarding any township unwilling to have a school, Jefferson thought that, if the pressure from the neighboring wards failed to change the situation, "it would become the duty of the alderman elected by the county, to take an active part in pressing the introduction of schools, and to look out for tutors."[183]

A couple of years later, the state eventually obtained enough extra assets to erect a state-run elementary education system. Then Jefferson insisted that half the available sum would suffice for the required 1,200 ward schools, because the "paupers" incapable of paying for tuition would require no more than an average of twenty-five dollars per school. Yet, even on this occasion, Jefferson acknowledged the need for a moderate, local tax increase on regular households. The other half of the new assets he needed for the University of Virginia.[184]

Jefferson's letters and memoranda dealing with the slavery issue provide even more telling examples of his politicking, as well as his flexibility on public spending. It is best to begin with a brief look at his Haitian policy both before and during his presidency. An epoch-making slave revolt had begun in St. Domingue in the aftermath of the French Revolution in 1791.[185] Even though the "Black Bonaparte" of the island of Hispaniola, General Toussaint L'Ouverture, eventually died in a French prison, the black insurgents won independence from France in 1804. Simultaneously, a whole series of slave insurrections occurred in Puerto Rico, Grenada, Curacao, and Venezuela. About 12,000 West Indian slaves were brought by their white masters to the United States in the early stages of the Haitian conflict. Even the Gabriel's slave rebellion of 1800 in Virginia was partially inspired by these events.[186]

As a slaveholder himself, President Jefferson sought to keep the Haitian rebels under constant pressure and even appeared to support the eventually disastrous French invasion of the island. It was important to prevent Toussaint's example from turning the whole of the West Indies into a theater of racial violence.[187] The Haitian war of independence provided Jefferson with an unsuspected success on another front, when Napoleon decided to sell the Louisiana Territory to the United States. However, throughout the Hispaniola turmoil, and even afterward, Jefferson embraced hopes that at least the Haitian part of the island would eventually fall into the hands of the Americans, so as to be turned into the long-awaited asylum for American slaves.[188]

Jefferson's lifelong commitment to the compulsory resettlement of the African-American population to the Caribbean or Latin America did not hinder him from paying lip service to the idea of sending a few freed men all the way back to Africa. In 1800, the Gabriel rebellion stimulated a wide discussion in the Virginia assembly about emancipation and deportation of the slave population. The task of seeking an appropriate colony was trusted to the newly elected President Jefferson, who vainly inquired whether British Sierra Leone or the Portuguese settlements in South America could receive the rebel captives.[189]

On this occasion, Jefferson noted that the Virginia legislature had failed to clarify whether the purpose was only to expel the few remnants of Gabriel's followers still in prison or to pave the way for a large-scale deportation of the whole slave population. No doubt he well understood that contrary intentions were in play in the Virginia legislature during the debate. Nevertheless, Jefferson's correspondence about the issue with the then Governor of Virginia, James Monroe, was later extolled as the constitutive step toward the formation of the American Colonization Society, which was dedicated to sending slaves "back" to Africa.[190] Although Jefferson mentioned Africa as the "last & undoubted resort" in passing, he clearly considered St. Domingo the most promising location for an asylum. Moreover, the African Colonization Society advocated voluntary migration, not compulsory expatriation as did Jefferson.[191]

Taking each and every line of Jefferson's statements at face value obscures his implicit disagreement with the implementation of a suggested policy – and sometimes with the policy itself. Jefferson's 1817 letter to Thomas Humphreys about purchasing Liberia as an asylum for freed slaves serves well to illustrate the point. Jefferson embraced the plan in apparently unreserved terms: "I concur entirely with your leading principles of gradual emancipation, of establishment on the coast of Africa, and the patronage of our nation until the emigrants shall be able to protect themselves."[192] He thus expressed no objections to the Liberia initiative – currently under discussion in the federal congress. He stated only that "for voluntary emigrations of people of color, [it] may be the corner stone of this future edifice."[193]

Edifying as the scheme appeared, Jefferson did not subscribe to it as the solution to the problem of slavery. What he said was this: "Personally I am ready and desirous to make any sacrifice which shall ensure their gradual but complete retirement from the State, and effectually, at the same time, establish them elsewhere in freedom and safety."[194] Although Jefferson committed only to sending the slaves "elsewhere," the letter has often been referred to as evidence that he saw Liberia as the solution to the problem.[195] He later even insisted that he had "ever deemed entirely impossible the idea that "any place on the coast of Africa should answer the purpose."[196]

Concurring with Humphrey's "leading principles" rather than with his actual plan, Jefferson lamented the failure of the rising generation of free Virginians to grasp the seriousness of the problem. He also remarked that, rather than the federal government, the slave states themselves should provide assets for the purchase of Liberia. Yet, Jefferson's goal was nothing less than the slave population's "complete retirement from the State."[197] He never cared "to go into all details of the burthens and benefits" of his own plan.[198] Finally, he remained particularly reluctant to speak of the funding of the education of slave children prior to their deportation, an idea that regularly appears in the Jefferson archive from the late 1780s to the early 1820s.[199]

Regardless of details, it is extremely difficult to reconcile Jefferson's huge emancipation program with any "Jeffersonian" ideal of minimal government with minimum spending. To the contrary, the fifty-year-long program that he suggested to Jared Sparks in 1824 entailed, alongside private donations, a dramatic increase in public spending on every level of government, from townships to counties, states, and the federal government.[200] Perhaps Jefferson had only by then grown willing to include the federal government in the implementation of the plan, but it is unclear whether that option was earlier excluded. In 1820, he had suggested that "the proceeds of the land office, if appropriated, would be quite sufficient" for deporting Virginia's slave population. But such assets most probably would have included more than only Virginia's proportionate share of all Western land sales. And even on this occasion, Jefferson brought up "the possible means of taxation aided by charitable contributions" from all the "Eastern states" of the Union as well as from European countries.[201]

Did Jefferson betray his antislavery ideals by gradually turning into an advocate of extending slavery to the Western territories? During the period from 1790 to 1820, numerous slave states had been incorporated into the Union and the American slave population had grown from about 600,000 to more than 1.5 million. At the same time, the free black population had grown from 59,000 to 234,000.[202] Most probably Jefferson's rationale for backing the extension of slavery was that, in the aftermath of the federal prohibition of slave imports (effective as of January 1808), it appeared possible to lower radically the proportion of the slave population in each slave state. Should the proportion of the black population in the southern states approach that of the northern states, Jefferson's program would have appeared a good deal easier to put into effect on the state level.[203] As Madison observed, "the States holding fewest slaves are those which most readily abolished slavery altogether."[204] Moreover, it is good to bear in mind that even Pennsylvania abolished slavery entirely only in 1847 and New Jersey in 1865.[205]

This so-called diffusion argument can be found in Jefferson's records from as early as 1807, when he argued that Congress should permit slave importation from other states to "the territory of Orleans" on the grounds that "dividing the evil, would lessen its danger."[206] To his former Secretary of the Treasury and trusted ally, Albert Gallatin, Jefferson explained in 1820 that spreading the institution to the West would ease the burden of the African Americans' future liberation "by bringing a greater number of shoulders under it."[207] Regardless of Jefferson's vague indications that even slaves' "happiness would be increased" in a projected, small-scale slave economy in the West, he was careful to claim no precise moral significance for the diffusion argument: "Moral the question certainly is not, because the removal of slaves from one state to another, no more than their removal from one country to another, would never make a slave of one human being who would not be so without it."[208]

In view of Jefferson's maxim that the essence of virtuous action stems from the happiness of those whom the act concerns, his stand made sense. The happiness of an individual slave could not function as justification for the diffusion argument. Jefferson sought to save his emancipation plan without destroying the southern states' loyalty to the Union. The principle of universal justice dictated only that no further harm would be caused to any slave in securing this end, particularly as the diffusion of slavery could eventually appear conducive to emancipation.

MORAL OBLIGATION AND SELF-REALIZATION

Finally, given that Jefferson claimed to have an ethical position beyond commitment to any simple classical political virtue, it is worth asking what that position was in the most elementary philosophical terms. All in all, the Jeffersonian conception of virtue can be viewed as evolving from individually variable, morally qualified human sociability. Virtue is an object of constant, lifelong training. As no one is virtuous or vicious at birth, a person's natural dispositions could only gradually be refined into the respective virtues. At first, virtue would only denote one's inborn capacity for acquiring desirable character traits, roughly equating with what Jefferson called either the inborn moral sense or, more simply still, conscience. Emulation and formal education had roles to play even in the person's orientation toward such a process. The process of internalizing any moral virtue as a permanent character trait entailed constant practice in morally commendable conduct.

Each component of this overall view – natural capacity, training in habits, and education – could prove abundant or scarce in the case of any individual. Still, prudence alone could make George Washington a character to be deemed genuinely great. Additionally, as Jefferson remarked, Washington's inborn talents were hardly comparable to those of Bacon, Locke, or Newton. Even these "three greatest men" of history had cultivated their inborn talents into specific excellences so as to earn their worldwide renown.[209] As noted, the Jeffersonian obligation appears to consist of an individual's constant effort toward self-betterment via the exercise of both intellectual and moral virtues.

Should Jefferson's moral position be characterized as deontic or teleological? It does not appear deontic in the Kantian sense of being primarily concerned with an abstract notion of good will. Yet, Jefferson can be viewed as a deontic thinker given his constant statements about benevolence and justice as the foremost duties of man – that is, as the primary obligations dictated by conscience, from which all other duties could be derived. On the other hand, if some more or less Epicurean notion of self-realization as the core conception of ethics is considered to represent teleological morality – as, for example, philosopher William Frankena maintains – Jefferson fits that characterization as well. His deist convictions assured him that, in the final analysis, our duties and true interests are reconcilable.[210]

In one of Jefferson's typical educational letters to his daughter Martha, he referred to "conscience" as the "faithful internal Monitor." Were Martha "always to obey it," she would "always be prepared for the end of the world: or for a much more certain event which is death."[211] Jefferson's ethics, in sum, arose from moral faith both in the primary duties of benevolence and justice and in human self-realization through action according to those principles – a kind of realization of character truly fulfilled only at the end of life.

Jefferson could acknowledge his own moral shortcomings in benevolent action, as his reminiscences in the Head and Heart letter show. What happened to the weary soldier whom Jefferson first refused to take into his carriage? After becoming "sensible" of his error in moral reasoning, Jefferson related, "I turned about to take up the souldier [sic], but he had entered a bye path, & and was no more to be found; and from that moment to this I could never find him out to ask his forgiveness."[212] The incident did not prove any failure to follow the rules of justice. Jefferson had asked himself whether he could practice equal benevolence toward all other weary soldiers on the road and concluded that his horses would fail in such an effort. His moral error lay solely in not viewing this particular opportunity to exercise partial benevolence as worth the trouble. The failure did not breach what his contemporaries would have called the perfect rights of the soldier. This is worth keeping in mind in turning to the subject of Jefferson's rights thinking.

4

The Perfectible Rights of Men

THE SELF-EVIDENT RIGHT OF RESISTANCE

As has been shown, Jefferson's belief in the moral progress of man rested on the view that once duly informed, no civilized man, savage, or barbarian would object to the two fundamental principles of morality: Justice for all and benevolence toward those in need of help. Yet as a Virginia slaveholder, Jefferson refused to follow the principle of equal justice as pertaining to his slaves when joining the War of Independence in order to preserve his own natural rights. His commitment to armed resistance as a revolutionary leader was not as radically at odds with his much-criticized patience in solving the slavery issue as at first it may appear. The purpose of this chapter is to clarify the nature of Jefferson's rights thinking in this context of justified violence. This entails exploring his use of such crucial concepts of contemporary jurisprudence as the state of nature and civil society, alienable and inalienable rights, consent and contract, and perfect and imperfect rights. Let us begin with certain repercussions of the Declaration of Independence regarding the notion of justified violence.

In their Declaration of Independence, the American revolutionaries held that "a decent respect to the opinions of mankind requires that they should declare the causes which impel them to the separation" from the British Empire. Their cause was just. It is noteworthy that on May 15, 1776 – well before the official proclamation of independence – the Continental Congress adopted John Adams's resolution according to which "it appears absolutely irreconcilable to reason and good Conscience" to support "any government under the crown of Great Britain."[1]

Jefferson was always proud of having chaired the committee that prepared the long-awaited Declaration of Independence during the summer of 1776.[2] His reliance on Locke's *Second Treatise* when drafting the declaration is well-documented, and John Locke remained a highly respected authority on both politics and ethics for Jefferson afterward.[3] Whether or not there is a break between the Jeffersonian and the Lockean concept of natural rights depends on what philosophical significance one gives to the fact that although Jefferson clung to the rights of life and liberty, he replaced the third Lockean natural right, "property," with "the pursuit of happiness." There are also a number of philosophically interesting differences between Jefferson's original draft and the final version of the Declaration. Truths that the Declaration holds "self-evident" were only "sacred and undeniable" in the more circumspect original draft. Nevertheless, Jefferson himself later insisted that the document was not about "new principles, or new arguments," but about "the common sense of the subject."[4]

Rather than a summary of the moral philosophy of its own time, the Declaration was originally written as a speech for delivery at the Continental Congress when proclaiming the independence of the United States.[5] Moreover, the document was drafted piecemeal by numerous persons and was eventually heavily re-edited by the Continental Congress. With so many coauthors, even Jefferson's own memorandum of his own original draft, as published in his *Notes on the State of Virginia*, was inaccurate. Historians have found an even earlier version, the "Original Rough Draught," today generally called the original draft. Even this actual original draft can be read as a careful recomposition of widely circulated earlier declarations of the natural rights of the colonists. In some of the numerous states' declarations of independence, for example, the right to the pursuit of happiness was phrased as a "right to obtain happiness."[6]

In essence, Jefferson's original draft seems to have been intended to circumvent rather than to resolve any debatable fine points about the divine or human foundation of morality. In this sense, the final draft did not compromise Jefferson's intentions regarding the interpretation of the document. His purposes were political in character, and they were maintained from the beginning to the end of this process, as can be shown by a brief look at the final version.

This is how the central passage, on the self-evident truths and natural rights, reads in what is usually considered the most authentic version of the document, called the parchment copy, that was signed on August 2, 1776:

> We hold these truths to be self-evident, that all men are created equal, that they are endowed by their Creator with certain unalienable Rights, that among these are Life, Liberty and the pursuit of Happiness. That to secure these rights, Governments are instituted among Men, deriving their just powers from the consent of the governed, That whenever any Form of Government becomes destructive of these ends it is the Right of the People to alter or to abolish it, and to institute new Government, laying its foundation on such principles and organizing its powers in such form, as to them shall seem most likely to effect their Safety and Happiness.

For anyone reading this central passage of the document for the first time, the most self-evident fact is its linguistic awkwardness. Even in view of the lack of standardization of contemporary English, the beginning of the second sentence in the form of "That to secure ..." seems grammatically clumsy. Also, why would one employ a comma prior to an apparently similar clause beginning as "That whenever any Form ..."? In the original draft, only semicolons were used for the same purpose: "We hold these truths to be sacred & undeniable; that all men are created equal & independant [sic], that from that equal creation they derive rights inherent & inalienable, among which are the preservation of life, & liberty, & the pursuit of happiness; that to secure these ends, governments are instituted among men."[7]

Be that as it may, the argument of both versions seems clear enough. In the final version the revolutionaries, after subscribing to the self-evident equality of men and, therefore, the unalienable rights of men, held it *just as self-evident* that "to secure these rights Governments are instituted among men." They went on to hold it similarly *self-evident* that "the Right of the People" not only to abolish a government but also "to institute a New government" would follow from the earlier premises. Most notable among the ensuing "Facts" to be "submitted to a candid world" was that the king was "waging War against us." The core interpretative point of the document is this notion of violence.

This declaration of a just, defensive war on the part of the colonies makes clear the Declaration's fundamental purpose. It was not to explain the self-evident fact that governments exist in order to secure the rights of free men, but to proclaim the not so self-evident fact that, there and then, "the consent of the governed" had been withdrawn from the British government.[8] Jefferson made it all the clearer that the Revolutionary War was fought for reestablishment of the political rights of free Americans when he later observed that, in refusing to free his slaves, the typical revolutionary slaveholder inflicted on these people "a bondage, one hour of which is fraught with more misery than ages of that which he [the planter] rose in rebellion to oppose."[9] Yet now all reforms needed to take place within the political system reestablished in the Revolution. What was genuinely "new under the sun" about the revolution of 1800 was simply the peaceful replacement of a reactionary, Federalist government with a progressive, Republican one. Even that revolution was achieved by free men, many of them still slaveholders.

Jefferson's rights thinking remained so tied to this early idea of only reclaiming free men's right to self-government that it is difficult to find a clear-cut natural rights' theory in his records.[10] Most of the time, he viewed natural rights as rightful powers of any man to act in association with his equals for the benefit of all. Such a mundane conception of rights did not evolve from any theoretically posited moral harmony waiting to be achieved, but from an understanding of conflict as a historically verifiable, central characteristic of human life. "In the course of human events," conflicts needed to be resolved according to more widely shared and fuller human understanding of equal justice and universal benevolence. The full scope of human rights remained so imperfectly known that as late as 1813 Jefferson proclaimed that there were natural rights that had "not yet entered any declaration of rights."[11]

In fact, Jefferson's breathtakingly long list of British violations of the colonists' rights to life, liberty, and the pursuit of happiness appear to degrade these theoretically perfect natural rights into imperfect rights. As imperfect rights, they would essentially be rightful powers of any individual to act according to the law of nature in the world of human conflicts. Similarly, at this point, the right to armed resistance and the right to the pursuit of happiness begin to appear as precisely the same kind of rights – rights that had to be constantly reinvigorated by their possessors.

In sum, as rightful powers to act collectively, the Jeffersonian natural rights evolved from the temporal consent of the governed in real history, where violence occasionally and politics generally prevailed. By the same token, these rights belonged exclusively to the living, making them absolutely independent of what previous generations had considered right and just under the law of nature. As this chapter shows, the free man's act of resorting to just violence already presumed his consent to some majority rule in Jefferson's thought. Although this majority rule was based on the equal rights of free men, innocents under their protection were excluded. From this perspective, Jefferson's patriarchal views on women, slaves, and children alike become readily comprehensible. This is also why one needs to question any straightforward reading of Jefferson as a modern, libertarian theorist of natural rights – one for whom contemporary social standards might have been of secondary interest.

INHERENT, MORALLY INALIENABLE RIGHTS

Modern moral philosophy centers on the notion of moral obligation. Jefferson could consider "our relations with others as constituting the boundaries of morality" to the extent that "to ourselves, in strict language, we can owe no duties, obligation requiring also two parties."[12] Even so, Jefferson's rights thinking did not amount to any doctrinaire libertarian position in which preference would go to individual rights over everything else. It is useful, nevertheless, to begin by delineating what in Jefferson's theoretical position accorded with such a libertarian reading.

In order to capture what Jefferson most probably thought of the purely obligatory character of natural rights, one may refer to his original draft of the Declaration of Independence, where the origins of rights are articulated in the following way:

> We hold these truths to be sacred & undeniable; that all men are created equal & independant [sic], that from that equal creation they derive rights inherent & inalienable, among which are the preservation of life, & liberty, & the pursuit of happiness; that to secure these ends, governments are instituted among men ...[13]

This short passage seems to suggest a pure theory of rights, connecting the twofold notion of men as "equal" and "independent" with the corresponding, twofold notion of rights as "inherent" and "inalienable."[14] Thus, being "equal" with others means being in the possession of the "inherent" rights. Correspondingly, being "independent" of others means that the individual possesses these rights as morally "inalienable."

The categories of inherence and inalienability refer only to two aspects of a single *moral obligation* (respect for others, not for oneself) from which these rights derived. First, inherent equality of all men was backed by the simple moral obligation to respect others as one's equals with regard to life, liberty, and the pursuit of happiness. Second, by calling the rights inalienable, Jefferson held them to be morally nontransferable from one person to another. Each individual was morally obligated not to consign his subjective rights to another person's responsibility. Rights, in short, were viewed as rightful powers and as such were self-obligating in character.

There is abundant evidence that Jefferson considered rights as both inherent and inalienable. Only two years before his death he famously exclaimed that "Nothing ... is unchangeable but the inherent and unalienable rights of man."[15] Jefferson's own memorandum of the original draft of the Declaration, as included in his autobiography, also referred to the notion of "inherent and inalienable" rights.[16] Similarly, his diplomatic memoranda from the 1790s include remarks about "inherent rights."[17] Finally, although Jefferson does not appear to have objected to the elimination of the term "inherent" from the Declaration of Independence, the at least equally loose final formulation does not contradict his attribution of that quality to rights.

Jefferson's linkage of the term "inherent" with "rights" most probably served to affirm the moral equality between men as possessors of natural rights. Nothing in the purely naturalistic view of self-interested people constantly prone to violate each other's rights could make them "equal." Indeed, Jefferson's draft for Virginia's criminal law begins with the simple presumption that because people "commit violations of the lives, liberties and property of others ... government would be defective in its principal purpose, were it not to restrain" them.[18] Some contemporary criticism of the wording of the Declaration of Independence held it unnecessary to invoke a specific natural "right to life" as if humans were not animated beings by definition.[19] For Jefferson, the wording was probably only about setting a kind of natural equality for all the living as possessors of the right to life. He himself attested that "*the dead have no rights*. They are nothing; and nothing cannot own something."[20] As for liberty, Jefferson saw a clear distinction between the naturalistic notion of liberty, consisting in "unobstructed action according to our will," and the "rightful liberty," consisting in "unobstructed action according to our will within limits drawn around us by the equal rights of others."[21] As for the pursuit of happiness, he averred that "the King of kings" had "made it a law in the nature of man to pursue his own interest."[22]

In sum, it appears evident that Jefferson's use of the term "inherent" was ethically charged, referring to a kind of inborn equality among the living as possessors of natural rights. As he held, no inborn deficiency of rationality can entitle a "superior" genius such as Isaac Newton to any power over a less talented individual's "exercise" of rights.[23] Moral respect for other people's liberty entailed "cherishing especially their freedom of conscience."[24] Despite Jefferson's outspoken suspicions about racial differences, slavery – because it denied the slave "the right of will" – was a violation of the inherent equality of all men.[25]

To move on to consider the connotations of the term "inalienable," it seems clear that Jefferson associated personal independence – as distinct from inherent equality of all people – with the inalienability of rights. The concept of inalienable right can be traced to Hugo Grotius's early seventeenth-century writings on natural law. As philosopher Morton White has pointed out, the term "alienation" did not primarily allude to losing a thing or becoming deprived of it, but to transferring it from one person to another.[26] That Jefferson understood the term in such a manner is evident in light of his later argument on the alienation of property rights. According to Jefferson's famous tenet, "the soil is the gift of God to the living" to the extent that the living cannot "alienate it from them[selves]" as security for such debts as their own labor cannot clear. Assuming such debts, he argued, "would be an alienation to the creditors."[27]

The only reason for Jefferson to call rights inalienable was that he regarded them *morally* inalienable. Again, in purely naturalistic terms, any individual was capable of alienating his right to life. Ancient writers, such as Cicero, did not consider suicide morally condemnable. One could also argue that no absolute obligation owed to others would be breached by such an act. Jefferson considered suicide as neither "justifiable" nor "felonious," but as an "excusable" homicide, and rather falling in the category of insanity than anything else.[28] Alienating one's right to life became a matter of morality when it meant the right to risk one's life. On this subject Jefferson could lean on, for example, Francis Hutcheson, according to whom alienation had to be fully unselfish to count as morally acceptable.[29] Risking one's right to life for self-regarding reasons would thus be reproachable. Jefferson's so-called Legal Commonplace Book includes a number of remarks against such self-centered notions of honor or reputation that could lead a man to risk his life in the "barbarious [sic] custom of duels."[30] By contrast, when the signers of the Declaration of Independence announced at the end of the document their intention to "mutually pledge to each other" their lives, they did something different.[31] Their professed willingness to alienate their right to life could be viewed as amounting only to risking their lives in order to preserve the rights of themselves as well as those of their fellow citizens.

The notion of liberty as a morally inalienable right Jefferson apparently equated with freedom of conscience. He once proclaimed "constitutional freedom of religion" to be "the most inalienable and sacred of all human rights."[32] But personally, Jefferson preferred not to "go to heaven" if that entailed submitting his own "opinions to the creed of any party of men whatever in religion, in philosophy, in politics, or in anything else."[33] Thus, he instructed his nephew Peter Carr to remain true only to himself when considering whether to believe in God.[34] In sum, Jefferson considered it immoral for an individual to transfer, or to entrust, the right of conscience to the hands of religious or secular authority, at least without personal conviction that such authority was trustworthy. One could not disclaim, or alienate, personal responsibility for one's own religious or philosophical convictions. "The rights of conscience," Jefferson famously insisted, "we could not submit" to government because "we are answerable for them to our God."[35] Given that "the true religion," discussed in the same passage of the *Notes on the State of Virginia*, could involve subscribing to no god, to one god, or to twenty gods, it is clear that the interpersonal criterion for the individual's right to liberty remained absolutely secular.[36]

What made the pursuit of happiness a morally inalienable right was simply that no man could morally disclaim his own responsibility for either succeeding or failing to attain happiness. No parish, neighborhood, society, or state could become morally accountable for this thoroughly individualized conception of the pursuit itself. Finally, no definition of happiness (whether rising from pure self-interest or disinterested motives) could alter the individual's own responsibility on matters of such an existentialist scope.

In essence, the theoretical moral obligation backing Jeffersonian natural rights consists of two elements: first, passive noninterference with other people's inherent rights and, second, active responsibility for one's own pursuit of the good, which entails a prohibition on alienating one's exercise of rights to other people. This dual obligation reconciles the individual's responsibility for laboring for oneself with one's inherent rights to life, to liberty, and even to material welfare. Indeed, Jefferson thought it absurd to assume that "a man had less right in himself than one of his neighbors."[37] This set of theoretical assumptions is compatible, too, with Jefferson's assessment of slavery as a moral wrong. As argued in the earlier chapters, the slave was unjustly "despoiled not only of all property," but also "of the faculties of acquiring it" as well as of "the right to dispose of his person."[38]

This key Jeffersonian notion of natural right – as every man's right to develop his inborn faculties – is well in accordance with the standard libertarian reading of his rights thinking. It recurs often enough in his records: When endorsing an early draft of the French declaration of the rights of man in 1789, for instance, Jefferson fully acknowledged the rights as entitling every man to "the entire disposal of his person and industry, as well as his faculties."[39] In 1795, Jefferson lectured Jean Nicolas Démeunier that the United States had become an asylum for many European refugees, offering them "an entire freedom to use their own means & faculties as they please."[40]

The same point was articulated in his first inaugural address in 1801, where one finds America described as a "chosen country," where all people may entertain "a due sense of our equal right to the use of our own faculties."[41] In a statement from 1817, Jefferson – after enumerating the rights to life, liberty, and the pursuit of happiness – again supplemented the list with the right to use "our faculties."[42] In light of all this, the Jeffersonian conception of natural rights provided equal footing and mutual respect for all men in their pursuit of happiness, regardless of whether they considered their own happiness in selfish or unselfish terms.

Up to this point, Jefferson's rights thinking remains fully reconcilable with the standard libertarian interpretation of the American founding-era ideals of negative freedom, equal opportunity, and minimal government.[43] Such an interpretation, however, fails to take into account the complexities of Jefferson's thought in regard to all kinds of potential and real conflicts between individuals as possessors of natural rights. Moreover, there is the question of how one should treat people who need help to take advantage of their basic rights.

The two reservations are worth keeping in mind because the central individual obligation of noninterference with other people's rights certainly does not exhaust Jefferson's moral thought – even when restricted to his use of the term "right." The right of resistance, for example, was sometimes included in Jefferson's summaries of the natural rights of man. This is how he bracketed the Marquis de Lafayette's draft for the French declaration of rights: "Every man is born with inalienable rights; such are [the right of property], the care of [his honor and] his life, the entire disposal of his person and industry, as well as his faculties, the pursuit of his own good, and resistance against oppression."[44] The notion of resistance could thus belong to the cluster of the inalienable rights of man.

Jeffersonian natural rights were never merely subjective rights of an individual. Instead, they arose from the notion of the present generation's common right to self-government. As Jefferson argued in 1816, the right to revise state constitutions every nineteen years could be derived from a single grand principle: "Each generation is as independent as the one preceding." It was the generation, not the individual alone, who had "a right to choose for itself the form of government" and "to accommodate to the circumstances in which it finds itself." "If they have not, who has?" Jefferson asked, "The dead? But the dead have no rights. They are nothing; and nothing cannot own something."[45]

In 1824, Jefferson repeated his fundamental premise of distinguishing between the rights of the living and those of the dead in this way:

Can one generation bind another, and all others, in succession forever? I think not. The Creator has made the earth for the living, not the dead. Rights and powers can only belong to persons, not to things, not to mere matter, unendowed [sic] with will. The dead are not even things. The particles of matter which composed their bodies, make part now of the bodies of other animals, vegetables, minerals, of a thousand forms. To what then are attached the rights and powers they held while in the form of men? A generation may bind itself as long as its majority continues in life; when that has disappeared, another majority is in place ... Nothing then is unchangeable but the inherent and unalienable rights of man.[46]

Again, nothing "is unchangeable, but the inherent and unalienable rights of man," when determined as "rights and powers" belonging "to persons" whose consequent obligation is to maintain them. Without the majority right to reinterpret the limits of such individual powers anew peacefully by every generation, Jefferson's whole doctrine would have resulted in a Hobbesian world of unrestricted, justified violence on the part of any individual differing on the correct interpretation of one's rightful powers. Thus, the living could – in absolute freedom from what once was legal and right – reinterpret the law of nature and its dictates. If people were enlightened enough, their reinterpretations could even manifest genuine human progress in understanding the law of nature in more detail.

With regard to generational sovereignty in 1776, the colonies, according to the Declaration of Independence, assumed "equal station among the Powers of the earth." Under the law of nature and nations, therefore, the revolutionaries were to regard their British brethren as nothing more than "Enemies in War, in Peace Friends."[47] In sum, conflict was presumed possible from the outset, and the notion of inherent and inalienable natural rights should be interpreted from that point of view. In this respect, the celebrated concept of the state of nature as the hypothetical ground for discerning the essential moral elements of human sociability appears marginal to Jefferson's rights thinking.

THE STATE OF NATURE IN JEFFERSON'S PARLANCE

Jefferson's records include surprisingly few references to the state of nature. What did the concept mean to him? To begin with a simplified reading of the Lockean theory as compatible with Jefferson's use of the concept, one may resort to Locke's famous maxim that in the state of nature, every man possesses the rightful power "*of doing whatsoever he thought fit for the Preservation of himself* and the rest of Mankind."[48] The concept of the state of nature, hence, readily accords with the essentially hermetic image of a self-sufficient man who – even if not truly isolated from others – works for himself and leaves all others to do the same. This self-sufficiency is what defines the state of nature as pre-political. It was the law of nature – governing the state of nature – that invested every man with the rightful power of doing what he pleased insofar as he respected other individuals' similar rights to life, liberty, and property.

Yet the concept of the state of nature changes radically once conflict is viewed as possible. And even in Locke's thought, conflict does appear in the state of nature. This is why Locke subscribed to what he himself called an odd doctrine, namely that in the state of nature "*every one has the Executive Power* of the Law of Nature."[49] "In the state of nature," Locke therefore held, "Man has two Powers": first, the right to self-preservation with regard to the rest of mankind and second, the right to punish those who violate that right.[50] Only with the assumption that conflict may arise in the state of nature itself, did it make sense for Locke to argue that insofar as the individual's own "Preservation comes not in competition, ought he, as much as he can, *to preserve the rest of Mankind*."[51]

It is because conflict is presumed possible in the state of nature that a certain kind of violence can be justified. Initially, this conception of just violence emerges in the state of nature as every man's subjective right against everyone else. Hobbes's famous thesis held that such a stance, if it did not preempt all human cooperation to begin with, would eventually dissolve the state of nature into every man's war against all others. This problem called for the social contract.

By and large, Hobbes's social contract theory deprived the individual of the right to justified violence and shifted it into the hands of the sovereign. Locke, by contrast, shifted it into the hands of the majority. Hence, the very notion of civil society resulted from the act of entrusting one's subjective rights to the political association, which necessarily rested on majority rule. As Locke insisted, the individual man must thus surrender both his rightful powers: "The first *Power, viz. of doing whatsoever he thought fit for the Preservation of himself*, and the rest of Mankind, he *gives up* to be regulated by Laws made by the Society" (e.g., by taxation and property regulations), but "the *Power of punishing* he *wholly gives up*."[52] Whereas the surrender of property rights to the fruits of one's own labor was partial, the surrender of the right to justified violence was absolute. It was entirely transmitted to the political association.

This was why the Lockean commonwealth evolved from the maxim that because "it is unreasonable for Men to be Judges in their own Cases" as would happen in the state of nature, "God hath certainly appointed Government to restrain the partiality and violence of Men."[53] Jefferson could go as far as to claim that no man has "a natural right to be the judge between himself and another"[54] or, as Jefferson's favorite authority in the field of natural law, Emer de Vattel, formulated the case, "as there does not exist in mankind a disposition voluntarily to observe towards each other the rules of the law of nature, they have had recourse to a political association." As Vattel further pointed out, "the law of nature itself approves of this establishment."[55] Sidestepping the scholarly debate about Locke's exact understanding of the concept, consider how James Madison characterized the state of nature. He saw it as sheer anarchy, "where the weaker individual is not secured against the violence of the stronger" and where "even the stronger individuals are prompted, by the uncertainty of their condition, to submit to government."[56]

How, then, does the concept figure in the Jefferson archive? It was clear to him that the "moral duties which exist between individual and individual in a state of nature, accompany them into a state of society." In effect, "the same moral duties exist" there "as did between individuals composing them while in an unassociated state."[57] In Jefferson's view, this simplified conception of the state of nature as an unassociated state of man could function as purely theoretical grounds for discerning the individual's absolute moral obligation to respect all mankind as one would respect oneself.

Yet this "unassociated state of man" occurs very rarely in Jefferson's records. Instead, one finds him regularly speaking of primitive and progressive stages of associations among people. Consider the imagined American landscape of progressive history that Jefferson so vividly painted to William Ludlow in 1824 – no "unassociated" people figured there. Instead, Jefferson's historical sketch "from the infancy of creation to the present day" began with hunting savages, representing the "earliest stage of association" in history, to be followed by nomadic, pastoral, and commercial stages of association.[58] To cast light on the socio-ethic presumptions behind the scheme, one may turn to Jefferson's famous contention from 1787 that "those societies (as the Indians) which live without government enjoy in their general mass an infinitely greater degree of happiness than those who live under the European governments." For the Indians, unlike the legally coordinated societies of orders in Europe, "public opinion is in the place of law & restrains morals as powerfully as laws ever did anywhere."[59]

In an even more telling 1816 statement, Jefferson held that American "Indians are evidently in that state of nature which has passed the association of a single family; and not yet submitted to the authority of positive laws." Two fundamental points need to be made on the Jeffersonian state of nature as it figures in this statement. First, Jefferson saw the Native Americans living *beyond* "that state of nature" that comprised "the association of a single family." Second, he depicted the earliest interfamily associations of Indians as a kind of a halfway house between a village-size society and civil society proper. The former was grounded on public opinion whereas the latter was grounded on the force of law. After all, even in this statement, Jefferson pointed out that every Indian brave was "perfectly free to follow his own inclinations, and if he violates the rights of another," he was punished by "public opinion."[60]

In the absence of legal institutions, public opinion alone counted as a shared, minimum standard for the reciprocal rights of men. All in all, Jefferson's remarks about Indian nations living under no law but that of public opinion do not imply some essentially "pre-political" stage of progress.[61] Rather, they indicate the exact opposite: Jefferson even discerned "parties among them adhering to different leaders, and governed by their advice, not by their command."[62]

Civil society, even among Native Americans was, in essence, an interfamily association between the equal heads of households. To be sure, the concept of society often referred to family relations, but primarily to an individual's relation to the whole family of mankind under God. As Locke had it, when a man leaves the state of nature and "joyns in a private, if I may so call it, or particular Political Society," he does it "separate from the rest of Mankind."[63] The Lockean history of the origins of the earliest governments could hence be conceived of as "*a Family*" gradually growing up "*into a Common-wealth*," or as "several Families" initially putting "the rule into the hands of a single person."[64] According to Francis Hutcheson's summary of the Hobbesian view of the origins of governmental powers, one could certainly imagine "a potent head of a family" compelling his neighbors "to submit to him." However, as Hutcheson went on, such a conception was hardly reconcilable with "the just causes of just power."[65]

Either way, a decent commonwealth necessarily separated its members from the rest of mankind. Jefferson's simplified conception of the state of nature as an "unassociated state of man" explains why all family allegories for civil society were fundamentally invalid. Civil society referred to the association of equal adults, but always via their voluntary consent. The principle with Locke was that "all men ... by their own Consents ... make themselves Members of some Politick Society."[66] Family relations were unequal relations between parents and children, and perhaps even servants, not equal relations between adults, the defining characteristic of civil society. Even the idea of a single family extending into a commonwealth required each son to give his consent to it as an adult.

The act of giving one's consent to political society provides the grounds of Jefferson's grand concept of generational independence, which could rest equally well on Lockean or Rousseauean theory. Rousseau's "Social contract" included explicit reference to the need for each generation to renew the contract as a justified basis of government.[67] In commonplace jurisprudential terms, all outsiders were respected under the law of nations (*jus gentium*), just as the insiders were to respect each other under civil law (*jus civile*).[68] From this scheme arises Jefferson's commitment to the notion of the law of the majority being the "fundamental law of every society," and remaining so for "every society of individuals of equal rights."[69] Moreover, his unequivocal subscription to the right of emigration, a tenet not be found in Locke's theory, suggests that the rising generation's consent to government was to be viewed as a genuinely individual, voluntary submission. After all, Jefferson claimed "the right of expatriation to be inherent in every man by the laws of nature, and incapable of being rightfully taken from him even by the united will of every other person in the nation."[70]

As for the historical ramifications of all this, it is notable that, in Jefferson's view, the American Revolution neither began in the state of nature, nor resulted in such a state. It was a moment of justified violence intended to restore the right to participate in peaceful discourse on conflicts over diverse interests – a right that by definition belonged to all free men in any decent civil society.

In fact, Jefferson never ceased arguing that the rebellious colonies had been "civil societies" prior to the Revolution, and that they wished to remain so.[71] In 1774, his rhetorical question posed to the king was this: "Shall these [colonial] governments be dissolved" and "their people reduced to a state of nature?" The question itself presumed that if parliament dissolved the colonial governments and hence reduced them to "a state of nature," the colonists could still appeal to the king as the ultimate supervisor of natural law. It was from this mock image of George III as a divine figure that Jefferson went on to ask, "does his majesty seriously wish" that the colonists should "submit themselves the absolute slaves of his sovereign will?"[72] When resorting to a just war, the colonists were not opting for a merely hypothetical, "unassociated" state of nature over the apparently dissolved colonial governments. At least in Jefferson's view, they opted for continuing their self-government over absolute slavery – the latter being nothing but a prolonged state of war.

THE CONSENT OF THE GOVERNED IN 1776

How did the celebrated Lockean right of armed resistance fit the revolutionaries' situation? The central deficiency of Locke's doctrine was that it offered no objective criteria for free men to judge in what precise circumstances the obligation to armed resistance arose.[73] Being a "Law antecedent and paramount to all positive Laws of men," the right of resistance was directly derivable from the moral law. Yet, as Locke also insisted that this very "judgment they cannot part with" and that "the Inconveniency" must be "so great, that the Majority feel it," it was obviously the right of someone who had already consented to one or another majority rule.[74] As Francis Hutcheson formulated the case, dethroning a tyrant does "not quite dissolve the political union," given that "civil polity" was "natural to man" owing to both his general "weakness" of will and his innate capacity for "reason."[75]

As noted, the message of the Declaration of Independence to "the candid world" was not so much about reiterating self-evident ethical truths as about explicating that the consent of the governed to British rule had been withdrawn. Whether or not Locke viewed (or should have viewed) the act of dissolving the government as equivalent to the termination of political society altogether, it seems clear that the right to armed resistance was derivable from the will of the majority in a given society.[76] Still, the criterion for justifiable violence remained the same as in natural jurisprudence generally: A single individual's moral judgment about the proper means of promoting justice and benevolence could not amount to the choice of violence. Only civil societies could make such a decision.

The notion of justified violence as arising from majority rule underlies the ethical presumptions of the Declaration of Independence. It is notable that the list of "self-evident" truths – beginning with all men having been "created equal" and hence all in the possession of "certain unalienable rights" – continues with the following ones:

That to secure these rights, Governments are instituted among Men, deriving their just powers from the consent of the governed, That whenever any Form of Government becomes destructive of these ends, it is the Right of the people to alter or to abolish it, and to institute new Government, laying its foundation on such principles and organizing its powers in such form, as to them shall seem most likely to effect their Safety and Happiness.[77]

In other words, it was self-evident that the sole function of government was to secure the unalienable rights of man, and that all its "just powers" to perform that function rested on "the consent of the governed." No particular constitutional form of government was recommended as the best to fulfill the only condition of a decent regime – the consent of the governed. Not only the right to resist, but also "the Right of the people to alter or to abolish" the present government resided in their common consent.

The central contention of Jefferson's revolutionary writings as well as of his later interpretations of the event was that only a legal, constitutional crisis had arisen within the British Empire because of its corrupt government. In his *Summary of the Rights of British America* from 1774, Jefferson considered it to be against "human nature" to suppose that the colonies' "political existence" could depend on the parliament's will. No tenet of British parliamentary sovereignty – comprised, according to Blackstone, of the orders of the king, the lords, and the commons – could determine the issue of constitutional division of governmental powers within the empire. Thus, Jefferson argued, even when acting in common and backed by the king, the houses of parliament possessed "no right to exercise authority over" the colonial legislatures.[78]

Consequently, in 1776, the king's refusal to continue political debate on taxes with the colonists – even if backed by the parliamentary majority – could justify armed resistance on the part of the Americans. One of the omitted parts of Jefferson's original draft of the Declaration stated that "in constituting our several forms of government," the colonists "had adopted one common king" with the British, whereas the "submission to their parliament was not part of our constitution."[79] From early on, in Jefferson's mind, the conflict was about just representation of the colonies as "several states of the British Empire." As all these states had their own legislatures, the English parliament was only "one legislature of the empire." The king's primary prerogatives were to either confirm or veto the laws adopted by the colonial legislatures and to prevent any of the empire's legislatures from enacting laws "which might bear injuriously on the rights and interests of another."[80]

In retrospect, Jefferson could well view the Revolution as a defensive act of violence against the imperial government that had refused to continue the discourse on such a minor political issue as "a two-penny duty on tea, unjustly imposed in a sequestered part" of the civilized world.[81] Obviously, the consent of the governed had been there and was only withdrawn in 1776. Given Jefferson's conviction that "Civil government being the sole object of forming societies, its administration must be conducted by comment consent," it is not so surprising to find him already in the midst of writing a new constitution for the state of Virginia when asked to draft the Declaration of Independence.[82] His draft constitution also provided a mechanism for its alteration "by the personal consent of the people" in county referendums.[83] As Jefferson formulated this seminal principle in 1790: "Every man, & every body of men on earth, possesses the righ[t] of self-government." Individuals exercise this right "by their single will" and "collections of men by that of their majority."[84] Despite that he was a slaveholder, Jefferson could consistently refuse to compromise with this free man's right to self-government.

The natural right to self-government is the stepping stone to all other natural rights in Jefferson's thought, excluding only the obligation to favor innocents. Innocents also figure in the Declaration of Independence, although only as victims of Indians' inhumane warfare. Their presence in the document, as victims, appears to rest on a twofold notion of consent – tacit and explicit. When entering civil society by explicit consent to government, one still tacitly consented to the Christian principle of universal benevolence – respecting the equal rights of the whole rest of mankind. The distinction between the innocent and the free men is crucial to the meaning of consent in the Declaration of Independence. A free man forfeits his innocence in order to protect himself as well as the innocents under his care. Even Locke argued that insofar as the individual's own preservation "comes not in competition, ought he, as much as he can, *to preserve the rest of Mankind*"[85] and whenever "all cannot be preserv´d, the safety of the Innocent is to be preferred."[86] Clearly, the protection of innocents was paramount, above even the obligation of a free man to reclaim his inherent and inalienable rights.

By voluntarily entering a society of laws of their own making, free men also changed their tacit consent to respect all of mankind into a jurisprudential commitment to the "law of nature and nations." The crucial point still held: no free man – endowed with equal, reciprocal rights – could count as innocent once he assumed the status of a free man. This was why no revolutionary could at once claim innocence and the capacity for self-government. The status of innocents was reserved to children, women, and slaves, not to those who gave their consent to wage a just war against the British. The war was waged for no less a political purpose than that of establishing "a new government."

In sum, the consent of the governed could not evolve from passive submission to government on the part of any free man. This is why Jefferson viewed the right of self-government as a universal principle applicable to individuals as free agents who voluntarily submit to majority rule, be its constitution monarchical, democratic, or something else. Innocents, however, remained excluded from political power even after the Revolution. Should a free man find such a majority rule personally unbearable, he possessed an inherent right to move elsewhere.

THE CONSENT OF THE GOVERNED OVER TIME

Jefferson's fundamental commitment to the right – or the rightful power – of every generation to enact laws anew according to its best understanding of natural law could not rest on historical precedents. In fact, the idea of generational popular sovereignty permeates all Jeffersonian historical thought, from immemorial Saxon liberties through the Revolution to the founding of the federal Constitution – and after. It is therefore useful to examine how, in his records, Americans' original consent to majority rule came into being and how it manifested itself over time.

To begin with the conventional beginning, namely the mythic, Teutonic origins of American freedom, it is notable that the natural right of expatriation was never questioned in Jefferson's history writing. In subscribing to the traditional historical claim that Anglo-Americans' "Saxon ancestors" once upon a time moved to Britain from "their native wilds and woods in the North of Europe," Jefferson insisted that they had done so under a "universal law." By that same law – or simply by the "right" – of "all men of departing from the country in which chance, and not choice, had placed them," the first British colonists had gone to America. There they had voluntarily established "new societies, under such laws and regulations as to them" had seemed "most likely to promote public happiness."[87] Not coincidentally, Jefferson argued that only when turning "into a nation" had Virginians voluntarily adopted common law as their law.[88]

As to any legal ordering of society, it was evident to Jefferson that even the immemorial, unwritten, British common law, or law by custom, had been "altered from time to time by proper legislative authority" up to the drafting of Magna Charta. That event initialized the period of statute, or written, law in British legal history. Nevertheless, even statute law's origins lay in ancient customary law or *jus commune*. Its equivalent among the Saxons was the concept of "folc-right," translated "the people's right" in Jefferson's memorandum.[89]

Hence, Jefferson had no problem in sharing the conventional view that the Norman Conquest had violated the Saxon "people's right." Even their unsuccessful rebellions against the Normans bespoke the idea that they never gave up their national right to self-government, for, as Jefferson pointed out, "force cannot change right." Eventually "the final re-conquest of their rights" took place under the Stuarts. Jefferson admitted that the legal documents of the period specified only some of the Saxon rights as truly restored, but jurisprudentially speaking, "the nation re-entered into all its rights."[90] In Jefferson's eyes, the Saxon endeavor to keep up national sovereignty manifested the natural, rightful power of every nation to interpret the law of nature to its best abilities. Well before the Norman Conquest, Saxons themselves had altered their laws by "proper legislative authority," obviously a political one.[91]

When holding that, legally speaking, the Saxons "doubtless had a constitution," Jefferson referred to what had been "practiced with approbation" among them – as evinced in the few surviving "fragments of their history and laws."[92] His wrestling with the specifics of the Saxon constitution amounted to nothing more than an affirmation of popular sovereignty as the historical manifestation of the natural right of any nation to alter its laws. The same principle was upheld in his memorandum on Sullivan's history of monarchical succession in medieval Europe. The long citation on this subject in Jefferson's Legal Commonplace Book ends with his own assertion that whenever a king appointed his successor, his choice "did not succeed by virtue of that appointment, which the king had no right to make, but of the approbation of the people which attended it."[93]

The actual purpose of this historical exegesis of legal conceptions was to derive the very meaning of law from temporal popular sovereignty, not to provide a reliable chain of legal precedents for the Americans to build on. Even Saxons had occasionally erred in their natural law interpretations, as had so many distinguished experts in natural jurisprudence after them.[94] As Jefferson maintained, the American revolutionaries had little need to "investigate the laws and institutions" of their "semi-barbarous ancestry," or search through "the musty records" of often centuries-old royal statutes.[95]

The Revolution, Jefferson later mused, "presented us an album on which we were free to write what we pleased." Instead of appealing to the erstwhile Saxon laws, he calmly noted, "We appealed to those of nature, and found them engraved in our hearts."[96] This 1824 statement was far from being only a retrospective effort to justify the revolutionaries' reinterpretations of natural law. The same line of argument is present in Jefferson's records dating back to the Revolution. In his *Notes on the State of Virginia*, written in the immediate aftermath of the Revolution, he lamented that the colonists had unnecessarily consented to the 1650 parliamentary "act for inhibiting their trade with foreign nations," an act amounting to a "fatal precedent which they continued to follow."[97] Moreover, Jefferson had favored popular sovereignty over sheer legalism in the very midst of the Revolution. This is best exemplified in his 1776 letter to Edmund Pendleton, which treated the question of legal ownership of colonial lands. Jefferson insisted that colonial lands were by all natural-law definitions "allodial" instead of feudal. As in his later writings on the issue, he here argued that the king had never possessed a right to regulate the colonists' free use, and hence full ownership, of the lands. Jefferson acknowledged that the colonists had occasionally consented to view their land possessions as "feuds." On these grounds any lawyer could argue that the lands were feudal possessions and taxable by the British Crown. When differentiating between the jurisprudentially valid character of these possessions and what they were by legal precedents, the young Jefferson drew this simple conclusion: "This matter is now become a mere speculative point; & we have it in our power to make it what it ought to be for the public good."[98]

Jefferson never let go of the idea of free, representative democracy as the core concept of all human progress, no matter how many times a people needed to change their laws or constitutions. When he fumed that "England has no constitution at all," because there is "not one principle of their government which the parliament does not alter at pleasure," he was not arguing for lessening the powers of the parliament in the British system. What he opposed was parliament acting as if independent of the people it represented.[99] Jefferson's rights thinking rested on the idea of a nation deploying its natural right to self-government according to its best contemporary understanding of the law of nature. The obvious concomitant of such a view was that human understanding of the law of nature was still imperfect.

To further verify the central role of popular sovereignty in Jefferson's rights thinking, it is worth considering how deeply his Virginia-centered reading of America's founding was constructed on the historically verifiable continuity of the consent of the governed. He traced the proper beginnings of civil society in the Commonwealth of Virginia back to the year 1621. That year, an agreement was achieved that, "after the government of the colony should be well framed and settled, no orders of council in England should bind the colony unless ratified" by the colony's own government.[100] In 1774, Jefferson himself informed the king about the colonies' actual "political existence."[101] Consequently, in 1776, the people of Virginia "chose to abolish their former organs of declaring their will" and to establish new ones.[102]

That Jefferson never viewed the 1776 Revolution as a return to the state of nature is further evinced by his argument that, even if the Virginia government was at the time dissolved, the Virginia nation was not:

> When, by the [Virginians'] declaration of Independence, they chose to abolish their former organs of declaring their will, the acts of will already formally & constitutionally declared, remained untouched. For the nation was not dissolved, was not annihilated; it's will, therefore, remained in full vigor; and on the establishing the new organs, first of a convention, & afterwards a more complicated legislature, the old acts of national will continued in force, until the nation should, by its new organs, declare it's will changed.[103]

The crucial theoretical point was that "the nation was not dissolved." There was a nation of Virginians, which, ever since its establishment under government in 1621, did not get dissolved for a moment throughout the War of Independence and all the consequent changes in its form of government. Neither did the situation essentially change when that nation joined the Union. According to Jefferson, all the "states composing" the federal association did so solely "for the management of their concerns with one another & with foreign nations, and ... chose to give it powers for those purposes & no others."[104]

The Union thus rested on the continuing flow of expressions of the will of its member states or nations. In the spirit of the Rousseau's concept of the general will, Jefferson proclaimed that "the law being law because it is the will of the nation, is not changed by their changing the organ through which they chuse [sic] to announce their future will."[105] "Civil government being the sole object of forming societies," it was evident to Jefferson that "its administration must be conducted by common consent."[106] Insofar as "the consent of the governed" prevailed, the enforcement of the law of nature and nations remained a government monopoly in the American federal republic as well. In this respect, Jefferson held only that the states were to remain the sole executive power of the civil law (*jus civile*), except in the few cases specifically listed in the Constitution, whereas the Union would have the executive power of international law (jus gentium), with its special prerogative of settling disputes between the member states.[107]

Jefferson never ceased to argue that mixing these two functions of civil government would only serve to submit any local democratic institution to the mercy of the federal Supreme Court justices. Besides appearing a small, elite council of the few, the justices were nominated for life. Jefferson never subscribed to the modern idea of judicial review as the Supreme Court's constitutional prerogative in the American federation of state republics. This is why he flatly denounced Chief Justice John Marshall's maxim that, because "there must be an ultimate arbiter somewhere," the arbiter of civil law predicaments should be Mr. Marshall's court. Instead, Jefferson invoked the authority of the constitutional convention: "The ultimate arbiter is the people of the Union, assembled by their deputies in convention, at the call of Congress or of two-thirds of the States."[108]

As for the general constitutional division of the federal government's powers between the executive, judicial, and legislative branches, Jefferson held that the principle of "check and balance" resolved all questions of judicial review among them. As he claimed, "each department is truly independent of the others, and has an equal right to decide for itself what is the meaning of the constitution in the cases submitted to its action."[109] The branches would check and balance each other thanks to their different powers.

In 1798, Jefferson attacked President John Adams's Alien and Sedition Acts, which appeared to prohibit all open criticism of the federal government and thus to violate freedom of speech. In his famous draft of the Kentucky Resolutions against these laws, Jefferson revealed his states' rights convictions in full. The document endowed each state with the power to review any federal law threatening those very rights the government was supposed to "secure" according to the Declaration of Independence.[110] Partly as a result of Jefferson's earlier perseverance, the argument now could concern the constitutional rights of the people rather than only their natural rights. James Madison had been initially unwilling to amend the 1789 Constitution with a Bill of Rights. Jefferson convinced him otherwise and argued that even if such written guarantees of rights hardly made them more secure, "[h]alf a loaf is better than no bread."[111]

PERFECT AND IMPERFECT RIGHTS

What was Jefferson's understanding of the natural lawyers' classic distinction between perfect and imperfect rights of man? The Jeffersonian natural rights can be construed as theoretically perfect rights, but only with the proviso that, in his eyes, all human rights were imperfect, even if perfectible over time under the guardianship of free government. The natural rights of man had been violated throughout history, whether from ignorance, error, or simple disrespect. Indeed, Jefferson appears never to have called natural rights perfect, except when speaking of the right of self-preservation. In Jefferson's parlance, the right of self-preservation remained superior even to the perfect rights of others.

To grasp the essential distinction between morally and jurisprudentially perfect rights, one may call on the two most renowned authorities in the field of the law of nature and nations, Hugo Grotius and Samuel Pufendorf. Both divided rights into perfect and imperfect. Perfect rights denoted the theoretically demonstrable minimum rights of every man. They called for respect even among different Christian denominations, whatever their disagreements on the means to salvation. Perfect moral rights were backed by correspondingly perfect, absolutely inviolable duties, whereas imperfect rights rested on less perfectly definable duties of benevolence and charity. To a large extent, therefore, this distinction rested on the pending epistemological problem of defining what true charity demands in terms of legislative action. Pufendorf sharpened the distinction by insisting that the perfect moral obligation to respect the rights of others essentially consisted in the negative obligation of an individual not to interfere with the perfect rights of others.[112]

Typically for an eighteenth-century lawyer, Jefferson read Grotius and Pufendorf rather as jurists than as moral theorists and compared their treatises on the law of nature and nations in detail with those of Emer de Vattel and Christian Wolff. Jefferson's memoranda on the revision of Virginia civil legislation from the late 1770s, as well as his much later diplomatic memoranda, teem with references to these authorities along with the less-known Cesare Beccaria and Jean Jacques Burlamaqui. Even so, Jefferson seems never to have paid any attention to Pufendorf's famous disagreement with Grotius about the nature of the human obligation to the moral law. Pufendorf insisted that God alone could be the obligator of man, whereas Grotius's rationalist "error" held that even if God did not exist, men, as rational creatures, could conceive of the minimum tenets of natural law.[113]

To offer a textbook example of the distinction between perfect and imperfect obligations from Jefferson's youth, this is how Lord Kames's *Principles of Equity* (1760) framed it:

> Gratuitous deeds are beneficial to society as exertions of kindness and generosity: but however beneficial, they are certainly not essential to society, which may subsist in vigour without them.[114]

In sum, beneficial deeds were morally necessary, but not proved by the theory of natural law to be something everyone justly could be compelled to perform. Even so, benevolence definitely belonged to the realm of morality. As Thomas Reid once pointed out, "it is evident that there is more worth in pure, unmerited benevolence than in compassion, more in compassion than in gratitude, and more in gratitude than in justice."[115] Lord Kames's probably ironic remark that human society is unlikely ever to attain such an elevated stage of refinement that "a law against hard-heartedness would be enacted" serves well to capture the complexity of the natural lawyers' legacy to the idea of moral progress.[116]

The distinction between the morally and jurisprudentially perfect (and imperfect) rights may appear problematic in reading the Declaration of Independence. Nevertheless, once the natural rights of man are viewed as simply morally defensible rights to act, Jefferson's distinction between perfect and imperfect rights seems fairly simple. The statement that "all men are created equal" and equally entitled to the inalienable, and hence perfect, rights of "Life, Liberty and the pursuit of Happiness" does not imply even the possibility of a conflict between people as possessors of rights.[117] But in the next phrase, "That to secure these rights, Governments are instituted among Men," there emerges a clear distinction between the theoretically perfect rights and the notion that "in the course of human events," all rights of man are imperfect human possessions, and hence must sometimes be protected even with violence. This is more easily discernible in Jefferson's original draft, where the rights of man consisted in "the preservation of life, & liberty, & the pursuit of happiness."

In 1789, Jefferson repeated this central point when lecturing Thomas Paine that, regardless of exact political forms, every "government should have for it's only end the preservation of the rights of man." In order to "recall constantly the government to the end proposed," even the French, monarchical constitution should "begin by a Declaration of the natural and imprescriptible [sic] rights of man."[118] In sum, even the perfect rights of man needed political backing, meaning that they were de facto imperfect, albeit perfectible within a free government. It is therefore not surprising that, in Jefferson's jurisprudential considerations, imperfect rights occasionally appear superior to the so-called perfect rights.[119]

Jefferson's famous foreign policy memorandum from 1793, known as his *Opinion on the French Treaties*, well illustrates how imperfect rights could overcome perfect ones.[120] The memorandum was written at the beginning of the two-decade long, Napoleonic wars following the French revolution. George Washington's cabinet soon realized that the Americans might be drawn into the European conflict as a result of their old treaties with France, dating back to the Revolution. Most members of the cabinet were willing to dissolve the treaties in order to prevent this, but Jefferson, the then secretary of state, argued against such a policy as "immoral." His conclusion was that by annulling the treaties precipitously, the Americans would give nothing less than "a just cause of war to France."[121]

In his long memorandum, Jefferson needed to point out that the Americans could not view the treaties as expired because of a mere change in the form of government in France. Again, he defined the governmental powers as directly derivable from the national will:

> I consider the people who constitute a society or nation as the source of all authority in that nation, as free to transact their common concerns by any agents they think proper, to change these agents individually, or the organisation of them in form or function whenever they please: that all acts done by those agents under the authority of the nation, are acts of the nation, are obligatory on them, & enure [sic] to their use, & can in no wise be annulled or affected by any change in the form of government, or the persons administering it.[122]

According to natural law, Jefferson here maintained, the treaties remained in force despite the fact that France had changed its form of government from a monarchy to a republic. In fact, the treaties bound the "nations," not only their governments, which were mere agents acting under "the authority of the nation." Only after pointing this out did Jefferson turn to consider the practical threat of the situation to the American nation, noting that "the danger which absolves us must be great, inevitable & imminent." His practical assessment that the danger was not yet as imminent as other cabinet members thought is difficult to prove or disprove. Eventually President Washington made American neutrality regarding these European developments one of the nation's most celebrated foreign policy doctrines.

Yet, Jefferson's memorandum also offers interesting statements about the obligatory character of "moral duties" as related to these practical considerations. It was in this document that he invoked the concept of "the state of nature" as an "unassociated" state of man so as to argue that the moral duties originating in the state of nature follow the individual upon entrance into civil society. He began with the following categories of the law of nations: "The Law of nations, by which this question is to be determined, is composed of three branches. 1. The Moral Law of our nature. 2. The Usages of nations. 3. Their special Conventions."[123]

"The first of these only," Jefferson asserted, concerned the Americans' right to retreat from their international treaties. The seminal question to be asked about this notion of "The Moral Law of our nature" is: What did Jefferson here claim to know about "our nature" regarding "the moral law"? Nothing was said about any natural, human inclination to happiness or about freedom of conscience. Jefferson here defined "moral duties" as something concerning equally the individual in the state of nature and any group of individuals comprising an association:

> The Moral duties which exist between individual and individual in a state of nature, accompany them into a state of society ... so that between society & society the same moral duties exist as did between individuals composing them while in an unassociated state....[124]

After noting that the moral duties are the same in both "states" of man, Jefferson turned to the notion of a compact or contract as that which truly binds individuals to their moral duties: "Compacts then between nation & nation are obligatory on them by the same moral law which obliges individuals to observe their compacts." Having thus shifted to the field of actual, voluntary contracts, he resorted to "the law of self-preservation" as the highest law, overruling even all "laws of obligation to others." This is Jefferson's account of the special circumstances in which contracts could be dissolved:

> There are circumstances however which sometimes excuse the non-performance of contracts between man & man: so are there also between nation & nation ... So if performance becomes *self-destructive* to the party, the law of self-preservation overrules the laws of obligation to others. For the reality of these principles I appeal to the true fountains of evidence, the head & heart of every rational & honest man.[125]

In sum, a contract that becomes "self-destructive" could turn one's jurisprudentially perfect duties into imperfect ones. Jefferson was here defining not natural law, but its applications in real life. The key point he quoted from Emer de Vattel, arguing that it "is demonstrated in natural law that he who promises another confers on him a perfect right to require the thing promised."[126] As for such a promise – here calling up the very notion of perfect right and the corresponding perfect duty – the excusing circumstances may free "man & man" just as "nation & nation" from their "perfect" duties.

Obviously, one should not confuse the theoretically perfect moral obligation to respect all mankind with the moral duty to perform a given promise, as derived from purely jurisprudential considerations. On this occasion, the concept of perfect duty arose out of a historically identifiable contract. Any such contract could become refutable under natural law if its performance appeared self-destructive. However, Jefferson went further than that.

To clarify the essentially imperfect character of the perfect right in Jefferson's use of the term, it is useful to resort to yet another diplomatic memorandum relating to a situation in which no contract yet existed. Well before his greatest diplomatic achievement as president, namely the purchase of the Louisiana Territory from Napoleon in 1803, Jefferson became involved in negotiations with Spain about American access to the lower Mississippi river. In 1792 – before the argument on the French treaties previously discussed – he drafted a memorandum for American negotiators on this issue.

This time Jefferson sought to establish nothing less than the natural right of a nation to reach certain kinds of compacts with others. Even on this occasion he referred to Grotius, Pufendorf, Vattel, and Wolff and freely admitted that "the natural right" of Americans to use the Mississippi River "would indeed be what those writers call an *imperfect right* because the modification of *it's exercise depends* in considerable degree on the conveniency [sic] of the nation thro' which they are to pass."[127] But his actual point was that the Americans living along the upper Mississippi possessed an "inherent" right to "innocent passage" of the river as a commercial water route.[128] This "natural right" he derived from Grotius's old natural-law precept about the open seas, dictating unequivocally that "the Ocean is free to all men, & the Rivers to all their inhabitants."[129] Eventually, Jefferson lectured the negotiators thus:

> It will probably be urged, because it was urged on the former occasion, that if Spain *grants* to us the right of navigating the Missisipi [sic], other nations will become entitled to it, by virtues of treaties giving them the rights of *the most favored nations*.
>
> Two answers maybe given to this:
>
> 1. When those treaties were made, no nations could be under contemplation but those existing, ... America did not then exist as a nation ... the treaties of that day were not adapted to any such being....
> 2. But the decisive answer is that Spain does not grant us the navigation of the river. We have an inherent right to it: & she may repel the demand of any other nation, by candidly stating her act to have been, what in truth it is, a recognition only, & not a grant.[130]

Jefferson's remarks about Spain's earlier agreements with colonial powers regarding access to the river served to confirm that Spain had already recognized such a right as pertaining to the Mississippi. It was thus a simple matter on Spain's part not to grant, but to recognize Americans' rightful access to this water route in its "whole breadth & length." Were this right to innocent use of the river repudiated, Jefferson further implied that Spain was handing a just cause of war to the Americans.[131]

Such wrestling with principles may well speak to morally insensitive patriotism on Jefferson's part. Yet the thrust of his argument was that extending the rights of one party without diminishing those of the other was fully compatible with natural law. Neither does the argument run counter to Jefferson's other statements on moral issues, such as that "the essence" of virtue is "in doing good to others."[132] Rather, the conception readily links Jefferson's language of natural rights to an ethically charged concept of progress – even if it concerned what moral philosophers usually call life goods rather than moral goods. As Jefferson held, virtuous action could be identified with its social utility, provided only that the bystander's situation was not weakened.

To extend the rights of one party without actually diminishing the rights of the other appeared simply progressive in Jefferson's eyes. The principle applied not just to use of water routes, but to use of any natural resource: "Whenever there are in any country uncultivated lands and unemployed poor," he proclaimed, "it is clear that the laws of property have been so far extended as to violate natural right."[133] Jefferson also linked such a natural right to the idea that the earth belonged exclusively to the living generation in genuine respect for its posterity: "[N]o man can by *natural right* oblige the lands … to the paiment [sic] of debts contracted by him" and therefore "eat up the usufruct of the lands for several generations to come."[134]

Indeed, without taking into account Jefferson's exalted notion of natural rights to material welfare, his war policies would breach the limits of his own moral principles. Shortly after assuming the presidency in 1801, Jefferson began the Barbary Wars against the North African Muslim nations. The North Africans' practice of collecting duties and even ransoms for ships entering the Mediterranean violated the natural-law principle of the open seas. Still, waging a war so far from American waters could hardly count as even a preemptive strike in the name of national security. Its sole rationale lay in keeping the Mediterranean open to international trade. From 1774 onward, Jefferson thought it evident that the Americans were in the possession of "a natural right" to free trade with the rest of the world.[135] The same natural right was at issue in the War of 1812 against the British, a war that Jefferson described as deplorable but "entirely justifiable."[136]

Or consider Jefferson's excuse for depriving the Native Americans of their ancestral lands: His Indian policy drew solely on the notion of extending the rightful use of land for effective cultivation. The Indian nations were either to change their barbarian form of life to that of farming or to move voluntarily beyond the Mississippi.[137] It was wrong, however, "to subject the Indians to our laws without their consent," particularly because "a little patience and a little money are so rapidly producing their voluntary removal across the Mississippi."[138]

THE SLAVEHOLDER'S CONSCIENCE

How was one to deal with the most conspicuous example of a whole group of people deprived of their theoretically perfect moral rights – the slaves?

It was clear to Jefferson that the slave enjoyed an unquestionable natural right to resist his enslaver, even if the very enslavement could result from the pre-political anarchy of the state of nature. In Jeffersonian free government, however, morality and moral progress remained dependent on free men's shared sense of benevolence in promoting universal equality. Innocents – all those not yet, or ever to be, endowed with equal rights – were entitled to benevolence and protection on the part of the empowered.

In Jefferson's view, the American institution of slavery was an unfortunate part of the revolutionaries' European inheritance.[139] Its sole justification resided in the errors of earlier experts in natural jurisprudence. The juridical line between criminal and erroneous behavior had been obscure enough to delude even the great John Locke into thinking that enslavement of captives of just wars could be in accordance with the fundamentals of the law of nations: "*Slavery*," Locke famously held, "*is* nothing else but *the State of War continued, between a lawful Conquerour, and a Captive*."[140] Jefferson, who does not seem to have ever subscribed to such a concept of lawful conquest, could hardly share this view in full.

To see the issue in terms of jurisprudence, it is useful to take a close look at Jefferson's marginal note on pages 147–149 of his copy of Lord Kames's *The Principles of Morality and Natural Religion* (1751).[141] There Jefferson offered a historical account of "the improvement in the moral sense" of man regarding just treatment of the prisoners of war. The note began with remarks that savage peoples had customarily killed their captives of war until "men became more humanized," and that the ancient Greeks began the practice of enslaving war prisoners. The Greeks had attained such a "stage of refinement," approximately by the Trojan War, whereas

> at this day it is perceived we have no right to take the life of an enemy unless where our own preservation renders it necessary. but the ceding his life in commutation for service admits there was no necessity to take it, because you have not done it. and if there was neither necessity nor right to take his life then is there no right to his service in commutation for it. this doctrine is acknowledged by later writers, Montesquieu, Burlamaqui &c. who yet suppose it just to require a ransom from the captive. one advance further in refinement will relinquish this also. if we have no right to the life of a captive, we have no right to his labor; if none to his labor we have none to his absent property which is but the fruit of that labor. in fact, ransom is but commutation in another form.[142]

In interpreting this passage, it is important to keep in mind that the practice of enslaving prisoners of war had been questioned only by such very recent authorities as Burlamaqui and Montesquieu. Moreover, as the extract suggests, they appeared to consider the ransoming of war prisoners as justifiable reparations of war, whereas Jefferson appears to hold that even such reparations were questionable.

The crucial three points of Jefferson's marginal note, as related to slavery and just warfare, are the following: First, contrary to earlier practices under the law of nations, the document states that "at this day it is perceived we have no right to take the life of an enemy unless where our *own preservation* renders it necessary." Second, abstaining from killing an enemy soldier "in commutation for service admits there was no necessity to take it, because you have not done it." Third, it is clear that "if we have no right to the life of a captive, we have no right to his labor."[143]

To the extent that this marginal note counts as a proof of Jefferson's personal convictions, he clearly objected to the notion of enslavement of an enemy guilty of unjustifiable violence, not to speak of enslavement of that individual's children or other relatives. Occasionally, at least, Locke himself argued that justified enslavement did not extend to the children or other relatives of the criminal.[144] Yet, none of these reservations about slavery brought into question the concept of justified violence.

Violence counted as a moral method of conflict resolution in natural jurisprudence. Just as Jefferson never ceased to view capital punishment as necessary in civil law, so in international law; violence remained an acceptable method when confined to the necessities of just warfare. In a battle situation, however, the mere capture of an enemy soldier sufficed to terminate the condition of just violence, unless actual war crimes were involved. Reparations of war and the modes of exchanging prisoners were issues to be solved solely between the combatant nations in their peace talks.[145] What made the enslavement of war prisoners (and perhaps even ransom for their release) unjust was the following principle: If one manages to capture an enemy combatant, that very fact proves that no further action is required to resolve the conflict in the case of that individual.

This view was quite conventional by Jefferson's time and remains consistent with the modern Geneva accords. Warfare in the eighteenth century was characteristically viewed as a kind of gentlemen's chess game played according to a myriad of regulations as to how, for example, an occupied "prize ship" becomes a "cartel ship" when its crew on oath assumes the obligation to sail the ship to the winner's port. The point was simply to keep the once-conquered ship out of the game, whereas the winner could continue to eliminate (rather than destroy) enemy forces elsewhere.[146] As the Americans' astonishment about the British burning of public buildings in the nation's capital in 1814 reveals, this chess game rarely included any such characteristically twentieth-century strategic aims as destruction of the enemy infrastructure or spreading terror among its civilian populace.[147]

The notion that a person's rights, in fact, arise from the assumed promise of another was of crucial importance in Jefferson's view of slavery. According to one of his most famous letters, the actual dilemma was that owners held their slaves like "the wolf by the ears," so that "[j]ustice is on one scale, and self-preservation on the other." Jefferson's lifelong conviction was that the masters' perfect right to self-preservation would be in immediate jeopardy if slaves were freed to live among their former masters. He was afraid that genocidal violence could erupt in Virginia, as the recent atrocities during the Haitian revolution appeared to validate.[148] Until Jefferson's own expatriation plan would be put into effect, the slaveholder's obligations remained in force. They consisted of the "moral duties which he owes to the slave, in return for the benefit of his service, that is to say, of food[,] clothing, care in sickness, and maintenance under age and disability."[149]

The jurisprudentially binding promise to be made to the slaves was not freedom for them but for their children, to be trained and sent to set up a government of their own as free people. Endowing black Virginians with perfect rights meant precisely what Jefferson wrote in his autobiography: The two races were to become "equally free" according to the principle of universal justice, even if not under the American government. But the Virginia legislature refused to make even this promise. In his efforts to politicize the problem, Jefferson confronted the fundamental anomaly of the natural lawyers' distinction between perfect and imperfect rights: It consisted in asking to what extent a civil society – by definition based on the "strict" notion of justice – should take Christian benevolence and charity as issues of public justice.

Jurisprudentially speaking, there was no valid pattern to demonstrate the true limits and extension of beneficent action without breaching the individualistic notion of freedom of conscience. Samuel Pufendorf's famous maxim on property rights serves well to illustrate the case. The maxim held that "a man of means is bound to come to the aid of one who is in innocent want by an *imperfect obligation* [only] which no one should, as a rule, be forced to meet."[150] This freedom remained something for which each individual was answerable to God – in the afterlife.[151] That was why, even for Locke, the linkage of benevolence with social justice could appear as a simple matter of proclaiming that slaves were to enter "what church or profession any of them shall think best," but not to step outside their given social order.[152]

Any legalistic doctrine of the individual's absolute freedom of conscience becomes stunningly problematic in the context of American slavery. Insofar as a law-abiding slaveholder found his peace of mind undisturbed, he could ignore all antislavery views as mere political opinions. Consider Jefferson's 1805 explanation of why he had long before given up hope for any early emancipation of slaves: "There are many virtuous men who would make any sacrifices to affect it, many equally virtuous who persuade themselves either that the thing is not wrong, or that it cannot be remedied."[153] Contrary to this apolitical notion of individual morality, Jefferson's own position can be summarized in the following manner: Frequent individual failures to obey "the Moral law" in all its details made political action absolutely necessary. The reason was that holding to the notion of moral obligation as an exclusively private matter could justify violence as the moral solution to every possible predicament of equal rights. By contrast, the Jeffersonian belief in human progress rested only on progressive political reforms that demanded the backing of majority opinion.

In considering the true origins of the moral obligation, it is notable that Emer de Vattel, for example, could view certain kinds of rights as imperfect, given that "the correspondent obligation depends on the judgment of the party in whose breast it exists."[154] As an admirer of Jean Jacques Burlamaqui, Jefferson may have encountered this crucial point about the modern understanding of moral autonomy in the following formulation: "[T]he whole force of external obligation ultimately depends on the internal."[155] One might also consider James Wilson as a likely source for Jefferson's implicit rejection of Samuel Pufendorf's famous voluntarist "maxim – *that a person cannot oblige himself*."[156]

Whether or not Jefferson was aware of these speculations, his conviction was that the ultimate moral obligation remained a matter of faith – a faith in a natural human sense of universal justice and benevolence. He could thus fully concur with Lafayette's declaration of the rights of man, that all people are "born with [an] inalienable right" to the "entire disposal" of their own "persons" and of their "faculties," even if they would mainly pursue only their "own good." As a result of the simple fact that even such "wise & honest" experts in the field of natural law as Grotius, Pufendorf, Vattel, and Wolff "often differ" on the specific rules of the exercise of natural rights, Jefferson noted, "we must appeal to our own feelings and reason to decide between them."[157] The reason was that constantly resolving "[q]uestions of natural right" about which the natural lawyers disagreed remained obligatory even in the course of human progress.[158] In solving them Jefferson frequently resorted to such conspicuously imprecise conceptions as "the tribunal of our consciences," or spoke of "judging ourselves" as "impartial & vigorous judges."[159] In his memorandum on the French treaties, he brought up no more objective criterion than that of "the opinion of the world."[160] Similarly, in his comments on navigation rights on the Mississippi, he eventually appealed to the general "judgment of mankind."[161]

No undisputable explanation of the "rules of our moral conduct," as natural or divine or wholly man-made, had yet been attained.[162] What Jefferson thought about "the true fountains of evidence" for the "reality" of the rules themselves was that they can be found in "the head & heart of every rational and honest man" where "[n]ature has written her moral laws and where every man may read them for himself."[163] This logic led him to maintain that any man may grasp even such an abstract idea as Grotius's precept of open seas as written in his "heart" as a "sentiment." Hence, Jefferson asked whether there can be "a man, savage or civilized, unbiassed by habit," who does not "feel & attest" to such a "truth" once informed of the proposition.

Nonetheless, not all people had been properly informed and some would never care even if they were. The provision about "habits" is of crucial importance in view of Jefferson's conviction that the institution of slavery corrupted the morals of the slaves as well as their masters. The people "are inherently independent of all but moral law," Jefferson proclaimed, and among them "habit alone confounds what is civil practice with natural right."[164] Eventually Jefferson admitted that the "revolution in public opinion" regarding slave emancipation was not about to be realized "in a day, or perhaps in an age," and consoled himself that "time will outlive this evil."[165] His fundamental problem with slavery was thus closely linked to his commitment to the contemporary will of the majority as the only secure basis for reciprocal justice and benevolence. Slavery was evil. Perhaps even women needed emancipation. Still, some groups of people, such as children and the mentally disabled, had to remain represented by others. In this sense, Jeffersonian civil society never ceased to be an ethical construction calling for benevolence on the part of the empowered in addition to the simple principle of reciprocal justice.

As Jefferson noted in 1813, some rights had yet to emerge – had "not yet entered any declaration of rights." Most notable among them was the right of the living generation to the use of land free from the debts resulting from the earlier occupiers' efforts to acquire a portion as a privately inheritable possession. To fully grasp this aspect of Jefferson's thought, it is necessary to examine his doctrine of generational sovereignty in the context of his republican statecraft. After all, the crucial political innovation of modern times was the concept of representative democracy.

5

Progressive Politics

BENEVOLENCE AND DISTRIBUTIVE JUSTICE

Jefferson's optimism about the moral progress of man rested on the apparently growing human sensitivity to the two fundamental principles of morally commendable conduct, equal justice for all, and benevolence toward those in need of help. However, Jeffersonian progress never worked on automatic pilot. This is why he viewed the eighteenth-century notion of free, representative government as the pivotal innovation in human history. It alone could bring about permanent, progressive changes in people's shared understanding of the two moral principles and of their practical ramifications.

As Jefferson insisted, "laws, to be just, must give reciprocation of right," otherwise "they are mere arbitrary rules of conduct, founded in force, and not in conscience."[1] What he thought of the ancient moralists was that "toward our neighbors & countrymen they taught justice, but scarcely viewed them within the circle of benevolence."[2] Enlarging the circle of reciprocal justice among the citizenry as well as showing benevolence to those in need of help was the essence of Jefferson's progressive politics. In this fundamental sense, Jeffersonian progress called for more, not less, control of society. The essential issue was not to diminish the power of free government, but to provide all free men with a voice in it. Moreover, as this chapter shows, Jefferson's political thought was far from the ideological commitment to minimum government with minimum spending often attributed to him.

Indeed, one should not too hastily distinguish Jeffersonian progressive politics from a broader conception of sound politics as constant discussion aimed at resolving the ever-present conflicts of interest among men. Jefferson's decades-long, passionate participation in American politics, as well as his outspoken insistence on "making every citizen an acting member of the government," cannot be reconciled with a supposedly apolitical, Jeffersonian notion of American freedom as settled by the Revolution.[3] Even after the Revolution, every citizen was supposed to remain an active member of society; that meant, just as it had meant from Aristotle onward, more-or-less direct citizen participation in government.

What distinguished Jefferson's political thought from ancient political science was his belief in universal human equality. What associated his republicanism with that of the ancients was the notion of distributive justice. Neither ancient democracies – nor the early modern societies of orders – were grounded on the notion of equality, but on that of equity. By and large, colonial lawyers understood "equity" to mean corrective justice, practiced by special equity courts resolving cases in which current written law appeared unjust in its consequences. But the term also carried another, crucially important meaning of distributive justice.[4] A telling example of this can be found in the writings of Arthur Lee, the brother of the famous Richard Henry Lee. By customarily drawing on the late classical Justinian code of Roman law, Lee defined the very term "Justice" as "*constans et perpetua voluntas jus suum cuique tribuendi*, a constant Endeavour to give every man his right."[5]

Here one has, in fact, a rough summary of distributive justice common to classical and modern political thought. Among the ancients, such a constant distribution of rights among citizens could be based on moral excellence or proved social merits. In the traditional society of orders, rights equated to privileges to be apportioned according to inherited social status. Even the Enlightenment-era ideal of rights, shared equally by all men, required constant human effort to so apportion them, at least in order to avoid justified civil violence on the part of the underprivileged. In the language of classical politics, the conception of distributive justice amounted to the simple notion that a corrupt government is one that fails to apportion rights among men justly. Jefferson could fully share this ancient idea of the ultimate purpose of government.

As Jefferson's own participation in the Revolution shows, violence could definitely count as an acceptable method of preserving reciprocity of rights among those already deemed free and equal. Yet, once the new machinery of distributive justice was in place, the principle obviously demanded the extension of reciprocal justice to any currently underprivileged group. The very idea of popular sovereignty – with its typical eighteenth-century concomitant that governmental representatives are not superior to the represented, but rather the servants of the public – assumed as much. None of this could render the ideal of free, representative democracy less of a power structure. Democratic discussion was embraced in order to achieve decisions that applied to all, including those who disagreed with the outcome of the debate. Even participatory democracy rested on majority rule, and only when all free men were entitled to equal political rights could they be treated as morally accountable for the common decisions.

What is more, in free, representative government, benevolence amounted to the obligation of the representative to represent not only his political equals, but all others as well. This conception underlay Jefferson's legendary commitment to the principle of generational independence. Innocents – all those not yet, or never to be, endowed with equal political rights – were entitled to benevolence on the part of the currently empowered. Were slaves freed and even women emancipated, there would always be children and other groups of people incapable of taking advantage of equal opportunity. This is why the Jeffersonian notion of progressive politics never ceased to be a moral endeavor.

In delineating Jefferson's political thought in this contextual framework, this chapter will explore several aspects of his politics anew, beginning with his belief in representative government as the crucial innovation in recent political science. The concept provided a radically new perspective on the classical, ancient statecraft known as republicanism. What it did not do was free Jefferson from the classical concern about the ever-present threat of the corruption of public morals.

Jefferson's so-called constitutional thought amounted to very little besides his morally charged, grand idea of generational independence. By and large, he viewed the Union as a coalition of independent states or nations, all of which should subscribe to the idea of periodical renewal of their constitutions in terms of equal justice and universal benevolence. Yet his statecraft was a good deal more profoundly linked to the legal forms of social control than his occasional outbursts against law being "but the tyrant's will" may suggest.[6]

To be sure, Jefferson never let go of his patriarchal notions about women's very restricted role in American democracy. Even so, his obstinate demands to extend democratic rights to all white male citizens and to subdivide "the federal republic" into state republics, "county republics," and "ward republics" for the "concerns of the neighborhood," were certainly meant to enlarge the power of the people in their own government.[7]

There are also good reasons to question Jefferson's fame as a champion of mere minimal government with minimum spending. The examples to the contrary include the 1803 purchase of the Louisiana territory and the 1808 embargo, as well as his open advocacy of publicly funded infrastructural improvements, general education, the care of the poor, and the hugely expensive plan of slave emancipation. Finally, as this chapter shows, although Jefferson's statecraft represented an almost unconditional surrender to the temporally variable will of the majority, this was not to argue that the statesman could not genuinely differ with public opinion on ethical issues.

JEFFERSONIAN REPUBLICANISM

Jefferson's first known reading list on "Politics and Trade" from 1771 offers no surprises to anyone familiar with the main trends of eighteenth-century political thought. It comprised different compilations of writings by Bolingbroke, Locke, Marmontel, Montesquieu, Sidney, Stewart, and the like.[8] In addition, Jefferson was at least superficially familiar with Aristotle, Cicero, Tacitus, and practically all other ancient authorities on politics and political history. Later on, he extolled Destutt de Tracy's writings on politics and economics and John Taylor's constitutional studies on states' rights. Still, Jefferson's comments on these and numerous other authorities are too few and scattered to offer a basis for any definite conclusions – particularly given the evidence that he rarely read any theoretical books all the way through.[9] It is hence best to resort to Jefferson's own sayings on the art of politics. He said a lot.

To start off with the very basics, it is useful to consider Jefferson's frequent use of jurisprudential terms when addressing the just origins of government. As a deist, he consistently subscribed to the Christian notion of mankind as one family under the divine law of nature. Yet what he preached to any utopian who suggested that humankind would one day get along without government was that any association of men, if "governed as a single family," will at some point "cease to be sufficient to preserve order, peace, and justice."[10] Even more telling is Jefferson's lamentation about the sorry state of political science in 1807: "I think there does not exist a good elementary work on the organization of society into civil government." What political science needed to determine was "the system of principles on which such an organization should be founded, according to the rights of nature."[11] The statement clearly distinguished between a society and its political ordering.

What was Jefferson's "system of principles" for organizing a given society according to the rights of nature? In essence, Jefferson's statecraft rested on majority rule as "the Natural law of every society" and thus, as "the only sure guardian of the rights of man."[12] His "first principle of republicanism" held that "*lex majoris partis* is the fundamental law of every society of individuals of equal rights."[13] Add to this his legendary commitment to the idea that each generation has the "right to choose for itself the form of government it believes most promotive of its own happiness," and one has Jefferson's political thought in a nutshell.[14] The single exception to this was every free man's right to publicly disagree with majority opinion.

Jefferson's frequent use of the term "republicanism" has led historians to read his politics in light of confusingly numerous classical, neoclassical, and modern conceptions of republicanism. But scholars also disagree on the exact contents of these republicanisms.[15] It is therefore best to gloss Jefferson's use of the term first and only then consider the similarities and differences between his republicanism and those of others.

In Jefferson's parlance, the "republic" denoted "a government by its citizens in mass, acting directly and personally, according to rules established by the majority."[16] Apart from this citizen-democracy definition of the term, Jefferson remained unconcerned about the erudite distinctions that scholars drew (and still draw) between ancient, early-modern, and modern republicanisms. No eighteenth-century politician needed to be intimately acquainted with Aristotle, Cicero, or Polybius in order to know that, by and large, all statecraft devolved from the Aristotelian, tripartite conception of decent government. The alternatives were monarchy, aristocracy, or democracy; and the republic proper usually meant some mixture of these. As one of Jefferson's favorite ancient Roman authorities, Tacitus, put it: "All nations and cities are ruled by people, the nobility, or by one man. A constitution, formed by selection of these elements, it is easy to commend but not to produce; or if it is produced, it cannot be lasting."[17]

Of the founding fathers, John Adams was the foremost expert in the history of republican modes of government in which he found several predecessors for his own convictions – for example, that bicameralism should rest on property qualifications. Jefferson, who professed to dislike political science in general, lamented that Adams's historical studies eventually sanctified the popular cry for the government of law and order "whether consistent or not with natural right."[18]

This complaint is not so surprising given Jefferson's use of republicanism and contemporary Whig political thought as synonyms – and particularly given his conviction that, deep down, the "parties of Whig and Tory" were universal, "whether called Aristocrats and Democrats, Coté Droite and Coté Gauche, Ultras and Radicals, Serviles, and Liberals."[19] In the American political landscape, the "toryism" of the 1770s thus differed but in name from the "federalism" of the late 1790s. By the same token, the inherent "Anglicism" of the Federalist conservatives resurfaced in their opposition to Jefferson's presidential embargo policy against the British in 1808.[20] Again, the Missouri crisis of 1819 appeared to Jefferson as a plot of old-school Federalists to divide the whole country over the issue of slavery, as if majority opinion in the southern states had been proved incapable of progressive changes.

Jefferson's fairly common, although imprecise equation of republicanism and Whig thought also appears in his interesting, jurisprudential concept of "Mansfieldism." In Jefferson's parlance, the concept originated in the flawed 1767 decree of the Earl of Mansfield (William Murray) that "the essential principles of revealed religion are part of the common law."[21] Jefferson condemned the doctrine as simply a Toryist stepping stone to criminalizing all speech "against Christianity" and the established religious authorities.[22] As late as 1826 he lamented the increasing popularity of the "Mansfieldism of Blackstone" among American lawyers, which served to weaken genuine understanding of "what whigism [sic] or republicanism means."[23]

Given Jefferson's outspoken belief in the natural moral sense of man and in the natural aristocracy of "the good and able," he could not subscribe to any Machiavellian notion of moral flexibility as the key virtue of the statesman. Neither could he sympathize with Mandeville's famous maxim that private "vices by the dextrous management of a skillful politician may be turned into public benefits."[24]

Jefferson definitely shared classical republican concerns about the dangerous potential for the corruption of governments, the degradation of civic virtue, the adverse influence of fortune, and the like. In addition to his occasional references to the menacing "revolution of the wheel of fortune," his writings convey quite commonplace fears of moral degradation among selfish rulers and among the too-careless people.[25] Fully acquainted as he was with the Aristotelian, numerical division of human regimes, he could customarily refer to the tyranny of "the many, the few, or the one" as the opposite of free government.[26]

The classic image of the statesman as the healer of the body politic was equally familiar to Jefferson, who occasionally spoke of the "disease of the imagination" among his fellow citizens that will soon "pass over, because the patients are essentially republican."[27] From the same context arose his use of "Solon to the Athenians" as a symbol of the wise statesman giving his people only as good a constitution as "they can bear."[28] According to this standard view, the statesman's task was only to deliberate which uncorrupt constitutional ordering of society would best serve the people in their current circumstances.

Nevertheless, the main link between classical republicanism and Jefferson's thought was his traditional conviction that active citizen virtue was the only guarantee against the inherent selfishness of officeholders. Jefferson famously insisted that "making every citizen an active member of the government, and in the offices nearest and most interesting to him, will attach him by his strongest feelings to the independence of his country, and to its republican constitution."[29] That was the plan, but the equally classical belief in the instability of all human governments kept Jefferson anxious about the feelings of the people.

Neither ancient history nor contemporary political developments offered Jefferson any unequivocal reasons to rely on the "common" people as the true guardians of liberty. Consider, for example, his language dismissing ancient Roman achievements in proper republican statecraft. He found little to admire in Ciceronian republicanism with its principled attachment to the already "degenerate Senate." "No government can continue good but under the controul [sic] of the people," Jefferson insisted, and the Romans "were so demoralised and depraved as to be incapable of exercising a wholesome controul" of their government.[30]

Jefferson's faith in the common man never grew into any utopian notion of human perfection. As late as 1821, he thought it better for the new Latin American republics to remain under the protection of Spain to "keep them in peace with one another." Their "essential powers of selfgovernment and selfimprovement [sic]," Jefferson argued, should be held at bay until the masses become "sufficiently trained by education and habits of freedom to walk safely by themselves."[31] In the aftermath of the Napoleonic wars, even the French appeared unprepared for full freedom. As Jefferson pointed out to Lafayette in 1817, for any nation the "government she can bear, depends not on the state of science, however exalted, in a selected band of enlightened men, but on the condition of the general mind."[32]

This classical concern about the condition of "the general mind" among his own countrymen is an omnipresent theme in Jefferson's records. In the early 1780s, his overall preference for an agrarian America over European social models drew on the simple conviction that men in manufacture and trade would unavoidably depend too much "on the casualties and caprice of customers." Such dependence could suffocate the very "germ of virtue," the only solid basis for the "the manners and spirit of a people which preserve a republic in vigour."[33]

Even if the idealized Virginia husbandman was free from such dependencies, the institution of slavery could ruin his character. As Jefferson mused, only a prodigy would grow up into a slaveholder while keeping his "manners and morals undepraved."[34] Eventually, "no man will labour for himself who can make another labour for him." Hence, along with the gradual erosion of the "morals of the people, their industry is also destroyed." Such "degeneracy" Jefferson called "a canker which soon eats to the heart of [the] laws and constitution" of the republic of Virginia.[35] Regardless of almost fifty more years of work for this particular republican experiment, the retired sage of Monticello found the Virginia husbandmen of the 1820s in need of salvation "from the degradation of becoming the Barbary of the Union." They were "sinking into the barbarism of our Indian aborigines," if not already "falling into the ranks of our own negroes."[36] No less frustrating was the moral "disposition in the rising generation" to fail to see the immorality of slavery.[37]

All in all, until his death Jefferson remained uncertain whether Americans would not one fine day concentrate all governmental "powers into the hands of the one, the few, the well-born, or the many."[38] The menacing image of traditional power politics – consisting in "the endless circle of oppression, rebellion, reformation; and oppression, rebellion, reformation again" – threatened something a good deal more profound than mere degeneracy of governmental agencies or officeholders.[39] In sum, Jefferson shared the ancients' concern about the corruptible "morals of the people."[40]

Despite these shared concerns, Jefferson's republicanism was not tantamount to the classical version. The difference lay not in the principle of majority rule, but in the idea of supplementing it with representation on all levels of government. In order to grasp the difference, one needs to take the ancient ideal of direct, citizen democracy seriously. The eighteenth-century notion of rights belonging to all men did not change the ancient conception of justice as a constant endeavor to provide every man his due rights. According to Madison's famous phrase, the "extended republic of the United

States, and the great variety of interests, parties, and sects which it embraces, a coalition of a majority could seldom take place on any other principles than those of justice and general good."[41]

As to the ideal of distributive justice, the Madisonian notion of politics as constant reconciliation of different interests of the people does not radically differ from the ancient conception of the public good. The Aristotelian, threefold sketch of proper governmental forms as rule by the one, the few, or the many envisioned all three as driven by the general good. Corrupt governments were not so driven. What the classic, Polybian tenet of the never-ending cyclical transience of governments essentially held was that all three constitutive forms of government necessarily corrupt regardless of the best human intentions to keep them true to the ideal of distributive justice. Hence, the classical view of all political history was comprised of three successive, endlessly recurring cycles, each of which saw the initial success in man's inherent ability to put attention to the public good above his selfish interests turn to failure.

The three consecutive phases of civic virtue comprised a cyclical whole in which one could discern six forms of government. The first cycle consisted in a virtuous monarchy falling into tyranny, which the virtuous few revived into an aristocracy. There followed the equally inevitable fall of the aristocracy into oligarchy and, in turn, the revival of civic virtue in the form of popular rule. Finally, even the popular rule was bound to fall into a lawless, self-interested mob-rule. From that sorry state of affairs, only a new (perhaps Machiavellian) prince could rise to save the people by establishing a virtuous monarchy – thus beginning the sixfold, governmental scheme anew.[42] As there was little to look forward to, beyond the inevitable return of the olden times, the meaning of all history resided in the eternal human wavering between virtue and vice.

But what often goes unnoticed among modern scholars is that the theory did not require any man's personal experience of time to be equally deterministic. No man could discern at which particular point of the current cycle he lived. This notion is best figured in the Roman imagery of the Goddess of Fortuna. Fortuna, not accidentally a female figure, kept on spinning the wheel of time, but whimsically – either quickening or slowing the wheel. Each full round of Fortuna's wheel – figuring as one cycle along a linear timeline – could hence take a month, a decade, or 100 years to complete. No individual could foresee how long the cycle would be for any given monarchy, tyranny, aristocracy, oligarchy, republic, or corrupt majority rule.[43]

From this conception of irregularity arose the classical image of the statesman – bound in the regular flow of linear time and hence incapable of forecasting the exact speed of Fortuna's wheel in the midst of its current turn. It was impossible for a virtuous revolutionary to foresee whether he was, in fact, joining a successful revolution of wise reformers or a hopeless rebellion of pathetic dreamers. In this sense, classical republicanism rendered political science a useless effort to escape the cyclical appearance and disappearance of the single significant aspect of all politics: public virtue. Jefferson did not share that pessimism.

Referring directly to Aristotle's writings on politics, Jefferson dryly remarked that the concept of "representative democracy has rendered useless almost everything written before on the structure of government."[44] Something genuinely novel had recently occurred in political science. To Jefferson, the eighteenth-century conception of free, representative democracy amounted to a wholesale refutation of classical republican pessimism. As early as 1776, he insisted that he had never subscribed to the "fantastical idea of virtue & the public good being a sufficient security of the state."[45] The ancients could have actually shared this view, for they found no universal remedy at all. Neither was this to deny that the ancient Greek city-states were citizen democracies according to Jefferson's definition of the republic as "a government by its citizens in mass, acting directly and personally, according to rules established by majority."[46] In his Federalist Number 10, James Madison defined the ancient, city-state model of participatory democracy similarly as "consisting of a small number of citizens, who assemble and administer the government in person."[47] But Madison's actual point was to contrast the ancient model with the properly modern, representative democracy.

It was equally clear to Jefferson that in the modern world, "numbers, distance, or force oblige" people "to act by deputy." Hence, "their government continues *republican in proportion only* as the functions they still exercise in person are more or fewer" than "those exercised by deputy."[48] Even if, as Jefferson claimed, "[c]orruption of morals in the mass of cultivators is a phaenomenon [sic] of which no age nor nation has furnished an example," it was clear that direct yeomen democracy had failed the test of genuinely progressive history.[49] In sum, representative democracy could efficiently address, if not fully correct, the fundamental problems of the ancient model of city-state democracy, namely its inapplicability to the world of modern, extended empires and its inherent tendency to fall into majority despotism.

One of Jefferson's main concerns about the legitimacy of the American government, on both state and federal levels, was to make the representatives of the judicial branch as "responsible to the people in their elective capacity" as the other branches.[50] In his imagination, the revolutionary notion of "the consent of the governed" was similarly linked to representation: "Civil government being the sole object of forming societies" entailed that "its administration must be conducted by common consent."[51] The Declaration of Independence itself was issued by the "Representatives of the United States of America, in General Congress, Assembled." The revolutionaries rejected the British tenet of the "virtual representation" of the colonies by parliament, thus asserting the actual right of the people to elect their representatives. In this fundamental sense, the notion of the consent of the governed could not denote passive submission to government – not before the Revolution, much less during it, and definitely not under the newly established government. Passive submission to government was reserved for those defined as innocent bystanders – women, slaves, and children; their husbands, masters, and fathers – whether electors of the representatives or representatives themselves – were supposed to guard the interests of those under their protection.

During the Revolution, it was comparatively easy to discern each man's ultimate consent to free government, for those who disagreed (the loyalists) left the country by the tens of thousands. Although loyalties became a good deal more obscure afterward, Jefferson's frequent calls for general male suffrage and for extending decision making downward to the municipal level clearly speak to his genuine wish to keep the consent of the governed not merely virtual, but actual – on all levels of government. In contrast to this primary goal, Jefferson's longing for an agrarian America over a manufacturing one appears a good deal less a principle than a matter of practical, political preferences.

Jefferson's election to the presidency in 1800, which he celebrated as a genuine triumph of democracy, took place under a still highly restricted national suffrage. As is well known, approximately 60 percent of free male Americans were entitled to suffrage on the national level. Although that was an exceptionally large figure compared to the European standards of the time, it is notable how variable the right to vote remained not only geographically but also at different levels of the government. In Virginia, no referendum was arranged on the state constitution, and free men's suffrage remained at approximately 50 percent. By contrast, in the state of New York, for example, suffrage included 100 percent of the adult male population when the ratification of the federal constitution was at issue. Owing, however, to property and other qualifications, only 30 percent of free male New Yorkers could cast a vote in the state senate elections. In the presidential elections they had no say at all, for the state legislature chose the electors on its own.[52]

In this context it is all the more conspicuous that as late as 1816 – in opposition to many leading politicians of even his own party – Jefferson was still urging America to extend suffrage to all free males and to strengthen local decision making across the country.[53] Even the 1830 constitutional convention of Virginia, held shortly after Jefferson's death, failed to extend suffrage to all white men in the state. Although Madison, Monroe, and Marshall attended this convention, its leading figure was John Randolph of Roanoke, who ridiculed old Madison's advocacy of equal suffrage and refused to regard the recently passed Jefferson as "an authority on any subject except the best method of constructing a plow."[54]

CHANGING CONSTITUTIONS

There has been a good deal of scholarly interest in Jefferson's constitutional thought.[55] When considered as a coherent doctrine of timeless guarantees for stable government, however, his constitutionalism inevitably falls apart. The reason is that even though Jefferson had a lot to say about contemporary state and federal constitutions, he never believed that constitutions could transcend the notion of politics as an unending pursuit of distributive justice.

What did the concept of a constitution mean in Jefferson's thought? In the spring of 1776, the thirty-three-year old Virginia lawyer would much rather have been in Williamsburg, where the Virginia Constitution was under preparation, than in the Continental Congress in Philadelphia. The reason was that just before authoring the celebrated lines about the equal rights of man, the young lawyer had drafted his own suggestion for a Virginia constitution.[56]

Jefferson's draft constitution was astonishingly radical by the standards of the time, and as there were many other proposals available, the state legislature paid little attention to it. Among other things, Jefferson suggested the adoption of general male suffrage in the election of the Virginia house of delegates, the election of the senate by the lower house, the appropriation of fifty acres of land to "every person of full age neither owning nor having owned" such property, and a law to secure religious liberty so that no one could "be compelled to maintain any religious institution."[57] Except the law of religious freedom, which Jefferson himself drafted later, none of these suggestions materialized in the state of Virginia in his lifetime.

Jefferson's lifelong, vain effort to change the state constitution explains his overall skepticism toward all legalistic beliefs resting on what he ridiculed as some "magic supposed to be in the word *constitution.*"[58] The state constitution was enacted in the midst of the War of Independence by the regular legislature instead of a constitutional convention. As Jefferson explained the paradoxical character of the case, it was as if "the ordinary legislature" could "establish an act above the power of the ordinary legislature."[59]

Jefferson's initial commitment to generational independence as pertaining to all kinds of constitutional arrangements dates back to 1776. In the Declaration of Independence, no particular form of government was named to fulfill the fundamental condition of a free government: "the consent of the governed."[60] Jefferson's draft constitution of Virginia included a mechanism to alter the constitution "by the personal consent of the people," namely whenever two-thirds of the county referendums should favor a proposed change.[61]

Like laws, all constitutions were to be viewed as articulations of the current will of the majority – and as liable to change according to that will. In 1785, Jefferson wrote Madison about "lessening the inequality of property."

Whenever private property rights violated the natural right of the poor to labor the earth, Jefferson held, "we must take care that other employment be provided to those excluded" from access to land.[62] In the famous "The Earth Belongs to the Living" letter from the fall of 1789, Jefferson further argued that members of each generation derive their property "rights not from their predecessors, but from nature."[63] Considering the principle in its full applications, he came to think that the large-scale confiscations of property of the Church and various other institutions currently going on in France were fully in accordance with the law of nature. "On similar ground," he exclaimed, "it may be proved that no society can make a perpetual constitution, or even a perpetual law."[64]

By 1816 it had become evident to Jefferson that all human

> laws and institutions must go hand in hand with the progress of the human mind. As that becomes more developed, more enlightened, as new discoveries are made, new truths disclosed, and manners and opinions change with the change of circumstances, institutions must advance also, and keep pace with the times.[65]

Among the "laws and institutions" to be renewed periodically were all state constitutions, because every generation had "the right to choose for itself" even its form of government. Most conspicuously, the opportunity to do so "every nineteen or twenty years" was important "for the peace and good of mankind."[66]

Jefferson's reading of the federal constitution was no less hostile to legalistic "magic" than in any state constitution. In his view, the federal government was primarily a defensive coalition of independent states, and thus answerable for all foreign policy issues under contemporary international law, known as the law of nature and nations. The states retained sovereignty on civil-law matters, as well as on the questions of citizenship. Moreover, the states were free, just as they pleased, to subdivide their sovereign powers among the lower levels of county and township administration regarding all questions of social justice, education, and charity.

A telling example of Jefferson's strict distinction between the functions of the federal government and the states is his response to a request of federal financial help for the white Santo Domingo fugitives at the height of the Haitian revolution. The then secretary of state explained that only state governments and private citizens could provide such ad hoc charity.[67] Notably, Jefferson never ceased to equate the concept of the American "federation" with that of a "confederacy." The War of 1812, he hoped, would result in "the addition of Canada to our confederacy."[68] During the Missouri Crisis, the retired sage of Monticello was terrified at the possibility that the United States would dissolve into conflicting "confederacies" in their own Peloponnesian Wars.[69]

It is important to note, however, that Jefferson's essentially jurisprudential approach to governmental powers was not aimed at stalling government action. Despite his restrictive interpretation of the exact powers of the federal government in relation to the states, he was very liberal about the use of those powers on other fronts. His behind-the-scenes involvement in the impeachment trials of two federal judges in 1804 speaks to the idea that the federal legislators should have a say in determining the "good Behaviour" required of the judges by the Constitution.[70]

Or consider Jefferson's much-discussed dodging of the limits of presidential powers during the 1803 purchase of the Louisiana Territory. It was the responsibility of the federal Congress to take action on such an issue. However, because all congressional representatives whom the president consulted refused to take any stand on the issue, he could well conclude that the nation was willing to double its landed property because that could now be achieved peacefully. Jefferson's long experience in diplomatic controversies with Britain, France, and Spain on issues related to the Ohio Valley, the Mississippi, and the Caribbean no doubt made the purchase look all the more desirable. Purchasing the area for 15 million USD, at less than 14 cents an acre, must have appeared an extremely good bargain even if only to keep rivals out.[71]

Interestingly, the concept of a protectorate – usually associated with the golden era of European imperialism at the end of the nineteenth century – also appears to jibe with Jefferson's constitutional principles. From the 1780s onward, his deportation plan for African Americans presumed that any future asylum would at first remain under American control.[72] In 1824, he still thought it evident that the expatriated freed men were to be held "under our patronage and protection" until capable of self-government.[73]

Still, Jefferson's fame as a Western expansionist, if not as the quintessential predecessor of Manifest Destiny, seems vastly exaggerated. He never quite made up his mind about whether the future states west of the Mississippi should join the original Union. In 1804, he observed: "Whether we remain in one confederacy, or form into Atlantic and Mississippi confederacies, I believe not very important to the happiness of either part."[74] As late as 1823, he still wondered whether to extend the American "confederacy" to include any new provinces, except perhaps Cuba.[75]

Neither did the Jeffersonian image of government by consent have much to do with any Tocquevillean conception of voluntary civil associations as the core of popular democracy.[76] In refusing to join Jedidiah Morse's nationwide society for "the civilization and improvement of the Indian tribes," Jefferson took great pains to explain why such an association was incompatible with his principles. Morse hoped to recruit hundreds of respected politicians, including all ex-presidents of the United States, to his organization. Jefferson deemed such membership highly problematic because these prominent figures would be "seceded from their constitutional stations as guardians of the nation, and acting not by the laws of their station, but by those of a voluntary society." Such an association could eventually be considered a half-official governmental institution, apt to constantly interfere with, if not "obstruct the operation of the [regular] government."[77] Jefferson's vision of politics was far from that of modern civil society in which politics is as much the business of the government as of all kinds of voluntary associations, trade unions, ad hoc pressure-group coalitions, corporation lobbyists, and the like.

To sum up Jefferson's so-called constitutional thought, his absolute commitment to generational popular sovereignty as the sole historically reliable basis for sustaining the minimum rules of natural law reduced constitutions to the same level as law.

PROGRESS THROUGH LAW

Insofar as the Revolution brought about a genuinely democratic American government, the fundamental challenge to individual freedom was not to be found in the government, but in popular sovereignty. As James Madison formulated the case: "In our Governments … the invasion of private rights is *cheifly* [sic] to be apprehended, not from the acts of Government contrary to the sense of the constituents, but from acts in which the Government is the mere instrument of the major number of the constituents."[78] Again, even democracy was a power structure.

Free government did not prohibit conflicts of opinions, but only violence as the method of solving them. In order to rectify evident injustices, one needed to participate in public discourse. If the government refused to change the law, one could insist on changing the government. The Jeffersonian understanding of politics ran counter to a misconception that would easily follow from Clausewitz's maxim of war being but a continuation of politics by other means. The means alone distinguished politics from justified violence, given that politics itself was about solving conflicts. In democracy, one needed only to count the heads, not break them.[79]

There was nothing particularly antigovernmental even in Jefferson's famous avowal that "a little rebellion now and then" is as "necessary in the political world as storms in the physical." He understood rebellions as "medicine of the sound *health of government*."[80] Neither did Jefferson's toleration for the recurrent small-scale insurrections of discontented war veterans in the late 1780s suggest that the former soldiers should go unpunished. He resisted precipitate hangings of these debt-ridden rebels. The most inveterate law-and-order party used to comprise their creditors – people who had risen to wealth and prestige as wartime speculators. Much as Jefferson resisted these law-and-order hotheads, he was most delighted by the "interposition of the people themselves *on the side of government*."[81]

Jefferson's stance was that of a classic statesman who, according to the Aristotelian definition, never deliberates whether to restore law and order.[82] In order to end the 1780s uprisings, Jefferson subscribed to the following, simple doctrine of democratic statecraft: "The basis of our government being the opinion of the people, the very first object should be to keep that right."[83] Were it possible to have "newspapers without government," Jefferson famously mused, he would have let the government go. But it was the notion of popular sovereignty itself that would be secured when "every man should receive those papers" – and "be capable of reading them."[84] After all, the American experiment was supposed to disprove "that freedom of the press is incompatible with orderly government."[85]

One of the few Jefferson quotations in *The Federalist Papers* stated that all "the powers of government, legislative, executive, and judiciary, result to the legislative body," and that an "elective despotism was not the government we fought for."[86] The proper limits of law within Jefferson's republicanism were determined by an uncompromised belief in two things: That the force of law is the basis of individual rights and the logical conclusion that whenever a law offends those rights, it is the law that must be mended. The rationale for this assumption was that the use of justified violence – as the ultimate guarantee of the otherwise peaceful execution of both civil and international law – belonged to the nation, not to an individual. Just how little Jefferson's idea of progressive politics had to do with any exclusively legalistic concerns becomes clear with his proclamation from 1776: "Let mercy be the character of the lawgiver, but let the judge be a mere machine."[87]

Legitimate majority rule could not resolve the dilemma of a private man who found his moral principles in absolute conflict with the contemporary legal order. The true patriot would endure this anomaly, because civil disobedience in Jefferson's republic consisted solely in every man's "right to expatriation." This right was to be considered "inherent in every man by the laws of nature, and incapable of being rightfully taken from him even by the united will of every other person in the nation."[88] For any man who found the contemporary legal system morally intolerable, the option to migrate to a country embracing higher moral standards remained open.

Similarly, for an individual statesman, there was no escape from the notion that popular sovereignty set the temporary yet real limits for his personal vision of progressive politics. Jefferson famously expressed this contradiction by asking "with what execration should the statesman be loaded" when incapable of persuading his fellow citizens to his side on the question of slavery?[89]

Jefferson's reliance on the force of law, when based on popular sovereignty, also characterizes his handling of the slavery question. In his view, the peculiar institution was an old-fashioned legal system of labor that necessarily restricted not only the freedom of the enslaved person, but also the slaveholder's autonomy, particularly in terms of property rights. Jefferson was against private manumissions because they would create a permanent class of free blacks who could not be legally compelled to leave the Union, which was the crucial stipulation in his abolition plan.

Only once does Jefferson appear to have considered the possibility of easing the legal burden of slavery in Monticello by turning his youngest slaves into semi-free tenants. His letter of January 26, 1789 to Edward Bancroft has been the pivotal evidence for scholars arguing that Jefferson customarily changed his mind about the proper solution to slavery.[90] Because of its peculiarity, this piece of evidence calls for a rereading.

In the letter, Jefferson first referred to the grim history of some Virginia Quakers' efforts to turn their slaves into tenants. These tenants tended to remain a "public nuisance" and "in most instances were reduced to slavery again." Then Jefferson went on to note that "I am decided on my final return to America to try this one. I shall endeavor to import as many Germans as I have grown slaves. I will settle them and my slaves on farms of 50 acres each, intermingled, and place all on the footing of the Metayers [Medietarii] of Europe."[91]

In short, Monticello slaves would live in partial freedom as "metayers," paying the land rent in kind, and would do so among imported German tenants sharing the same condition – obviously without the right to leave their station. These lines were followed by Jefferson's suggestion that the children of the tenants could acquire citizenship in the commonwealth of Virginia. But Jefferson's formulation of the idea is ambiguous:

> Their children shall be brought up, as others are, in habits of property and foresight, and I have no doubt but that they will be good citizens. Some of their fathers will be so: others I suppose will need government. With these, all that can be done is to oblige them to labour as the labouring poor of Europe do, and to apply to their comfortable subsistence the produce of their labour, retaining such a moderate portion of it as may be a just equivalent for the use of the lands they labour and the stocks and other necessary advances.[92]

Clearly, the African Americans at Monticello were supposed to gain a half-free tenant status amid, and in emulation of, the immigrant German peasants. Unstated is whether the African-American children were supposed to qualify for citizenship together with the German children. But if the reference to "some of their fathers" pertained to slave fathers as well as German, it would be strikingly at odds with everything else Jefferson ever said about African Americans – whether slave or free.

It is far from evident that Jefferson thought of even every German peasant father worthy of American citizenship. Rather, all the tenants were to be accustomed to "habits of property and foresight" before naturalization. Jefferson had been suspicious of any large-scale European immigration to Virginia since the early 1780s. Any mass immigration would infuse into the local legislation "their spirit, warp and bias its direction," and generally render it an "incoherent distracted mass."[93] Given that in the Bancroft letter Jefferson also compared the emancipation of slaves to "abandoning children," it remains fully possible that the children of his black tenants, if supposed to be eventually freed, were also supposed to leave the country. All in all, Jefferson had in mind some temporal, manorial style of economic arrangements to replace the slave-labor force.

Instead of turning his slaves into half-free tenants, Jefferson soon after his return from France embarked on an astonishingly expensive rebuilding of the Monticello manor to satisfy his newly refined architectural tastes. Together with his taste for expensive European wines, handmade telescopes, and other gadgets, his failure to make his two plantations profitable led him to practical bankruptcy in his old age.[94] Even if he had been a good deal stingier, it remains unclear whether he would have been able to finance any private attempt to deport his slaves from Virginia. Later on, he confessed that he had "often thought" about replacing slaves with German immigrants, namely "at the general expense" of the slave states.[95]

That Jefferson's opposition to private manumissions was a matter of principle, not of private expediency, becomes most apparent in his 1814 letter to Edward Coles, cited earlier. Coles, a former secretary of James Madison, planned to free his slaves and to migrate with them to Illinois. Jefferson wanted Coles to keep his slaves and stay in Virginia as a public advocate for Jefferson's plan of compulsory expatriation of slaves.[96]

Given Jefferson's grand plan for eradicating slavery by sending African Americans out of the Union, it is little wonder that he never faltered in upholding the color line as a prerequisite for his long-term abolition program. In his own words, the contemporary Virginia race codes considered "two crosses with the pure white, and a third with any degree of mixture, however small, as clearing the issue of negro blood."[97] As slavery was inheritable through mothers, white blood alone could make no slave free against the will of the master. Jefferson's own suggestion was that any white woman having "a child by a negro or mulatto" should be expelled from Virginia by law. The mother would be punishable by a fixed term of involuntary servitude only if failing to leave the state, which was a remarkable step forward compared to earlier statutes. Although the draft aimed at maintaining racial segregation, it was also intended to prevent the commonplace early practice of subjecting both the mother and the child to a long-term compulsory servitude, which could easily turn into permanent slavery in the case of the child.[98]

Institutionalized slavery was only one form of compulsory labor in eighteenth-century Virginia. Conventional hard work was used as punishment for various crimes, and even indentured servants who fled the usually seven-year-long compulsory service to cover their trip to America were hunted after like runaway slaves. In Jefferson's draft revision of the Virginia poor laws, unfree labor remained an integral part of the general control system of the poor, orphans, and vagabonds – white persons who were compelled to work for their livelihood under guardians.[99]

Later laws that added restrictions unique to slavery received Jefferson's support because they further distinguished the institution from other forms of compulsory servitude and, therefore, made more feasible a future legislative act that could abolish slavery at one blow. This explains why Jefferson appears to have had no objections to criminalizing the masters' right to allow their slaves to "hire their own time" in 1792.[100] By the same token, his much-discussed endorsement of the Federal Fugitive Act of 1793 falls in line with his general willingness to place slavery under more comprehensive legal control throughout the country.[101] Given this general tendency to streamline slavery legislation, it is hardly surprising that, after the 1803 purchase of the Louisiana Territory, President Jefferson showed no interest in favoring the milder slave codes of the French masters over those of the Anglo-Americans.[102]

Neither does Jefferson appear to have had anything against banning the practice of "self-hiring" in 1808. This law should not be confused with the earlier prohibition on slaves occasionally working for themselves. In legal terms, self-hiring denoted the slaveholder's right to let his skilled slaves find the best-paid jobs in the work markets, so as to maximize the master's profits. After the Virginia slave conspiracies of 1800 and 1801, the common practice of slaves staying in towns to seek jobs was deemed too dangerous. In sum, with Jefferson's full accord, the state gradually restricted the slaveholder's private property rights in numerous ways.[103] That was majority rule with law.

DEMOCRACY THROUGH REPRESENTATION

Jeffersonian democracy assumed equal diffusion of power among those deemed equal. Representation denoted the idea that those deemed temporarily or permanently incapable of self-government would remain under the protection of the free citizenry. Progressive politics was about extending the class of equals so as to attain genuine reciprocity between the government and its citizenry as well as to keep the free citizens aware of their duties of benevolence toward those under their protection.

The ethical rationale for Jefferson's advocacy of general, male suffrage is perhaps best discernible in his diplomatic memoranda. As he lectured Washington's cabinet members, "people who constitute a society or nation" remained absolutely free to "transact their common concerns by any agents they think proper," all such agents being but "officers of high trust."[104] Regardless of "any change in the [mere] form of government," Jefferson explained, "all the acts done by those agents" were "acts of the nation."[105] No free man could hence claim innocence regarding the actions of the officers of high trust. Conversely, any restrictions of universal suffrage violated the reciprocity of the rightful powers between the free man and his government. The goal was that of "making every citizen an active member of the government, and in the offices nearest and most interesting to him."[106]

In clear distinction from the European societies of orders, Jefferson's advocacy of equal suffrage was, above all, an endeavor to turn American society into one political order, into one electoral body in each state. This primary goal had little to do with favoring either unicameral or bicameral legislature. Jefferson's 1776 draft constitution of Virginia already suggested the creation of a single constituency to periodically elect all the representatives of the people. This essential point was not altered by his further suggestion to leave it to the elected to divide themselves into two legislative chambers. Similarly, Jefferson praised the French revolutionaries' goal of the creation of "one [political] order only," although the legislature was divided into two legislative chambers.[107] The American constitutional provision for the states to assume "a Republican Form of Government" did not exclude unicameral legislature, a form tried in both Georgia and Pennsylvania in the aftermath of the Revolution.[108]

Rather than seeking to divide the legislature into different orders by the criteria of property, age, or virtue, Jeffersonian bicameralism drew solely on the idea of making the representatives think twice: Such "double deliberation," Jefferson explained, was obtainable "either by requiring a greater age in one of the bodies, or by electing a proper number of representatives of persons, dividing them by lots into two chambers."[109] The fundamental task of the legislature was that of deliberating over the means of distributive justice, not over that end. It thus had little to do with the number of legislative chambers. The notion of "peaceful deliberation" was in simple opposition to general "violence rash and ruinous innovations."[110] None of this was to deny that "in every free & deliberating society there must" be discords, opposite parties, and the like.[111]

Historians sometimes speak of Jefferson's "less than fully democratic sensibilities" when commenting on his conviction that the Virginia representatives and senators should remain independent of popular pressure in their deliberations.[112] Representation was not supposed to suppress the conscience of a representative, and Jefferson understood the complexities that could result from representatives' independence. He admitted that he had "never indeed thought" that vice president Aaron Burr was "an honest, frank-dealing man," but as long as Burr "possessed the confidence of the nation," Jefferson considered it his "duty to respect in him their confidence, & to treat him as if he deserved it."[113] Compared to any such problems, the various, precise etiquettes of gentlemanly discussion were of secondary importance, although it was eventually Jefferson himself who took the trouble to write *A Manual of Parliamentary Practice* for the federal Congress in 1801.

As for Jefferson's belief in equal democratic rights of all free men, it is worth emphasizing that as early as 1776 he proclaimed his goal to be "extending the right of suffrage (or in other words the rights of a citizen) to all who had a permanent intention of living in the country."[114] The "permanent intention" in question was not qualified by literacy or property. Any man alone or "having a family," who paid his taxes or served the military, qualified.[115] To no big surprise, the young lawyer was immediately attacked for his radical idea not to demand any property qualifications for the members of even the upper house of the Virginia legislature, or the constituency itself. In his defense, Jefferson insisted that he had never subscribed to any "fantastical idea of virtue & the public good being a sufficient security of the state."[116] In later depicting the contemporary Virginia legislative system as one in which "wealth and wisdom have equal chance for admission into both houses," Jefferson's critical point was that, unfortunately, the constituency itself still consisted of the wealthy alone.[117]

Obviously, many people still thought that property interests would function as somehow less "fantastical" grounds for stable government than political virtue. Consider Alexander Hamilton's speech in the 1787 Constitutional Convention on behalf of lifelong Senatorial appointments of the wealthy: "All communities divide themselves into the few and the many. The first are the rich and well born, the other the mass of the people ... The people are turbulent and changing; they seldom judge or determine right. Give therefore to the first class a distinct, permanent share in the government ... Nothing but a permanent body can check the imprudence of democracy."[118]

The commonplace rationale for excluding the poor from the electorate entirely can be traced to Blackstone's classic tenet, which was cited, for example, in Hamilton's *The Farmer Refuted* (1775). The principle held that "the true reason of requiring any qualification, with the regard to property, in voters, is to exclude such persons as are in so mean a situation that they are esteemed to have no will of their own."[119] By contrast, Jefferson thundered: In any country where "only one man in ten has a right to vote," all nominees inclined to buy their way to the assembly simply "get nine-tenths of their price clear."[120]

Jefferson's general wish to have as few artisans as possible among Virginia yeomen drew on the commonplace wisdom of the time that mechanics and manufacturers were too dependent on their employers to be fully independent in their voting decisions. This conventional wisdom was brought up, for example, by such an outright Federalist as Gouverneur Morris in the Philadelphia Convention.[121] Even with his outspoken "moral and physical preference of the agricultural, over the manufacturing man," however, Jefferson had no intention to exclude the latter from the ballots.[122] Whenever the people were considered "not enlightened enough to exercise their control with a wholesome discretion, the remedy is not to take it from them, but to inform their discretion by education."[123]

Jefferson's advocacy of equal male suffrage and local decision making was closely linked to his equally consistent advocacy of general elementary education. "Every government," he maintained, "degenerates when trusted to the rulers of the people alone. The people themselves therefore are its only safe depositories. And to render even them safe their minds must be improved to a certain degree."[124] With the "basis of our government being the opinion of the people," it was clear that, particularly under still unequal suffrage, a free press was necessary for a free government, provided only that every man would become "capable of reading."[125] General education was needed for the people "to understand their rights, to maintain them, and to exercise with intelligence their parts in self-government."[126]

When Jefferson defined the very "object of the township schools" in 1805, it was to offer "a degree of learning given to every member of the society as will enable him to read, to judge & to vote understandingly on what is passing."[127] Interestingly, the Spanish liberals' idea of setting literacy as a qualification for citizenship was "entirely new" to Jefferson even in 1816. It remains unclear what he eventually thought of it.[128] Clearly, in the meantime, even illiterate American farmers qualified to elect the few directing "the county republics, the States republics, and the republic of the Union."[129]

Jefferson's commitment to the so-called natural aristocracy was not an embrace of elitist social ideals. Rather, it was acknowledgment that even majority democracy remained an association between genuinely different individuals.[130] Representative democracy did not mean that each and every individual was equally capable of running the government. Neither did Jefferson believe in some utopian disappearance of socioeconomic elites. But an elite without any other than socioeconomic qualifications was, in Jefferson's terms, an "artificial aristocracy" based solely "on wealth and birth without either virtue or talents, for with these it would belong to" what he called "natural aristocracy."[131]

Still, Jefferson could not see any point in John Adams's stubbornly held tenet that the republic would gain some extra stability by devoting the upper house to the natural aristocracy of "a few in whom all advantages of birth, fortune, and fame are united."[132] Such a tenet resembled the British version of bicameralism that Jefferson mocked as making sense only "if honesty were to be bought with money, and if wisdom were hereditary."[133]

Neither could equal education eradicate the natural, inborn differences in talents and inclinations among the populace. Equal elementary education was intended, instead, to guarantee that "[w]orth and genius would [be] sought out from every condition of life," so that the most talented would be "completely prepared by education for defeating the competition of wealth and birth for public trusts."[134] Jefferson's democratic vision certainly included those lucky few who were both wealthy and well born, albeit to qualify for office they should also be "good and wise."[135] The criterion for qualification, however, was not metaphysical. A rich man qualified for office just as the poor man did – namely, by earning the public trust. Given that the constituency of common men would occasionally err in such judgments (just as the educated would), the constant rotation of offices would keep representatives aware that they were bound to "return into the mass of the people."[136]

In elaboration of his contention that Americans were "constitutionally and conscientiously democrats," Jefferson made clear that, by and large, the general public was "unqualified for the management of affairs requiring intelligence above common level." It had proved "safer, for the mass of individuals composing the society, to reserve to themselves personally the exercise of all rightful powers to which they are competent, and to delegate those to which they are not competent to deputies."[137] The long-term goal of democratizing America was the "distributing to every one exactly the functions he is competent to."[138] There was no belittling of the common man, but only Jefferson's call for America to adapt to the modern world of complicated socioeconomic issues requiring expertise in public management.

Democratization was not about making people equally intelligent, but about viewing them all as capable of moral responsibility. The recipe was simple: "Divide the counties into wards of such size as that every citizen can attend, when called on, and act in person."[139] Rather than attempting to free the people from authoritarian modes of thought derived from the ancien régime, Jefferson insisted that the people come to exercise that authority over themselves. They needed to become political, active participants in democratic government – on all levels of society.

How was the principle of representation supposed to supplement local democracy within the federal system of government? Jefferson's most thorough explication of this seminal point can be found in his 1816 letter to Samuel Kercheval, then wrestling with the problem of how to democratize the state of Virginia without touching its sovereignty over such issues as citizenship under the federal government. Jefferson suggested to his correspondent this simple thought experiment:

> Were our state a pure democracy, in which all inhabitants should meet together to transact all their business, there would yet be excluded from their deliberations, 1, infants until arrived at years of discretion. 2. [sic] Women, who to prevent depravation of morals and ambiguity of issue could not mix promiscuously in the public meetings of men. 3, Slaves, from whom the unfortunate state of things with us takes away the right of will and property. Those then who have no will could be permitted to exercise none in the popular assembly; and, of course, could delegate none to an agent in the representative assembly ... So, slaves with us have no powers as citizens; yet in representation in the General Government, they count in the proportion of three to five; so also in taxation. Whether this is equal, is not here the question.[140]

This statement provides the key to Jefferson's conception of democratic representation as applicable throughout the American federal system of government. What he felt necessary to explain even to Kercheval was that the Constitution was but a "compromise" in which Virginia slaves counted only as three-fifths of persons in determining the state's representation on the federal level. The clause thus shrank the population basis on which Virginia representation in the federal House of Representatives was formed. On the other hand, the fiscal responsibility of the Virginia slave masters to the central government was determined on the same basis. Jefferson would have preferred that each state be represented in Congress according to the true number of population, but this position did not entail surrendering the state's exclusive right to decide on the issue of citizenship. In regard to the federal republic and any foreign nation, all inhabitants of the state – slaves, free and freedmen, women, and children alike – should be "men to them," he argued.[141]

To sum up Jefferson's understanding of the representative American government, one may view it as consisting of four main points. First, representation on the federal level should have been based on the number of inhabitants in each state. Second, decisions about civil-law issues, including citizenship, were to remain in the hands of state governments, which hopefully would provide all white men with equal suffrage. Third, free republican males needed to represent all women as well. The fourth point concerned representation of all "infants until arrived at years of discretion" – an idea clearly related to Jefferson's grand concept of generational independence.

Indeed, even if children were to be considered as innocent bystanders belonging rather to the domestic than the public sphere, Jefferson constantly spoke of protecting posterity from debt service possibly resulting from overconsumption by preceding generations. As he explained the principle in 1789, "no man can by *natural right* oblige the lands ... to the paiment [sic] of debts contracted by him" and therefore "eat up the usufruct of the lands for several generations to come."[142] As no feasible constitutional or legal measure could perform such a task, the only recourse was to hold on to the purely temporal principle that every generation possessed the inherent right to reconsider even property arrangements anew.

Jefferson's faith in representative government was thus inextricably linked to the doctrine of generational independence: Judging who truly belonged to the aristocracy of "good and wise" was to be solely the responsibility of the constituency of all free men of the states – who were to make such judgments periodically, generation after generation. Deep down, all questions of justice, as duly arising from obligation to sociability, could be turned into constant deliberation about the means for distributive justice here and now. It was the foremost duty of the politically empowered to extend reciprocity of rights to all male citizens alike and to show benevolence to those incapable of taking advantage of equal opportunity. Hence, one arrives at Jefferson's famous summary of the desired reforms of the Virginia state constitution – obviously appropriate to any state of the Union:

> The sum of these amendments is, 1. General Suffrage. 2. Equal representation in the legislature. 3. An executive chosen by the people. 4. Judges elective or amovable [sic]. 5. Justices, jurors, sheriffs elective. 6. Ward divisions. And 7. Periodical amendments of the constitution.[143]

In short, future developments could go as far as abolishing slavery and even providing women with full political rights. Jefferson never embraced women's political rights, although Mary Wollstonecraft's book on the issue had been openly discussed in the republican clubs in the early 1790s. Even if women were emancipated, however, children, paupers, idlers, people with serious disabilities, and the like would still remain to be represented by the politically empowered. The statesman's ongoing responsibility to solve such questions of distributive justice and benevolence peacefully comprised the essence of progressive politics – and always for the sake of the future. After all, as Aristotle had noted, no one deliberates about the past.[144]

REGULATING PROPERTY RIGHTS

In Jefferson's eyes, politics was not about building a utopian social order – yeoman or otherwise. Neither is there much reason to view him as the foremost American champion of small government. The question was how to keep the government true to the fundamental law of nature – that the "earth is given as a common stock for man to labor and live on," generation after generation.[145] According to Jefferson's records, the actual, contemporary inequalities in wealth and welfare were so grave that whenever uncultivated land was not available, "we must take care that other employment" is offered. Otherwise, "the fundamental right to labor the earth returns to the unemployed."[146] The government's very mandate to maintain peace and order could be questioned if it tolerated the violation of such a "fundamental right."

In order to secure a just government – which by definition should defend this elemental natural "right to labor the earth" – Jefferson considered a wide range of means. Among them were compulsory equal division of individual property among heirs and even progressive taxation. He also pondered the legal possibility of compelling large landowners to rent out their unused lands.[147] None of this made Jefferson even a proto-socialist. It was evident to him that "an equal division of property is impracticable."[148] However, it is equally important to note that the Jeffersonian yeoman did not need to be a landowner; a cultivator "paying a moderate rent" could do.[149] It is far from clear whether yeomen, husbandmen, or "the cultivators of the earth" ever excluded leaseholders in Jefferson's parlance. Even Adam Smith's definition of the "farmer" required no more than an independent status for a man renting land for cultivation.[150]

Jefferson's emphasis on the land as "the gift of God to the living" generation was not meant to belittle the significance of trade and a free-market economy.[151] As he insisted from early on, even under British rule Atlantic commerce had brought welfare to the colonies. What the British Parliament had endangered was "the constitutional security we have for the enjoiment [sic] of that wealth."[152] By the same token, Jefferson's 1792 argument on Americans' "inherent right" to navigate the Mississippi, when still under

Spanish control, was that such an innocent extension of natural rights to the use of natural resources did not lessen Spain's subjects' enjoyment of the same.[153]

Nevertheless, the potentially conflicting claims of a man's natural right to inheritable private property in land and other men's right of access to labor on natural resources created a genuine dilemma. Jefferson's position on the matter was clear from the 1780s onward: In principle, any portion of land "occupied by an individual ceases to be his when he himself ceases to be, and reverts to the society."[154] If other options for employment were not available, "the fundamental right to labor the earth returns to the unemployed."[155] There is no evidence in the Jefferson archive that he ever substantially changed his mind on the issue.

The jurisprudential grounds of Jefferson's view originate in the ancient principle, called Cato's theater argument, according to which a man occupying a seat obtains a right to use it – a right ceasing at the very moment he leaves it unoccupied.[156] The similarities to Jefferson's position are striking. What he stated on property rights in general and patent rights in particular was that by a "universal law, indeed, whatever, whether fixed or moveable, belongs to all men equally and in common, is the property for the moment of him who occupies it; but when he relinquishes the occupation, the property goes with it."[157]

Christian natural lawyers turned Cato's theater argument into the doctrine of taking the best possible care of the earth as the divinely given, common property of mankind. The line of argument is traceable back to Thomas Aquinas, and it was afterward modified by practically every natural lawyer from Hugo Grotius to John Locke himself.[158] Given the natural lawyers' genuine disagreements on the details of how the individuation of property takes place according to natural law, it is best to focus on Jefferson's own statements. Not surprisingly, when considering the fundamental, ancient division of things into "mine" and "yours," the law of "*meum* & *tuum*," Jefferson's ultimate criterion was the law of self-preservation:

> The law of self-preservation authorizes the distressed to take supply by force. In all these cases, the unwritten laws of necessity, of self-preservation, and of the public safety, control the written laws of *meum* and *tuum*.[159]

To be sure, this statement was written to justify the government's interference with private property in any wartime crisis. However, the essential repercussions of the argument comply with what Jefferson said of property rights elsewhere. The extract suggests a fully temporalized understanding of the natural right to private property as ultimately derivable from every man's right to the necessary means of living. It does not contradict the essential Lockean claim that the individuation of property may take place in the state of nature. That is precisely the ground upon which "written laws" of private property would comply with natural law.[160]

What Jefferson suggested here was that the natural laws of "self-preservation, and of the public safety" together – not one after the other – should control all property legislation. As all property rights were de facto imperfect, any genuinely "civil" society would cling to the absolute primacy of the "inherent" right of every man to self-preservation. After all, the notion of civil society under government drew on the idea that rational men voluntarily submit to such a government. Moreover, according to Jefferson, all rules of commendable conduct needed to draw on the reciprocity of all rights in order to bind citizens "in conscience."[161]

All so-called radicalism in Jefferson's political thought devolved from a belief that property relations were instrumental in insuring that the republic served distributive justice. In the simplest economic terms, Jefferson viewed every individual as a natural member of society as well as of a household – a notion shared with ancient republican thinkers. In his eyes, this basic economic unit – the household – could equally well be a farm, a plantation, or a trading house. This is why small-scale subsistence farming could endow even a tenant with independence enough to be counted a responsible member of any political council.

This notion of every man being a representative of his own household among other men is the key to grasping Jefferson's patriarchal attitudes toward women. This conception made it difficult for him to view women's *political* rights in any clear-cut sense as a moral question, particularly in comparison to slavery. Slavery was a simple violation of the reciprocity of rights among men as the heads of households.

BIG LITTLE GOVERNMENT

Jefferson's central commitment to the subdivision of the federal republic into state republics, counties, and ward republics had nothing to do with any ideological advocacy of little government. The idea of dispersing political authority by dividing the whole nation into ward republics did not aim to deprive the central government of its constitutional functions or to diminish political activity on other levels. Instead, it was meant to extend the citizenry's political control over all social developments. In addition, Jefferson's actual political initiatives show no general tendency to lessen the overall tax burden of the people. Rather, one finds only a constant effort to shift all expenditure under more direct political control of the citizenry itself.

As early as in his *Notes on the State of Virginia*, written shortly after the Revolution, Jefferson called for equal responsibility of the whole Virginia citizenry for all "public expenses, whether of the general treasury, or of a parish, or county" for such various purposes as the "maintenance of the poor, building bridges, court-houses &c."[162] On the local level of government, Jefferson sought nothing less than immediate citizen control.

This central feature of his progressive policies is clearly discernible in the often overlooked statements he made on the maintenance of the poor in Virginia. There was a social-security system even in 1780s Virginia, and, as Jefferson explained the workings of the system, each parish appointed regularly special representatives, called vestrymen, to take care that

> [t]he poor who have neither property, friends, nor strength to labour, are boarded in the houses of good farmers, to whom a stipulated sum is annually paid. Vagabonds, without visible property or vocation, are placed in workhouses, where they are well cloathed, fed, lodged, and made to labour.[163]

As the allegedly "anti-government" Jefferson was careful to point out here, the vestry system worked well precisely because every corner of every Virginia parish "may be under the immediate eye of some one of them."[164] It was thanks to the effectiveness of the system in Virginia's small municipalities and village neighborhoods – as opposed to urban centers, which abounded with unattended poor and vagabonds – that Jefferson proclaimed: "I never yet saw a native American begging in the streets or highways." Notably, immigrant paupers and vagabonds, even from other American states, were explicitly excluded from the rights of citizenry in Virginia.[165]

What did Jefferson wish to alter in this evidently well-working system of social control? A more often quoted statement on the subject occurs only a couple of pages later in the *Notes on the State of Virginia*. There Jefferson noted that "the maintenance of the poor ... being merely a matter of charity, cannot be deemed expended in the administration of government." What was argued was not that the maintenance of the poor should be deemed a moral matter of private conscience, as if the commonwealth had no interest in such a striking social issue. Instead, Jefferson was suggesting that the Commonwealth of Virginia would save $20,000 in its administrative expenses by eliminating a whole item from its budget, namely the "voluntary contributions" received by clergy "on 200,000 tythes."[166]

In other words, Jefferson sought to eliminate the Anglican clergy's free use of taxpayers' money without political control and to replace the parish-based control system of the poor with a secular one. According to Jefferson's own drafts for revised state laws from the 1770s onward, the poor were not only to be put to labor for their own subsistence but also entitled to some elementary public education. Only in the cases of definite incapacity for acquiring any subsistence for themselves were they to be placed in poorhouses.[167] None of this is likely to affirm the traditional image of Jefferson as the quintessential champion of little government.

Jefferson's much-discussed retirement-years doctrine of "ward-republics" included very minor alterations of his earlier views. This seemingly new doctrine from 1816 held simply that under the federal government, one should divide the country not only into state republics and county republics, but also into smaller, local political neighborhoods called ward republics, townships, or hundreds. As early as 1778, Jefferson had demanded for dividing the counties into "hundreds" in each of which there would be an elementary public school.[168] Moreover, the actual tasks of each level of the governmental system were hardly altered at all from those described in the *Notes on the State of Virginia* thirty years earlier. On the "ward-republic" level, Jefferson again in 1816 attributed to the citizen body such familiar tasks as maintaining a "justice, chosen by themselves, in each, a constable, a military company, a patrol, a school, the care of their poor, their own portion of the public roads, the choice of one or more jurors to serve in some court, and the delivery, within their own wards, of their own votes for all elective officers of higher sphere."[169]

There was a minor, new preference for the ward republics over county meetings. In this respect, Jefferson's main concern appears to have been that "the drunken loungers at and about the court houses" tended to prevail in the county meetings, "the distances being too great for the good people and the industrious generally to attend."[170] Economically, no wholesale reduction of public spending was at issue even here. The purpose was simply to shift the general burden of common expenditure to the lower levels of democratic decision making in the hope that local communities would use the assets more effectively than the upper strands of state government.

All in all, there is not much truth in the conventional image of Jefferson as an advocate of little government with minimum spending and minimum taxation. Jefferson's radical cuts in federal government expenditures during his presidency do not clear his record on the issue. His most-often hailed achievement in the Oval Office, the 1803 purchase of Louisiana Territory, again increased the national debt and the consequent debt service expenditures, but in return, the nation acquired huge property in public lands. For once, even Alexander Hamilton was pleased.

A particularly costly national effort was Jefferson's embargo policy against the British restrictions of Atlantic trade during his second term in the presidential office. The administration declared the embargo in December 1807. In diplomatic terms, it meant calling all American vessels to home ports in apparent preparations for war. In effect, the embargo measure halted all American trade with other nations, although the main aim was to compel the British to retract their measures forbidding Americans' neutral trade with Napoleon's Continental system.[171] As the embargo continued, it turned into nothing more than an experiment in commercial coercion – an ineffective one at that. At the same time, its consequences for the American economy began to appear catastrophic. More serious than the expected criticism on the part of the northern trading houses was the sudden boom of large-scale contraband and smuggling across the Canadian border. To Jefferson's astonishment, his policies appeared to weaken rather than strengthen the sense of a common cause in the nation. This phenomenon he immediately attributed to the inherent "Anglicism" of the remnants of the Federalist Party adherents.[172]

As to the much-discussed issue of public investments for internal improvements and the long-standing struggle over the so-called Welfare clause of the Constitution (Article I, §8), Jefferson was never an opponent of building intrastate or interstate roads and canals. One of his very first public tasks in Virginia had been to lead the effort to clear the Rivanna River for commercial use in the 1760s, an achievement he still in 1800 listed as one of his top "services to the country."[173] During his presidency, new public assets were provided to connect Ohio and New Orleans to the federation and money appropriated for building new post roads. Both Jefferson and Madison also spoke on behalf of building national roads and canals as well as the establishment of a national university. The only provision on which they both insisted was that whenever the Constitution needed to be reinterpreted – say, on the federal government's constitutional powers regarding the states – such an interpretative change could not be entrusted to Congress or to the judiciary; it called for a constitutional amendment.[174]

On the state level, Jefferson's lifelong insistence on establishing a school in every Virginia township would have inevitably increased the general financial burden of the citizenry. As late as 1820 he still insisted that each school district had to provide the funding for its own schoolhouse and a teacher's salary. In addition, he admitted that a general tax increase was needed to carry out such a reform.[175]

Finally, Jefferson's lifelong commitment to the general deportation of the African-American population would have entailed a huge increase in public spending over a period of fifty years. First of all, Jefferson forcefully argued that no imaginable increase in taxes would suffice for his deportation plan if full compensation to the masters for the emancipated slave children was also required. Even in the midst of the Missouri Crisis, he rejected such compensation. In suggesting that moderate tax increases and public land sales might cover the basic costs of deportation, he admitted that additional financial assistance would be required from free states, from individual donors, and even from Europe.[176] Similarly, his preference for deporting American blacks to the West Indies instead of distant Africa resulted from clear-cut financial considerations.[177]

In his most explicit statement on the issue to Jared Sparks, written only two years before his death, Jefferson insisted that he had never changed his mind on the subject. He again noted that compensating the masters for the real value of the freed slaves, in addition to covering the costs of the deportation, was impossible. Instead, he resorted to his now half-a-century old plan, put forward in the *Notes on the State of Virginia*: Emancipate only the slave children with "due compensation" to the masters for the nourishment of the infants only until separated from their parents and put to work "at the public expense."[178] Once reaching adulthood, they would be deported as free people. The plan, Jefferson lectured Sparks, would not violate slaveholders' true property rights, although he admitted that their actual "surrender of property would" equate to a 50 percent increase in their contemporary direct taxes.[179]

Stripped of the rhetoric, Jefferson's suggestion in the Sparks letter was that the slaveholders must surrender the slave children for free. This, he supposed, they would do willingly once the whole organization for emancipation had been put together. In legal terms, the plan would have cost "nothing" to the non-slaveholding citizenry. Nonetheless, even the Union needed to contribute to the cause via public land sales and perhaps provide vacant lands for each new generation of young blacks to work on before their deportation.[180] The whole project would have taken fifty years to complete, the costs diminishing annually because the number of fertile slave women would lessen year by year.[181]

What Jefferson neglected to bring up in his 1824 statement to Sparks was one more requirement for the program mentioned in the *Notes on the State of Virginia*. That was the "encouragements" to bring an equal number of free white immigrants to the country to compensate for the consequent labor shortage.[182] There is also a passing remark about bringing German peasants to replace slaves "at the general expense" of the slave states in Jefferson's records from 1805.[183] A politician to the bone, Jefferson did not care to be too explicit on this point, although in yet another statement, dating to 1814, he referred to this aspect of his plan as consisting of the "gradual extinction of that species of labor & substitution of another."[184] All this indicates that, in his view, not only the deportation, but also the importation of free labor required some additional public funding.

Jefferson's plan for slave emancipation remained essentially the same over a period of fifty years. It was a clear-cut political program to be implemented by the government, which certainly could not go forward with anything less than an unprecedented increase in public spending. Yet Jefferson's ultimate failure to persuade his fellow citizens on the importance of solving the problem was far from being the only one of its kind. He failed in changing public opinion on numerous other issues as well.

STATESMAN'S CONSCIENCE

It would be "strangely absurd," Jefferson mused in 1816, "to suppose that a million of human beings collected together are not under the same moral laws which bind each of them separately." Furthermore, it was "a great consolation" to the retired president that the American "government, as it cherishes most it's duties to it's citizens, so is it the most exact in it's moral conduct towards other nations."[185] These apparently self-serving views of agreement with the public provide one little insight about Jefferson's personal attitudes, for he spent decades in the service of the people with whom he still disagreed on a great many issues.

Jefferson's fully republican conviction that "every man is under the natural duty of contributing to the necessities of the society" did not mean that the performance of one's civic duties would comprise one's highest end as an individual. Any such a notion can well be distinguished from Jefferson's ideal of the man of wisdom and virtue.[186] The moral dictates of a statesman's conscience, whether made publicly known or not, could not be submitted to the will of the majority, which, whenever "oppressing an individual, is guilty of crime."[187]

To cast light on Jefferson's own moral stance in regard to his disagreements with the will of the majority, it is useful to turn back to John Chester Miller's central conclusion from 1977 on Jefferson's stand on slavery. From early on, Miller argues, "it was impressed upon Jefferson that he must choose between the preservation of his political 'usefulness' and his active opposition to slavery."[188] Miller's conclusion draws on Jefferson's refusal to subscribe to Thomas Brannagan's political pamphlet advocating abolition. In his letter to George Logan about the issue, the president responded that his public support of the pamphlet would in the circumstances prove harmful for Brannagan's goal, which he supported:

> The cause in which he embarks is so holy, the sentiments expressed in his letter so friendly that it is highly painful to me to hesitate on a compliance which appears so small. But that is not it's true character, and it would be injurious even to his views, for me to commit myself on paper by answering his letter. I have most carefully avoided every public act or manifestation on that subject. Should an occasion ever occur in which I can interpose with decisive effect, I shall certainly know & do my duty with promptitude and zeal. But in the meantime it would only be disarming myself of influence to be taking small means.[189]

In sum, when a realistic opportunity to reach a political agreement on abolition appeared, the president would definitely "know his duty" and back it. In the meantime, it would be irrational to infuriate the many proslavery slaveholders in high positions. The moral responsibility for providing African Americans with their natural right to self-government lay in the hands of those currently empowered with political rights.

It was only the Missouri Crisis of 1819 that compelled Jefferson to seriously consider the threat that the United States could dissolve into conflicting "confederacies" over the issue of slavery.[190] Indeed, it has often been argued that Jefferson's moral thought failed him when he attempted to reconcile emancipation with state sovereignty.[191] He can be accused of an overly rigid position on states' rights, but his ultimate moral failure with the slavery question would then lie only in his constitutional opinions. Jefferson held that each slave state needed to reach an agreement about abolition on its own. Just as Virginia could not impose its own statute of religious freedom on other any other state, other states could not dictate to free Virginians on slavery.

As noted, Jefferson's ultimate nightmare was precisely the situation in which Abraham Lincoln later found himself: An open, national conflict about the political meaning of equal rights, which, were the slaveholders to have their way, would end the federal experiment without ending slavery. Nor is there much evidence to support the contention that Jefferson would have agreed with the constitutional stand of many slave states in 1861, namely that a state was free to secede from the Union because it was not pleased with the outcome of an undisputed presidential election.

In sum, Jefferson's hope was that once Virginia would decide to put into effect his abolition plan, at least most other slave states would follow suit so that it would be possible to build up a whole federation-wide program for implementing deportation. This is the niche from which it could appear ethically defensible for Jefferson to lay his hope in winning the majority to his side peacefully – at least once all Virginians, and not only the slaveholding elite, had gained equal suffrage. To be sure, even according to his own principles, one could have expected him to free and send abroad all Monticello slave children at the risk of his own poverty, although with at least a couple of provisions – namely, that he would have escaped his debtors as potential shareholders of his slave property and that there would have been American or a Virginian protectorate to which to send them.

None of this is to offer excuses to Jefferson's moral failures. There were slaveholders who fared much better on a purely moral scale. Edward Coles, for example, did not follow Jefferson's advice to stay in Virginia so as to advocate abolition there. He moved to Illinois, freed his ten slaves, and eventually fought a long political antislavery fight there. For better or worse, Coles kept on insisting that his old friends, Madison and Jefferson, were sincere in their antislavery sentiments.[192]

In fact, the question about women's political rights was more complicated than slavery when seen from Jefferson's "niche." When refusing to appoint a woman to a governmental office in 1807, Jefferson stated that the "appointment of a woman to office is an innovation for which the public is not prepared, nor am I."[193] As a mere trustee of public opinion, he settled the issue by invoking public preference. Nevertheless, it is worth keeping in mind that Jefferson's progressive thought called for "knowing" less rather than more. His falling back on his personal prejudices did not argue against such an innovation appearing consistent with natural law in the eyes of future generations.

Meanwhile, every male representative of free government was under the obligation to represent not only his constituency, but also women, slaves, and children – as well as all those thousands of white male Virginians still lacking full democratic rights. Politics was not about denying the present as brought about the often misguided past, but about collectively changing the future.

As late as 1821, Jefferson found the United States in need of "moral emancipation" in addition to its "physical liberty." The problem was not the insufficient legal protection of minority rights, but the practical "inquisition of public opinion" against all kinds of religious and nonreligious political dissenters.[194] Jefferson hated easy conformism with public opinion, especially when that opinion took the odious form of censorship of books. This hatred is reflected in his 1814 reaction to a censorship case in Philadelphia. The book in question, de Becourt's *Sur la Création du Monde, un Systême d'Organisation Primitive*, was about no less a subject than the origins of the universe. Although this work, totally forgotten today, appeared to question even Newtonian physics, it was not the book, but the censorship that got the sage of Monticello absolutely furious:

> I am really mortified to be told that, *in the United States of America*, a fact like this can become a subject of inquiry, and of criminal inquiry too, as an offence against religion; that a question about the sale of a book can be carried before the civil magistrate. Is this then our freedom of religion? and [sic] are we to have a censor whose imprimatur shall say what books may be sold, and we may buy? And who is thus to dogmatize religious opinions for our citizens? Whose foot is to be the measure to which ours are all to be cut or stretched? Is a priest to be our inquisitor, or shall a layman, simple as ourselves, set up his reason as the rule for what we are to read, and what we must believe? It is an insult to our citizens to question whether they are rational beings or not, and blasphemy against religion to suppose it cannot stand the test of truth and reason. If M. de Becourt's book be false in facts, disprove them; if false in it's reasoning, refute it. But for God's sake, let us freely hear both sides, if we choose.[195]

Thus, Jefferson preached against the appalling fact that "in the United States of America," religious conformists could still think it their business to determine which questions were worth asking and which were not. Even on this occasion, Jefferson did not call for the Federal government to correct the situation. Each state was responsible for securing civil liberties for its inhabitants. Largely thanks to Jefferson himself, religious freedom was now in force in Virginia, unlike in most other states at the time.[196] There was no extra-human guarantee that even Virginia would not lose that freedom again. This is why Jefferson's statute could only recommend that future generations would not alter the law providing everyone with freedom of conscience.

Conclusions

THE JEFFERSONIAN ETHICS OF THE LIVING

Jefferson's grand concept of human progress rested on three basic elements: The evidently rising general standard of living among common Americans, the equally evident increase in human knowledge, and people's apparently increasing general sensitivity to the ethical aspects of their everyday lives. There were cultural restrictions that could prevent people from grasping the idea of progress. In Jefferson's eyes, Native-American cultures often appeared incapable of genuine innovations. However, the most dangerous enemies of progress were timid conservatives, whether European traditionalists or secrete American Tories. All signs of positive historical changes appeared insignificant in the face of the core conservative belief in the unalterably sinful and selfish human condition. By contrast, Jefferson believed in human perfectibility, although he made very few claims as to what perfection would, or even should, look like.

As has been argued throughout the preceding chapters, Jefferson's intellectual position was characteristically that of a politician. For a politician it was, as it still is, unwise to present oneself as a philosopher or a moralist. Jefferson did not seek to publicize his personal understanding of either the ultimate ordering of the universe or the ultimate nature of the good. Instead, he held that one could subscribe with equal consistency to either a deist notion of a divinely created universe or to the atheist notion of it being a self-regenerating whole. Both conceptions could still be viewed as reconcilable with further scientific research, rather than used for fruitless philosophical speculation. Neither did Jefferson have any professed view of what the recent innovations in natural and moral sciences would prove about the actual construction of history as a whole.

Personally, Jefferson was a materialist and a deist for whom the material, atomistic, self-regenerating universe appeared to be in a constant state of turmoil in which whole races of animals and even stars could disappear without the system itself falling into chaos. This is why he was confident that there must be some constructive, divine rationale behind all matter, motion, and their relations. The assumption that there is a supreme being, in turn, provided him with a belief in the fundamentally twofold, physical and moral ordering of the whole universe – an ordering in which a person's moral respect for others would eventually converge with his/her true interests. Jefferson's deism included a belief in the afterlife as well. He made passing remarks about his hope of entering the Elysium fields, with at least John Adams as his companion, and even of receiving thanks for his lifelong advocacy of human happiness on earth.[1] Yet, even though Jefferson personally embraced such deistic beliefs, he strictly distinguished them from what others should hold true.

Jefferson was not a preacher of his own deism, but of human progress. There were matter, motion, void, and, eventually a sensitive, individual human being in a constant, inductive attempt to grasp how these elements made up a reality that imposed sense-experience on the human being. The Baconian notion of increasing human knowledge meant that one was constantly dealing with imperfect knowledge of that reality. This is why Jefferson carefully distinguished his own beliefs from those he thought all should agree on.

To begin with a set of extra-historical truth claims to which Jefferson thought any man of the Enlightenment could submit, he readily admitted that he had no proof for his position as a "material deist" – namely, the kind of proof that could appear methodologically incontestable. The contemporary disputes in natural sciences required only suspension of judgment until further research could resolve, say, the ultimate character of the genetic differences between the African, American, Asian, and European varieties of man. The extra-historical foundation of human morality, including such notions as the moral sense, natural rights, moral law, or the obligation to universal benevolence, could be similarly left for theoreticians to quarrel about.

Turning to the claims that historical experience appeared to confirm, Jefferson's understanding of humanity evolved from the apparent historical fact that as particular social animals destined to live in society, humans had always shared some notion of justice and of justified violence against those breaching the minimum rules of human sociability. From this historically, if not anthropologically, verifiable notion of sociability and conflict colliding all the time and everywhere, even the natural rights of man appeared as imperfect rights and, in essence, perfectible only through human regulation. Jefferson could hence tolerate the atheist's belief in a self-regenerating, apparently purposeless universe, even if that would make the cosmological moral ordering a matter of mere faith, and faith in mere humanity at that.

For a lawyer like Jefferson, the simplest and safest approach to human morality was to cling to the Lockean doctrine that each man possesses the rightful power to labor the earth for his own happiness and the corresponding obligation to allow the rest of mankind to do the same, while simultaneously committed to protect the innocents. This twofold principle of equal justice for all and benevolence toward those in need of help qualified as the only interpersonally valid principle in Jefferson's moral faith. Hence, he happily shared what John Adams found to be the crucial lesson of all "religious" thinking: That the human being should seek to become both "just and good."[2]

History proved, indeed, that all efforts to perpetuate the human ordering of justice had failed thus far. But the eighteenth-century innovation of representative government could perhaps change all that, and there was plenty of evidence that people could better their lot through cumulative knowledge of nature and of themselves as part of that nature. The most telling intellectual examples of this development Jefferson found in books on natural jurisprudence, a discipline within which it only recently had become apparent that, regardless of contemporary racist beliefs, the institution of slavery lacked any justifiable basis. What kept Jefferson's worldview progressive was the simple presumption that the historically verifiable is not inevitably the whole truth.

It is this future orientation that undergirds the ultimate temporal aspect of Jefferson's progressive worldview. In the simplest terms, temporality arises from the notion of a human being as necessarily oriented to the future in the eternal present of constantly advancing time. A traditionalist's future orientation would typically consist of hopes for return to the olden times and thus escape from a degenerate present; a utopian would embrace an abstract vision of a distant future liberated from the equally erroneous past and present. The progressive sees the eternal present as a result of the past and thus the only meaningful context of his future orientation, while sharing the utopian's belief in the possibility of genuine innovations. To fully come to grips with the temporal aspect of Jefferson's individualistic ethics of the living – ethics that humans must re-enact all the time – it is worth recalling his key conception of the cultivation of human capacities.

What does the Jeffersonian notion of cultivation of the faculties of the head and heart mean in modern language? It means this: Every human being has inborn capacities – intellectual and moral. These given, instinctive capacities do nothing by themselves. Once an individual comes into contact with the surrounding world through sensations, s/he simultaneously begins a lifelong exercise of emotional reflection and reasoning on those sensations. That the rational and emotional capacities of reflection can be consciously trained like muscles is why they serve as the source of human intellectual and moral virtues, the Jeffersonian "qualities of the head and heart." It is this existential opportunity to develop one's capacities into respective virtues that underlies the Jeffersonian obligation of the individual to seek self-betterment. Surely, if this was not what one should seek, then why care about other people being deprived of the opportunity altogether, whether oppressed by the European aristocratic elites or by the Virginia slaveholders?

Both kinds of inborn human capacities varied individually. To come to an understanding of this crucial notion of a natural, individual inequality in Jefferson's moral outlook, consider, for example, his lifelong advocacy of general elementary education: The point was that the nation should "avail the state of those talents which nature has sown as liberally among the poor as the rich, but which perish without use, if not sought for and cultivated."[3] Although intellectual capacities were disseminated among people regardless of social status, they were still dispersed. Different individuals were differently capacitated in the pursuit of intellectual virtues. As Jefferson saw it, Isaac Newton's inborn intellectual capacities were obviously superior to those of, say, George Washington.

As for inborn moral capacities, Jefferson could go as far as to claim that some people probably lacked the moral sense entirely. Be that as it may, the individual differences in the realm of commendable conduct clearly depended on conscious, human self-improvement in discerning between harmful, indifferent, and genuinely desirable action. This is why it made little difference whether the foundation of human morality was emotional rather than rational in character. In Jefferson's eyes, man was "an imitative animal, who learns to do what he sees others do" and keeps on doing so "from his cradle to his grave."[4] This inward socio-ethical orientation to the outside world continued throughout life, although it remained at the mercy of varying historical circumstances.

At this point, another Jeffersonian set of concepts becomes readily comprehensible – namely, the morals and manners of a given society. Jefferson's paragraphs on "particular customs and manners" in *Notes on the State of Virginia* were devoted to demonstrating the genuinely harmful impact of the institution of slavery on the masters' white children. At their initial stage of moral orientation, these children were taught to trump the rights of their black brethren. The prevailing morals and manners reflected poorly what Jefferson at the very beginning of the same paragraph referred to as a simple, universal "standard" of equal rights.[5] Such a standard was obviously attainable by the savage, the deist, and the atheist alike, provided that sheer habits had not thoroughly eroded the person's inborn capacities for self-betterment.

The wise man would endure his own limitations and consent to making most out of his given capacities. For Jefferson, the historical Jesus personified "the best qualities of the human head and heart," namely "wisdom," on the one hand, and "justice" and "goodness," on the other hand.[6] But, as in the case of George Washington's character, an individual could be deemed "wise" without Newton's intelligence and "good" without any reference to Jesus as the ideal personification of all virtues. Washington, whose heart was not "warm in its affections," nonetheless exhibited such character traits as prudence and an exceptionally "inflexible" sense of justice, which sufficed to make him "a great man."[7] Wisdom was attainable for a man also willing to get to know himself. It was for Peter Carr alone to decide, although hopefully after a careful scrutiny of all the arguments, whether he believed in God. With respect to his fellow humans, he was "answerable not for the rightness but uprightness of the decision."[8]

In Jefferson's imagination, people were not equally capacitated and their common effort to respect each other in the face of this fact was what made them moral beings distinct from the rest of animate nature. This is why the notion of individual self-realization comprised a process of the internalization of scientific truths through education as well as the internalization of the morals and manners of one's own society. Finally, the scientific standard of free enquiry and the moral standard of equal rights remained the twofold cornerstone for an individual's critical adjustment to the world as it was and as it might become.

Jefferson's often misunderstood commitment to natural aristocracy did not contradict his egalitarian faith in the reciprocal rights of all men. That such aristocracy of the "real good and wise" could only evolve from among the talented was fully compatible with the ideal of representative democracy. The ideal rested on the simple principle that the superior natural capacities of some individuals were neither denied nor embraced as the organizing principle of a society based on human equality. The commitment to the inherent independence and equality of all humans entailed that even Isaac Newton could not be deemed "lord of the person or property of others."[9]

Neither was there any reason to appeal to nature or providence in discerning the real good and wise. Democracy provided the best empirical test available for filling the highest offices of the nation to exercise justice at home and abroad. The candidate's actual behavior qualified as the sole proof of his competency. The mass of the people could err in their character assessments, but hardly more often than any elitist electorate qualified by wealth or higher education.[10] And this testing was to go on in periodical elections, ad infinitum.

As for the limits of Jefferson's optimism, it is worth keeping in mind that he did not share the twenty-first century's characteristically apocalyptic concerns with chronic global overpopulation, climate change, or the spread of the weapons of mass destruction. The ultimate challenge in Jefferson's struggles with conservatives was not that of reaching any absolute truth about nature, about humans, or about morality. Rather, the issue was recognizing that absolute knowledge was not in the reach of an individual living in human time. This is why even the never-ending democratic process of measuring the candidates' intellectual and moral qualities could not warrant the breach of freedom of conscience as the cornerstone of free government.

The Jeffersonian freedom of conscience was not an instrumental, but an end value. It is important not to identify, for example, Jefferson's caution in promoting Unitarianism in the United States with his legendary "patience" in persuading his fellow revolutionaries to eliminate slavery, as if the similar means would imply parity between the ends. Jefferson could certainly hold that once the majority would abolish slavery as incompatible with justice, the government might compel dissenters to comply, whereas national Unitarianism, no matter how pure a faith and how widely embraced, could never justify compulsory conversion of any American.

Jefferson's ultimate commitment to the key virtue of prudence – the disposition to avoid hasty epistemic conclusions about either naturalistic or moral truths – warrants attention in the context of the huge variety of eighteenth-century speculations about race, gender, cosmology, religion, and morality. Jefferson never ceased to believe that something genuinely significant might still unfold on these issues in the future. On the basis of this epistemic prudence alone, a latter-day Jeffersonian individual could reconsider the eighteenth-century understanding of "electricity," once informed of Faraday's findings, and ridicule the eighteenth-century legends about orangutans' interest in mating with humans, given what is now known about animal behavior. Similarly, the Jeffersonian understanding of "matter" and its "qualities" would definitely alter when thought of in Einstein's terms of matter and energy, as well as in view of the now prevalent hypothesis that dark energy comprises at least 65 percent of the universe's entire composition.

Such an open-ended perspective on epistemologically valid claims is applicable to history itself. Eventually Americans failed to end slavery without resorting to war. But Jefferson did not know that. Instead, he compromised even on his short-term goal of attaining equal, white male democracy in Virginia. It entailed a legal reform, which he never saw. Jeffersonian progress was always human progress, something people might attain in the future, and only together. Its ethical characteristics do not weaken in the slightest just because Jefferson's main concern was that his contemporaries refused to grasp what the standards of equality and benevolence would politically require from them.

Jefferson's suggestions – about progressive taxation, the distribution of vacant lands to the unemployed, public funding for a large-scale emigration of slave children, and establishment of a public elementary educational system – went well beyond any simple doctrine of minimal government with minimum spending. Enlarging the circle of people deemed genuinely free and independent, as well as exercising benevolence toward all others, was the central hope of Jefferson's essentially political notion of human progress.

Despite the fact that he was a slaveholder, Jefferson believed in the equality of all men according to the simple premise that individual moral responsibility could only rest on reciprocal freedom. Slavery was unnatural as well as unjust because it prevented slaves from even seeking intellectual and moral improvement. Jefferson's racist convictions were no less dependent on contemporary scientific speculations on human origins than was his stated belief that rocks grow. As to the actual extent of his prejudices, it is worth bearing in mind that he also harbored doubts about the Native Americans' genetic equality with white Americans, which explains his constant dodging the issue of how to persuade Indians to move west of the Mississippi. His undeniable racism may explain his segregationist position, but not his insistence that the African Americans deserved the possibility to establish free government for themselves, even if outside the United States. In the midst of free Virginians' own attempt to achieve mass democracy, it appeared too risky to set the freed slaves under the same civil government with their former masters.

Throughout his life, Jefferson remained convinced that the immediate abolition of slavery would lead to a full-scale race war among Americans. In order to correct the situation, he suggested a hugely expensive, fifty-year long, nationwide program for sending the African-American population out of the United States so as to provide it with self-government elsewhere. The more regulated and more unified the institution of slavery would become, the easier it would be to eradicate it with a single legal act. In addition to entailing unprecedented increase in public spending, Jefferson's plan compromised slaveholders' property rights, for they were obliged to surrender slave children to the state without remuneration so that the children could be prepared for freedom and eventual expatriation.

Jefferson was too much of a politician to go into all the details of his abolition program, and too much of a Virginian to suggest that some other slave state could manage to set up one. His commitment to states' rights also kept him from explicating how big a majority it would take for the federation or public opinion around the country to compel the rest of the states to follow suit. Leaving aside his other possible, unstated motives for all these provisions, he seems to have held that, without a political majority decision to put up a fully coordinated system of slave children's compulsory expatriation in Virginia or in some other slave state of equal importance, no such majority decision could be achieved elsewhere. That was the Jefferson problem the South never solved.

Even in purely historical terms, Jefferson's slaveholding cannot be justified, for there were people born into slaveholding families who freed their slaves. Moreover, given that he saw slavery as a moral problem and insisted on a political solution to it, he definitely could have pressed the issue more openly and more frequently. Yet how many open pleas would have cleared his moral bill in our eyes, given his segregationist program? For him, the ethical dilemma lay elsewhere, namely in the widely shared notion that a man fostering charity toward the oppressed in his heart could hence regard benevolence as a matter of his private, rather than his political, sentiments. The paradoxical character of such a position is readily discernible in Jefferson's characterization of his problem in persuading his fellow citizens to abolish slavery: "There are many virtuous men who would make any sacrifices to affect it, many equally virtuous who persuade themselves either that the thing is not wrong, or that it cannot be remedied."[11]

Political self-government entailed the forfeiture of one's innocence about all issues of social justice. Unlike the preservation of justice, benevolence could never rest on violence. Jefferson's commitment to free government was a commitment to non-violent conflict resolution, a genuinely political conception – under which the social concomitants of benevolence, rather than the concept itself, remained at the core of forward-looking ethical discourse. That is why the Jeffersonian notion of ethics belonged to the living alone.

Notes

Acknowledgments

1 Isaak Dinesen (Karen Blixen), *Out of Africa and Shadows on the Grass* (New York: Vintage Books, 1987), 323–324.

Introduction

1 Quotes, respectively, from Peter S. Onuf, *The Mind of Thomas Jefferson* (Charlottesville: University of Virginia Press, 2007), 1; Scott A. French and Edward L. Ayers, "The Strange Career of Thomas Jefferson: Race and Slavery in American Memory, 1943–1993," in Peter Onuf (ed.), *Jeffersonian Legacies* (Charlottesville: University of Virginia Press, 1994), 419.

2 For a useful, introductory account of this historiographical issue and for the Parton citation, see Gordon Wood, "Trials and Tribulations of Thomas Jefferson," Onuf (ed.), *Jeffersonian Legacies*, 395–417.

3 TJ to P.S. Dupont de Nemours, April 24, 1816, in Merrill D. Peterson (ed.), *Thomas Jefferson Writings* (New York: Library of America, 1984) [Hereafter cited as *TJW*], 1387.

4 Thomas Jefferson, *Notes on the State of Virginia* (London, 1787 edition), as in *TJW* [Hereafter cited as *Notes*], Query XVIII, 288.

5 John Chester Miller, *The Wolf by the Ears: Thomas Jefferson and Slavery* (New York: New American Library, 1980), 279.

6 TJ to Don Valentin de Foronda, October 4, 1809, Paul Leicester Ford (ed.), *The Works of Thomas Jefferson*, 12 vols., federal edition (New York, 1904–1905) [Hereafter cited as *Ford*], 11: 120.

7 Consider, for example, Richard K. Matthews's offhanded remark about Jefferson's "naïve belief that science cannot produce anything evil." It serves well to illustrate how easily Jefferson's belief in progressive, cumulative scientific knowledge can be lost from sight. To view eighteenth-century racist theories or the later eugenics or, say, the Hiroshima bombing as resulting from some innately *scientific* ambitions is not entirely logical. Scientific research did not bring about such events, no matter which particular individuals are to be blamed or praised for them. Quotation in Richard K. Matthews, *The Radical Politics of Thomas Jefferson: A Revisionist View* (Lawrence: University Press of Kansas, 1984), 125.

8 Stanley Elkins and Eric McKitrick, *The Age of Federalism: The Early American Republic, 1788–1800* (New York: Oxford University Press, 1995), 198.

9 For the later "textbook image," see Alan Brinkley, Richard N. Current, Frank Freidel, and T. Harry Williams, *American History: A Survey*, 8th edition (New York: McGraw-Hill, 1991), 205. As to contemporary appraisals of Jefferson, see *Richmond Enquirer*, September 6, 1822, as in Dickinson W. Adams and Ruth W. Lester (eds.), *Jefferson's Extracts from the Gospels: The Papers of Thomas Jefferson, Second Series* (Princeton, NJ: Princeton University Press, 1983) [Hereafter cited as *Extracts*], 408n. On the origins of this image, see, for example, a reference to the "retired philosopher of Monticello" in Saul K. Padover's renowned biography, *Jefferson* (New York: Harcourt, Brace and Company, 1942), 110. On the general claim of Jefferson's "own philosophy" including "unquestionable inconsistencies," see, for example, Dumas Malone, "The Life of Thomas Jefferson," in Merrill D. Peterson (ed.), *Thomas Jefferson: A Reference Biography* (New York: Charles Scribner's Sons, 1986), 24. On Jefferson's political "theory" lacking consistency, see Henry F. May, "The Enlightenment," in ibid., 51. On his writings in general conveying inconsistencies, see Robert B. Dawidoff, "Man of Letters" in ibid., 195. For Jefferson being incapable of self-criticism regarding his inconsistencies, see Leonard Levy, "Civil Liberties," in ibid., 343. On Jefferson simply being accustomed "to say one thing and to do another," see Judith Shklar, "Review of Garry Wills's *Inventing America*," *New Republic*, August 26, 1978, 34.

10 *Notes*, Query XVII, 287.

11 TJ to James Madison, March 15, 1789, *TJW*, 944.

12 TJ, Notes on Prof. Ebeling's Letter, July 30, 1795, *TJW*, 700.

13 TJ to Judge Spencer Roane, September 6, 1819, *TJW*, 1425.

14 Quotations, TJ to Madame de Staël, May 24, 1813, *TJW*, 1272 and TJ to Governor John Langdon, March 5, 1810, ibid., 1219.

15 Emer de Vattel's name has been misspelled since Jefferson's time, as Dr. Petter Korkman pointed out to me.

16 TJ to Thomas Law, June 13, 1814, *Extracts*, 356.

17 TJ to Thomas Law, June 13, 1814, *Extracts* 355–358; quotation in ibid., 355.

18 TJ to Francis Hopkins, March 13, 1789, *TJW*, 941. For a well-documented account of Jefferson's eclecticism, see Allen Jayne, *Jefferson's Declaration of Independence: Origins, Philosophy and Theology* (Lexington: University Press of Kentucky, 1998), esp. 168.

19 Herbert Sloan's *Principle and Interest: Thomas Jefferson and the Problem of Debt* [Oxford University Press, 1995] (Charlottesville: University of Virginia Press, 2001) is definitely one of the most thorough and methodologically rigid achievements in all Jefferson scholarship. Sloan shows that Jefferson's obsession with the idea of getting rid of debt on both personal and national levels was fully consistent with his larger concern for generational, political independence. Contrary to many scholars interested in Jeffersonian pastoral ideals, Sloan's book also testifies to Jefferson's full awareness of living in a capitalist world and to his genuine interest in such issues as stable currency and internal improvements – regardless of his personal failure to make ends meet (see ibid., e.g., 211–218). Richard Matthews's intriguing book, *The Radical Politics of Thomas Jefferson* (1984), is

still the most insightful account of Jefferson's true "calls for mass participatory democracy" (see ibid., 126). Matthews is right on almost everything he claims on Jefferson's personal beliefs: Namely, on Jefferson being a Stoic rather than an Aristotelian thinker (ibid., 94), on his moral-sense beliefs as related to human sociability (ibid., 75), on his reliance on participatory politics as an inevitable part of the good life (ibid., 91), and on his view that natural rights were primarily the means for every man's freedom to pursue happiness (ibid., 122). What Matthews fails to do is to distinguish between what Jefferson believed and what he insisted others should agree on. While I would disagree on some of Matthews's haphazard characterizations of the moral and social topics, my main disagreement arises with his attempt to turn the Jeffersonian vision into an allegedly open-ended, yet oddly fixed, Marcusean kind of spirited pastoralism. From that vision evolves the apparently fixed Jeffersonian image of a small-scale economic entrepreneur whose highest occupation remains in the Aristotelian kind of philosophical contemplation. Deep down, Matthews offers us a Jeffersonian "dream" of a harmonious pastoral future of humankind carefully distinguished from Hamilton's "dream" of powerful central government as well as from Madison's "nightmare" of people proving incapable of the republican virtue (see ibid., 116–117). As this study shows, Jefferson's hopes lay in a feasible, democratic government within the already present commercial world markets, not in some kind of romanticized "communitarian anarchism" (see ibid., 17, 124). Contrary to Matthew's interpretation, it seems that Madison and Jefferson knew precisely on what they agreed – namely on the idea of a free, representative, democratic government. Such a government needed the elite of the wise and the good, even if the only available criterion for discerning true wisdom and virtue was that of leaving the people to find it among the candidates for the offices of the government.

20 TJ to Samuel Kercheval, July 12, 1816, *TJW*, 1402 (emphasis added).

21 TJ, Bill for Establishing Religious Freedom, *TJW*, 347.

22 In the now classic book, *The Philosophy of the American Revolution* (New York: Oxford University Press, 1978) by Morton White, Jefferson is depicted primarily as a moral rationalist, although partially resting his assumptions on what is called intuitionism in modern moral philosophy (ibid., e.g., 77). The central thesis is that the Jeffersonian, inalienable rights arise from a given set of perfect moral duties from which the enactors cannot morally alienate themselves. In contrast, Garry Wills, in his *Inventing America: Jefferson's Declaration of Independence* (Garden City, NY: Doubleday, 1978), sees Jefferson's moral beliefs devolving from Hutchesonian moral sentimentalism rather than from any Lockean-derived moral rationalism. Michael Zuckert in his *The Natural Rights Republic: Studies in the Foundation of the American Political Tradition* (Notre Dame, IN: University of Notre Dame Press, 1996), attacks both White's and Wills's views. In his well-argued effort to turn Jefferson into a modern libertarian, Zuckert states, for example, that "no person who understands property as Jefferson does would accept a positive right to life." Such a right, he claims, "would amount to a blank check on one's own life and liberty that a rational being would not accept" (ibid., 79). As for an excellent Epicurean account of Jefferson's moral thought, see Charles L. Griswold, Jr.'s extensive article, "Rights and Wrongs: Jefferson, Slavery, and Philosophical Quandaries"

in Michael J. Lacey and Knud Haakonssen (eds.), *A Culture of Rights: The Bill of Rights in Philosophy, Politics, and Law – 1791 and 1991* (Cambridge: Cambridge University Press, 1991), 144–214.

23 Even Garrett Ward Sheldon, in his brilliant *The Political Philosophy of Thomas Jefferson* (Baltimore, MD: Johns Hopkins University Press, 1993), finds Jefferson guilty of self-deception in respect to slavery. Unfortunately, Sheldon constructs the argument awkwardly by first setting among Jefferson's "hierarchy of values" such a value as "his personal lifestyle." The question whether that "value" should be viewed as a terminal or an instrumental value is not addressed. Still, Jefferson allegedly set this "value" on a higher scale than the value of "the emancipation of slaves." No wonder that "Jefferson's ideas and action on slavery ... tell us more about the human capacity for self-deception than anything else" (see ibid., 139–140). Some scholars have found this self-confessedly religious man guilty of self-deception because of his refusal to subscribe to the theological tenet of the trinity. Alas, Paul Conkin, who makes this accusation, offers no explanation of why Jefferson's self-proclaimed deism should entail the belief in a tripartite God. See Paul A. Conkin, "The Religious Pilgrimage of Thomas Jefferson," in Onuf (ed.), *Jeffersonian Legacies*, 25.

24 For example, speculations abound about Jefferson growing into a more religious person over the years. What is known is that from early on, he regarded the historical Jesus as a great moralist, who brought the principle of universal benevolence to moral philosophy. Richard Samuelson, for example, claims that "Jefferson's disposition towards Jesus changed" substantively in the early 1790s, but refers only to his growing interest in biblical exegesis; Richard Samuelson, "Jefferson and Religion: Private Belief, Public Policy," in Frank Shuffelton (ed.), *The Cambridge Companion to Thomas Jefferson* (New York: Cambridge University Press, 2009), 145. On Jefferson's gradual shift to essentially "Christian ethics," see, for example, Sheldon, *The Political Philosophy*, 104. See also Jean M. Yarbrough, *American Virtues: Thomas Jefferson on the Character of a Free People* (Lawrence: University of Kansas Press, 1998), 15.

25 As to Jefferson allegedly changing his political principles, Garrett Ward Sheldon finds a gradual shift from the younger Jefferson's Lockean thought to the later Jefferson's more classically republican concerns over public virtue and corruption; Sheldon, *Political Philosophy*, 50–52. Michael Zuckert, by contrast, sees Jefferson's political philosophy evolving from its outset in opposition to all kinds of communitarian modes of thought, whether or not derived from classical republicanism. According to Zuckert, it was only in 1816 that Jefferson's political thought matured into genuinely democratic thinking from his allegedly earlier, English-derived notion of the bicameral legislature "as the specific home of wisdom, talent, and virtue"; Zuckert, *Natural Rights Republic*, 231.

26 Quoted in Joseph. J. Ellis, *American Sphinx: The Character of Thomas Jefferson* (New York: Alfred A. Knopf, 1997), 297.

27 Gordon S. Wood, *The Creation of the American Republic 1776–1787* (Chapel Hill: University of North Carolina Press, 1969), 604. As Sheldon writes, "for Wood the American experiment began as classical republicanism, but ended as Lockean liberalism"; Sheldon, *Political Philosophy*, 153.

28 As if illuminating the analytic problems of any too-generalized approach to the founding legacy, Wood later, offhandedly – and without any suggestion for

comparative research – opined that "following the Declaration of Independence, the United States became the most egalitarian nation in the history of the world, and it remains so today, regardless of its great disparities of wealth." Gordon S. Wood, *The Radicalism of the American Revolution* (New York: Vintage Books), 223. Whether the United States was the most egalitarian nation in the world at the time is not self-evident. More importantly, however, Wood here appears to embrace a kind of evolutionary view of American history in which all the good things evolve from the egalitarian ideals put forward in the Declaration of Independence. As for the repercussions of such a perspective, it is worth noting that any view of American history as if destined to fulfill the founders' liberal, libertarian, or classically republican vision too easily tames the grand national narrative into a gradual manifestation of the "true" meaning of the founding via, say, the emancipation of slaves, women's suffrage, the 1960s civil rights legislation, and Barack Obama's election to presidency. The problem is that such a reading of history confuses the study of a specific historical meaning of the founding era to a given historical agent with the metahistorically "true" meaning of the founding. Consider, for example, what Joyce Appleby once stated about the ultimate goal of writing intellectual history of the founding era: "What remains to be resolved in the scholarly dispute about republicanism in America is whose republicanism we are talking about – that of the founding fathers or ours? And if theirs is ours, which one of ours?" If this is a call for viewing "our republicanism" as a criterion of what should interest us in the no doubt numerous republicanisms of the founders, it has very little to do with genuine interest in history. Quotation in Joyce Appleby, "Republicanism in Old and New Contexts," *The William and Mary Quarterly*, 43 (1, 1986), 33.

29 Wood, "Trials and Tribulations," 406.

30 See, for example, Ellis, *American Sphinx*, 296.

31 One may also illuminate this disturbingly antipolitical attitude in early American history writing by drawing attention to Joyce Appleby's famous thesis that in the 1800 presidential elections, the forward-looking, liberal Jeffersonian movement – ultimately relying on the notion that "consumers form the nation" – crushed the backward-looking Hamiltonian vision of a mercantilist, centralized American state, while the movement itself aimed at nothing less than "retreat from politics." Quotations, respectively, in Joyce Appleby, *Capitalism and a New Social Order: The Republican Vision of the 1790s* (New York: New York University Press, 1984), 89, 33. Or consider how political scientist Judith Shklar once summed up the meaning of the American founding by stating that, with the Constitution, sheer "bargaining replaces the tumult of popular assemblies, as order and freedom are reconciled pre-politically." Quotation in Judith Shklar, "Montesquieu and the New Republicanism," in Gisela Bock, Quentin Skinner, and Maurizio Viroli (eds.), *Machiavelli and Republicanism* (Cambridge: Cambridge University Press, 1990), 270. At least with Jefferson, it is difficult to discern what is apolitical, pre-political, or antipolitical in his persuasion of Madison to include the Bill of Rights in the Constitution. Even after the constitutional, allegedly "pre-political" reconciliation of "order and freedom," Jefferson's records are replete with political claims about the meaning of the concept of "constitution." No constitutional framework prevents a politician from politicizing a constitution, if he or she so wishes. By the same token,

one may view each and every advocate of the 1960s civil rights movement as one ready to question and hence to politicize the then-customary, social view of equality in America.

32 Daniel T. Rodgers, "Republicanism: The Career of a Concept," *The Journal of American History*, 79 (June 1992), 14.

33 On the conceptually important link between conflict and politics, see, for example, Kari Palonen, *Quentin Skinner: History, Politics, Rhetoric* (Cambridge: Polity Press, 2003), 2–3; Palonen, "Four Times of Politics: Policy, Polity, Politicking, and Politicization," *Alternatives*, 28 (2003), 171–186; Bernard Yack, *The Problems of a Political Animal: Community, Justice, and Conflict in Aristotelian Political Thought* (Berkeley: University of California Press, 1993), e.g., 1–3.

34 TJ to John Taylor, June 4, 1798, *TJW*, 1050.

35 Perhaps the methodological point can be phrased more simply still: In accepting the doctrinaire belief in the conception of free society as inherently distinct from the conception of free government, one loses the need to ask why Jefferson, like so many contemporaries, thought it justifiable to exclude children, slaves, as well as women from the political sphere as innocents, just as children and mentally disabled remain, by and large, excluded from full political powers today.

36 TJ, Autobiography (1821), *TJW*, 44.

37 This problem simply evades such straightforward summaries as that of Joseph Ellis, according to whom "it was Lincoln's expansive revision of the original Jeffersonian version of natural rights philosophy that broadened the message to include blacks." If Ellis is right, Lincoln simply nationalized this natural rights philosophy so that the principle now covered all male Americans within the borders of the United States. Quotation in Ellis, *American Sphinx*, 297.

38 *Notes*, Query VI, 155–156.

39 TJ to Isaac H. Tiffany, April 4, 1819, Joyce Appleby and Terence Ball (eds.), *The Political Writings of Thomas Jefferson* (New York: Cambridge University Press, 1999), 224.

40 TJ, Draft Constitution for Virginia, June 1776, *TJW*, 338, 343.

41 Michael Zuckert, for example, on the basis of this document, says only that Jefferson "sought an indirect election for the upper house – not the popular electorate directly." For the quotation, see Zuckert, *Natural Rights Republic*, 230. In fact, Jefferson's draft clearly advocated equal suffrage, even if the elected would divide themselves into two houses. On Jefferson's constant claims that half of free, white males were unfairly excluded from the ballot in Virginia, see *Notes*, Query XIII, 244; TJ to John Taylor, May 28, 1816, *TJW*, 139; TJ to Samuel Kercheval, July 12, 1816, ibid., 1396.

42 Brinkley et al., *American History Survey*, 898 (emphasis added).

43 On Hamilton's remarks about Jefferson's "womanish attachment to France," see Sloan, *Principle and Interest*, 185. On other accusations, see, for example, Douglas R. Egerton, *Gabriel's Rebellion: The Virginia Slave Conspiracies of 1800 and 1802* (Chapel Hill: University of North Carolina Press, 1993), 8.

44 See Max Edling, A Revolution in Favor of Government: Origins of the U.S. Constitution and the Making of the American State (New York: Oxford University Press, 2003).

45 Sheldon, *Political Philosophy*, 98.

46 A.J. Beitzinger, "Political Theorist," in Peterson (ed.), *A Reference Biography*, 98. Sometimes Jefferson's ethical precepts have been identified with those of Lenin and Mao and even Pol Pot, as if his moral failures amounted to genocidal aspirations. On Leninist and Maoist features of Jefferson's thought, see Ellis, *American Sphinx*, 127. For Conor Cruise O'Brien's argument that Jefferson, in light of his statements on the French Revolution, would have admired Pol Pot, see Peter S. Onuf, *Jefferson's Empire: The Language of American Nationhood* (Charlottesville: University of Virginia Press, 2000), 226, n66. As for genuinely philosophical aspects of Jefferson's moral thought, it is worth considering Jean Yarbrough's statement about Jefferson's "general failure to recognize the tensions between doing good for others and doing good for oneself, moral virtue and intellectual virtue, the duties we owe to God and the duties we owe to others, as well as to ourselves" (Yarbrough, *American Virtue*, 194). The referred "tensions" must be true prior to Jefferson's failure to recognize them as such. But modern moral philosophy hardly agrees, for example, on the existence of certain moral duties everyone owes to some god. Neither do all moral theories acknowledge the duties that people owe to themselves as strictly speaking moral to begin with, because morality should be about the respect for others. What Yarbrough means when stating that both Jefferson and Madison "mistake the nature of the good" (ibid., 173) remains a bit mysterious in her otherwise insightful analysis of Jefferson's virtue ethics.

47 Joyce Appleby, "Introduction: Jefferson and His Complex Legacy" in Onuf (ed.), *Jeffersonian Legacies*, 2.

48 Hence, my epigraph from Hannah Arendt's *The Human Condition* (1958), 2nd edition, Introduction by Margaret Conovan (Chicago: Chicago University Press, 1998), 234: "No man can be sovereign, because not one man, but men, inhabit the earth." For the essentially unintended results of politics, see Palonen's intriguing article, "Four Times of Politics."

49 Notably, Leonard Levy's famous accusations that Jefferson betrayed all his "libertarian" principles of free speech and minimal government draw on a stunningly simplified view of not only Jefferson, but of history. According to Levy, Jefferson's eighteenth-century world "regarded truths as immutable and self-evident" and by "1800 or thereabouts the standards of his own time did not noticeably differ from those of ours on the kind of civil-liberties questions he confronted" (quotations in Levy, "Civil Liberties," 345, 347.) As this study shows, none of the previously mentioned claims holds true, beginning with the common error of dubbing Jefferson as a modern-day libertarian thinker who only failed to act accordingly.

50 For Morton White's speculations on Jefferson's original draft of the Declaration of Independence suggesting a government that would aid men in attaining their suggested "ends" rather than a minimal government that only secures their "rights," see White, *The Philosophy of the American Revolution*, esp., 249–251. What distinguished Jefferson's vision from a modern welfare society is perhaps not so much his sceptical attitude toward big government as his conviction that the consent of the governed as its moral basis would also mean considering general welfare in moral terms. Modern welfare society – when viewed as a society that primarily aims at diminishing the socioeconomic differences among people – can well be motivated by merely the best interest of the well-to-do to

keep the less wealthy peaceful. Paradigmatically speaking, the modern welfare state aims at cost-efficient health care and welfare services for the population as a whole, and hence views all individuals as potentially gained or lost economic resources for the system itself. That the outcome of such policies can prove ethically sustainable and economically competitive on a global scale is rarely even questioned today, except in the United States.

51 In this respect, the recent discussion about the ethical dimensions of torturing prisoners of war brings to mind Jefferson's principle of generational sovereignty. As early as 1776, Jefferson thought it evident that at least the Virginia assembly shall *not* "have power to prescribe torture in any case whatever." TJ, Draft Constitution of Virginia from 1776, *TJW*, 340. On the issue of torture, see an exemplary column "Necessary Roughness" by Max Boot, a senior fellow of the Council of Foreign Relations, published in *Los Angeles Times* on January 20, 2005. Boot's argument is that "waterboarding may well meet the United Nations' definition of torture," but nevertheless raises the question: "Should this be permitted?" To this question, Mr. Boot replies: "I'm not sure. It's hard to know exactly where to draw a line here. But I am sure that I reject the absolutist understanding of so many of the president's critics, who would turn international law into a suicide pact." On much later, veiled thanks for "the so-called enhanced interrogation techniques" for acquiring information that led to the killing of Osama bin Laden, see David Von Drehle's "Death Comes for the Terrorist," *Time*, May 20, 2011.

1 History, Progress, and Politics

1 TJ to Joseph Priestley, March 21, 1801, *TJW*, 1086.

2 Quotations respectively from TJ to John Adams, June 15, 1813, *TJW*, 1278 and from TJ to Bishop James Madison, January 31, 1800, ibid., 1076–1077.

3 TJ to William Green Munford, June 18, 1799, *TJW*, 1064.

4 Similarly, in concentrating on Jefferson's progressive beliefs, I will set aside most of the scholarly disagreements on the true character of the Enlightenment among such luminaries in eighteenth-century studies as Karl Löwith, Peter Gay, Reinhard Koselleck, and Jonathan Israel.

5 TJ to William Green Munford, June 18, 1799, *TJW*, 1065.

6 TJ to Joseph Priestley, January 27, 1800, *TJW*, 1073.

7 TJ to Joseph Priestley, March 21, 1801, *TJW*, 1085.

8 TJ to P.S. Dupont de Nemours, April 24, 1816, *TJW*, 1387.

9 TJ to Miles King, September 26, 1814, *Extracts*, 360 (emphasis added).

10 Even this novelty Jefferson was ready to rely on only "till a change in circumstances shall take place." TJ to Joseph Priestley, March 21, 1801, *TJW*, 1085–1086.

11 TJ to Judge Spencer Roane, September 6, 1819, *TJW*, 1425.

12 On this view, see Michael J. Lacey and Knud Haakonssen, "Introduction: History, Historicism, and the Culture of Rights," in Lacey and Haakonssen (eds.), *A Culture of Rights: The Bill of Rights in Philosophy, Politics, and Law – 1791 and 1991* (New York: Woodrow Wilson Center and Cambridge University Press, 1991), 14.

13 For example, historian David Brion Davis noted that "Quite frankly, I am not at all sure what 'progress' means," in the introduction to his *Slavery and Human Progress* (Oxford and New York: Oxford University Press, 1984), xvi.

14 TJ to John Norvell, June 14, 1807, *Ford* 10: 416.
15 Quotation in TJ to John Norvell, June 14, 1807, *Ford* 10: 416. For further criticism of Hume as a historian, see TJ to William Duane, August 12, 1810, *TJW*, 1229 and TJ to Major John Cartwright, June 5, 1824, ibid., 1491. See also TJ to an unknown correspondent, October 25, 1825, in Andrew A. Lipscomb and Albert Ellery Bergh (eds.), *The Writings of Thomas Jefferson*, 20 vols. (Washington, DC, 1903–1904), [Hereafter cited as *L&B*], 16:125–129. See also Douglas L. Wilson, "Jefferson vs. Hume," *The William and Mary Quarterly* 16 (1, 1989), 49–70.
16 On Jefferson's keen interest in contemporary history writing about the Revolution, see, for example, TJ to Samuel Adams Well, May 12, 1819, *TJW*, 1417–1422. On Jefferson's very critical reading of John Marshall's long biography of George Washington, see TJ to Joel Barlow, October 8, 1809 (including a long memo on Marshall's errors), *Ford* 11: 120–124. See also, TJ to John Adams, June 15, 1813, *TJW*, 1279. For a valid discussion on Jefferson's views of historiography, see Andrew Burstein, *Jefferson's Secrets: Death and Desire in Monticello* (New York: Basic Books, 2005), 219–225.
17 *Notes*, Query XIV, 274. Jefferson's habit of reading Tacitus indicates that he was perfectly familiar with the notion of history repeating itself. The old paradigm of history as *magistra vitae* is also present in Jefferson's remark that the lessons of history are too "unfrequent" to qualify as a "moral exercise" for which he preferred pure fiction. TJ to Robert Skipwith, August 3, 1771. See on Jefferson's use of history as providing essentially extra-historical examples on governmental issues, TJ to Destutt de Tracy 1811, *Ford* 11: 184,186.
18 See also the 1778 Virginia Bill for the More General Diffusion of Knowledge, where the committee's curriculum for a three-year, free education for both boys and girls consisted of writing, reading, and arithmetic as well as Greek, Roman, English, and American history. TJ et al., Virginia Bill for the More General Diffusion of Knowledge, *TJW*, 367.
19 TJ to Caesar A. Rodney, February 10, 1810, *TJW*, 1217.
20 TJ to Caesar A. Rodney, February 10, 1810, *TJW*, 1217.
21 TJ to Caesar A. Rodney, February 10, 1810, *TJW*, 1217.
22 That Jefferson's deism had little to do with any particular religious denominations is strongly indicated in the several-page-long extracts from Lord Bolingbroke's philosophical writings in the young Jefferson's memoranda book, called Literary Commonplace Book. For a remark, copied from Bolingbroke, on "the phenomena of nature, physical and moral, which we know to be the work of god," although not of the biblical one, see Douglas L. Wilson (ed.), *Jefferson's Literary Commonplace Book, The Papers of Thomas Jefferson, Second Series* (Princeton: Princeton University Press, 1989), [Hereafter cited as *Literary CB*], (§8), 30. The vastness of truly important questions is well conveyed in this extract: "I combat the pride and presumption of metaphysicians in a most flagrant instance, in the assumption that man is made the final cause of the whole creation. [F]or if the planets of our solar system are worlds inhabited like ours, and if the fixed stars are other suns about which other planets revolve, the celestial phaenomena were no more made for us than we were made for them." Unfortunately, Jefferson never commented on these formulations. See ibid., (§16), 29.

23 TJ to William Ludlow, September 6, 1824, *TJW*, 1496–1497.

24 On the Ludlow letter as an expression of the Jeffersonian pastoral ideals see, for example, Henry Nash Smith, *Virgin Land: The American West as Symbol and Myth* (Cambridge, MA: Harvard University Press, 1950, 1970), 219–222; Leo Marx, *Machine in the Garden: Technology and the Pastoral Ideal in America* (Oxford and New York: Oxford University Press, 1967), 125; Matthews, *Radical Politics*, 122–125.

25 Jefferson did not need learn this four-stage notion of civilization from Adam Smith because it was included in Lord Kames's history of property, which Jefferson meticulously excerpted in his Legal Commonplace Book [Hereafter cited as *Legal CB*]. See Gilbert Chinard (ed.), *The Commonplace Book of Thomas Jefferson: A Repertory of His Ideas on Government* (Baltimore: Johns Hopkins University Press, 1926), (Entry 559), 107–113. Notably, it was not by the ancients but by medieval feudal laws that "land was withdrawn from commerce and could not be attached for paiment [sic] of debt," for example. Ibid., (Entry 565), 130. Adam Smith no doubt viewed ancient Rome as a civilization. On his comparison of the schism between the American colonies and the mother land to the ancient Roman civil wars, see Andrew Skinner (ed.), Adam Smith, *The Wealth of Nations, Books IV–V*, 1776 (London: Penguin Books, 1999), 205. On Smith's comparison of the American, Greek, and Spanish colonies with each other, see ibid., 147–149. On the notion that the Roman educational system promoted "refinement" among them, see ibid., 364–365. On some early indications of the four-stage theory as present in Pufendorf's writings, see Istvan Hont, "The language of sociability and commerce: Samuel Pufendorf and the theoretical foundations of the 'Four-Stages Theory'" in Anthony Pagden (ed.), *The Languages of Political Theory in Early-Modern Europe* (Cambridge: Cambridge University Press, 1990).

26 TJ to Jean Babtiste Say, February 1, 1804, *TJW*, 1144. As Leo Marx argues, Jefferson probably became acquainted with this pastoral image of the yeoman, originally Virgil's, via the works of Joseph Addison, Hugh Blair, Richard Price, and James Thomson. See Marx, *Machine in the Garden*, 95–105.

27 TJ to William Ludlow, September 6, 1824, *TJW*, 1496–1497.

28 *Notes*, Query VI, 185.

29 TJ to Joseph C. Cabell, January 22, 1820, *Ford* 12:155.

30 TJ to John Adams, June 11, 1812, *TJW*, 1264.

31 TJ to John Adams, June 11, 1812, *AJL*, 307.

32 TJ to John Lynch, January 21, 1811, *TJW*, 1240.

33 TJ to John Adams, January 11, 1816, *AJL*, 458–459.

34 TJ to Joseph Priestley, March 21, 1801, *TJW*, 1085.

35 TJ, Notes on Prof. Ebeling's Letter, July 30, 1795, *TJW*, 700.

36 TJ to Joseph Priestley, January 27, 1800, *TJW*, 1973.

37 TJ to John Adams, June 15, 1813, *TJW*, 1278.

38 TJ to John Adams, September 12, 1821, *AJL*, 575.

39 TJ to John Adams, October 28, 1813, *TJW*, 1309.

40 Historian Charles A. Miller suggests that in Jefferson's title, *Notes on the State of Virginia*, the term "state" probably referred not to a juridical state but to the present "condition" of Virginia. See Charles A. Miller, *Jefferson and Nature: An Interpretation* (Baltimore: John Hopkins University Press, 1993), 17. This is

notable particularly in view of the title *A True Discourse of the Present State of Virginia* by Ralph Hamor from as early as 1615. See on this, Joseph Boskin, *Into Slavery: Racial Decisions in the Virginia Colony* (Washington, DC: University Press of America, 1979), 33.

41 TJ to James Madison, August 28, 1789, Julian P. Boyd et al. (eds.), *The Papers of Thomas Jefferson* (Princeton: Princeton University Press, 1950), [Hereafter cited as *Papers*], 15: 367. Here Jefferson speaks of "the dark ages which intervened between antient [sic] and modern civilisation," and of the corrupt "principles" that were "held in just horror in the 18th century." On Jefferson's positive view of the intellectual legacy of Aristotle and Plutarch, see TJ to A. Coray, October 31, 1823, *L&B* 15: 481.

42 For Jefferson's familiarity with all these standard conceptions, see, for example, *Legal CB*, (Entries 740 and 771), 190, 251. In this respect, Jefferson's remark about "our original barbarism" (TJ to Madame de Tessé, March 20, 1787, *TJW*, 893) carries evident connotations of the specifically Anglo-American Saxon ancestry roaming the "wilds and woods in the North of Europe" (TJ, A Summary View of the Rights of British America, 1774, *TJW*, 105–106). I see Jefferson's references to the Teutonic, barbarian origins of Anglo-Saxons less important than does Maurizio Valsania, for even this mode of barbarism was barbarian only in comparison to the Greco-Roman civilization. Cf. Maurizio Valsania, "'Our Original Barbarism': Man vs. Nature in Thomas Jefferson's Moral Experience," *Journal of the History of Ideas*, Vol. 65 (4, 2004), 627–645.

43 Jefferson's Legal Commonplace Book includes similarly conventional accounts of the barbarian nations destroying the ancient Roman civilization only to end up establishing what Jefferson called a "new system of polity," namely the feudal one. Notably, achieving "a just taste" in architecture, sculpture, and the art of writing was still the distinction of the ancient Greeks. See *Legal CB* (Entries 859–860), 339–342.

44 TJ to John Adams, September 12, 1821, Lester J. Cappon (ed.), *The Adams-Jefferson Letters: The Complete Correspondence between Thomas Jefferson and Abigail and John Adams*, 2 Vols. (Chapel Hill: University of North Carolina Press, 1959), [Herafter cited as *AJL*], 575.

45 TJ to John Adams, September 12, 1821, *AJL*, 575.

46 TJ to Benjamin Rush, January 16, 1811, *TJW*, 1236.

47 TJ to John Trumbull, February 15, 1789, *TJW*, 939–940.

48 Bacon found only three revolutions of learning in history, occurring in the Greek, in the Roman, and in the seventeenth-century European scientific thinking. See Fulton H. Anderson (ed.), Francis Bacon, *The New Organon and Related Writings* (Indianapolis and New York: Bobbs-Merrill Company, 1960), 75 [Bk. I, Ch. 78].

49 TJ, Syllabus on the Doctrines of Jesus, April 1803 (as attached to TJ to Benjamin Rush, April 21, 1803), *TJW*, 1124.

50 TJ to Samuel Kercheval, January 10, 1810, *TJW*, 1214.

51 TJ to Benjamin Rush, April 21, 1803, *TJW*, 1124–1125.

52 TJ to Benjamin Rush, April 21, 1803, in the enclosed "Syllabus of the Doctrines of Jesus Compared to Others," *Extracts*, 332. On the word "over" before "learned" as interlined later, see ibid., 335n.

53 *Notes*, Query XVII, 286.

54 Jean Barbeyrac, "An Historical and Critical Account of the Science of Morality; and the Progress it has Made in the World, from the Earliest Times Down to the Publication of Pufendorf's the Law of Nature and Nations," in Samuel Pufendorf: *The Law of Nature and Nations* [*De jure naturae et gentium*, 1672], translated by Jean Barbeyrac (London: 1729), 36. On Jefferson's owning both editions, see E. Millicent Sowerby (ed.), *Catalogue of the Library of Thomas Jefferson* (Washington, DC, 1951–1953), Vol. II, 69n. In quoting Pufendorf, Jefferson usually made the translations himself, and appears to have known Pufendorf's writings as early as 1770, when he quoted Pufendorf on the concept of servitude as grounded either on a compact or capture in war. See TJ, *Howell v. Netherland* case file, April 1770, *Ford* 1: 475.

55 Quotations respectively from Barbeyrac, "An Historical Account," 36, 18. To be sure, Barbeyrac also used much ink to oppose Bayle's apparently too skeptical position.

56 Knud Haakonssen, "Introduction," in Haakonssen (ed.), *Thomas Reid: Practical Ethics, Being Lectures and Papers on Natural Religion, Self-Government, Natural Jurisprudence, and the Law of Nations* (Princeton: Princeton University Press, 1990), 30–31. As Haakonssen characterizes Thomas Reid's view in this respect, "The apparently paradoxical notion of duties to ourselves is explained by the fact that these duties are only prima facie self-regarding ... The duties to ourselves are thus really owed to God." Ibid., 57.

57 See *Legal CB* (Entry 797), 291. The famous formulation in Grotius's *On the Law of War and Peace* was the following: "Just as, in fact, there are many ways of living, one being better than another, and out of so many ways of living earth is free to select that which he prefers, so also a people can select the form of government which it wishes; and the extent of its legal right in the matter is not to be measured by the superior excellence of this or that form of government, in regard to which different men hold different views, but by its free choice." Notably, Grotius was not denying the hypothesis that one denomination might be best suited to provide the best possible human government. He held that we have no objective criteria even on a natural-law basis to define that best form of government. Quotation from Grotius in J.B. Schneewind (ed.), *Moral Philosophy from Montaigne to Kant: An Anthology*, 2 Vols. (Cambridge: Cambridge University Press, 1990), [Hereafter cited as *Anthology*], 102. Pufendorf approached the same issue in stating, "Hence the decrees of the natural law are adapted only to the human forum, which does not extend beyond this life, and they are wrongly applied in many places to the divine forum, which is the especial care of theology." Pufendorf, *The Duty of Man and Citizen*, as in ibid., 159.

58 Peter H. Nidditch (ed.), John Locke, *An Essay Concerning Human Understanding* [1690, 1700], (Oxford: Oxford University Press, 1979), [Hereafter cited as *Essay*], (1:3:4), 68–69.

59 Locke, *Essay* (1:3:9–10), 70–72.

60 On the state of war, Locke states clearly that "by the *Fundamental Law of Nature* ... when all cannot be preserv'd the safety of the Innocent is to be preferred." John Locke, *The Second Treatise of Government* (1690, 1698) in Peter Laslett (ed.), *John Locke: Two Treatises of Government* (Cambridge: Cambridge University Press, 1994), (§ 16), 279. See also ibid. (§ 20), 281–282.

61 Locke, *Second Treatise* (§129), 352.

62 Locke, *Second Treatise* (§13), 275–276.
63 TJ to John Randolph, August 25, 1775, *TJW*, 749.
64 TJ's original draft of the Declaration of Independence, *Papers* 1: 423.
65 TJ to P.S. Dupont de Nemours, April 24, 1816, *TJW*, 1385–1386.
66 TJ to James Madison January 30, 1787, *TJW*, 882.
67 Quotations, TJ to Samuel Kercheval, July 12, 1816, *TJW*, 1401–1403.
68 TJ to Judge Spencer Roane, September 6, 1819, *TJW*, 1425.
69 TJ to George Logan, November 12, 1816, *Ford* 12:43.
70 TJ to Peter Carr, August 10, 1787, *Papers* 12: 14–15. As noted, scholars often disagree on the direction of the presumed changes in Jefferson's ethical thought – most of which, as I would argue, never occurred. According to Garrett Ward Sheldon – and, he claims, Richard Matthews and Forrest McDonald agree – the Scottish moral-sense doctrine was still absent in Jefferson's so-called "philosophy" during the Revolution. (See Sheldon, *Political Philosophy*, 155.) Even if Jefferson had some prior moral philosophy, it is hard to see why he should have attempted to include, say, a moral-sense theory in the Revolutionary-era documents. Focusing on the dictates of natural law could well serve all his purposes at the time. As Jean Yarbrough has pointed out, Jefferson's early memoranda collections, the so-called Legal and Literary Commonplace Books, mostly completed by 1775, teem with references to Scottish moral sentimentalism. Yarbrough, *American Virtues*, 17. In addition, a letter from as early as 1771 conveys Jefferson's hearty commitment to the exercise of "moral feelings" that "produces a habit of thinking and acting virtuously." TJ to Robert Skipwith, August 3, 1771, *TJW*, 741.
71 Jefferson attributed the doctrine of the artificiality of justice to Hobbes. TJ to Francis W. Gilmer, June 7, 1816, *Ford* 11: 535. The notion of man being created for society was of course fully acceptable to such authorities as Lord Kames, Adam Smith, and others – even if not evidently the basis of properly moral, disinterested behavior. See Kames 1751, passim., e.g., 114. See also D.D. Raphael and A.L. Macfie (eds.), Adam Smith, *The Theory of Moral Sentiments* [1759, 6th ed., The Glasgow Edition], (Oxford: Oxford University Press, 1982), [Herafter cited as *TMS*], e.g., 116, 177.
72 TJ to John Adams, October 14, 1816, *AJL*, 492.
73 On Jefferson's claim that the notion of "justice" results from "the construction of man," and is "instinct, and innate" in being "as much a part of our construction as necessary in an animal destined to live in society," see TJ to John Adams October 14, 1816, *AJL*, 492. Or consider Jefferson's statement that "Man was destined for society. His morality therefore was to be formed to this object. He was endowed with a sense of right and wrong merely relative to this. This sense is as much a part of his nature as the sense of hearing, seeing, feeling … [and is] given to all human beings in a stronger or weaker degree [so as to] be strengthened by exercise." TJ to Peter Carr, August 10, 1787, *Papers* 12: 14–15. Notably, this statement includes one of Jefferson's few Homerian nods in the sense that he here made a direct claim about the moral sense as the "true foundation of morality." Contrary to this letter, written to his own nephew, Jefferson was elsewhere conspicuously consistent in arguing that the tenet of the moral sense was only his own belief. As I will explicate, Jefferson's moral-sense beliefs dismissed some common distinctions drawn by contemporary moral scientists.

It was widely held that genuinely moral concerns must arise from disinterested motivation as distinct from equally natural, but self-interested social instincts. See on this elementary point about Francis Hutcheson's moral sense philosophy, J.B. Schneewind, *The Invention of Autonomy: A History of Modern Moral Philosophy* (Cambridge: Cambridge University Press, 1998), 339.

74 TJ to Caesar A. Rodney, February 10, 1810, *TJW*, 1217.

75 TJ to Jean Baptiste Say, February 1, 1804, *TJW*, 1144.

76 TJ to Madame d'Enville, April 2, 1790, *TJW*, 965.

77 Here, the parentheses around "rights" are in Jefferson's hand. See TJ, Notes on Locke and Shaftesbury, *Papers* 1: 545. The list of interests as copied from Locke consisted here of "life, health, indolency of body, liberty, property." See ibid.

78 TJ to Peter Carr, August 19, 1785, *TJW*, 814.

79 What historians, suggesting that Jefferson used the separation to publicly promote his own deistic beliefs rather than freedom of conscience, tend to leave out of the equation is precisely this new natural-law paradigm of moral sciences. On the scholarly debate on the idea that Jefferson intended to create an American "civil religion" based on his own Unitarian convictions as if equaling "natural" morality, see, for example, Johann M. Neem, "Beyond the Wall: Reinterpreting Jefferson's Danbury Address," *Journal of the Early Republic*, 27 (1,2007), esp. 141n.7.

80 As even the Earl of Shaftesbury argued, the fear of hell cannot imply conscience, "unless where there is an apprehension of what is wrong." He thus concluded that "religious conscience supposes moral or natural conscience." Quotation in Schneewind, *Invention of Autonomy*, 498. On the same issue, Lord Kames stated that "the very supposition of the purity and rectitude of the nature of the Divine Being presupposes a taste, feeling, or knowledge in us of an essential difference betwixt virtue and vice." Lord Kames (Henry Home), *Essays on the Principles of Morality and Natural Religion*, Edinburgh 1751, (Facsimile reprint: London 1981), [Hereafter cited as *Essays*], 93. According to Hutcheson, we need first approve benevolence as the basic motive of all morality and goodness so as to truly grasp the unbound benevolence of God. On this view, see, for example, Schneewind, *Invention of autonomy*, 339; Knud Haakonssen, *Natural Law and Moral Philosophy: From Grotius to the Scottish Enlightenment* (Cambridge: Cambridge University Press, 1996), 78. Pierre Bayle was one of the initiators of the idea that religious understanding only follows moral understanding. As Schneewind formulates Bayle's position, "It is morality that must tell us what religious doctrines to accepts, not the other way round." Schneewind, *Invention of Autonomy*, 283.

81 TJ to P.S. Dupont de Nemours, April 24, 1816, *TJW*, 1387.

82 *Notes*, Query XVII, 286.

83 TJ to John Adams, September 12, 1821, *AJL*, 575.

84 *Notes*, Query XVII, 285–287.

85 TJ to John Adams, August 22, 1813, *AJL*, 368. On the same, see also Yarbrough, *American Virtues*, 177.

86 *Notes*, Query XVII, 286. As a youngster, Jefferson copied in his so-called Literary Commonplace Book passages from John Tillotson, who mocked biblical truths that "may be taken in historical, mystical, literal, and allegorical" senses simultaneously. Interestingly, Tillotson noted that even if the "divinely

inspired" Moses could not explain to the people the Copernican worldview, there was no reason that "he should give them an absurd account" instead. See Jefferson, *Literary CB* (§58), 55. See also, for example, Adam Smith mocking the French for believing in Descartes's theory of vortices, Smith, *TMS* (Part VII), 313.

87 See for D'Alembert's classic remark about the difference between "le véritable esprit systématique qu'il faut bien se garder de prendre pour l'esprit de système." Jean Le Rond d'Alembert, "Discours Préliminaire des editeurs" in *Encyclopédie ou dictionnaire raisonné des sciences, des arts et des métiers* (Tome premier, Paris, 1751), vi. This is what Ernst Cassirer claimed to be the most essential distinction for the very notion of the Enlightenment itself. Ernst Cassirer, *The Philosophy of the Enlightenment* (*Die Philosophie der Aufklärung*, 1932), transl. by Fritz C.A. Koelln and James P. Pettergrove (Princeton: Princeton University Press, 1979), esp., vii. Let me add that this is not to claim anything about the true historical character of the Enlightenment itself: whether that was about some all-embracing idea of progress or only about "clarification" of philosophical concepts is not my concern in this book, which is dedicated to understanding Jefferson. For one classic interpretation, see Peter Gay's two-volume study on the Enlightenment, the first of which ends with a Humean notion of modernism as distinguishable from all mythic thinking and the second volume with what Gay takes to be the Madisonian, decisively modern, conception of politics. See Peter Gay, *The Enlightenment: An Interpretation, The Rise of Modern Paganism* (New York: W.W. Norton, 1966), esp., 418–419; Peter Gay, *The Enlightenment: An Interpretation, The Science of Freedom* (New York: W.W. Norton, 1969), esp., 563–568.

88 Dugald Stewart, *The Elements of the Philosophy of the Human Mind* (1792) in *The Works of Dugald Stewart*, Vol. I (Cambridge: Hilliard and Brown, 1829), 5.

89 *Notes*, Query XVII, 286.

90 TJ to John Adams, April 11, 1823, *TJW*, 1466–1469.

91 TJ to John Adams, April 11, 1823, *TJW*, 1466.

92 Kames, *Essays*, 319.

93 In considering the philosophical ramifications of the Declaration of Independence, philosopher Morton White, for example, objects to Jefferson's conception of the pursuit of happiness as a given, human inclination posited as prior to any obligatory notion of morality. Such a position, according to White, entails the epistemologically questionable presumption that we actually have some knowledge about the essence of man. White, *Philosophy of the American Revolution*, passim., e.g., 206–213, 233, 238.

94 Jefferson's Syllabus on Epicureanism, TJ to William Short, October 31, 1819, *TJW*, 1433.

95 TJ to James Smith, December 8, 1822, *Extracts*, 408.

96 TJ, First Inaugural Address, March 4, 1801, *TJW*, 494.

97 There is nothing particularly radical in this claim. As Merrill D. Peterson argued long ago, "There could be no objective definition of this good, therefore no way a government could obtain it for the multiplicity of citizens." Peterson, *Thomas Jefferson and the New Nation: A Biography* (New York: Oxford University Press, 1975), 94.

98 TJ to James Smith, December 2, 1822, *Extracts*, 409.
99 TJ to Peter Carr, August 10, 1787, *Papers* 12: 16–17.
100 TJ to Francis Hopkinson, March 13, 1789, *TJW*, 941.
101 My proposition about Jefferson's overall moral position is reminiscent of what historian Charles Griswold calls "a 'prudential' theory of moral deliberation." See Griswold, "Rights and Wrongs," 151. The difference arises from Griswold's use of the term "theory," which, I think, Jefferson's prudence would seek to avoid altogether.
102 Jefferson's pejorative remarks about "Stoic apathy" did not preempt his interest in such Stoic-inspired philosophers as Epictetus, Cicero, and Epicurus, for example. Epictetus, Jefferson held, had said all that "was good with the stoics," while Cicero misrepresented Epicurus because of his too-keen Stoic leanings. TJ to William Short, October 31, 1819, *TJW*, 1430.
103 Conkin, "Religious Pilgrimage," 27.
104 TJ to William Short, October 31, 1819, *TJW*, 1433.
105 TJ to Doctor Walter Jones, January 2, 1814, *Ford* 11: 375.
106 *Papers* 1:429–430. At this point, the original draft is practically identical with the final formulation. Cf. *Papers* 1:424.
107 TJ to Major John Cartwright, June 5, 1824, *TJW*, 1493.
108 TJ to Lafayette, February 14, 1815, *TJW*, 1361.
109 TJ to Monsieur A. Coray, October 31, 1823, *L&B* 15:484.
110 Smith, *TMS*, 187.
111 James Madison, National Gazette, January 20, 1792 in Jack N. Rakove (ed.), *James Madison Writings* (New York: Library of America, 1999), 520.
112 TJ to Joseph C. Cabell, February 2, 1816, *TJW*, 1378.
113 In fact, there was no reason to inquire whether "true virtue" can be "any where out of its place." Antoine Louis Claude Destutt de Tracy, *A Commentary and Review of Montesquieu's Spirit of Laws*, transl. by Thomas Jefferson [et al.], 1811 (Reprint, New York: Burt Franklin, 1969), 16–17.
114 Destutt de Tracy, *Commentary*, 148–149. This notion of savages occasionally enjoying the blessings of pure democracy is potentially present even in the Rousseauean notion of savagery as the universal, prehistoric condition of man, a view that Voltaire shared. Or consider Locke's famous remark that the whole world was once like pre-European America.
115 TJ to Isaac H. Tiffany, August 26, 1816, *Jefferson Political Writings*, Appleby & Ball (eds.), 218.
116 TJ to John Adams, June 11, 1812, *AJL*, 307.
117 TJ to Francis W. Gilmer, June 7, 1816, *Ford* 11: 535. Notably, when Jefferson asserted that some Indian nations had not submitted to "any shadow of government," he clearly referred to legal social arrangements as opposed to the non-governmental, cultural control of individual behavior and the natural "moral sense of right and wrong" that the Indian nations shared with the rest of mankind. *Notes*, Query XI, 220.
118 TJ to John Adams, June 11, 1812, *TJW*, 1263–1264.
119 The remarkably persistent image of Jefferson as the quintessential proponent of minimal government is well summed up by Gordon Wood: "Jefferson's faith in the natural sociability of people also lay behind his belief in minimal government.... He believed in nationhood, but not the modern idea of a state. He

hated all bureaucracy and all the coercive instruments of government" (see Wood, "Trials and Tribulations," 407). How far one should consider Jefferson's belief in human sociability to be pointing toward the concept of minimal government depends on what one understands by its opposite, maximal government. For many Americans today, the varying European welfare-state models seem to represent variations of socialist dictatorship. Unfortunately, Wood's statement does not invoke Jefferson's well-documented animosity to contemporary European societies of social orders. Jefferson's hatred of bureaucracy is suggested as an extra-historical truth as if bureaucracy was somewhere presented as an end in itself.

120 Consider, for example, Hannah Arendt's view that secularization was essentially nothing more than "the separation of politics from religion," and that the "first stage of this secularization was the rise of absolutism, and not the Reformation." Hannah Arendt, *On Revolution* (New York: Viking Press, 1968), 18.

121 TJ, Autobiography (1821), *TJW*, 64.

122 On Jefferson's long-standing concern for reliable currency and on his hostility toward local banks issuing paper money, see, for example, Sloan, *Principle and Interest*, passim.; Burstein, *Jefferson's Secrets*, 84–85.

123 On the depiction of Jefferson as a backward-looking agrarian by, for example, Forrest McDonald, Thomas D. Govan, and (to an extent even by) Drew McCoy on the one hand and on Joyce Appleby's effort to rectify this picture on the other hand, see Matthews, *Radical Politics*, 10.

124 *Notes*, Query XIX, 291.

125 TJ, Summary View of the Rights of British America, 1774, *TJW*, 108. When Jefferson was finally compelled to subscribe to domestic manufacturing instead of importation, he asserted simply that in political economy "no one axiom can be laid down as wise and expedient for all times." TJ to Benjamin Austin, January 9, 1816, *TJW*, 1371.

126 TJ to Benjamin Austin, January 9, 1816, *TJW*, 1370–1371.

127 For an interesting methodological debate on the political aspects of utopian literature between Reinhardt Koselleck, John Pocock, and Melvin Richter, see Helmut Lehmann and Melvin Richter (eds.), *The Meaning of Historical Terms and Concepts, New Studies on Begriffgeschichte* (Washington, DC: German Historical Institute, 1996). As John Pocock has noted, even Harrington's utopian view of England in the *Oceana* may be "read as an attempt to change history and not to stop it." J.G.A. Pocock, "A Discourse of Sovereignty" in Nicholas Phillipson and Quentin Skinner (eds.), *Political Discourse in Early Modern Britain* (Cambridge: Cambridge University Press, 1993), 405–406.

128 TJ to John Adams, June 15, 1813, *TJW*, 1278.

129 See for Jefferson's early suggestions that general suffrage be adopted in Virginia, TJ, Draft Constitution for Virginia, June 1776, *TJW*, 338.

130 Wood, *Radicalism of the American Revolution*, 367. For example, Peter Onuf concurred with this view in a speech held at the Thomas Jefferson and the Founding Fathers in Retirement conference, The International Center for Jefferson Studies, March 3, 2005.

131 *Notes*, Query XVII, 287.

132 TJ to James Madison, September 6, 1789, *TJW*, 959–964.

133 TJ to William Short, January 3, 1793, *TJW*, 1004.
134 TJ to Littleton Waller Tazewell, January 5, 1805, *TJW*, 1149 (emphasis added).
135 *Notes*, Query XIII, 246.
136 TJ to Samuel L. Smith, September 21, 1814, *TJW*, 1353.
137 TJ to John Holmes, April 22, 1820, *TJW*, 1434.
138 TJ's Draft Declaration and Protest of the Commonwealth of Virginia, December 1825, *TJW*, 484. (Notably, Jefferson never published this famous paper in defense of states' rights.)
139 TJ's Draft Declaration and Protest of the Commonwealth of Virginia, December 1825, *TJW*, 484.
140 TJ to Joseph C. Cabell, November 28, 1820, *Ford* 12: 170.
141 TJ to Samuel Kercheval, July 12, 1816, *TJW*, 1402.
142 TJ to P.S. Dupont de Nemours, April 24, 1816, *TJW*, 1387.
143 TJ to Samuel Kercheval, July 12, 1816, *TJW*, 1403.
144 TJ, First Inaugural Address, March 4, 1801, *TJW*, 493.
145 This is the point that Johann N. Neem, like many others, misses in reading Jefferson as an enlightened utopian, who believed not only that man is essentially good but also that some specific "history's logic" would entail an outcome in which "natural goodness of man would finally flourish" (Neem, "Beyond the Wall," 143). Jefferson never claimed that man is essentially good rather than selfish or sinful. He claimed that individuals need to learn to control their inherent self-love.
146 From such a temporalized position, disagreeing on what is progressive and what is not is definitely a value choice and thus, also a political matter. Moreover, disagreeing on what is progressive must be kept distinct from such totalitarian assertions about history that President George W. Bush, for example, put forward in his Second Inaugural Address: "History has an ebb and flow of justice, but history also has a visible direction, set by liberty and the author of liberty." The claim is that history's direction is clearly visible, which also implicates that the end of history is foreseeable for a normal human being. The claim is epistemologically absurd.
147 TJ to Abigail Adams, January 11, 1817, *AJL*, 504. On human improvement, see also TJ to Bishop James Madison, January 31, 1800, *TJW*, 1076–1077 and TJ to Dupont de Nemours, April 24, 1816, ibid., 1387.
148 For a good, book-length study of these events, see Egerton, *Gabriel's Rebellion*.
149 TJ to James Monroe, November 24, 1801, *TJW*, 1096.
150 TJ to (Governor of Virginia) James Monroe, June 2, 1802, as accessed from *The Online Library of Liberty* on March 19, 2011 at: http://oll.libertyfund.org/title/757/87347.
151 TJ to Jared Sparks, February 4, 1824, *TJW*, 1484.
152 "The Fundamental Constitutions of Carolina," in *The Works of John Locke*, Vol. X (London, 1823; Reprint, Aalen, Germany: Scientia Verlag, 1963), (§ CVII) 196. Jefferson thought that the "organizations of Locke were impracticable for Carolina." TJ to William Lee, January 16, 1817, *L&B* 15: 101.
153 *Notes*, Query XVIII, 288.
154 On this point, see Wills 1978, 306. Quotations, TJ, Autobiography, *TJW*, 44.

155 For example, John Chester Miller condemns Jefferson at various points for failing to promote racial equality. See John Miller, *The Wolf by the Ears*, e.g., 141, 143–145, 208–209. For particularly harsh verdicts on Jefferson's racism as related to his position on slavery, see for example, Paul Finkelman, "Jefferson and Slavery: 'Treason Against the Hopes of the World,'" in Onuf (ed.), *Jeffersonian Legacies*, 181–224 and Egerton, *Gabriel's Rebellion*.

156 *Notes*, Query XIV, 264.

157 TJ to Doctor Thomas Humphreys, February 8, 1817, *L&B* 15: 103.

158 Duncan J. Macleod, *Slavery, Race, and the American Revolution* (New York: Cambridge University Press, 1974), 22.

159 TJ, Summary View of the Rights of British America, 1774, *TJW*, 115.

160 Oddly enough, historians often argue that by excluding the extract from the document, the Continental Congress saved Jefferson from contradicting himself as the spokesman of the natural rights of man. For the only scholarly account that I know to agree with me on this point, see Eric Slauter, "The Declaration of Independence and the New Nation," Frank Shuffelton (ed.), *The Cambridge Companion to Thomas Jefferson* (New York: Cambridge University Press, 2009), 22.

161 *Notes*, Query XIV, 264. For Jefferson's repeated claim that there had been such an early proposal of abolishing slavery, see also TJ to Jean Nicolas Démeunier, June 26, 1786, *TJW*, 591–592; and TJ, Autobiography (1821), ibid., 44. To be sure, Jefferson also held that the "value of our lands and slaves, taken conjunctly, doubles in about twenty years" (*Notes*, Query XXII, 302). Whether this brief remark proves his early disillusionment about abolition is questionable, given that the quoted edition of the *Notes* was published in 1787. At that time he probably still hoped for the emancipation to begin to take place around the year 1800, which was the suggested timing for prohibiting slavery in new western territories in his early draft for the Northwest Ordinance of 1787. See TJ, Report on Government for Western Territory, March 1, 1784, *TJW*, 377.

162 TJ, Report on Government for Western Territory, March 1, 1784, *TJW*, 377. Notably, as early as 1790 a group of abolitionists, mainly Quakers, demanded that the first Federal Congress enact a national law of emancipation. James Madison characterized the debate on the idea as "shamefully indecent." Elkins & McKitrick, *Age of Federalism*, 152.

163 For an earlier view that Jefferson's slave codes were "milder but more comprehensive" than the colonial statutes, see John T. Noonan, *Persons and Masks of the Law: Cardozo, Holmes, Jefferson, and Wythe as Makers of the Masks* (New York: Farrar, Straus, and Giroux, 1976), 51.

164 TJ to Jared Sparks, February 4, 1824, *TJW*, 1484.

165 TJ to John Lynch, January 21, 1811, *TJW*, 1241.

166 A well-known abolitionist and later professor of law at the University of Virginia, St. George Tucker advocated a large-scale plan of turning the Virginia slaves into tenants. George Tucker – cousin of St. George Tucker and later professor of moral philosophy at University of Virginia – suggested a large-scale involuntary deportation of no less than 400,000 blacks out of Virginia. But contrary to Jefferson's program, Tucker's colony could have been established in the American West. See Egerton, *Gabriel's Rebellion*, 151–154. On St. George Tucker's "A Dissertation on Slavery" (Philadelphia, 1796) and George Tucker's

"A Letter to the Member of the General Assembly … with a Proposition for Colonization" (Baltimore 1801), see Gary B. Nash, *Race and Revolution: The Inaugural Merrill Jensen Lectures* (Madison, WI: Madison House Publishers, 1990), 151–165.

167 Drew R. McCoy, *The Last of the Fathers: James Madison & the Republican Legacy* (New York: Cambridge University Press, 1996), 301; Quotation in ibid., 279.

168 TJ to Edward Coles, August 25, 1814, *TJW*, 1345.

169 On Jefferson's own claim that he had never thought of the distant Africa as the asylum for the entire African-American population, see TJ to Jared Sparks, February 4, 1824, *TJW*, 1484. To Thomas Humphreys, Jefferson spoke of being "desirous to make any sacrifice" to solve the question, while not personally committing himself to Humphreys's idea of sending them to Africa, but to "elsewhere." TJ to Doctor Thomas Humphreys, February 8, 1817, *L&B* 15: 102–103.

170 TJ to J.P. Reibelt, December 21, 1805, *Ford* 10: 205.

171 Notably, Jefferson did not free even all skilled Hemings-family slaves, which makes it possible to speculate that light skin color was an additional qualification for Jefferson to allow a slave at least to run away. On this interesting, although apparently unanswerable question, see, for example, Annette Gordon-Reed, *Thomas Jefferson and Sally Hemings: An American Controversy* (Charlottesville: University of Virginia Press, 1997), e.g., 39, 202; John C. Miller, "Slavery," in Peterson (ed.), *A Reference Biography*, 426; Egerton, *Gabriel's Rebellion*, 11.

172 For a thorough historical discussion of the Sally Hemings issue, see, for example, the compilation of articles in Jan Ellen Lewis & Peter Onuf (eds.), *Sally Hemings & Thomas Jefferson: History, Memory, and Civic Culture* (Charlottesville: University of Virginia Press, 1999). For the generally accepted formulation that "DNA evidence now come close to proving that Jefferson fathered at least one of Sally Hemings's children," see Jan Ellen Lewis and Peter Onuf, "Introduction," ibid., 16n. For a good summary of all evidence on the case, see Burstein, *Jefferson's Secrets*, 115–117. On Jefferson's partial, and hence questionable, denial of the liaison with Sally Hemings, see Gordon-Reed, *Thomas Jefferson and Sally Hemings*, 141–145. On Gordon-Reed's later, I think questionable, epistemological premise that a historian (as a storyteller) should consent to some declarations "of new truths" even when "drawing reasonable inferences" only, see Gordon-Reed, "'The Memories of a Few Negroes': Rescuing America's Future at Monticello" in Lewis & Onuf (eds.), *Sally Hemings & Thomas Jefferson*, 251.

As I have often been pressed to take a stand on the Hemings issue, let me state the following: Whether the famous Y chromosome tests (matching Jefferson's father's brother's descendants with Eston Hemings's descendants) remove any doubt of Jefferson's fatherhood of at least one of Sally Hemings's children, namely Eston, is difficult for a layman to judge. Genealogist Herbert Barger has noted that Jefferson's brother, the brother's sons, and perhaps some other male relatives, cannot be excluded on this basis. (See *U.S. News*, January 18, 1999, "The Tom-and-Sally Miniseries" by Lewis Lord.) Almost all circumstantial evidence speaks to Jefferson fathering all of Hemings's children. Among other things, he clearly favored Hemings family members over other Monticello slaves. Still, on Thomas's and Sally's personal feelings toward each other, we have no direct evidence whatsoever. Should it one fine day be proven that not all (or any of) Sally Hemings's children were fathered by Jefferson, we would still lack any substantial evidence on how she truly conducted and viewed her own life. As to the ethical aspects of the very likely relationship between them, one may turn to Annette Gordon-Reed's profound account of scholars' questionable prejudices. As she makes clear, numerous distinguished Jefferson scholars have managed to embarrass themselves with their poorly documented and downright offensive characterizations of Sally Hemings as a lying, light-skinned harlot claiming to be the great Jefferson's lover. (See Gordon-Reed, *Thomas Jefferson and Sally Hemings*, passim., esp., 11–19, 169). Most importantly, however, Jefferson never changed his openly racist account of African Americans in his *Notes on the State of Virginia*, which was originally written well before his relationship with Hemings could have begun. Jefferson hoped to remove all African Americans out of the country so as to prevent any further "mixing of races." The long-standing liaison with Hemings would, of course, appear contradictory to such a public stand, but Jefferson could hardly offer his own (mis)behavior against his own principles as an excuse for others.

173 After the elections of 1800, the Hemings-Jefferson liaison was brought into public again in 1802, this time by the journalist James Callender, a former Jefferson adherent who had become a political enemy. Callender's motives for condemning the liaison probably resulted from what he saw as the general corruption of morals in Richmond, where he engaged himself in a campaign against white gentlemen openly escorting their black mistresses in theaters and dance halls. See Gordon-Reed, *Thomas Jefferson and Sally Hemings*, 60–61 and Joshua D. Rothman, "James Callender and Social Knowledge of Interracial Sex in Antebellum Virginia," in Lewis & Onuf (eds.), *Sally Hemings and Thomas Jefferson*, 95. Callender hardly lacked ideological, personal, and political motives for his anti-Jefferson campaign, but he could have had purely racist motives as well.

174 Egerton, *Gabriel's Rebellion*, 73. As Peter Onuf, in his *Jefferson's Empire: The Language of American Nationhood* (Charlottesville: University of Virginia Press, 2000), has persuasively argued, Jefferson was also a nation-builder with nascent nation-state ideals, which he mainly derived from his studies of the law of nature and nations. This explains his views on enslaved African Americans as a distinct "nation in chains." Onuf's conceptualization of a "nation in chains" arises solely from a historical interest in grasping Jefferson's thought. This interpretation partly follows Garry Wills's earlier arguments about Jefferson's principles on slavery. But such a purely historical interest, surprisingly enough, runs directly counter to the standard argument on the issue. For example, Judith Shklar once stated that "Wills's apology for Jefferson's airy deportation schemes, which gave the blacks their rights as 'a people,' but not, of course, as 'men,' who were individuals, is condescending and pointless" (Judith Shklar on *Inventing America: Jefferson's Declaration of Independence* by Garry Wills in *The New Republic*, August 26, 1978: 32–34). Leave off the notion of offering apologies for Jefferson and you have at hand that "oddly … convincing picture of Jefferson" Shklar herself found in Wills's book (ibid., 34).

175 Quotations, Onuf, *Jefferson's Empire*, 226, n63.

176 Let me add that subscribing to Jefferson's racism *in order to be true to the Jeffersonian tradition today* would be tantamount to claiming that in order to subscribe to any Kantian-inspired modern moral philosophy, one has to deny that women are genuinely capable of moral autonomy, because Immanuel Kant in effect did.

2 Progress in Natural and Moral Sciences

1 Charles Miller, *Jefferson and Nature*, 41–45. See ibid., esp. 41, n47.

2 On the amusing tale about garden peas, see Jack McLaughlin, *Jefferson and Monticello: A Biography* (Lawrence: University Press of Kansas, 1977), 5.

3 See TJ to (Rev.) Professor James Madison, July 19, 1788, *TJW*, 924. On Jefferson's persistent interest in astronomy, see also TJ to Dr. Ezra Stiles, July, 17, 1785, *Papers* 8: 298–300; TJ to Professor James Madison, 1785, *Papers* 8: 575–576; Rev. James Madison to TJ, March 27, 1786, *Papers* 9: 355–356.

4 TJ to Reverend (Professor) James Madison, July 19, 1788, *TJW*, 924.

5 Much later, Jefferson himself noted that ancient nations had no word for oxygen. His additional remark that they also lacked the idea of electricity illustrates how far his world of ideas was from our post-Faraday world of physics. See TJ to John Adams, August 15, 1820, *AJL*, 567. Thomas Kuhn's classic study on paradigm shifts in science used Priestley's and Lavoisier's quarrel as an example of how empiricist experiments were, and still are, related to conceptual understanding. As Robert D'Amico points out, "it is hopeless to ask who made the first discovery of oxygen." Lavoisier's claim that there is such a thing as oxygen was "a change in conceptual order rather than a triumph of observational acumen." Robert D'Amico, *Historicism and Knowledge* (New York: Routledge, 1989), 48–49.

6 TJ to John Adams, October 14, 1816, *AJL*, 491.

7 *Notes*, Query VI, *TJW*, 156.

8 See, for example, Haakonssen, Introduction to *Thomas Reid*, 38; Haakonssen, *Natural Law and Moral Philosophy*, 182–183.

9 TJ to Benjamin Rush, October 10, 1820, *L&B* 15: 284. Contrary to this view, historian Charles A. Miller over-interprets Jefferson's deistic beliefs about the embedded rationalism of nature. According to him, Jefferson's concept of nature comprised a strictly predetermined whole of both physical and moral natural laws. Miller also claims that by "adhering to the authority of nature, Jefferson ... accepted a basically deterministic [ethical] position," and ends up with an extraordinary conclusion that "in all the regions of value, Jefferson was ignorant of any problems associated with deriving a statement of value from a statement about being." For quotations, see Charles Miller, *Jefferson and Nature*, 98, 91.

10 TJ to John Trumbull, February 15, 1819, *TJW*, 939–940.

11 TJ to John Adams, August 15, 1820, *TJW*, 1443–1444. It is in this letter that Jefferson spoke of his "creed of materialism" and rejected immaterialism as a mode of atheism, the advocates of which he thought differed "from the material Atheist only in their belief that 'nothing made something,' and from the material deist who believes that matter alone can operate on matter." Obviously, Jefferson here refers to his own position as that of a material deist.

12 John Adams to TJ, January 20, 1820, *AJL*, 559–560. TJ to John Adams, March 14, 1820, ibid., 562.
13 TJ to John Adams, March 14, 1820, *AJL*, 562.
14 TJ to John Adams, May 12, 1820, *AJL*, 569. Interestingly, Jefferson's early memorandum on Bolingbroke's epistemological assumptions held that the ideas of primary qualities of matter, namely solidity and extension, while not precisely including the idea of thought or even motion, "exclude neither." Hence, one may cling to the essential properties of matter "tho' it becomes a sensitive plant, a reasoning elephant, or a refining metaphysician." *Literary CB* (§§9–11), 26–27. Bolingbroke spoke of "a substance" – some properties of which are known in contrast to a substance of which men pretend "merely to know what it is not." Ibid. (§10), 26.
15 TJ to John Adams, May 12, 1820, *AJL*, 569. For another example of Jefferson's resorting to the answer "ignoro" on the question of whether "all things have existed without beginning in time as they now exist, and may for ever exist, producing and reproducing in circle," see TJ to John Adams on May 27, 1813, *AJL*, 324. In one of the latest letters on the subject, Jefferson suggested simply that in the beginning God as well as "reason (or mind)" existed and "that mind was God." From this argument one could contend that such a mind would equal logic, (which of course represented the third kind of science even to Locke) and thus view the divine ordering of the universe as devolving from God's will so as to end up with Leibniz's famous notion of our world being the best of all the logically possible worlds. But Jefferson did not draw on Leibniz here. He aimed only at keeping himself in the middle ground between the spiritualist's position and the atheist's "simpler hypothesis of a self-existent universe." See TJ to John Adams, April 11, 1823, *TJW*, 1468.
16 TJ to John Adams, August 15, 1820, *TJW*, 1443.
17 According to Berkeley, the divine spirit could be seen as the single substance from which all qualities, primary and secondary, derived their existence as the kinds of "powers" that Locke himself held them to be. As Michael Ayers writes, Locke's "argument [on sensitive knowledge] implies that the world immediately known through sense-experience is entirely a world of powers," and on this implication Berkeley constructed his idealism. Michael Ayers, *Locke: Epistemology and Ontology* (London: Routledge, 2001), 180.
18 Jefferson's reading of the French Encyclopedia is well beyond any controversy given his numerous references to many of its most famous contributors and his own contributions to the later editions of the series regarding the history of Virginia. See for example, Douglas L. Wilson, "Jefferson and the Republic of Letters," in Onuf (ed.) *Jeffersonian Legacies*, 55.
19 See D'Alembert, "Discours Préliminaire des editeurs," *Encyclopédie* (Tome Premiere, 1751), ii, xxvii. [For a translation, see D'Alembert, *Preliminary Discourse to the Encyclopedia of Diderot*, transl. by Richard N. Schwab and Walter E. Rex (New York: Bobbs-Merrill, Library of Liberal Arts, 1963), 6–8, 83.] Or consider Dugald Stewart's remark that whenever a particular sensation excites the mind, one must be aware of "two facts at once: that of the existence of the sensation, and that of his own existence, as a sentient being." See Stewart, *The Elements of the Philosophy* (1792) in *The Works of Dugald Stewart*, 74. Lucretius could well have been one source for Jefferson's approach

to sensationalism, as historian Miller claims. Charles Miller, *Jefferson and Nature*, 27. For Thomas Reid quoting Lucretius approvingly when attacking the Humean reading of Locke, see Timothy Duggan (ed.), Thomas Reid, *An Inquiry into the Human Mind* [1764] (Chicago: Chicago University Press, 1970), 34, 258 [in other editions, see chapters 2 and 7].

20 TJ to John Adams, August 15, 1820, *TJW*, 1444. As for the term "reality," it is notable that Jefferson's correspondent, Adams, defined Berkeley's position as denying not the existence of matter, but a definite proof of its existence. John Adams to TJ, May 12, 1820, *AJL*, 563–564.

21 On Jefferson's conviction that, "Truth can stand by itself," see *Notes*, Query XVII, 286. Paradoxically, one may think that the proverbial "whole truth" should include all errors as well. What I think Jefferson's positivist epistemological position would imply today is approximately this: One may always argue that we have no guarantees that the world necessarily makes sense at all, but that it is only us humans who try to make it make sense. Even so, the sole object of scientific understanding is observable reality. Should science some day provide us with an undeniable proof about some ultimate "ontological incompleteness of reality itself" – as Slavoj Žižek suggests about the reality – such a truth, to be scientific, would still need to apply to genuinely observable reality. Natural science calls for nothing else but continued research to enrich our understanding of observable reality, which has proven to include a huge amount of things unknown to eighteenth-century scientists, such as X-rays, magnetic fields, the so-called quantum foam in the so-called voids of subatomic space-time, the Higgs boson, and the like.

As in Jefferson's time, so today, the link between scientific inquiry into observable reality and human morality lies simply in *not* linking the two. In the simplest terms, this means making a choice to believe in something beyond any scientifically observable reality or an "ontologial incompleteness of reality itself." As for ethics, the fundamental problem with the Kantian categorical imperative – which, as Žižek among others, confirms, "compels us to reject any reference to duty as an excuse"– is whether or not my conscious notion of wishing all others well is of any help to anyone else but me. A number of ethicists, from Aristotle onward, have suggested that virtue does not make itself manifest primarily in thought, but rather in right conduct, while admitting that even the truly wise and good man only "makes the best of circumstances" – a point obviously relevant to Jefferson and his circumstances. Quotations respectively from Slavoj Žižek, *Interrogating the Real*, ed. by Rex Butler and Scott Stephens (London: Continuum, 2006), 335, 331; Aristotle, *The Nicomachean Ethics* (I, 10), transl. by David Ross, J.L. Ackrill, and J.O. Urmson (Oxford: Oxford University Press, World's Classics, 1980), 21.

22 TJ to John Adams, August 15, 1820, *TJW*, 1444–1445.

23 TJ to Chastellux, June 7, 1787, *TJW*, 801.

24 In this same Chastellux letter, historian Daniel Boorstin – who famously traced a tension between Jefferson's "egalitarian faith" and his apparently scientific belief in black people's intellectual inferiority – found nothing but inconsistencies: "Since the equality of creatures had been determined once and for all by the qualities of the species at the Creation, it was nonsensical [on Jefferson's part] to express a hope that the Negro after favorable influences might 'become' equal.

Individuals not equals in the original order of creation could not by any later circumstances become so." See Daniel J. Boorstin's 1948 classic, *The Lost World of Thomas Jefferson* (Boston: Beacon Press, 1963), 94–95. In short, Boorstin's argument is that, in Jefferson's view, the given "qualities" of a black individual simply must have been determined once and for all at the Creation of all natural species. Again, what Jefferson held certain and what only probable should not be confused with one another. As this chapter shows, the main element neglected in this widely accepted general interpretation is Jefferson's conception of human faculties as capable of development.

25 For Linnaeus's definitions of the races, see MacLeod, *Slavery, Race and the American Revolution*, 171.

26 TJ to John Adams, April 11, 1823, *TJW*, 1467.

27 TJ to John Adams, March 21, 1819, *AJL*, 536. On Jefferson's taking notice of Laplace's achievements in astronomy from early on, see TJ to Professor James Madison, July 19, 1788, *TJW*, 926.

28 Peter Gay, *The Enlightenment: An Interpretation, The Science of Freedom* (New York: W.W. Norton, 1969), 143. For a similar interpretation on this issue, see Timothy Sweet, "Jefferson, Science, and the Enlightenment," in Shuffelton (ed.), *The Cambridge Companion to Thomas Jefferson*, 102. This elementary point about eighteenth-century cosmological notions is not even mentioned in, for example, Silvio A. Bedini's, *Thomas Jefferson: Statesman of Science* (New York: MacMillan, 1990). For Jefferson, it appeared quite possible that the currently incalculable routes of comets might "require renovation under some other laws" than the familiar Newtonian laws of motion. TJ to John Adams, April 11, 1823, *TJW*, 1467. There is nothing too surprising in Jefferson's awe about early nineteenth-century cosmology, given that the occurrence of novas and supernovas was not a familiar subject in contemporary astronomy. The same held true of the non-gravitational causes of minor irregularities in comets' courses. During his stay in Paris, Jefferson showed occasional interest in speculating whether the stars in outer space were "suns which have their orbits of revolution too," to the effect that the "motion of our sun would be a miniature" of some "attracting powers" that could not be thought of as conventionally existing "within the orbit" only. TJ to Professor James Madison, 1785, *Papers* 8: 575–576. See also Rev. James Madison to TJ, March 27, 1786, *Papers* 9: 355–356. Professor Madison does not here deny Jefferson's hypothesis, but notes only that no evidence can yet prove it.

29 Moreover, Jefferson was aware of Buffon's, if not also of Laplace's, historical views of the solar system as emerging from different compositions of gases millions of years ago. Jefferson's statement about the infinitude of time could have referred to the Newtonian conception of absolute linear time, the hypothetical clockwork of mere inertial motion of a piece of matter in empty space with nothing to cause a change in its speed. Rather, Jefferson seems here to have aimed solely to point out that there was no way to disprove the atheist belief in an eternally preexisting universe, just as there was no way to refute the creation of the material universe in view of some time conception independent of the current ordering of the solar system.

30 Hence, it is not at all unproblematic to state that the Jeffersonian "Nature's God" once "created the universe with law to govern it and then left it alone,"

as, for example, Allen Jayne characterizes Jefferson's religious deism. See Jayne, *Jefferson's Declaration*, 23–26, quotations in 139.

31 When translating John 1:1 as "in the beginning God existed, and reason (or mind) was with God, and that mind was God," Jefferson came very close to viewing God and the rational ordering of the universe as one and the same thing. Given that this was followed by a remark about the atheist's refusal to subscribe to the very notion of teleological causation and to prefer "the simpler hypothesis of a self-existent universe," very little was left of any purposeful immutability in nature besides the ever-transforming compositions of matter. See TJ to John Adams, April 11, 1823, *TJW*, 1467.

32 See Charles Louis Secondat, baron de Montesquieu, *The Spirit of Laws* (*L'Esprit de lois*, 1748) as in David Wallace Carrithers (ed.), *A Compendium of the First English Edition*, transl. by Thomas Nugent, London, 1750 (Berkeley: University of California Press, 1977), 99 [Bk. I, Ch. 1]. On Calvin being "indeed an Atheist," see TJ to John Adams, April 11, 1823, *TJW*, 1466.

33 For Jefferson's numerous references to Lord Kames, see, for example, his long quotations in *Legal CB* (§§ 557–565), 95–135. See also TJ to Robert Skipwith, August 3, 1771, *TJW*, 744–755; TJ to John Garland Jefferson, June 11, 1790, *TJW*, 967; TJ to Peter Carr, June 22, 1792, where he admits that Kames might be a bit too metaphysical, but still provides the "ideal system of equity," as quoted in Gilbert Chinard's 1926 "Introduction" in Chinard (ed.), *Legal CB*, 17; TJ to Thomas Law, June 13, 1814, *Extracts* 1983, 358; *Catalogue of the Library of Thomas Jefferson*, Sowerby (ed.), Vol. I, 11–12; TJ to John Minor, August 30, 1814, *Ford* 11: 420–423n.

34 Kames, *Essays*, 327.

35 On Kames being accused of the heretical doctrine of deceitful free will, see Ian Simpson Ross, *Lord Kames and the Scotland of His Day* (Oxford: Clarendon Press, 1972), 155–157.

36 TJ to John Adams, April 11, 1823, *TJW*, 1467.

37 As for this concept, it is notable how the British Royal Society formulated the ultimate premises of progressive natural sciences in 1667, "Such is the dependance among all the orders of creatures; the animate, the sensitive, the rational, the natural, the artificial; that the apprehension of one of them, is a good step towards the understanding of the rest." See Arthur O. Lovejoy's 1936 classic, *The Great Chain of Being: A Study of the History of an Idea* (Cambridge, MA: Harvard University Press, 1978), 227. The notion of the great chain of being was also referred to in the *Encyclopédie*, although the basic distinction between the epistemic ideal of classifying things and the metaphysical pursuit of linking them was recognized. Especially interesting in this context is John Locke's statement that man probably "is one of the lowest of all intellectual beings." Locke, *Essay* (4:3:23), 354. The young Jefferson's memoranda included excerpts of Bolingbroke, who argued not only that humans should perceive in other species the power of thinking, but also that "the distance between the intellectual faculties of different men, is often greater, than that between the same faculties in some men and some other animals." *Literary CB* (§12), 27–28.

38 By and large, this metaphysical notion provided an answer to the basic question of all ontology, namely, as Gottfried Wilhelm Leibniz once put it: "Why is there something rather than nothing?" *Anthology*, 315.

39 *Notes*, Query VI, 176.

40 See the statement as quoted at length in Boorstin, *The Lost World*, 36. The statement is from Jefferson's paper, which he presented at the Society in 1797. Jefferson's "whole system of things" clearly handled the concept of animate nature as something more than a mere food chain where any given animal species could be conceived of as living and reproducing in "a never ending circle" while being nothing but a source of nutrition for other species. Interestingly, the young Jefferson had copied long extracts from Bolingbroke, who insisted that, within the larger view of the entire universe – possibly including multiple worlds such as our solar system, it was rational to presume that the earth was not created for man's purposes, but instead to think that the human being was created for earth with all other animate species. See *Literary CB* (§16) 1989, 29; see also ibid. (§46), 43–44.

41 For Jefferson's constant references to the "excess of population in Europe and want of room" as opposed to America where "room is abundant" and "population scanty," see, for example, TJ to William Short, August 4, 1820, *TJW*, 1439.

42 Regarding Virginia rivers freezing for months during wintertime only a generation earlier, see *Notes*, Query VII, 207. On later climatic changes, see TJ to Lewis E. Beck, July 16, 1824 as in Charles Miller, *Jefferson and Nature*, 42.

43 Alexander Boulton, "The American Paradox: Jeffersonian Equality and Racial Science," *American Quarterly* 47 (1995), 480.

44 *Notes*, Query VI, 176.

45 Quotation from Boorstin, *The Lost World*, 256n.

46 TJ to John Adams, April 8, 1816, *AJL*, 467–468.

47 Lovejoy, *The Great Chain of Being*, 269.

48 *Notes*, Query VI, 170.

49 TJ to John Adams, April 8, 1816, *AJL*, 467–468.

50 TJ to John Adams, April 11, 1823, *TJW*, 1467.

51 TJ to Dr. John Manners, February 22, 1814, *TJW*, 1329.

52 TJ to John Adams, August 15, 1820, *TJW*, 1444.

53 TJ to John Adams, March 14, 1820, *AJL*, 562.

54 See Stewart (1792) *The Elements of Philosophy*, 295.

55 See Vol. I, Sec. II in Antoine Louis Claude, Destutt de Tracy, *A Treatise on Political Economy to which is Prefixed a Supplement to a Preceding Work on the Understanding or, Elements of Ideology*, translation edited by Thomas Jefferson 1817 [with Jefferson's Compliments dated as October 28, 1818], (Reprint, New York: Augustus M. Kelley Publishers, 1970), 40. Apparently following Reid, Dugald Stewart contended that external objects cause different kinds of impressions on different senses of the observer, and given that these different cause-effect relations of different senses were largely unknown, one should speak only of various kinds of sensations occurring in the mind. Hence, one could even hold that the sense-perception only follows sensation. Stewart, *The Elements of Philosophy*, 68, 258. Charles Miller remarks that Jefferson acquired a conceptualist position without realizing that it derived from the medieval nominalism-realism controversy. This reading appears to presume that Jefferson had not read Dugald Stewart, who depicted this position as more or less the proper reading of Locke. Cf. Charles Miller, *Jefferson and Nature*, 34, n35 and Stewart, *Elements of Philosophy*, 142.

56 TJ to John Adams, March 14, 1820, *AJL*, 562.
57 TJ to John Adams, March 14, 1820, *AJL*, 562. Later on, Jefferson noted that Flourens had managed to prove the cerebrum to be the thinking organ in the absence of which, certain primitive animals could still be kept alive. TJ to John Adams, January 8, 1825, *AJL*, 606.
58 TJ to John Adams October 14, 1816, *AJL*, 492.
59 *Notes*, Query VI, 182.
60 *Notes*, Query VI, 190.
61 *Notes*, Query VI, 170.
62 See Boulton, "The American Paradox," 481. On the question of whether the elephant and the mammoth represented the same species, neither Buffon nor Jefferson had any evidence from the criterion of fertility. But Jefferson does not appear to have given any notice to this criterion, which was presented only in the 6th volume of Buffon's *History of Nature*. Instead, Jefferson drew on circumstantial evidence in arguing that the animals cannot be of the same species: "Thus nature seems to have drawn a belt of separation between these two tremendous animals ... to have assigned to the elephant the regions South of these confines, and those North to the mammoth, founding the constitution of the one in her extreme of heat, and that of the other in the extreme of cold. When the Creator has therefore separated their nature as far as the extent of the scale of animal life allowed to this planet would permit, it seems perverse to declare it the same, from a partial resemblance of their tusks and bones." *Notes*, Query VI, 169. When speaking of the mouse and the mammoth, Jefferson referred to the influence of environment on "every race of animals," thus using the term race as a synonym for species. See ibid., 169.
63 *Notes*, Query VI, 156. For Jefferson's later statement that "it is generally agreed that rocks grow," see TJ to Charles Thomson, September 20, 1787 as in Charles Miller, *Jefferson and Nature*, 47.
64 *Notes*, Query VI, 170.
65 *Notes*, Query XIV, 267.
66 *Notes*, Query XIV, 270. Whether Jefferson had other, nonscientific, motives for advocating such a research cannot be decided on the basis of this statement. He made it perfectly clear elsewhere in the *Notes on the State of Virginia* that the institution of slavery itself debilitated both the masters and the slaves. To the extent that slavery had fostered Jefferson's racism, one may infer that he would have rather seen science proving his preconceptions than forcing him to change them. As for the vast historical literature dealing with the origins of racism as related to American slavery and to the burgeoning, eighteenth-century "scientific" notion of race, see, for example, David Brion Davis, *Slavery and Human Progress* (1984); Robert Fogel, *Without Consent or Contract: The Rise and Fall of American Slavery* (1992); Eugene D. Genovese, *The World the Slaveholders Made* (1971); Winthrop Jordan, *White over Black: American Attitudes Toward the Negro 1550–1812* (1969). See also the good collection of classic articles on the theme, Peter Charles Hoffer (ed.), *Africans become Afro-Americans: Selected Articles on Slavery in the American Colonies* (1988) in which particularly interesting are Stanley Elkins and Eric McKitrick, "Institutions and the Law of Slavery: Slavery in Capitalist and Non-Capitalist Cultures" (*American Quarterly*, No. 9, 1957) and Carl N. Degler, "Slavery and

the Genesis of American Race Prejudice" (*Comparative Studies in Society and History*, No. 2, 1959). A fruitful starting point for anyone interested in the complexity of these issues is Eric Williams's debatable remark from as early a date as 1944 that slavery "was not born of racism: rather, racism was the consequence of slavery." See Eric Williams, *Capitalism & Slavery*, ed. by Colin A. Palmer (Chapel Hill: University of North Carolina Press, 1994), 7. The debate over the scientific premises of the biological determinants of human behavior as related to human differences in ethnic origin, sex, and intelligence is very much alive. For a renowned introduction to the topic, see Ullica Segerstråle, *The Defenders of the Truth: The Sociobiology Debate* (Oxford and New York: Oxford University Press, 2001).

67 *Notes*, Query XIV, *TJW*, 264–265.

68 *Notes*, Query XIV, *TJW*, 265. Here the term "Orang Outang" did not refer to the East-Indian species, but to African apes or anthropoids. Whether it had anything to do with distinguishing between monkeys and apes is equally difficult to decide from Jefferson's statements.

69 MacLeod, *Slavery, Race and the American Revolution*, 174. On this eighteenth-century "problem" about the Africans' humanity as discussed by Charles de Bonnet, Edward Long, Lord Monboddo, and many others, see, for example, Kaija Tianen-Anttila, *The Problem of Humanity: The Blacks in the European Enlightenment* (Helsinki: SHS, 1994), 103–111.

70 For a direct reference to Linnaeus by Jefferson, see *Notes*, Query VI, 187.

71 The basic categories were thus classes, orders, genera, and species. The *class of mammals* was divided into the *orders of primates and other mammals*, such as "*Bruta*" (e.g., elephants and sloths), "*Ferae*" (e.g., seals and cats), "*Bestiae*" (e.g., pigs and moles), and so forth. The order of primates itself was divided into the two *genera*, *Homo* and *Simia*. Finally, the *genus Homo* was divided into two *species* of humans and anthropoids, and the *genus Simia* into different species of monkeys and apes generally.

72 Boorstin, *The Lost World*, 82.

73 On Linnaeus's catalogue of the races, as arranged according to "*varians cultura, loco*" see, for example, Tianen-Anttila, *The Problem of Humanity*, 104. Notably, historian Duncan J. MacLeod considers the Primates to be the genus and Homo to be the species. Be that as it may, Linnaeus's characterizations of the four main races of man are interesting reflections of ethnic conceptions of his time: The Indians he described as "reddish," "choleric," "nervy and free," and as "regulated by custom." The Europeans were "white, sanguine, muscular," "gentle," and "governed by law." The Asians were "sallow, melancholy," "avaricious," and "ruled by opinions." The Africans were "black, phlegmatic," "crafty, indolent," their "women without shame," and they were generally "governed by caprice." See MacLeod, *Slavery, Race and the Revolution*, 71. One may compare MacLeod's summary to that of Gould's, which is clearly drawn from pages 21–22 of the standard, 10th edition of Carolus Linnaeus, *Systema Naturae* (Holmiae, Editio Decima, Reformata, Vol I, 1758): "... in his last line of description for every variety ... [Linnaeus] tries to epitomize supposed behavior in a single word following the statement *regitur* (ruled) – for the American, *consuetudine* (by habit); for the European, *ritibus* (by custom); for the Asian, *opinionibus* (by belief); for the African, *arbitrio* (by caprice)." Stephen Jay Gould, *I Have*

Landed: The End of a Beginning in Natural History (Harvard University Press, 2011), 360. Let me add that Senior Lecturer in Classics Timo Sironen from the University of Oulu informed me that the term, "*ritibus*," means ceremonies. Perhaps Linnaeus's reference to the specific European mode of "rule" simply denoted the Christian rule(s) of Calvinist, Catholic, and Lutheran clergy.

74 See Lovejoy, *Great Chain of Being*, 230–236. Edward Long's widely read *The History of Jamaica* (1774) suggested directly that the Negro and the "orang outang" would together comprise the missing link. See on this, MacLeod, *Slavery, Race and the American Revolution*, 173. MacLeod also refers to an anonymous pamphlet, "Personal Slavery Established," published in Pennsylvania in 1773, which serves well to further illustrate this trend of thought. After noting that the human race has been divided into four or five species of men, the anonymous author limits them to four: the Europeans, the Asians, the Americans, and the Africans. The fundamental thesis, however, is that of "retracting the word *species*, substitute *genus*, which is more expressive" as a "general term" for distinguishing "the Africans as only a species of that *genus*," and then dividing the genus into five "*classes*" of Africans, orang outangs, apes, baboons and monkeys. *Personal Slavery Established by the Suffrages of Custom and Right Reason*, Anonymous, (Philadelphia, 1773), 18–19.

75 See Lovejoy, *Great Chain of Being*, 227–241; MacLeod, *Slavery, Race and the American Revolution*, 170–182. It is equally important to bear in mind that even modern scholars cannot always agree on how to categorize the eighteenth-century thinkers in terms of their racial views. Voltaire has been regarded as an advocate of both polygenesis and monogenesis. See Tiainen-Anttila, *The Problem of Humanity*, 76n.

76 *Notes*, Query XIV, 270.

77 Yet, none of this warrants Daniel Boorstin's classic claim that, according to Jefferson's scientific beliefs, "individuals not equals in the original order of creation could not by any later circumstances become so." Boorstin, *The Lost World*, 94–95. As late as 1825, Jefferson endorsed Frances Wright's famous experiment of a black cooperative colony in Tennessee by a confusingly "well-meaning" statement that "it would be a solecism to suppose a race of animals created, without sufficient foresight and energy to preserve their existence." Again, black people could be of distinct, genetic origins from the whites. TJ to Frances Wright on August 9, 1825 as in Boorstin, *The Lost World*, 97.

78 TJ to John Manners, February 22, 1814, *TJW*, 1329.

79 *Notes*, Query XIV, 269. One of Jefferson's most respected authorities in the field, Benjamin Rush, speculated about leprosy being a generic disease among the Africans causing their skin color. Boorstin, *The Lost World*, 90–91.

80 As late as 1814, Jefferson referred to Buffon's "no-system" of natural species and to the "*tout ensemble*, which Buffon makes his sole principle of arrangement." Instead of relying on the latest elaborations of natural science by Blumenbach and Cuvier, Jefferson simply preferred holding to Linnaeus's system as "sufficient as a ground-work" owing to its having obtained "the general consent." TJ to Dr. John Manners, February 22, 1814, *TJW*, 1330–1332.

81 Quotations in *Notes*, Query XIV, 268, 270.

82 See MacLeod, *Slavery, Race and the American Revolution*, 174, 181. Interestingly, Lord Kames claimed that, for Buffon, man and dog were of the same genus.

Moreover, Kames consistently held the concept of race as equivalent to not only the species but also to the "kinds" of men. See Lord Kames (Henry Home), *Six Sketches on the History of Man* (Philadelphia, 1776), e.g., 7, 13, 45.

83 *Notes*, Query XIV, 270 (emphasis added).

84 *Notes*, Query XIV, 270.

85 This conception was not outright refuted even by Darwin, even though it has very little to do with what is today counted as biological evolution.

86 Lovejoy, *Great Chain of Being*, 269.

87 *Notes*, Query VI, 187 (emphasis added). With this reservation in mind, it is interesting that Jefferson does not appear to doubt at all that certain "radical changes of language having taken place among the red men of America, proves them of greater antiquity than those of Asia." Ibid., 227.

88 *Notes*, Query XIV, 269 (emphasis added).

89 *Notes*, Query VI, 191. Rittenhouse was known for his model of the planetary system, called the "Orrery." Moreover, Jefferson insisted that Hadley's quadrant was first invented by an American named Godfrey.

90 *Notes*, Query VI, 189.

91 On the terms used here, see *Notes*, Query XIV, 264.

92 *Notes*, Query XIV, 264.

93 *Notes*, Query XIV, 264–265.

94 *Notes*, Query XIV, 265.

95 *Notes*, Query XIV, 267.

96 *Notes*, Query VI, 187. Jefferson speculated about the racial determinants of the Indian in this earlier chapter of his book. Even there his evidence was mainly cultural.

97 For the term "genius" as related to the Indian and Euro-Americans compared to the French, see *Notes*, Query VI, 189, 191.

98 *Notes*, Query XIV, 266

99 *Notes*, Query XIV, 273–274.

100 TJ to John Langdon, March 5, 1810, *TJW*, 1221–1222.

101 TJ to John Adams, Jauary 8, 1825, *AJL*, 606.

102 *Notes*, Query XIV, 264.

103 TJ's Notes from Condorcet on Slavery, January 1789, *Papers* 14: 496.

104 *Notes*, Query XIV, 269.

105 TJ to Peter Carr, August 10, 1787, *TJW*, 901–902.

106 TJ to Peter Carr, August 10, 1787, *TJW*, 901–902. TJ to Peter Carr, August 10, 1787, *Papers* 12: 15. In the *Essays on the Active Powers of Man*, Thomas Reid's principles of morals involved both the notion of paying "attention to moral instruction" and that of "maintaining a lively sense of the beauty of right conduct." *Anthology*, 642.

107 Wills, *Inventing America*, 149–150.

108 As in Smith, *TMS*, 320.

109 As noted, according to Hutcheson, people must first and foremost approve benevolence as the basic motive of all morality and goodness, and only then may grasp the unbound benevolence of God. On this elementary point, see Schneewind, *Invention of Autonomy*, 339. Whether Hutcheson was "truly" a moral sentimentalist as Schneewind argues or a "moral sense cognitivist" as Knud Haakonssen believes, or a "moral realist" as David Norton holds, one

need not decide here. On this problem, see, for example, ibid. and Haakonssen, "Introduction" in Haakonssen (ed.), *Thomas Reid*, 53. Hutcheson's "moral realism" would consist of believing, first, that benevolence and self-love together comprise the *quality* of human nature as the object of moral judgment, and, second, that the correlation between the moral quality involved and the judgment is objective in character (true and false), not a subjective feeling in the mind of the observer. Haakonssen, *Natural Law and Moral Philosophy*, 73–74. In Jefferson's eyes, Hutcheson most probably was a moral sentimentalist, particularly in comparison to natural lawyers.

110 As noted earlier, Shaftesbury argued that the fear of hell cannot imply conscience, "unless where there is an apprehension of what is wrong" and, thus, concluded that "religious conscience supposes moral or natural conscience." Quotation in *Anthology*, 498.

111 Smith, *TMS* (Part VII), 322.

112 For this summary explanation of Hutcheson's position, see Haakonssen, *Natural Law and Moral Philosophy*, 73–74, 79.

113 Schneewind, *Invention of Autonomy*, 334.

114 Smith, *TMS*, 326.

115 On Reid's moral faculty in comparison to that of Hutcheson, see Haakonssen, "Introduction" in Haakonssen (ed.), *Thomas Reid*, 52–53.

116 Both Smith's *Theory of Moral Sentiments* and Reid's *Inquiry on the Human Mind* are included in Jefferson's first known list of recommended readings for his friends and acquaintances from 1771. Jefferson probably came to know Hutcheson's doctrines first through these authors as well as through Lord Kames, whose "Natural Religion" is included as well. TJ to Robert Skipwith, August 3, 1771 (with the enclosure of the recommended books), *TJW*, 740–745. Later on, Jefferson recommended Hutcheson's *A Short Introduction to Moral Philosophy* in the field of ethics and natural religion, TJ to John Minor, August 30, 1814, *Ford* 11: 422n.

117 On this elementary point, see, for example, Schneewind, *Invention of Autonomy*, 339.

118 TJ to John Adams October 14, 1816, *AJL*, 492 (emphasis added). In this letter, Jefferson explicitly connected the moral sense with the origins of justice by stating that justice results from "the construction of man." As usual, he referred to his own position as a mere belief.

119 *Notes*, Query XIV, 269. See for Jefferson's use of the natural "moral sense of right and wrong," as something even all savage Indians share with the rest of humankind. *Notes*, Query XI, 220.

120 For example, James Wilson's famous writings on natural law teemed with references to Bacon, Bolingbroke, Kames, and other favorite authorities of Jefferson's. Preferring Thomas Reid over John Locke, Wilson unequivocally refuted the Lockean notion of knowledge as based solely on ideas. See James Wilson, *The Works of the Honourable James Wilson, L.L.D.* [Published by Bird Wilson, Vol. 1] (Philadelphia: Bronson and Chauncey, 1804), passim., e.g., 73, 260. Although Wilson's views appear reconcilable with Jefferson's formulations, I have no evidence that Jefferson ever read this particular work.

121 TJ to Thomas Law, June 13, 1814, *Extracts*, 355–358.

122 To offer a more or less conventional reading of Locke's basic claims about moral concepts: Even though Locke admitted that the notions of good and evil devolve from the (simple) ideas of pleasure and pain, he also maintained that moral ideas are attainable only by reconciling the sensations with the complex idea of law. According to Locke, therefore, people first acquire the notions of good and evil through the sensations of pleasure and pain, which could amount to what are often called life goods. Still, one attains proper moral notions only as the complex ideas of good and bad. These ideas, in turn, are fully comprehensible only through the tripartite view of the term "law" as God's law, civil law, and the law of opinion. See Locke, *Essay* (2:28:5–7), 351–352. On the Scottish writers' effort to deepen this view beyond sheer law-conceptions, see Haakonssen, *Natural Law and Moral Philosophy*, 52–53. On Locke's allegedly voluntarist position, see Schneewind, *Invention of Autonomy*, 145–151.

123 TJ to Richard Price, July 11, 1788 as in Jefferson's *Catalogue of the Library*, Sowerby (ed.), Vol. II, 9.

124 TJ to Edward Bancroft, January 12, 1789, *Papers* 14: 492–493.

125 TJ to Thomas Law, June 13, 1814, *Extracts*, 355–358 (quotation in ibid., 355). See also Thomas Law, *Second Thoughts on Instinctive Impulses* (Philadelphia, 1813, "printed for the author," 143 pages.) [Micprint 8, No 28918, University of Virginia]. In his essay, Law frequently speaks of "the benevolent system of Providence" (ibid., e.g., 125) and general "moral improvement" (ibid., e.g., 3).The essay also includes brief comparisons of Hutcheson, Reid, and Stewart as well as a fairly standard account of classical republicanism. Law clearly favors Hutcheson's position over Reid's contention that moral judgments must precede the actual moral feelings.

126 Jefferson stated that "of all the theories on the question, the most whimsical seems to have been that of Woollaston, who considers truth as the foundation of morality." TJ to Thomas Law, June 13, 1814, *Extracts*, 355.

127 TJ to Thomas Law, June 13, 1814, *Extracts*, 355–358 (quotations in ibid., 356).

128 Helvétius, *De l'Esprit* as in *Anthology*, 417.

129 TJ to Thomas Law, June 13, 1814, *Extracts*, 356–357.

130 TJ to Robert Skipwith, August 3, 1771, *Papers* 1: 76–77. Indeed, Jefferson here held that "a lively and lasting sense of filial duty is more effectually impressed on the mind of a son or daughter by reading King Lear, than by all the dry volumes of ethics."

131 TJ to John Adams, October 14, 1816, *AJL*, 492.

132 TJ to Thomas Law, June 13, 1814, *Extracts*, 356–357.

133 On Hutcheson, see Haakonssen, *Natural Law and Moral Philosophy*, 71.

134 Smith, *TMS*, 9.

135 Kames, *Essays*, 57.

136 In sum, Kames's moral sense distinguished three kinds of qualities of deliberate human action. The qualities comprised first, the agent's intention being *right* (just); second, the agent's deliberation being *fit* (morally acceptable); and third, the agent's particular choice of action being *meet* (effective) in terms of sheer utility. All the conditions of just motivation, moral acceptability of the chosen means, and their effectiveness had to apply simultaneously. See *Essays*, 49–52.

137 *Essays*, 146–147. Notably, Jefferson referred to savage Indians' inhumane warfare even in the Declaration of Independence.
138 TJ to Edward Bancroft, January 12, 1789, *Papers* 14: 492–493.
139 TJ to Thomas Law, June 13, 1814, *Extracts*, 358. Kames himself stated that "No action therefore is a duty, to the performance of which we are not prompted by some natural principle," *Essays*, 77. Kames's natural principles consisted of two kinds: self-regarding principles and principles regarding others. As the natural principles for any individual human being they always apperared together, and hence comprised of self-preservation, self-love (or a desire for one's own happiness), fidelity, gratitude and benevolence "in proportion to the distance of particular objects." Ibid., 87–90.
140 TJ to Thomas Law, June 13, 1814, *Extracts*, 357.
141 TJ to Joseph Priestley, April 9, 1803, *TJW*, 1121.
142 *Notes*, Query XVIII, *TJW*, 288–289.
143 *Notes*, Query XVIII, *TJW*, 288.
144 Miriam Brody Kramnick (ed.), Mary Wollstonecraft, *Vindication of the Rights of Woman* [1792] (Harmondsworth: Penguin Books, 1978), 86. On Wollstonecraft's lamentation that soldiers (educated only to gallantry) and (women educated only to please) "both acquire manners before morals," see ibid., 106.
145 *TMS* (Part V), 209. On Smith's view that an uninterrupted *custom* may authorize a permanent *practice* to the extent that such superior philosophers as Aristotle and Plato erroneously approved of the barbarous practice of killing infants, see ibid., 210–211. As noted, the difference between "morals" and "manners" was not self-evident. For the notion that customs, for example, would generally refer to "exterior conduct" and "manners" to interior conduct, see Nugent's 1750 translation of Montesqueiu's *Spirit of Laws*, 294 [Bk. XIX, Ch. 16]. It is worth noting that Nugent also translated Burlamaqui's "moeurs" as "mores or manners." See J.J. Burlamaqui, *The Principles of Natural Law in which the True Principle of Morality and Civil Government are Established* (*Principes du droit naturel,* Geneva 1747), translated by Mr. Nugent, London, 1748 (Reprint Clark, NJ: The Lawbook Exchange, 2003), 111.
146 *Notes*, Query XVIII, 288. For Jefferson speaking of "daily habits" as preventing people from properly "reflecting" moral issues, see, for example, TJ to Edward Coles, August 25, 1814, *TJW*, 1344.
147 *Notes*, Query XVIII, 288.
148 TJ to Joseph Priestley, April 9, 1803, *TJW*, 1121.
149 TJ to John Adams, October 12, 1813, *TJW*, 1300–1301. (Jefferson relied here on William Enfield's abridged translation of Brucker's huge volume.)
150 TJ to John Adams, October 12, 1813, *TJW*, 1300.
151 TJ to John Adams, May 27, 1813, *AJL*, 323.
152 *Notes*, Query VI, 185–186. Jefferson's explanation for the apparent fact than an "Indian man is small in the hand and wrist" was that the Native-American woman, by contrast, is "submitted to unjust drudgery" of manual work, and was thus also "habituated to labour and formed by it."
153 TJ to Dugald Stewart, April 26, 1824, *TJW*, 1488.
154 Stewart, *Elements of Philosophy*, 287. At this point, Stewart approvingly quotes Archbishop King.
155 TJ to Thomas Earle, September 24, 1823, *L&B* 15: 471.

156 *Notes*, Query XIV, 268–269.
157 *Notes*, Query XIV, 269.
158 TJ to Edward Bancroft, January 12, 1789, *Papers* 14: 492–493.
159 TJ to Edward Coles, August 25, 1814, *TJW*, 1344–1345.
160 Garry Wills famously argued that although Jefferson considered black people inferior to the whites, the inequalities were of "head and body, not of heart, not of the affective basis for all equality, the moral sense." (Wills, *Inventing America*, 217; see also ibid, 225, 304.) The problem with Wills's fully sentimentalist reading of Jefferson's morality is that even if a white slaveholder acknowledges such "an affectionate basis for all equality" with his black slave, he may still argue for other inequalities between them to the effect that no moral obligation to free the slave would necessarily follow. That was certainly not Jefferson's position, for moral equality had to be grounded on equal freedom. In other words, Wills's conceptualization is dangerously close to justifying any practical application of a merely *theoretical* moral equality arising from one or another set of presumed human characteristics.
161 TJ to Edward Coles, August 25, 1814, *TJW*, 1344–1345.
162 TJ to Edward Bancroft, January 12, 1789, *Papers* 14: 492–493.
163 TJ to John Lynch, January 21, 1811, *TJW*, 1240.
164 TJ to Thomas Earle, September 24, 1823, *L&B* 15:471.
165 *Notes*, Query XIV, 264.
166 TJ to Edward Coles, August 25, 1814, *TJW*, 1345.
167 TJ to Albert Gallatin, December 26, 1820, *TJW*, 1450.
168 TJ to Jared Sparks, February 4, 1824, *TJW*, 1484.
169 TJ to Thomas Law, June 13, 1814, *Extracts*, 335.
170 TJ to Thomas Law, June 13, 1814, *Extracts*, 355. Notably, presuming truth to be the foundation of morality was in Jefferson's view "as if a tree taken by its roots, had its stem reversed in the air, and one of its branches planted in the ground." The symbol most probably denoted the traditional "tree of knowledge" used by Francis Bacon as well as the Encyclopedists. It can also be associated with Thomas Reid's epistemology of the common sense. In Reid's tree of knowledge, "the root" represented the commonsense perceptions, "the trunk" mankind's common understanding, and "the branches" the various philosophical and scientific results of human inquiry. See on this argument, for example, Wills, *Inventing America*, 185. On Reid's view, see his *An Inquiry into the Human Mind* (1764), 212–214.
171 The concept of equity devolved from the very notion that human knowledge of natural law remains imperfect. A Bill for Establishing Religious Freedom, *Papers* 2: 545.
172 Destutt de Tracy, *A Commentary*, 97. The problem was handled in Chapter XI, which was the only one Jefferson personally translated.
173 White, *The Philosophy of the American Revolution*, 201. Jefferson might also have had in mind the distinction between the notions of consciousness and attention made by both Thomas Reid and Dugald Stewart. According to Stewart, our consciousness is "an involuntary state of mind," whereas attention would refer to "a voluntary act." Stewart, *The Elements of Philosophy* (1792), 89. According to Thomas Reid, ignoring this distinction was one of Locke's most serious errors. See ibid., 89n.

174 TJ to John Adams, August 22, 1813, *AJL*, 368. See also Yarbrough, *American Virtues*, 177.

175 TJ to John Adams, April 11, 1823, *Extracts*, 410.

176 TJ to John Adams, October 14, 1816, *AJL*, 492. Destutt de Tracy's catalogue of the faculties, common to both man and animal, consisted of feeling, recollecting, judging, and willing. Destutt de Tracy, *A Treatise of Political Economy* (1817), Part I, 37–38.

177 TJ to Peter Carr, August 10, 1787, *TJW*, 900–906.

178 TJ to Peter Carr, August 10, 1787, *TJW*, 901. After this remark, Jefferson went on to explain that man was destined for society and his morality was formed to this object, and that the moral sense, rather than truth or beauty, indeed, "is the true foundation of morality." This comment, which was offered to the young Peter Carr, is conspicuously exceptional among Jefferson's numerous, more restricted statements on the issue. In fact, it looks like one of his rare Homeric nods given his general unwillingness to subscribe to particular theoretical doctrines. Even in his most outspoken statement on the issue, the letter to Thomas Law, Jefferson referred to the general theory of the moral sense numerous times only as compatible with his "belief" or "creed," but not once as definitely "true."

179 Thomas Reid in the *Essays on the Active Powers of the Human Mind* (1788), Essay V, Ch. 4, as in *Anthology*, 646.

180 In essence, the Frenchman held that, because people are often unaware of their precise motives in behaving as they do, they are essentially neither evil nor altruistic. Instead, people are driven by a number of motives – all of which can be reduced to self-interest in the final analysis. Eventually, even public virtue coincides with the genuine human self-interest, which also includes helping one's fellow citizens, because of the natural emotional pain that any humane man feels at "the sight of another's misfortunes." As Helvétius states the case, men "are not cruel and perfidious, but carried away by their own interest." Moralists should therefore not complain about people's wickedness but about the ignorance of legislators placing private interest ahead of the public one. Eventually, a "man is just when all his actions tend to the public welfare," the criterion of justice being "the public utility." True virtue, in turn, is "desire of general happiness." As to the factual state of things, Helvétius notes that there "is not that penurious wretch on earth which has not once behaved with generosity," meaning that "no perfection, either with regard vice or virtue, is to be found on the earth." Quotations respectively in Helvétius, *De l'Esprit* as in *Anthology*, 418n, 419, 421, 416–417.

181 Jefferson certainly believed in the seminal idea of all virtue ethics that one should get in the control of one's own passions and affections. But, as Helvétius notes, "we cannot judge of intentions.... It is seldom or never that action is the effect of a sentiment; we ourselves are often ignorant of the motives by which we are determined." Helvétius, *De l'Esprit* as in *Anthology*, 417. Alternatively, think of Reid's argument against Hume's famous maxim that morality is "more properly felt than judged of." Reid insisted that when "I exercise my moral faculty ... I am conscious that I judge as well as feel.... That other men judge, as well as feel ... I am convinced, because they understand me when I express

my moral judgment." Hence, one may first judge another man's conduct as highly approvable, and then consider how agreeable a feeling it provided for the observer. Such words as "decision, determination, sentence, approbation, disapprobation, applause," and the like "necessarily imply judgment in their meaning," whereas Hume erroneously thought that they "signify feelings only." Reid, *Essays on the Active Powers of the Human Mind* (1788) as in *Anthology*, 646–648. Thus, Reid concluded that the "first principles of morals are not deductions. They are self-evident." Ibid., 649. In sum, Reid considered Hume's view as simply and thoroughly subjective, whereas Reid held, as Knud Haakonssen states, that "the goodness of the action itself does not depend on the motive." Haakonssen, "Introduction" in Haakonssen (ed.), *Thomas Reid*, 54–55.

182 TJ to Mrs. Samuel H. Smith, August 6, 1816, *TJW*, 1404. Or, as Jefferson here also noted, "it is in our lives, and not from our words, that our religion must be read."

183 TJ to John Adams, October 14, 1816, *AJL*, 492.

184 For Smith's famous endorsement of Grotius and other natural lawyers, see the end of *TMS* (Part VII), 341–342. What Smith said about the real facts of life was that in "no country do the decisions of positive law coincide exactly, in every case, with the rules which the natural sense of justice would dictate." Hence, "[s]ystems of positive law," although they deserve to be seen as "the records of the sentiments of mankind in different ages and nations, yet can never be regarded as accurate systems of the rules of natural justice." Smith also defined "a system of what might properly be called natural jurisprudence" here as "a theory of the general principles which ought to run through and be the foundation of the laws of all nations." Ibid., 341.

185 TJ, Opinion on the French Treaties, April 28, 1793, *TJW*, 428.

186 TJ to John Adams, October 14, 1816, *AJL*, 492.

187 TJ to John Adams, October 14, 1816, *AJL*, 492.

188 TJ to Thomas Law, June 13, 1814, *Extracts*, 355.

189 Kames, *Essays*, 55, 121. Kames argued first against Hutcheson's benevolence as apparently excluding justice and then against Shaftesbury's view that "partial benevolence" would not be "benevolence at all." Ibid., 121.

190 *Notes*, Query XVIII, 289.

191 TJ to Edward Carrington, January 16, 1787, *TJW*, 880.

192 TJ to Samuel Kercheval, July 12, 1816. *TJW*, 1401.

193 TJ to John Bannister, Jr., October 15, 1785, *TJW*, 839.

194 TJ to P.S. Dupont de Nemours, January 18, 1802, *TJW*, 1101. (Here Jefferson also gave Hamilton the credit as the originator of false principles, although he – in the midst of his administration's efforts to pay off the national debt – somewhat ambiguously went on to state that "we can never get rid of his financial system.")

195 TJ to Monsieur A. Coray, October 31, 1823, *L&B* 15: 484.

196 TJ to John Adams, April 11, 1823, *TJW*, 1466–1469.

197 TJ to John Adams, April 11, 1823, *TJW*, 1467.

198 TJ to Jared Sparks, February 4, 1824, *TJW*, 1487.

199 *Notes*, Query XIV, 264.

200 "Suarez puts forward," says Haakonssen, "the old chestnut, now mainly known from Hume, that the same form of behavior in an animal and in a person ... has no moral significance in the former case." Haakonssen, *Natural Law and Moral Philosophy*, 19. Similarly, Pufendorf held that without "the guidance of natural law, human volition and human action would be natural, non-moral phenomena like those we find in the rest of animal creation." Ibid., 38.

201 Emer de Vattel in the Preface to *Le Droit de gens* (1758) as in Emerich de Vattel, *The Law of Nations: Or Principles of the Law of Nature Applied to the Conduct and Affairs of Nations and Sovereigns*, transl. by Joseph Chitty (6th American edition, Philadelphia, 1844), v.

202 For example, Adam Smith appeared to hold the incapacity to discern moral qualities as a disability when noting that a man "so absurdly constituted as to approve of cruelty and injustice as the highest virtues," simply has "such a constitution of mind" as to be regarded "unnatural in itself." See *TMS* (Part VII), 323. As Reid put it, "I take it for granted ... that every man of real honor feels an abhorrence of certain actions, because they are in themselves base." Reid, *Essays on the Active Powers of the Human Mind* (1788) as in *Anthology*, 636. Similarly, Reid noted that to "reason about justice with a man who sees nothing to be just or unjust ... is like reasoning with a blind man about color." Ibid, 639. Or consider Helvétius's remark that "He who to be virtuous must always conquer his inclinations, must necessarily be a wicked man." Helvétius, *De l'Esprit* as in ibid., 427.

203 On the moral realm appearing to Hutcheson as that of qualities and to Reid as that of relations, see Haakonssen, "Introduction" in Haakonssen (ed.), *Thomas Reid*, 54.

204 TJ to John Adams, March 14, 1820, *AJL*, 562. A brief note on the qualities of moral action as related to historical views is in place here. As Knud Haakonssen puts it, Dugald Stewart (one of Jefferson's favorite authorities) perhaps ended up simply claiming "that mankind has always and everywhere had some sort of morality" as a result of its capacity to distinguish some, but not all the simple qualities of action. Haakonssen scorns this because of Stewart's strong brand of objectivism (being a realist rather than an idealist kind of objectivism). Stewart's theoretical view appears to have been that all qualities of action are simple qualities, meaning that they are God-given and hence truly existing regardless of man's incapability of always discerning them. (See Haakonssen, *Natural Law and Moral Philosophy*, 230–231.) If Haakonssen's view of Stewart is correct, there is a gap between the intellectual outlook of Jefferson and Stewart. According to Haakonssen, "Stewart's historicist notion of the march of the mind is combined with a realist and cognitivist moral theory" indicating "that politics and the law increasingly will become marginal as the morally well-ordered society emerges spontaneously" (ibid., 256–257, 264.) This, however, tells us nothing about Jefferson's problems in putting general education and equal rights in force until such spontaneous development would take place, not to mention that Jefferson does not appear to have ever submitted to such spontaneity. Here Haakonssen's "historicist" appears to refer to simply a deterministic view of history.

205 TJ to John Heaton, May 20, 1826, *TJW*, 1516.

3 Progress and the Wise Man's Virtue

1 TJ to Benjamin Rush, September 23, 1800, *TJW*, 1081.

2 TJ to John Adams, October 28, 1813, *AJL*, 388. Even with its elitist implications, Jefferson's definition appears a good deal easier to grasp than John Adams's confusingly conservative definition of natural aristocracy as comprising "a few in whom all [the] advantages of birth, fortune, and fame are united." See Adams, *A Defence of the American Constitutions* (1787) as in George A. Peek Jr. (ed.), *The Political Writings of John Adams* (New York: The Liberal Art Press, 1954), 138–139. That John Adams did not regard "talents" as inborn individual capacities to be cultivated is implicated in his oddly liberal list of talents including "Education, Wealth, Strength, Beauty, Statute, Birth" as well as such notions as "Genius and Science and learning." Adams to TJ, November 15, 1813, *AJL*, 398.

3 TJ to William Short, August 4, 1820, *TJW*, 1437.

4 TJ to Thomas Law, June 13, 1814, *Extracts*, 356. Jefferson made it fully clear here that self-love was "the sole antagonist of virtue, leading us constantly by our propensities to self-gratification in violation of our moral duties to others. Accordingly it is against this enemy that are erected the batteries of moralists and religionists, as the only obstacle to the practice of morality. Take from man his selfish propensities, and he can have nothing to seduce him from the practice of virtue." Ibid.

5 On the young Jefferson's acquaintance with ancient virtue ethics, see his several-pages-long excerpts from Greek and Roman moralists in *Literary CB*, 56–89. The extracts include, for example, Cicero's statement that the "seeds of virtue are inborn in our dispositions, and, if they were allowed to ripen [*quae si adolescere liceret*], nature's own hand would lead us on to happiness of life [*ad beatam vitam natura perduceret*]; as things are, however, as soon as we come into light of day and have been acknowledged, we at once find ourselves in a world of iniquity amid a medley of wrong beliefs… [T]hen we become infected with deceptions so varied that truth gives place to unreality and the voice of nature itself to fixed prepossessions." Ibid., 60n (extracts in Latin, translation by the editor, Douglas Wilson).

6 TJ William Branch Giles, February 3, 1807, *TJW*, 1175.

7 TJ to Joel Barlow, January 24, 1810, *Ford* 11: 131. The "Dr. Mason" referred to here is most probably John Mitchell Mason, who wrote a strongly anti-Jefferson pamphlet in 1800 with a revealing title, "The Voice of Warning, to Christians, on the Ensuing Election of a President of the United States." (I owe thanks to Professor John C. Stagg for this suggested identification.)

8 On the former Girondin general Dumouriez (Dumourier), who took the side of counter-revolution by joining the Austrian army, see TJ to Martha Jefferson, May 26, 1793. *Ford* 7: 344.

9 TJ to Dr. Benjamin Rush, January 16, 1811, *TJW*, 1236.

10 TJ to John Adams, May 5, 1817, *AJL*, 513.

11 For a thorough study of dueling, see Markku Peltonen, *The Duel in Early Modern England: Civility, Politeness and Honour* (Cambridge: Cambridge University Press, 2003).

12 See, for example, Jefferson's excerpts from Lord Kames in *Legal CB* (Entries 557, 558), 99, 106 (quotation on page 106). On Hamilton bringing up the issue

of honor in his latest statement before the duel, see Joanne B. Freeman "Dueling as Politics: Reinterpreting the Burr-Hamilton Duel," *The William and Mary Quarterly*, LVIII, (2, 1996), 229–318. For a conceptual division between rank, fame, character (name or reputation), and honor as "reputation with a moral dimension and an elite cast" in Jefferson's America, see Joanne B. Freeman, *Affairs of Honor: National Politics in the New Republic* (New Haven: Yale University Press, 2001), xx.

13 *Notes*, Query XIII, 245.

14 TJ to Cesar A. Rodney, February 10, 1810, *TJW*, 1217.

15 TJ to Peter Carr, August 19, 1785, *TJW*, 815. The commonplace metaphor about the opposing forces of "head and heart" figures frequently, for example, in Lord Kames's *Essays on the Principles of Morality* (1751), e.g., 98, 132, 134. See on the same use of terms, Smith, *TMS* (1790), e.g., 67, 81, 86, 70–71, 90–91, 323, 329.

16 TJ to Peter Carr, August 19, 1785, *TJW*, 815.

17 TJ to Martha Jefferson, May 21, 1787, *TJW*, 896–897.

18 TJ to Peter Carr, August 10, 1787, *Papers* 12: 16.

19 Jefferson, *Literary CB* (Entry 39), 41.

20 TJ to Peter Carr, August 10, 1787, *Papers* 12: 17. As this letter was written from France, Jefferson probably reflected some of his own sentiments regarding the intellectually exciting atmosphere in Paris. The very next year he rejected, without hesitation, Martha's wish to become a Catholic nun and to stay in France for the rest of her life. See Fawn M. Brodie, *Thomas Jefferson: An Intimate History* (New York: W.W. Norton, 1974), 236–240. For the phrase on "its good dispositions," see TJ to Peter Carr, August 19, 1785, *TJW*, 815.

21 TJ to Martha Jefferson, May 21, 1787, *TJW*, 896–897. In view of this notion, it is hardly evident at all that, according to Jefferson, human nature was essentially good. On the contrary views, see, for example, Charles Miller, *Jefferson and Nature*, 255.

22 TJ, Syllabus on the Doctrines of Jesus, April 1803 as attached to TJ to Benjamin Rush, April 21, 1803, *TJW*, 1124.

23 Jefferson went on to supplement this lesson with the old witticism that where there is bread, there is God. TJ to John Adams, January 11, 1817, *AJL*, 506. For Adams's original statement on his "moral and religious Creed" as abbreviated "in four short Words '*Be just and good*,'" see ibid., 499.

24 Jefferson evidently drew much open contempt for the doctrine of tripartite God from Bolingbroke. In the young Jefferson's excerpts from Bolingbroke, one finds him ridiculing the idea of God "sending his only begotten son, who had not offended him, to be sacrificed by men … to satisfy his anger," and the idea of "a god who was himself his own father and his own son." Jefferson, *Literary CB*, 42–43. One could just as well ask, for example, whether heaven is "beyond all the solar systems of universe," or whether "hell is in the center of every planet," or whether the death "wander in air" or "reside latent in every element." Ibid., 29.

25 TJ to John Adams, April 11, 1823, *TJW*, 1469.

26 TJ to William Short, April 13, 1820, *Extracts*, 391.

27 TJ to William Short, April 13, 1820, *Extracts*, 391–392.

28 TJ to William Short, April 13, 1820, *Extracts*, 391–392.

29 TJ to Francis Hopkins, March 13, 1789, *TJW*, 941 (emphasis added).

30 For an exceptionally well-balanced summary of Jefferson's religious views, see E.S. Gaustad, "Religion" in Peterson (ed.), *A Reference Biography*, 277–294. On the significance of Christianity to Jefferson, scholars are unlikely to reach a consensus. Given that their source materials overlap considerably, a simple comparison between Paul K. Conkin's conclusion that "Jefferson was authentically religious" and Andrew Burnstein's insistence that Jefferson was an "unreligious man" suggests different standards for religious thinking. One way to solve the dilemma might be to invoke Henry F. May's remark that for Jefferson, "a just and benevolent creator and ruler was an essential intellectual need." Paul K. Conkin's conclusive remarks that "Jefferson was authentically religious" and that "in his age, when so many people were indifferent to religion ... he stands with that small cadre of religious seekers ... who have graced each period of human history," suggests that any person interested in the moral message of the Gospels is a religious person. Cf. Andrew Burstein, "Jefferson and the Familiar Letter," *Journal of the Early Republic* 14 (1994), 220; Conkin, "The Religious Pilgrimage," 47; and May, "The Enlightenment," 53.

31 See Charles B. Sanford, *The Religious Life of Thomas Jefferson* (Charlottesville: University of Virginia Press, 1992), 3–5. As Sanford also notes, Jefferson was probably buried with the Episcopal service. Contrary to Sanford's implication, however, Jefferson's service as a vestryman tells nothing of his religious faith. See ibid., 4–5.

32 TJ to Benjamin Rush, April 21, 1803, *Extracts*, 331–335. As this letter well validates, Jefferson simply considered Jesus the most perfect example of a man manifesting moral virtues in deeds and words throughout his life. Within the expression "human excellence," the word "human" was underlined. Ibid., 335n.

33 Quotation, TJ to Dr. Benjamin Waterhouse, June 26, 1822, *TJW*, 1458–1459.

34 Jefferson continued collecting different translations of the Gospels until approximately 1820. The so-called Jefferson Bible was published only in the early twentieth century and the larger version – including both the early "The Philosophy of Jesus" and the later version, "The Life and Morals of Jesus" – in the 1920s. See Eugene R. Sheridan, Introduction in Dickinson W. Adams and Ruth W. Lester (eds.), *Jefferson's Extracts from the Gospels: The Papers of Thomas Jefferson, Second Series* (Princeton, NJ: Princeton University Press, 1983), 28, 104. The content of both Jefferson collections remained the same, including the Sermon on the Mount and other main texts, but excluding all references to miracles and to resurrection. See Gaustad, "Religion," 286–287. Contrary to Sheridan's claims, it is hence difficult to see why Jefferson's continuous interest in the Greek, Latin, French, and English translations of the Bible would have been "strictly for his own moral and religious instruction." See Sheridan, "Introduction," *Extracts*, 38. Rather, it seems to speak to his conviction that it was worth getting the simple morality of the historical Jesus right so as to see its validity within the contemporary scholarly discussion on "the natural religion."

35 On this point of disagreement, see, for example, Yarbrough, *American Virtues*, 184. Indeed, Jefferson later wrote that we "well know that among Unitarians themselves there are strong shades of difference, as between Doctors Price and

Priestley for example." TJ to Timothy Pickering, February 27, 1821, *Extracts*, 403. He eventually consented to the idea that Jesus "might conscientiously believe himself inspired from above," but only in the sense that "he might readily mistake the coruscations of his own fine genius for inspirations of an higher order" just as "our wisest men still believe in the reality of these inspirations, while perfectly sane on all other subjects." TJ to William Short, August 4, 1820, *TJW*, 1438.

36 TJ to Alexander Smyth, January 17, 1825, *Extracts*, 416.

37 TJ to Isaac Story. December 5, 1801, *L&B* 10: 299.

38 TJ to John Adams, May 5, 1817, *AJL*, 512.

39 TJ to William Short, April 13, 1820, *Extracts*, 391–392.

40 TJ to Dr. Thomas Cooper, November 2, 1822, *TJW*, 1465. Contrary to John Adams's suggestion, Jefferson had no intention to include theology in the curriculum of the University of Virginia. See John Adams to TJ, March 2, 1816, *AJL*, 466.

41 TJ to James Smith, December 8, 1822, *Extracts*, 409.

42 TJ to Mrs. Samuel H. Smith, August 6, 1816, *TJW*, 1404. Here, again, Jefferson noted that "it is in our lives, and not from our words, that our religion must be read."

43 TJ to Miles King, September 26, 1814, *Extracts*, 360.

44 TJ to John Adams, January 11, 1817, *AJL*, 506. On Jefferson holding that "the Creator has made no two faces alike, so no two minds, and probably no two creeds," see TJ to Timothy Pickering, February 27, 1821, *Extracts*, 403.

45 TJ to John Adams, January 11, 1817, *AJL*, 506.

46 Quotations, TJ to William Short, August 4, 1820, *TJW*, 1437 and TJ to Benjamin Rush, April 21, 1803, ibid., 1125–1126.

47 TJ, Syllabus on the Doctrines of Jesus, April 1803 as attached to TJ to Benjamin Rush, April 21, 1803, *TJW*, 1125. Jefferson's belief in benevolent sentiments as natural to man should not be too hastily related to the theological conception of the love commandment as written in the heart of every Christian and of every Gentile. This tenet – which was drawn from St. Paul's letters (Romans 2.14–15) and shared by St. Thomas Aquinas and many Protestant natural lawyers alike – was often understood in the sense that God must impose love as the law on sinful men, whose natural benevolence could never appear sufficient on its own. See, for example, Schneewind, *Invention of Autonomy*, 21–25.

48 TJ, Report on Negotiation with Spain, March 18, 1792, *Ford* 6: 425.

49 Jefferson's "Notes on Locke and Shaftsbury" was prepared in 1776 to consider the reasons for disestablishing the Anglican Church in Virginia, *Papers* 1: 548. (In this quotation, the brackets and parentheses are Jefferson's own.)

50 TJ, Autobiography, 1821, *TJW*, 40.

51 TJ, Opinion on the French Treaties, April 28, 1793, *TJW*, 423. Even the term "conscience" could require the qualification of "good" in some of Jefferson's most philosophically oriented letters. See TJ to Miles King September 26, 1814, *Extracts*, 361.

52 TJ, Opinion on the French Treaties, April 28, 1793, *TJW*, 429.

53 TJ, Opinion on the French Treaties, April 28, 1793, *TJW*, 432.

54 TJ, Opinion on the French Treaties, April 28, 1793, *TJW*, 432. On interesting Lockean implications of such a use of terms, see John Dunn, "The concept of

'trust' in the politics of John Locke" in Richard Rorty, J.B. Schneewind, and Quentin Skinner (eds.), *Philosophy in History: Essays on the Historiography of Philosophy* (New York: Cambridge University Press, 1984), 279–302.

55 TJ to George Logan, November 12, 1816, *Ford* 12:43.

56 TJ to Cesar A. Rodney, February 10, 1810, *TJW*, 1217.

57 Jefferson, *Literary CB* (Entry 39), 41.

58 TJ to Benjamin Rush April 21, 1803, *TJW*, 1124.

59 TJ to John Adams, April 8, 1816, *AJL*, 467.

60 TJ, A Bill for Proportioning Crimes and Punishments, Sec. XII (approx. 1779), *TJW*, 349.

61 On "useless miseries," see Jefferson's letter to Eliza House Trist, probably of December 2, 1783 (the date is uncertain) in Andrew Burstein, *The Inner Jefferson: Portrait of a Grieving Optimist* (Charlottesville: University of Virginia Press, 1996), 65. On "proper bounds," see TJ to John Adams, April 8, 1816, *AJL*, 467. On the idea that grief was an anomaly within Jefferson's conviction that the whole issue of happiness was matter of self-control, see Burstein, *The Inner Jefferson*, passim.

62 TJ to Thomas Law, June 13, 1814, *Extracts*, 356.

63 TJ to Martha Jefferson, May 21, 1787, *TJW*, 897.

64 TJ to Martha Jefferson, November 28, 1783, *TJW*, 781–782. In the postscript, Jefferson wrote: "Keep my letters and read them at times that you may always have present in your mind those things which will endear you to me." Ibid., 783. On Jefferson's recommendations that women should read, for example, the works of Maria Edgeworth and William Godwin, see Burstein, *Jefferson's Secrets*, 94–109.

65 On, for example, historian Fawn Brodie's appalled reaction to this letter, see Brodie, *An Intimate History*, 171.

66 TJ to Martha Jefferson, November 28, 1783, *TJW*, 782. The notion of developing "the qualities" of both the head and the heart can also be found in Destutt de Tracy's writings. This is what he had to say about uneducated women: "In respect to women, it is too true that the misfortune of being marriageable when almost in a state of childhood, and to be in a state of decline on the verge of youth, must prevent them in general, from having *many good qualities of head and heart*; and consequently, they easily become the playthings and victims of man, and rarely their companions or friends. This is, without doubt, a very great obstacle to true morality, and true civilization; for if man becomes *corrupted* when he oppresses his fellow creature, he yet more extremely perverts his nature, when he reduces the object of his most lively desires to a state of servitude. The passion for sensuality being destructive of maturity, by prematurely *preventing beings from becoming perfect* [... is one of the] great evils." Tracy, *Commentary*, 196 (emphasis added).

67 TJ to Peter Carr, August 19, 1787, *Papers* 12: 15.

68 *Notes*, Query XIV, 265.

69 TJ to Natheniel Burwell, March 14, 1818, *TJW*, 1411.

70 *Notes*, Query XIV, 267.

71 TJ to William Short, January 3, 1793, *TJW*, 1004.

72 TJ to George Logan, May 11, 1805, *Ford* 10: 141.

73 TJ to James Madison, July 14, 1793, *Ford* 7: 449.

74 TJ to Jared Sparks, February 4, 1824, *TJW*, 1487.
75 TJ to John Holmes, April 22, 1820, *TJW*, 1434.
76 Quotations from TJ to John Adams, May 17, 1818, *AJL*, 524 and from TJ to Lafayette, May 14, 1817, *TJW*, 1409.
77 As Aristotle remarked about confusing theoretical moral studies with proper ethical upbringing, "it is by doing just acts that the just man is produced" and "without doing these no one would have even a prospect of becoming good." Aristotle, *Nicomachean Ethics* (II, 5), 35.
78 TJ to Robert Skipwith, August 3, 1771, *Papers* 1: 76–77.
79 In his summary of the Aristotelian use of the term virtue, Alasdair MacIntyre points out that there are two kinds of virtue, both describable in terms of rationality as exercised in human activities: "Intellectual virtue is the consequence of explicit instruction; moral of habit. Virtue is not inborn, but a consequence of training. The contrast with our natural capacities is plain: first we have the natural capacity, and then we exercise it; whereas with virtues we acquire the habit by first performing the acts." Alasdair MacIntyre, *A Short History of Ethics: A History of Moral Philosophy from the Homeric Age to the Twentieth Century* (London: Routledge, 1995), 64.
80 Document in Sarah N. Randolph (ed.), *The Domestic Life of Thomas Jefferson: Compiled from Family Letters and Reminiscences by His Great-Granddaughter* (New York: Frederick Ungar Publishing, 1958), 337. On the same incident, see also, for example, Gordon-Reed, *Thomas Jefferson and Sally Hemings*, 139.
81 TJ to Peter Carr, August 19, 1785, *TJW*, 815.
82 *Notes*, Query VI, 189–191.
83 Smith, *TMS* (Part VII), 324.
84 *TMS* (Part VII), 320.
85 Francis Hutcheson, *A Short Introduction to Moral Philosophy*, anonymously translated from Latin in Glasgow in 1747 (Reprint: Hildesheim, Netherlands: Georg Olms Verlagsbuchhandling, 1969) 68.
86 Kames, *Essays*, 51.
87 *Essays*, 66.
88 *Essays*, 146.
89 In *A Treatise of Human Nature* (1749), David Hume said that "the sense of justice and injustice is not derived from nature, but arises artificially, though necessarily, from education and human convention." See *Hume's Moral and Political Philosophy*, ed. by Henry D. Aiken (New York: Hafner Press, 1948), 54.
90 By "artificial systems," Jefferson referred, for example, to such "immaculate" religious tenets as the trinity, original sin, and resurrection. See TJ to William Short, October 31, 1819, *TJW*, 1431.
91 *Notes*, Query XIV, 269.
92 TJ to Thomas Law, June 13, 1814, *TJW*, 1338. Given Jefferson's view that it was in people's true interest to behave morally and that it was more likely that there is a supreme being than not, Jean Yarbrough's claim that Jefferson here approves of deluding people to act from the fear of God seems erroneous. Jefferson did not talk of these assumptions as truths. See on Yarbrough's remark about Jefferson committing a "noble lie," Yarbrough, *American Virtues*, 186.
93 TJ to Peter Carr, August 19, 1785, *TJW*, 815.
94 TJ to Thomas Jefferson Randolph, November 24, 1808, *TJW*, 1194–1195.

95 Concurring with a fairly common view among modern scholars, Gordon Wood notes that the term "refinement" represented a "new mingling of politeness and morality" within eighteenth-century thought. Politeness was, in sum, "a new social virtue" (Wood, "Trials and Tribulations," 40). Regarding Jefferson's moral outlook, this generalization appears too broad. That human sentiments regarding taste and manners developed alongside civilization was a common theme of the time regardless of what kind of politeness one was advocating. Adam Smith saw it as evident that among the barbarians, virtues of self-denial were prevalent whereas among civilized nations, virtues were more generally built on humanity. See Smith, *TMS*, 205. As for the much-discussed connection between politeness and the rise of sentimentalism, Smith also noted, for example, that "Cicero, in the times of the highest Roman politeness, could, without degrading himself, weep with all the bitterness of sorrow in sight of the whole senate and the whole people." Smith's probably fully conventional view was that "the two most polished nations upon the continent" – which embraced the idea of expressing emotions publicly – were the French and Italians. Ibid., 207.

96 TJ to Charles Bellini, September 30, 1785, *TJW*, 833–834.

97 TJ to Thomas Jefferson Randolph, November 24, 1808, *TJW*, 1194–1195.

98 TJ to Thomas Jefferson Randolph, November 24, 1808, *TJW*, 1194. Jefferson later extolled his professor of mathematics at the College of William and Mary, William Small, as one who "probably fixed the destinies of my life." George Wythe was the professor of Law and Jefferson's later mentor as well as perhaps his closest associate, along with James Madison. Peyton Randolph was the King's attorney. In addition to them, the young Jefferson came to know intimately Francis Fauquier, the then British Governor of Virginia.

99 TJ to Peter Carr, August 19, 1785, *TJW*, 815.

100 *Notes*, Query XVIII, 288.

101 *Notes*, Query XVIII, 288.

102 C.L.R. James, *The Black Jacobins: Toussaint L'Ouverture and the San Domingo Revolution*, 2nd revised edition, 1963 (New York: Vintage Books, 1989), 180.

103 TJ to John Adams, October 28, 1813, *TJW*, 1309. An example of utter depravity among a group of seventeenth-century New Englanders – generally feasting as ancient Romans in their bacchanalia and adhering to atheist doctrines – is vividly pictured in one of Jefferson's letters on colonial history to Adams. TJ to John Adams, December 28, 1812, *AJL*, 317.

104 TJ to Peter Carr, August 10, 1787, *Papers* 12: 14–15.

105 On Hutcheson speaking of ethics as "the art of regulating our whole life," see Hutcheson, *A Short Introduction to Moral Philosophy* (1747), 1. Lord Kames spoke of a "great refinement in the art of living" when referring to gradually developing property regulations among civilized nations (Kames, *Essays*, 109). For Jefferson's reference to ethical considerations as "the art of life," see TJ to Maria Cosway, October 12, 1786, *TJW*, 872. Or consider philosopher Julián Marías's statement that, by and large, the Stoics turned the Greek conception of philosophy itself into "the practice of *an art*, the aim of which is the proper governing of one's life." Julián Marías, *History of Philosophy* [*Historia de la Filosofía*, 1966], transl. by Stanley Applebaum and Clarence C. Strowbridge (New York: Dover Publications, 1967), 88 (emphasis changed).

106 On Jefferson's use of these terms, see TJ to Benjamin Rush, April 21, 1803, *TJW*, 1124. In Jefferson's list of ancient authors, Marcus Aurelius is referred to as "Antoninus." The official title was "Imperator Caesar Marcus Aurelius Antoninus Augustus pontifex maximus." On Jefferson's continuing interest in ancient philosophy, see also TJ to Martin van Buren, June 29, 1824, *Ford* 12: 372.
107 TJ to John Adams, June 17, 1813, *AJL*, 335.
108 TJ to William Short, October 31, 1819, *TJW*, 1432. On the tension between consolation and active virtue, see also Reinhold, 1986, 153.
109 TJ to John Adams, April 8, 1816, *AJL*, 467. Even Adam Smith spoke of differently appropriate manners for the young and old. See *TMS* (Part V), 201–202.
110 TJ to John Langdon, March 5, 1810, *TJW*, 1221–1222. Jefferson obviously did not share Epicurus's alleged opposition to political activity. Perhaps, as Richard Matthews suggests, Epictetus is mentioned in the letter in order to add that aspect to Jeffersonian Epicureanism, although it is not clear whether Jefferson himself ever thought of Epicureanism as an essentially antipolitical strand of thought. Matthews, *Radical Politics*, 94.
111 TJ to Martha Jefferson, May 21, 1787, *TJW*, 896–897. "A mind always employed is always happy," Jefferson lectured Martha. By the same token, the ease of body entailed its exercise, as becomes clear in Jefferson's many references to his own habits of daily horse riding and his advice to the young Peter to take long walks with a gun so as to relax his mind as well as strengthen the body. "A strong body makes the mind strong," Jefferson insisted. TJ to Peter Carr, August 19, 1785, *TJW*, 816.
112 TJ to William Short, October 31, 1819, *TJW*, 1432.
113 TJ to William Short, October 31, 1819 with the Syllabus of the Doctrines of Epicurus, *TJW*, 1430–1433.
114 TJ to William Short, October 31, 1819, *TJW*, 1433.
115 TJ to William Short, October 31, 1819, *TJW*, 1432.
116 TJ to James Smith, December 8, 1822, *Extracts*, 409.
117 TJ to John Adams, May 5, 1817, *AJL*, 513.
118 Smith, *TMS* (Part VI), 297.
119 TJ to Maria Cosway, October 12, 1786, *TJW*, 872.
120 As to my knowledge, Jefferson's genuine love of his wife, Martha Wayles Jefferson, has never been questioned.
121 TJ to Maria Cosway, October 12, 1786, *TJW*, 870.
122 TJ to Maria Cosway, October 12, 1786, *TJW*, 869. On the Head stating to the Heart, "how imprudent it is to place your affections, without reserve, on objects you must soon lose," see ibid., 871.
123 TJ to Maria Cosway, October 10, 1786, *TJW*, 869.
124 On scholars arguing that sentiments prevail in Jefferson's moral thought at the expense of reason, see Wills, *Inventing America*, 290–303; Burstein, *The Inner Jefferson*, e.g., 95. For an opposite view of Jefferson favoring intellect, see White, *Philosophy of the American Revolution*, e.g., 115–116.
125 TJ to Maria Cosway, October 12, 1786, *TJW*, 866–877.
126 For the view that the Epicurean temperance is "nothing but prudence with regard to pleasure," see Smith, *TMS* (Part VII), 297. Notably, the Heart's exclusively secular line of argument does not deny that the Head could, in its

monkish ethos of "visionary happiness," grasp the pleasures of the afterlife. Yet Jefferson left such concerns out of the equation.

127 TJ to Doctor Walter Jones, January 2, 1814, *Ford* 11: 375.

128 TJ to Maria Cosway, October 12, 1786, *TJW*, 866–877.

129 TJ to Maria Cosway, October 12, 1786, *TJW*, 869, 875.

130 Quotation from Reid's *Essays on the Active Powers*, as in *Anthology*, 641. In addition, Reid notes that neither "can we conceive a greater depravity in the heart of man, than it would be to see and acknowledge worth without feeling any respect to it." Ibid., 641.

131 TJ to Dr. Walter Jones, January 2, 1814, *TJW*, 1319.

132 As noted in the famous Thomas Law letter, Jefferson implicitly sided with Hutcheson's sentimentalist position against Reid's more rationalist morality when subscribing to Law's account of the two. Even more directly, however, Jefferson subscribed to Lord Kames's teachings, which were considerably closer to Reid's than to Hutcheson's position.

133 See Smith, *TMS* (Part VII), 322. See also Schneewind, *Invention of Autonomy*, 339.

134 Kames, *Essays*, 70.

135 TJ to William Short, April 13, 1820, *Extracts*, 391–392.

136 TJ to Major John Cartwright, June 5, 1824, *TJW*, 1490–1491.

137 TJ to Peter Carr, August 19, 1787, *TJW*, 902.

138 As for the use of the term "common sense" here, it is notable that Jefferson appears never to have subscribed to Thomas Reid's common sense concept. He rarely explicated his use of terms in ways philosophers tend to do. As for the definition of the concept one may, for example, resort to Knud Haakonssen's studies of the topic. According to him, Reid linked his two fundamental categories of truths – necessary and contingent truths – with a set of human, intellectual capacities to grasp them. All the three together comprise, Haakonssen states, what "Reid calls Common sense." The sciences of necessary truths were grammar, logic, mathematics, aesthetics, morals, and metaphysics. All the six sciences were derivable from their own self-evident principles whose opposites were impossible. In the field of contingent truths, one should study, for example: Mental world, personal identity, memory, free agents, the external world, other minds as agents, the uniformity of nature, and "reliable signs and evidence." Haakonssen, *Natural Law and Moral Philosophy*, 186.

139 Haakonssen, "Introduction" in Haakonssen (ed.), *Thomas Reid*, 48–49.

140 Quotes from Burlamaqui, *The Principles of Natural Law: In which the True Principle of Morality and Civil Government are Established* (*Principes du droit naturel*, Geneva 1747), translated by Mr. Nugent (London, 1748, reprint Clark, NJ: The Lawbook Exchange, 2003), 16. Jefferson's acquaintance with Burlamaqui's views is commonly accepted and well-documented. For example, Burlamaqui was included in Jefferson's list of book purchases for Madison. See TJ to James Madison, September 1, 1785, *TJW*, 823.

141 Adam Smith explained the theories of the foundation of this human capacity under the title, "the principle of approbation." Among the theorists who found the principle of approbation in self-love, Smith enumerated Hobbes, Mandeville, and Pufendorf. Cudworth he took to be the principal champion of approbation arising from human reason, whereas Hutcheson saw it arising

from a particular sentimental capacity or "a power of perception called a moral sense." Hume, according to this classification, saw approbation arising from sympathy for other people's sentiments, but left justice beyond the domain of morality proper. Smith's own view concentrated on the approval (or disapproval) itself as arising from genuinely different kinds of sympathetic sentiments of approbation in different situations, which only after becoming thus noticed, could also be considered as "part of a system of behavior" including utility of action, according to both individual and social happiness. *TMS* (Part VII), 314–325.

142 TJ to Maria Cosway, October 12, 1786, *TJW*, 874–875.

143 See, for example, MacIntyre, *A Short History of Ethics*, 74.

144 Aristotle, *Nicomachean Ethics* (III, 7), 65.

145 See Cicero, *On Duties* (*De officiis*), translated by M.T. Griffin and E.M. Atkins (Cambridge: Cambridge University Press, 1991), 7, 105 [Bk. I, 14; Bk. III, 13–14].

146 TJ to Thomas Law, June 13, 1814, *Extracts*, 357. In Merrill D. Peterson's edited volume of Jefferson's writings, this particular phrase is misspelled as "the standard and best of virtue." See *TJW*, 1338.

147 TJ to Thomas Law, June 13, 1814, *Extracts*, 357.

148 Helvétius, *De l'Esprit* as in *Anthology*, 427.

149 TJ to John Adams, October 14, 1816, *AJL*, 492.

150 TJ to William Short, August 4, 1820, *TJW*, 1437.

151 TJ to Thomas Law, June 13, 1814, *Extracts*, 357. See also TJ to William Short, October 31, 1819, *TJW*, 1433.

152 TJ to John Adams, October 14, 1816, *AJL*, 492. For another definition of the essence of virtue as "social utility," see TJ to William Short, August 4, 1820, *TJW*, 1437. Such references to essences are exceptional in the context of Jefferson's repeated claim to be a materialist, at least if he spoke of essence in the ancient sense of the term as that which precedes being. As he once lectured John Adams, "to talk of immaterial existences is to talk of nothing." TJ to John Adams, May 12, 1820, *AJL*, 567.

153 See, Hutcheson, *A Short Introduction* (1747), e.g., 109, 118, 120.

154 Quotations respectively from Aristotle *Nicomachean Ethics* (X.9, I.4.), 271, 4. Contrary to the proper method of becoming just by doing just acts, Aristotle noted that most people "take refuge in theory and think they are being philosophers and will become good in this way, behaving somewhat like patients who listen attentively to their doctors, but do none of the things they are ordered to do." Ibid. (II, 5), 35.

155 On the view, for example, that the Aristotelian understanding of good life was not codifiable in any simple rational or emotional terms, see John McDowell's intriguing article, "Virtue and Reason" (*The Monist* 62, 1979, 331–350) in Roger Crisp and Michael Slote (eds.), *Virtue Ethics* (New York: Oxford University Press, 1997), 141–162.

156 TJ to Thomas Paine, July 15, 1789, *Papers* 15: 268.

157 TJ to Edward Coles, August 25, 1814, *TJW*, 1345.

158 TJ, Opinion on the French Treaties, April 28, 1793, *TJW*, 423.

159 TJ to William Green Munford, June 18, 1799, *TJW*, 1064.

160 TJ to Lafayette, February 14, 1815, *TJW*, 1361.

161 See Aristotle, *Nicomachean Ethics* (I.4), 4.
162 Smith, *TMS*, 214.
163 TJ to Dr. Benjamin Rush, January 16, 1811, *TJW*, 1236.
164 TJ to Peter Carr, August 10, 1787, *Papers* 12: 14–15.
165 This elitism had its roots in Adams's oddly old-fashioned definition of natural aristocracy as consisting of "a few in whom all [the] advantages of birth, fortune, and fame are united." See, *Political Writings of John Adams*, ed. Peek, Jr., 138–139. Even Richard Bushman's renowned study of the various modifications of politeness and refinement in early America does not draw any clear distinction between Jefferson's and Adams's conceptions of the so-called natural aristocracy when characterizing the concept as a combination of genteel manners and classical aristocratic societal beliefs. See Richard L. Bushman, *The Refinement of America: Persons, Houses, Cities* (New York: Vintage Books, 1993), e.g., 414–415.
166 Thucydides, *The History of the Peloponnesian War*, translated from Greek by R. Crawley (London: J.M. Dent & Sons, 1910, 1940), 123.
167 This approaches what Kari Palonen labels politicking, the performance of politics in the Arendtian sense of art in conquering time as an extended present rather than as mere tactics of playing for time on behalf of a given a policy. Palonen, "Four Times of Politics."
168 TJ to Charles Clay, January 27, 1790, *Papers* 16: 129, as quoted in Elkins & McKitrick, *Age of Federalism*, 197.
169 TJ to Peter Carr, August 19, 1785, *TJW*, 815.
170 TJ to John Taylor, June 4, 1798, *TJW*, 1048–1051.
171 TJ to Edward Coles, August 25, 1814, *TJW*, 1344–1346.
172 TJ to John Taylor, June 4, 1798, *TJW*, 1048–1051. The standard lamentation that Jefferson was not outspoken enough in all his wishes is out of touch with what successfully playing politics is all about. Historian Leonard Levy, for example, considers it ethically questionable that, as the vice president of the United States, Jefferson wrote under a pseudonym against President Adams's Alien and Sedition acts. See Levy, "Civil Liberties," 341. Historian Jay Fliegelman may well be right in speculating that Jefferson's legendary headaches were associated with his problems in adapting to the eighteenth-century's new public rhetoric of authentic self-expression. But whether genuinely persuasive political rhetoric was about "expressing one's self publicly" in contemporary political discourse is quite another matter. Quotation from Jay Fliegelman, *Declaring Independence: Jefferson, Natural Language & the Culture of Performance* (Stanford, CA: Stanford University Press, 1996), 200.
173 See Jefferson's complaint about the hard-core Federalists propagating this image to Hamilton, TJ to Dr. Walter Jones, January 2, 1814, *TJW*, 1321. On Hamilton's remarks about Jefferson's "womanish attachment to France," see Sloan, *Principle and Interest*, 185. On Jefferson being "sensitive and thin-skinned, with an easily bruised ego," see John C. Miller, *The Wolf by the Ears*, 199; or that he was in general "thin-skinned and touchy at the smallest impeachment of himself," see Elkins & McKitrick, *Age of Federalism*, 205.
174 TJ to Charles Clay, January 27, 1790 as quoted in Elkins & McKitrick, *Age of Federalism*, 197.

175 TJ to Albert Gallatin, November 14, 1818, *Ford* 12: 104–105. Similarly, Jefferson argued that no courthouse should be taken as the ultimate arbiter between nations concerning such questions as cessions of landed property, given that "neither party thinks of calling the other to a trial of the fact in a court of its own, where it would be both party and judge." Jefferson to Henry A. Dearborn, January 6, 1806, *Ford* 10: 221.

176 On "pure morality," see TJ to Benjamin Hawkins, February 18, 1803, *TJW*, 1116. On the idea of secretly running the tribes into debt, see TJ to William H. Harrison, February 27, 1803, ibid., 1118.

177 TJ to Lafayette, May 14, 1817, *TJW*, 1409. For a later statement of the same kind, see TJ to John Adams, January 22, 1821, *AJL*, 570.

178 TJ to John C. Breckinridge, August 12, 1803, *TJW*, 1137.

179 TJ to Albert Gallatin, November 14, 1818, *Ford* 12: 104–105.

180 TJ to George Logan, November 12, 1816, *Ford* 12: 43.

181 The plan was supplemented with the idea of providing the best student of each school district free education on the higher levels also. That only very few would be so provided has led scholars to argue that Jefferson's educational ambitions were far from democratic. John Howe proclaims that "Jefferson's aristocracy of talent" was not "class-neutral" because the system as a whole remained open for all children who could pay for tuition. Such accusations seem misleading, for Jefferson had no reason to think that even poorer talented students would inevitably remain dependable on only public funding. See John Howe, "Republicanism" in Peterson (ed.), *A Reference Biography*, 70. For similar accusations, see May, "The Enlightenment," 55; Wills, *Inventing America*, 146–147.

182 TJ, A Bill for the More General Diffusion of Knowledge, 1778, *TJW*, 365–373. Quote, TJ, Autobiography 1821, *TJW*, 43. Even if Jefferson's argument here was self-serving, given his need for funds for his university, nothing in this or other documents related to the issue (that I know of) justifies Darren Staloff's conclusion that Jefferson somehow drastically "shifted priorities from educating the masses through primary education to training statesmen at the university level" or that his university curriculum speaks to some "narrow political indoctrination." See Staloff, "The Politics of Pedagogy: Thomas Jefferson and the Education of a Democratic Citizenry" in Shuffelton (ed.), *The Cambridge Companion to Thomas Jefferson*, 138–139. For example, Jefferson's well-known hopes for getting Dugald Stewart and a number of other European scholars as lecturers at the University of Virginia hardly bespeaks any particularly narrow political interests.

183 TJ to Joseph C. Cabell, February 2, 1816, *TJW*, 1378–1379.

184 TJ to Joseph O. Cabell, November 28, 1820, *Ford* 12: 171.

185 The term of St. Domingo referred to the island of Hispaniola, that is, to both French Saint Domingue (San Domingo) and Spanish Santo Domingo, of which the first was renamed Haiti.

186 See Egerton, *Gabriel's Rebellion*, 45–47; John C. Miller, *The Wolf by the Ears*, 133.

187 Jefferson's cabinet declared a trade embargo against the rebels, and the president's son-in-law, John Wayles Eppes, publicly proclaimed that Haiti's "Negro government should be destroyed." John C. Miller, *The Wolf by the Ears*, 140.

It appears that, despite the official trade embargo, the Jefferson administration did little to prevent American traders from supplying Toussaint's armies with war materials; whether the trade embargo was ever meant to become effective remains questionable. In Jefferson's eyes, it probably served both as a threat to the black republic and as a public expression of support for Napoleon without costing anything to the United States. Many historians have failed to find consistency in Jefferson's Haitian policy precisely because they abstain from taking into account the president's long-range plan for general slave emancipation by means of colonization.

188 See for a similar argument, John C. Miller, *The Wolf by the Ears*, 139. See also Clifford L. Egan, *Neither Peace nor War: Franco-American Relations, 1803–1812* (Baton Rouge: Louisiana State University Press, 1983), 55–59.

189 See for Jefferson's own account of these efforts, TJ to John Lynch, January 21, 1811, *Ford* 11: 178–181.

190 American Colonization Society, "The Sixth Annual Report of the American Society for Colonizing the Free People of Color of the United States," issued in Washington City, 1823, *The American Review*, 42, January 1824, 41.

191 TJ to James Monroe, November 24, 1801, *TJW*, 1098. On later claims, see TJ to Jared Sparks, February 4, 1924, *TJW*, 1484.

192 TJ to Thomas Humphreys, February 8, 1817, *L&B* 15: 102–103.

193 TJ to Thomas Humphreys, February 8, 1817, *L&B* 15: 102–103.

194 TJ to Doctor Thomas Humphreys, February 8, 1817, *L&B* 15: 103.

195 See on the earlier intepretations of this letter, for example, Sheldon, *Political Philosophy*, 133 and John C. Miller, "Slavery," in Peterson (ed.), *A Reference Biography*, 420–421.

196 TJ to Jared Sparks, February 4, 1824, *TJW*, 1487.

197 TJ to Thomas Humphreys, February 8, 1817, *L&B* 15: 102–103.

198 TJ to Jared Sparks, February 4, 1824, *TJW*, 1487.

199 On education of the slave children as part of Jefferson's abolition plan for decades, see *Notes* (from 1787), Query XIV, 264; TJ to Edward Coles, August 25, 1814, *TJW*, 1345; TJ to Albert Gallatin, December 26, 1820, *TJW*, 1450.

200 TJ to Jared Sparks, February 4, 1824, *TJW*, 1486–1487.

201 TJ to Albert Gallatin, December 26, 1820, *TJW*, 1450.

202 On the figures, see Ira Berlin, *Slaves without Masters: The Free Negro in the Antebellum South* (New York: Oxford University Press, 1981), 46, 136–137.

203 On Madison's position, see McCoy, *The Last of the Fathers*, 265–278.

204 James Madison to Robert Walsh, November 27, 1819, *James Madison Writings*, Rakove (ed.), 743.

205 Peter Charles Hoffer, *The Brave New World: A History of Early America* (Baltimore, MD: Johns Hopkins University Press, 2006), 459.

206 TJ to John Dickinson, January 13, 1807, *TJW*, 1169.

207 TJ to Albert Gallatin, December 26, 1820, *TJW*, 1449.

208 TJ to Albert Gallatin, December 26, 1820, *TJW*, 1449.

209 On Washington, TJ to Dr. Walter Jones, January 2, 1814, *TJW*, 1317. On "the three greatest men that have ever lived," see TJ to John Trumbull, February 15, 1789, *TJW*, 939.

210 See William Frankena, *Ethics*, 2nd edition (Englewood Cliffs, NJ: Prentice Hall, 1973), e.g., 14–15, 45, 65–67, 71.

211 TJ to Martha Jefferson, December 11, 1783, *TJW*, 784.
212 TJ to Maria Cosway, October 12, 1786, *TJW*, 874–875.

4 The Perfectible Rights of Men

1 Pauline Maier, *American Scripture: Making the Declaration of Independence* (New York: Vintage Books, 1998), 37–38.
2 As for the question of originality, Jefferson clearly thought it proper to deploy the widely used formulations of John Locke's *Second Treatise* when drafting the Declaration. The natural right of man to decide the form of his own government became articulated in the preamble of the Declaration, and that was what mattered. Whether Jefferson was the committee's draftsman rather than the main author of the document is an interesting historical problem in itself. Pauline Maier gives great weight to the fact that Jefferson asked advice from other members of the committee when preparing his draft. The other members were John Adams, Benjamin Franklin, Robert L. Livingston, and Roger Sherman. See Maier, *American Scripture*, 1998.
3 That Jefferson respected Lockean philosophy in general is beyond controversy. In 1814 he sent an exceptionally short, and probably exceptionally representative, list of recommended readings for a young law student. As with other such lists, the topics varied from mathematics to belles lettres, with remarks about the most appropriate study material. Under two topics, the recommended readings started with Locke: "Ethics. & Natl. Religion" and "Politics, general." The former subject was to be studied in Locke's *Essay Concerning Human Understanding* and to be complemented by his "conduct of the mind in the search after truth." For politics, Jefferson recommended the *Two Treatises of Government*. TJ to John Minor, August 30, 1814, *Ford* 11: 420–425. In a similar list written to his nephew, Peter Carr, Jefferson placed Locke's *Essay Concerning Human Understanding* under the heading "Morality." TJ to Peter Carr, August 10, 1787, *Papers* 12: 18.
4 TJ to Henry Lee, May 8, 1825, *TJW*, 1501.
5 See for a thorough discussion of this aspect of Jefferson's thinking, Fliegelman, *Declaring Independence*.
6 The point about the more extensive "right to obtain happiness" in George Mason's Virginia Declaration of Rights was probably made for the first time in Arthur M. Schlesinger [Sr.], "The Lost Meaning of the 'The Pursuit of Happiness,'" *The William and Mary Quarterly* 23 (1964), 325–327. It has often been noted that Jefferson's original draft was probably inspired by George Mason's earlier document. See, for example, Noble E. Cunningham, Jr., *In Pursuit of Reason: The Life of Thomas Jefferson* (Baton Rouge: Louisiana State University Press, 1987), passim., esp., 49.
7 See TJ's "original Rough draught" and the parchment copy of the final Declaration of Independence, the latter generally considered the authoritative version of the document, *Papers* 1: 423–427, 429–432.
8 On the argument that "the Declaration's chief verbal performance" was a declaration of war, see J.G.A. Pocock, "States, Republics and Empires: The American Founding in Early Modern Perspective" in Terence Ball and J.G.A. Pocock (eds.), *Conceptual Change and the Constitution* (Lawrence: University Press

of Kansas, 1988), 58. On Richard Beeman's argument that, indeed, "the punch line" of the whole second paragraph of the Declaration is "the assertion of the right to rebel against the government of England," see Richard Beeman, *The Penguin Guide to the Unites States Constitution: A Fully Annotated Declaration of Independence, U.S. Constitution and Amendments, and Selections from the Federalist Papers* (Walbaum, MT: Penguin Books, 2010), 5.

9 TJ, Miscellany, Answer to Jean Nicolas Démeunier, June 26, 1786, *TJW*, 592.

10 Stephen Conrad is absolutely right to question Jefferson's fame as *a philosopher* of rights. Stephen A. Conrad, "Putting Rights Talk in Its Place: The Summary View Revisited" in Onuf (ed.), *Jeffersonian Legacies*, 273. On viewing Jefferson as "the leading natural rights theorist of the day," see Michael J. Lacey and Knud Haakonssen, "Introduction: History, Historicism, and the Culture of Rights," in Lacey and Haakonssen (eds.), *A Culture of Rights: The Bill of Rights in Philosophy, Politics, and Law – 1791 and 1991* (New York: Woodrow Wilson Center and Cambridge University Press, 1991), 13. For the most thorough discussion on Jefferson's philosophical intentions and the meaning of the Declaration of Independence, see Morton White, *The Philosophy of the American Revolution.*

11 TJ to John Wayles Eppes, June 24, 1813, *TJW*, 1282.

12 TJ to Thomas Law, June 13, 1814, *Extracts*, 356.

13 TJ's original draft of the Declaration of Independence, *Papers* 1: 423.

14 This line of argument has been suggested by a number of scholars, although not with fully identical conclusions to mine. For slightly varying but generally valid theoretical accounts of the topic, see Carl L. Becker's 1922 classic, *The Declaration of Independence: A Study in the History of Political Ideas* (New York: Random House, 1970); Adrienne Koch, *Power, Morals, and the Founding Fathers: Essays in the Interpretation of the American Enlightenment* (Ithaca, NY: Cornell University Press, 1961); White, *Philosophy of the American Revolution*; Wills, *Inventing America*. For exceptionally well-documented accounts of Jefferson's views of the natural rights over the years, see Conrad "Putting Rights Talk in Its Place," and John Zvesper, "Jefferson on Liberal Natural Rights" in Gary L. McDowell and Sharon L. Noble (eds.), *Reason and Republicanism: Thomas Jefferson's Legacy of Liberty* (Lanham, MA: Rowman & Littlefield, 1997).

15 TJ to Major John Cartwright, June 5, 1824, *TJW*, 1494. Jefferson here followed the spelling of the final, printed version of the Declaration. In fact, the change from "inalienable" to "unalienable" was probably a mere printing error. See Maier, *American Scripture*, 144. As for some of the confusing punctuation of the document originating in Jefferson's intention to write a speech rather than a written document, see Fliegelman, *Declaring Independence*, 5–20.

16 TJ, Autobiography (1821), *TJW*, 19.

17 TJ, Report on Negotiation with Spain, March 18, 1792, *Ford* 6: 435.

18 TJ, A Bill for Proportioning Crimes and Punishments, Sect. XII (approx. 1779), *TJW*, 349.

19 See White, *Philosophy of the American Revolution*, 206–208, 286.

20 TJ to Samuel Kercheval, July 12, 1816, *TJW*, 1401–1402 (emphasis added).

21 TJ to Isaac H. Tiffany, April 4, 1819, *Political Writings of Thomas Jefferson*, Appleby and Ball (eds.), 224.

22 TJ to Doctor John Manners, June 12, 1817, *Ford* 13: 66.
23 TJ to Henri Gregoire, February 25, 1809, *TJW*, 1202.
24 TJ to Miles King, September 26, 1814, *Extracts*, 360.
25 TJ to Samuel Kercheval, September 5, 1816, *L&B*: 15: 71.
26 White, *Philosophy of the American Revolution*, e.g., 242; Richard Tuck, *Natural Rights Theories: Their Origin and Development* (Cambridge: Cambridge University Press, 1981), 71. Like Jefferson, John Witherspoon thought it clear that our "alienable rights," we may "according to justice and prudence, surrender or give up by our own act." See Jack Scott (ed.), John Witherspoon, *An Annotated Edition of Lectures on Moral Philosophy of John Witherspoon* [1800–1801], (London and Toronto: Associated University Presses, 1982), 111.
27 TJ to John Wayles Eppes, June 24, 1813, *TJW*, 1282.
28 On suicide, TJ, A Bill for Proportioning Crimes and Punishments, Sect. XII with notes (approx. 1779), *TJW*, 349–364, quotes, 353–354n. Neither did Adam Smith see suicide as punishable, see *TMS*, 287.
29 For Hutcheson's qualifications for alienable rights, see White, *Philosophy of the American Revolution*, 209. See also Francis Hutcheson, *An Inquiry Concerning Moral Good and Evil* [1725, 1726] in L.A. Selby-Bigge (ed.), *British Moralists: Being Selections from Writers Principally of the Eighteenth Century* (Indianapolis, IN: Bobbs-Merrill, 1964), 163; Hutcheson, *Short Introduction*, 124. For Jefferson being familiar with at least the latter volume – even before the Revolution – see, for example, Jayne, *Jefferson's Declaration*, 67.
30 See, for example, Jefferson's excerpts from Lord Kames's writings, *Legal CB* (Entries 557–558), 99, 106 (the quotation from the latter).
31 See on Morton White's solution to this dilemma, White, *Philosophy of the American Revolution*, 203, 209.
32 Minutes of the Board of Visitors to UVA, October 7, 1822, *TJW*, 478.
33 TJ to Francis Hopkinson, March 13, 1789, *TJW*, 941.
34 TJ to Peter Carr, August 10, 1787, *TJW*, 904.
35 *Notes*, Query XVII, 285.
36 *Notes*, Query XVII, 285. As for Jefferson's attempt to circumvent the question of divine origins of natural rights in his original draft of the Declaration of Independence, it is notable that George Mason's somewhat earlier Virginia Declaration of Rights circumvented the issue as well. Mason stated simply that "all men are by nature equally free and have certain inherent rights," and then went on to describe these rights as "the enjoyment of life and liberty, with the means of acquiring and possessing property, and pursuing and obtaining happiness and safety." For Mason's declaration, see for example, Kermit L. Hall, William M. Wiecek, and Paul Finkelman (eds.), *American Legal History: Cases and Materials, Second Edition* (New York: Oxford University Press, 1996), 69.
37 TJ to James Madison, May 20, 1782, *TJW*, 779.
38 TJ's Notes from Condorcet on Slavery, January 1789, *Papers* 14: 496.
39 Lafayette's formulation as edited by Jefferson (with the second bracket missing) was: "Tout homme nait avec des droits inaliénables; tels soint [le droit de propriété, le soin [de son honneur et] de sa vie, la disposition entier de sa personne, de son industrie, de toutes ses facultés, la recheche du bien ëtre et la résistance à l'oppression." Lafayette's Draft of a Declaration of Rights, June–July 1789

as incompletely bracketed by TJ in *Papers* 15: 230. Garry Wills claims that he could discern the second of the four brackets in the original document after the word "propriété." See Wills, *Inventing America*, 230. One may, of course, also speculate that Jefferson changed his mind in the midst of bracketing, and eventually thought that one should exclude all the lines between the first and the last bracket. Even such radical editing would not change what I think is essential, for the document would then read: "Every man is born with inalienable rights; such are [...] his life, the entire disposal of his person and industry, as well as his faculties, the pursuit of his own good, and resistance against oppression." (Translation from Wills, *Inventing America*, 230.)

40 TJ to Jean Nicolas Démeunier, April 29, 1795, *TJW*, 1028.

41 TJ, First Inaugural Address, March 4, 1801, *TJW*, 494.

42 TJ to John Manners, June 12, 1817, *Ford* 12: 66.

43 For example, in his *The Natural Rights Republic* (1996), Michael Zuckert clearly attempts to turn Jefferson into a modern libertarian. He claims, for example, that "no person who understands property as Jefferson does would accept a positive right to life." Such a right "would amount to a blank check on one's own life and liberty that a rational being would not accept" (Ibid., 79). Eventually, Jefferson is turned into a mere predecessor of Zuckert's somewhat bleak libertarian humanism under which "personhood" and "human dignity" are solely derivable from "labor" by which human beings "become owners of themselves" (Ibid., 318–319). The connections of Zuckert's philosophy with C.B. McPherson's originally critical view of Locke's "possessive individualism" from 1962 are too obvious to need detailing. Nevertheless, it is not easy to bring Zuckert's allegedly Jeffersonian "morality that begins with and builds upon self-love" (ibid., 72) into compliance with Jefferson's insistence, for example, that the very term "obligation" requires "two parties" and that "[s]elf-love therefore is no part of morality" (TJ to Thomas Law, June 13, 1814, *Extracts*, 356). Neither do Zuckert's other central formulations easily fit with Jefferson's statements on private-property rights. Among other things, Jefferson held it evident that the "law of self-preservation authorizes the distressed to take supply by force" and thereby controls "the written laws of *meum* [mine] and *tuum* [yours]" (TJ to John B. Colvin, September 20, 1810, *TJW*, 1232).

44 Lafayette's Draft of a Declaration of Rights, June–July 1789 as bracketed by TJ, *Papers* 15: 230.

45 TJ to Samuel Kercheval, July 12, 1816, *TJW*, 1402.

46 TJ to Major John Cartwright, June 5, 1824, *TJW*, 1493–1494.

47 Notably, this notion is involved in Jefferson's original draft as well. See *Papers* 1: 427. See also, TJ, Autobiography (1821), *TJW*, 19.

48 Locke, *Second Treatise* (§ 129), 352.

49 Locke, *Second Treatise* (§ 13), 275. On the numerous scholarly interpretations of the Lockean concept of the state of nature, one may begin with Richard Ashcraft's famous suggestion that there is a special "second state of nature" in Locke's thought. This is to argue that Locke could view regular government as inescapable for mankind because of a historical emergence of monetary institutions, which made labor the basis of accumulating wealth. This notion of accumulating wealth, in turn, perhaps served to distinguish civil government from the ad hoc regimes of American Indians, who, according to Locke, agreed only

to temporary civil contracts in the case of war with alien tribes. See Richard Ashcraft, "Locke's Political Philosophy" in Vere Chappell (ed.), *The Cambridge Companion to Locke* (Cambridge: Cambridge University Press, 1995), 247. On Locke's view about Indians' temporary submission to war regimes, see also James Tully, *A Discourse on Property: John Locke and His Adversaries* (Cambridge: Cambridge University Press, 1980), 225. The idea that Locke had two different kinds of states of nature seems doubtful, but the question does not need to be solved here. To my knowledge, Jefferson never argued that modern monetary institutions had in some fundamental way distinguished Euro-Americans' right to self-government from that of Native Americans.

50 Locke, *Second Treatise* (§§ 128–130), 352–353.
51 Locke, *Second Treatise* (§ 6), 271.
52 Locke, *Second Treatise* (§§ 129–130), 352–353 (emphasis added).
53 See Locke, *Second Treatise* (§13), 275–276.
54 TJ to Francis W. Gilmer, June 7, 1816, *Ford* 11: 534.
55 Vattel (transl. Chitty), *The Law of Nations*, xi.
56 James Madison, The Federalist Number 51, *The Federalist Papers*, Rossiter (ed.), 324.
57 TJ, Opinion on the French Treaties, April 28, 1793, *TJW*, 423.
58 TJ to William Ludlow, September 6, 1824, *TJW*, 1496.
59 TJ to Edward Carrington, January 16, 1787, *TJW*, 880. On Jefferson's speculations about a society without government "as among our Indians" being perhaps the best "condition" for the Americans in general, see TJ to James Madison, January 30, 1787, *TJW*, 882.
60 TJ to Francis W. Gilmer, June 7, 1816, *Ford* 11: 535. Regarding the same kind of use of "public opinion" among the Native Americans, see *Notes*, Query XI, 220.
61 On this surprisingly common scholarly view, see, for example, Ellis, *American Sphinx*, 115.
62 TJ to Francis W. Gilmer, June 7, 1816, *Ford* 11: 535.
63 Locke, *Second Treatise* (§ 128), 352.
64 Locke, *Second Treatise* (§ 110), 341–342.
65 Hutcheson, *Short Introduction* (1747), 282.
66 Locke, *Second Treatise* (§ 15), 278.
67 Rousseau remarked about the imposition of government on the young when coming into their "years of discretion": It is "necessary, in order to legitimize an arbitrary government, that in every generation the people should be in a position to accept or to reject it; but were this so, the government would be no longer arbitrary." Jean-Jacques Rousseau, *The Social Contract and Discourses* [*Du Contrat Social*, 1762], transl. by G.D.H. Cole and updated by P.D. Jimack (London: Everyman, 1993), 186.
68 John Locke was explicit that commonwealths remain "in the state of nature" regarding each other. Once divided into nations, individuals' obligations to the rest of mankind would be handled as issues in ancient jus gentium, a term later used to refer to the laws of nations. On Locke's view that every person becomes a subject to one's commonwealth and as such a subject, remains in the state of nature with regard to other commonwealths, see Locke, *Second Treatise* (§ 145), 365. See also ibid. (§ 183), 390.

69 TJ to Alexander von Humboldt, June 13, 1817, *Thomas Jefferson: Political Writings*, Appleby and Ball (eds.), 221.
70 TJ to Albert Gallatin, June 26, 1806, *Ford* 10: 273. On the same point, see also TJ, Summary View of the Rights of British America, 1774, *TJW*, 105; TJ, Autobiography (1821), ibid., 9, 36. Jefferson was not alone in this view. Emer de Vattel, for example, argued that every "man has a right to quit his country," although not in order to avoid defending it. The footnote there mentioned that England had not submitted to this right. See Vattel (trans. Chitty), *The Law of Nations*, 103–104.
71 Jefferson's Composition Draft of the Declaration of the Causes and Necessity for Taking up Arms, June–July 1775, *Papers* 1: 193.
72 TJ, A Summary View of the Rights of British America, 1774, *TJW*, 117. Regarding J.G.A. Pocock's seemingly opposite thesis that the colonies had been settled in the state of nature, it is notable that such a state of nature would then include "the space jointly occupied by sovereigns in the *jus gentium*." See J.G.A. Pocock, "Political Thought in the English-speaking Atlantic, 1760–1790: The Imperial Crisis," in J.G.A. Pocock with the assistance of Gordon J. Schochet and Lois G. Swoerer (eds.), *The Varieties of British Political Thought* (Cambridge: Cambridge University Press, 1993), 279. Pocock thinks that Jefferson here implicitly offered the king the position of an emperor of the British Empire, as if it were a confederation of independent English-speaking states and hence of independent peoples – the notion the colonists learned from Grotius, Pufendorf, and Vattel (who came respectively from Dutch, German, and Swiss confederations). As Pocock notes, "if a 'people' existed only as represented and embodied in its own sovereign government, there must be as many 'peoples' as there were 'states'." Ibid., 274–275.
73 On this elementary point, see, for example, Csaba Lévai's insightful review of Péter Hahner's *Thomas Jefferson és a francia forradolom*, Lévai, "A Moderate Reformer?" *Budapest Review of Books*, No. 4, 1999, 203.
74 Locke, *Second Treatise* (§ 168), 380.
75 Hutcheson, *Short Introduction*, 306, 279.
76 James Tully is one of those scholars who would insist that "Locke distinguishes between the dissolution of government and the dissolution of political society" and holds that "virtually the only way political society is dissolved is by foreign conquest." James Tully, "Locke," in J.H. Burns with Mark Goldie (eds.), *The Cambridge History of Political Thought 1450–1700* (Cambridge: Cambridge University Press, 1991), 636.
77 The Declaration of Independence, *Papers* 1: 429.
78 TJ, A Summary View of the Rights of British America, 1774, *TJW*, 109–110. On Jefferson clearly favoring James Wilson's position on popular sovereignty over Blackstone's apparently erroneous understanding of the concept, see *Legal CB* (Entry 832), 316.
79 TJ, Autobiography (1821), *TJW*, 23.
80 TJ, A Summary View of the Rights of British America, 1774, *TJW*, 115.
81 TJ, Autobiography (1821), *TJW*, 97. Jefferson definitely saw the principles of the Revolution as of world historical significance, but it is notable that even the Declaration of Independence calls for "prudence" in deciding whether or not a denial of the consent of the governed could be deemed justified in the summer of 1776.

82 *Notes*, Query XVII, 211.
83 TJ, Draft Constitution for Virginia, June 1776, *TJW*, 345.
84 TJ, Jefferson's Opinion on the Constitutionality of the Residence Bill, July 15, 1790, *Papers* 17: 195.
85 Locke, *Second Treatise* (§ 6), 271.
86 Locke, *Second Treatise* (§ 16), 279.
87 TJ, A Summary View of the Rights of British America, 1774, *TJW*, 105–106. The central point is well captured by John Zvesper: "Choosing to remain where one is, or choosing to set up elsewhere, is a right held by individuals, the exercise of which creates peoples." Zvesper, "Jefferson on Liberal Natural Rights," 19. This principle could not apply to people of African origin in Jefferson's thought for obvious practical reasons. It is worth keeping in mind, however, that the restricting of immigration and the regulation of naturalization were generally viewed as natural rights of any independent nation. Madison, for example, argued in 1787 that all questions concerning naturalization should be left entirely in the hands of state legislatures. See Madison on August 9, 1787 in Adrianne Koch (ed.), *Notes of Debates in the Federal Convention of 1787 Reported by James Madison*, Bicentennial Edition (New York: W.W. Norton, 1987), 419. The federal naturalization acts of 1795 and 1798, of course, aimed to regulate the immigration of white Europeans. See Elkins and McKitrick, *Age of Federalism*, 694.
88 TJ to Edmund Randolph, August 18, 1799, *TJW*, 1068.
89 On alterations in common law, see TJ to Thomas Cooper, February 10, 1814, *TJW*, 1325 and the same in Jefferson, *Legal CB* (Entry 873), 354. For the etymology of *jus commune* as *folc-right*, see ibid. (Entry 896), 348. Jefferson's conventional definition of the common law of England was "that part of the English law which was anterior to the date of the oldest statutes extant." *Notes*, Query XIV, 263. The more complicated question of Jefferson's exact understanding of the extent to which the concept of common law rested on immemorial custom instead of being created over time by different authorities is beyond the scope of this study. In general terms, however, he clearly held that because there were now available not only legal yearbooks, but also critical studies of law, "we take no judge's word for what the law is." TJ to Thomas Cooper, February 10, 1814, *TJW*, 1324. Finally, Jefferson's consistent attempts to shift to milder punishments in criminal law appear to have evolved from the idea that it is the lawgiver who is supposed to be enlightened in such issues, whereas the judge should "be a mere machine." TJ to Edmund Pendleton, August 26, 1776, *TJW*, 757.
90 TJ to Major John Cartwright, June 5, 1824, *TJW*, 1490.
91 TJ to Doctor Thomas Cooper, February 10, 1814, *TJW*, 1325. (The summary Jefferson offered here to Cooper was drawn from his own Legal Commonplace Book.)
92 TJ to Major John Cartwright, June 5, 1824, *TJW*, 1490.
93 *Legal CB* (Entry 770), 257. According to this same statement, the principle of primogeniture originated in this medieval monarchical practice of appointing the eldest son of the king to the crown. See ibid. (Entry 770), 256.
94 Even Grotius, Pufendorf, Vattel, and Wolf "often differ," Jefferson noted, on the specific details of natural law. TJ, Opinion on the French Treaties, April 28, 1793, *TJW*, 428.

95 TJ to Major John Cartwright, June 5, 1824, *TJW*, 1491. As to Saxons' moral shortcomings, there is a passing remark in Jefferson's memoranda that they also had slaves. See Jefferson, *Legal CB* (Entry 596), 135.

96 TJ to Major John Cartwright, June 5, 1824, *TJW*, 1491. My reading is here at odds with H. Trevor Colbourn's widely shared view of Jefferson as an advocate of so-called Whig history, according to which one would paradigmatically consider "one's forefathers as exponents of democracy and liberty." See Trevor H. Colbourn, *The Lamp of Experience: Whig History and the Intellectual Origins of the American Revolution* (New York: W.W. Norton, 1974), 183.

97 *Notes*, Query XIII, 238.

98 TJ to Edmund Pendleton, August 13, 1776, *TJW*, 751.

99 TJ to Diodati, August 3, 1789, *TJW*, 958.

100 *Notes*, Query XIII, 237–238.

101 TJ, Summary View, 1774, *TJW*, 111.

102 TJ to Edmund Randolph, August 18, 1799, *TJW*, 1068. As Jack Rakove once formulated the case, "the concept of equality that Jefferson evoked in the declaration ... was tied less to notions of liberal individualism than to the collective right of the American people to govern itself." Jack Rakove, "Our Jefferson," in Lewis and Onuf (eds.), *Sally Hemings and Thomas Jefferson*, 230.

103 TJ to Edmund Randolph, August 18, 1799, *TJW*, 1068–1069

104 TJ, Summary View of the Rights of British America, 1774, *TJW*, 111. Jefferson's states' rights doctrine should be taken seriously. Consider, for example, his (at least apparently hyperbolic) statement to Adams on whether to continue the War of 1812 against the British: "Peace would seem now to be an easy work," Jefferson mused in 1814, but went on by asking, "[w]hat will Massachusetts say to this? I mean her majority, which must be considered as speaking, thro' the organs it has appointed itself ... Will she now sacrifice the fisheries to the same partialities? This question is interesting to her alone ... Take this question ad referendum. It concerns you alone. If you would rather give up the fisheries than war with England, we [the other states] give them up. If you had rather fight for them, we will defend your interests to the last drop of our blood." TJ to John Adams, July 5, 1814, *TJW*, 1340–1341.

105 As to the universal repercussions of this principle, according to Jefferson, the change of the form of government did not alter the status of a nation as a sovereign power in terms of international law. See TJ, Opinion on the French Treaties, April 28, 1793, *TJW*, 423–429.

106 *Notes*, Query VIII, 211. Practically speaking, Jefferson equated the consent of the governed with regular elections under universal male suffrage. In a letter to John Taylor, he lamented that in contemporary Virginia, "one half of our brethren who fight and pay taxes, are excluded ... from the rights of representation" to the effect that this half was submitted to the state "without their consent." TJ to John Taylor, May 28, 1816, *TJW*, 1393.

107 See, for example, TJ to Edmund Randolph, August 18, 1799, *TJW*, 1068–1069.

108 TJ to William Johnson, June 12, 1823, *TJW*, 1476.

109 TJ to Judge Spencer Roane, September 6, 1819, *TJW*, 1426.

110 See TJ, Draft of the Kentucky Resolutions, October 1798, *TJW*, 449–456.

111 TJ to James Madison, March 15, 1789, *TJW*, 944.

112 For a good introduction to this elementary point of natural law theory, see, for example, Istvan Hont and Michael Ignatieff, "Needs and Justice in the Wealth of Nations: An Introductory Essay" in Hont and Ignatieff (eds.), *Wealth and Virtue: The Shaping of Political Economy in the Scottish Enlightenment* (Cambridge: Cambridge University Press, 1983), 1–44. See also Haakonssen, *Natural Law and Moral Philosophy*, e.g., 29–30, 39–43.

113 The only occasion that Jefferson ever uttered the slightest indication that he preferred one of the natural lawyers over others is when he accused Emer de Vattel (his otherwise most often cited authority in the field) of being imprecise about the "moral duty" of a nation to abide its international treaties. See, TJ, *Opinion on the French Treaties,* April 28, 1793, *TJW*, 422–434. Yet, as late as 1814, Jefferson recommended Vattel as elementary reading in the field of "Natural Law." TJ to John Minor, August 30, 1814, *TJW*, 1558.

114 Kames (Henry Home), *Principles of Equity* (Edinburgh: A. Kincaid, 1760), 10–11, 46.

115 See Thomas Reid, *Essays on the Active Powers of Man* (1768), in Sir William Hamilton Bart (ed.), *The Works of Thomas Reid*, Vol. II, 8th edition (Edinburgh, 1880), 640.

116 Kames, *Essays*, 134.

117 It is precisely when turning Jefferson's rights thought into clear-cut philosophy of perfect and imperfect rights that his use of terms begins to appear confusing. For example, philosopher Morton White runs into insurmountable problems in claiming that Jefferson's inalienable right to the pursuit of happiness, in order to appear a perfect right (and hence as truly moral), would require an individual to submit to a corresponding *moral* obligation to the pursuit itself. Given Jefferson's Epicureanism, one could just as easily consider the pursuit of happiness as a natural human inclination, or more simply still, view happiness as nothing less than "the aim of life" (TJ to William Short, October 31, 1819, *TJW*, 1433). White seeks the Jeffersonian distinction between perfect and imperfect rights at a wrong place in the Declaration of Independence. The statement that "all men are created equal" and equally entitled to the inalienable – and hence perfect – rights of "Life, Liberty and the pursuit of Happiness" does not imply even the possibility of a conflict. On the Declaration's phrase regarding happiness, Morton White states that "man has a right to pursue happiness if he pleases," meaning that man is not "caused" to do so. He then goes on to state that "I think Jefferson would have to treat it [the pursuit of happiness] as unalienable on moral grounds, arguing that since it is our duty and therefore a right to pursue happiness, we would be violating that duty in transferring that right to another" (see White, *Philosophy of the American Revolution*, 213). With regard to Jefferson's thought, White's mistake in this formulation consists in the phrase "if he pleases." In Jefferson's eyes, the pursuit of happiness was beyond our will, and Jefferson treated such pursuit as natural for man as a living thing and as a free agent. A man committing suicide would thus be doing something unnatural rather than something morally reproachable. White, in fact, even though resisting Jefferson's view as philosophically inconsistent, conceded to its probably being closest to his own line of thought. Interestingly, White also brings up the possibility of viewing Jefferson's "rights" as Aristotelian kinds of powers to act regarding the "ends" of life, liberty, and

the pursuit of happiness. This is close to my overall interpretation of Jefferson's moral thought, albeit one cannot dub Jefferson an Aristotelian in any strict sense of the term (see ibid., e.g., 288.).

118 TJ's "Rough draught" of the Declaration of Independence, *Papers* 1:423. See also TJ to Thomas Paine, July 11, 1789, *Papers* 15: 268.

119 Whether Jefferson's position would accord with what Knud Haakonssen claims about Thomas Reid's theory in this respect – namely, that Reid gave the perfect and imperfect rights equal epistemological status – is beyond the focus of this study. Jefferson never offered a consistent theory on the issue. Judging strictly from Jefferson's statements, it seems clear that if Reid truly saw it as the government's task to legally enforce the imperfect rights along with the perfect ones, Jefferson would have agreed. See on Reid's views, Haakonssen, *Natural Law and Moral Philosophy*, e.g., 203–204.

120 TJ, Opinion on the French Treaties, April 28, 1793, *TJW*, 422–434.

121 TJ, Opinion on the French Treaties, April 28, 1793, *TJW*, 434.

122 TJ, Opinion on the French Treaties, April 28, 1793, *TJW*, 422–423.

123 TJ, Opinion on the French Treaties, April 28, 1793, *TJW*, 423.

124 TJ, Opinion on the French Treaties, April 28, 1793, *TJW*, 423.

125 TJ, Opinion on the French Treaties, April 28, 1793, *TJW*, 423.

126 TJ, Opinion on the French Treaties, April 28, 1793, *TJW*, 432.

127 TJ's Report on Negotiation with Spain, March 18, 1792, *Ford* 6: 414–445. For the quotation, see ibid., 426 (emphasis added).

128 TJ's Report on Negotiation with Spain, March 18, 1792, *Ford* 6: 435.

129 TJ's Report on Negotiation with Spain, March 18, 1792, *Ford* 6: 425, 435.

130 TJ's Report on Negotiation with Spain, March 18, 1792, *Ford* 6: 433–435 (the formulation of the paragraphs is slightly altered here in order to clarify the line of argument).

131 TJ, Report on Negotiation with Spain, March 18, 1792, *Ford* 6: 435.

132 TJ to John Adams, October 14, 1816, *AJL*, 492. For another definition of virtue as linked to "social utility," see TJ to William Short, August 4, 1820, *TJW*, 1437.

133 TJ to James Madison, October 28, 1785, *TJW*, 841–842.

134 TJ to James Madison September 6, 1789, *TJW*, 959–960.

135 TJ, Summary View of the Rights of British America, 1774, *TJW*, 108.

136 TJ to William Short, November 28, 1814, *TJW*, 1357.

137 On "pure morality," see TJ to Benjamin Hawkins, February 18, 1803, *TJW*, 1116. On the idea of secretly running the tribes into debt, see TJ to William H. Harrison, February 27, 1803, *TJW*, 1118.

138 TJ to Albert Gallatin, November 14, 1818, *Ford* 12: 104–105. It was equally evident to Jefferson that no courthouse could be taken as the ultimate arbiter between nations concerning such questions as cessions of landed property because "neither party thinks of calling the other to a trial of the fact in a court of its own, where it would be both party and judge." Jefferson to Henry A. Dearborn, January 6, 1806, *Ford* 10: 221.

139 On Jefferson's statement about slavery and "Europe, which has forced this evil on us," see TJ to Albert Gallatin, December 26, 1820, *TJW*, 1450.

140 See Locke, *The Second Treatise* (§ 24), 284. As for the Lockean concept of the state of nature, one might argue that in that state of affairs, human sociability

would prevail only until disagreements arise even among the law-abiding people about the true dictates of God-given natural law and, as a result, the preservation of peace becomes impossible. The European religious wars had well proved for natural lawyers that governmental monopoly of violence should not be extended to solve disagreements on the details of divine natural law. By the same token, it seems evident that Locke's own reading of the precise dictates of the natural law (as prevailing in the state of nature) could include slavery.

141 Jefferson's marginal note on page 147 in Lord Kames's *Essays on the Principles of Morality and Natural Religion* (1751) as in Jefferson, *Catalogue*, Sowerby (ed.), Vol. II, 11–12. Given Jefferson's own testimony that he had not touched the book after studying it as a young man, the note could have been dictated by some of his teachers at the College of William and Mary. Be that as it may, it bears remarkable resemblance to Jefferson's other statements on human progress and on the injustice of slavery.

142 For Jefferson's marginal note on page 147 in Lord Kames's *Essays*,see Sowerby (ed.), *Catalogue*, Vol. II,11–12. The note's core argument may have been drawn from Montesquieu's *Spirit of Laws* (Bk. XV, Ch. 2), where it is stated that, even in war, killing is lawful only "in case of absolute necessity, but when a man has made another his slave, he cannot be said to have been under a necessity of taking away his life." See Montesquieu, *Spirit of Laws*, 259. (This quotation follows Jefferson's own practice of not using capital letters at the beginning of sentences. Unlike other editors of Jefferson's writings, E. Millicent Sowerby retains this practice.)

143 Jefferson's marginal note on page 147 in Lord Kames's *Essays*, Sowerby (ed.), *Catalogue*, Vol. II, 11–12 (emphasis added).

144 See Locke, *Second Treatise* (§ 183), 390. On this argument, see also Helo and Peter Onuf, "Jefferson, Morality, and the Problem of Slavery," *The William and Mary Quarterly* 60 (3, 2003), 583–614.

145 It was similarly evident to Arthur Lee that "it is not true that a Captive may be slain, unless in [the] case of absolute necessity." But the enslavement of an enemy soldier proved simply that "no such necessity existed" in the first place. Arthur Lee's "Address on Slavery" in *Virginia Gazette*, March 19, 1767 as quoted in Nash, *Race and Revolution*, 93.

146 For cartel-ship principles as actually practiced during wartime, see, for example, David F. Long, *Nothing too Daring: A Biography of Commodore David Porter, 1780–1843* (Annapolis, MD: United States Naval Institute, 1970), 67.

147 For such prevalent eighteenth-century notions of warfare "as an extension of diplomacy," see, for example, Elkins and McKitrick, *Age of Federalism*, 583.

148 TJ to John Holmes, April 22, 1820, *TJW*, 1434.

149 TJ to Clement Caine, September 16, 1811, *Ford* 11: 214. Here the point was also to emphasize that a good slave master would take better care of the slave than a typical European manufacturer would of his paid workers.

150 Quotation in Hont and Ignatieff, "Needs and Justice," 30 (emphasis added). As Kari Saastmoinen has clarified, Pufendorf's understanding of human equality in terms of moral duties should be held strictly separate from his thought on social justice. For example, Pufendorf thought it unfortunate that Christians had abolished slavery among themselves and had, instead, resorted to the system of "public workhouses, in which lazy rascals are constrained to a life of labour."

See Kari Saastamoinen, "Pufendorf on Natural Equality, Human Dignity, and Self-Esteem," *Journal of the History of Ideas*, Vol. 71 (1, 2010), 44.

151 This fundamental, early modern turning point in Western moral philosophy has provided the basis for most modern theories of natural rights as well. Even today this notion of perfect human rights, albeit often deprived of its purely religious ramifications, provides the moral backing for various theoretical conceptions of minimal government as one not interfering with the absolute individual right to self-determination.

152 See "The Fundamental Constitutions of Carolina," as in *The Works of John Locke*, Vol. X, 196.

153 TJ to William A. Burwell, January 28, 1805, *Ford* 10: 126. Cynically speaking, one needs only to replace the emancipation of slaves in this quotation with, say, the idea of providing every American with minimum health coverage in order to have at hand the definition of "the progressive" as *political*.

154 Vattel (transl.by Chitty), *Law of Nations*, lix [Introduction, § 17].

155 Burlamaqui (transl. by Nugent), *The Principles of Natural Law*, 67. See also ibid., 95.

156 Wilson, *The Works of Wilson*, 211. I have no evidence that Jefferson ever read or commented on Wilson's view in this respect. On his familiarity with Wilson's revolutionary writings from 1774, see *Legal CB* (Entry 833), 317. On Knud Haakonssen's explanation of this developing notion of self-imposed obligation as at least implicitly argued by Burlamaqui, Wilson, and Jefferson alike, see Haakonssen, *Natural Law and Moral Philosophy*, 336–341. On these developments in the theory of obligation, see also Petter Korkman, "Voluntarism and Moral Obligation: Barbeyrac's Defence of Pufendorf Revisited," in T.J. Hochstrasser and Peter Shröder (eds.), *Early Modern Natural Law Theories: Contexts and Strategies in the Early Enlightenment* (Dordrecth: Kluwer Academic Publishers, 2003), 195–226. I would emphasize, however, that it is of crucial importance to keep Jefferson's progressive view of morality as distinct from what Knud Haakonssen (on purely theoretical grounds) argues about the self-imposed obligation, as implicitly concerning Jefferson as well: "Burlamaqui and cognate spirits among rational dissenters, who were finding their way to the idea of moral autonomy and the possibility of self-imposed obligation, found it hard to accept the implication that self-government makes moral harmony an open-ended task and not a justifying ideal" (see Haakonssen, *Natural Law and Moral Philosophy*, 340). Jefferson could agree with Burlamaqui's general views, whether or not he is considered as a "rational dissenter." However, nothing in the socio-political realities of early American history would imply the need for some clear-cut distinction between an "open-ended" task to attain moral harmony and moral harmony as "a justifying ideal." For Jefferson, the idea of a self-imposed obligation could easily appear as a mere hope in view of the socio-political inequalities present in the America of his day, where so many free, white males were still viewed as incapable of genuine independency. Jefferson's vision was about enabling all male citizens "by their single will" (or "by that of their majority") to exercise "the right of self-government." Such a vision could well remain a justifying ideal with or without any commitment to some presumed moral harmony as either a closed or an open-ended task. As the next chapter shows, Jefferson, for example, never refuted the idea that women

might some day be endowed with equal political rights. What he contended was that he was not yet personally ready for such an innovation.

157 TJ, Opinion on the French Treaties, April 28, 1793, *TJW*, 428.

158 TJ, Opinion on the French Treaties, April 28, 1793, *TJW*, 428.

159 TJ, Opinion on the French Treaties, April 28, 1793, *TJW*, 423.

160 TJ, Opinion on the French Treaties, April 28, 1793, *TJW*, 424.

161 TJ, Report on the Negotiations with Spain, May 18, 1792, *Ford* 6: 425. Charles A. Miller finds an apparently major shift in Jefferson's thought on natural law occurring in a memorandum dating to 1818. According to Miller, Jefferson's earlier conception of the law of nature and nations as derivable from natural law suddenly fell apart in this particular document. The law of nature and nations now "found a home with politics, where, under the name of international law, it has largely remained" (Charles Miller, *Jefferson and Nature*, 195). What this erudite point supposedly means is that Jefferson eventually chose practical politics over his earlier, more comprehensive notion of nature as the foundation of all facts and values – which notion of nature itself Miller (I think erroneously) derives from Jefferson's alleged ignorance of the distinction between statements of facts and values (see ibid., e.g., 91).

162 TJ to Peter Carr, August 10, 1787, *TJW*, 901. After this remark, Jefferson went on to explain that man was destined for society and his morality was formed to this object, and that the moral sense, rather than truth or beauty, indeed, "is the true foundation of morality." As noted, this comment is truly exceptional among Jefferson's numerous, more restricted statements on the issue. Even in the letter to Thomas Law, Jefferson referred to the general theory of the moral sense numerous times only as compatible with his "belief" or "creed."

163 TJ, Opinion on the French Treaties, April 28, 1793, *TJW*, 423.

164 Quotes respectively from TJ to Judge Spence Roane, September 6, 1819, *TJW*, 1426 and TJ to Thomas Earle, September 24, 1823, *L&B* 15: 471.

165 TJ to John Heaton, May 20, 1826, *TJW*, 1516.

5 Progressive Politics

1 *Notes*, Query XIV, 269.

2 TJ, Syllabus on the Doctrines of Jesus, April 1803 as attached to TJ to Benjamin Rush, April 21, 1803, *TJW*, 1124.

3 TJ to Samuel Kercheval, July 12, 1816, *TJW*, 1399. Nevertheless, the standard scholarly view of Jefferson's political thought runs directly counter to this central contention that every free man needed to participate in politics as an "active member of the government." An illuminating example of the treatment of Jefferson as a champion of little government – if not as an essentially anti-political intellectual – is Gordon Wood's claim that "Jeffersonian modern virtue flowed from the citizen's participation in society, not in government," and should hence be held distinct from any ancient notion of "participation in politics" (Wood, "Trials and Tribulations," 406). In this respect, it is equally difficult to reconcile Jefferson's views with Joyce Appleby's generalized Jeffersonian vision in which "Democratic values were invoked not to enlarge the people's power in government but rather to justify the abandonment of the authority traditionally exercised over them" (Appleby, "Republicanism in Old and New

Contexts," *The William and Mary Quarterly* 43 [1, 1986], 25). For Jefferson, the essential problem in contemporary Virginia was that only "freeholders" were entitled "to vote, not including the half of those on the roll of the militia, or of the tax-gatherers," given, for example, that "all able-bodied men" were in fact enrolled in the state militia. Quotations respectively from *Notes*, Query XIII and Query IX, 244, 216. In his draft of the later Northwest Ordinance, Jefferson suggested universal male suffrage without any property or tax qualifications in the Western territories. See TJ, Report on Government for Western Territory, March 1, 1794, TJW, 376–378.

4 Interestingly, Jefferson referred to Lord Kames as the best authority on the law of equity. TJ to Peter Carr, June 22, 1792 as quoted in Gilbert Chinard's Introduction to *The Commonplace Book of Thomas Jefferson* (Baltimore, MD: Johns Hopkins University Press, 1926) [*Legal CB*], 17. In Kames's early writings one finds a Jeffersonian kind of distinction between the functions of the legislator and the judge, namely that "it belongs to the legislature only, to enact regulations for advancing the positive good or happiness of society," whereas the court of equity acts "upon the principle of utility." Kames, *Principles of Equity*, 46.

5 See "Address on Slavery" in *Virginia Gazette*, March 19, 1767 as in Nash, *Race and Revolution*, 92. That Jefferson regarded Lee's "The Monitor Letters" from 1769 as one of the predecessors of his own "A Summary View of the Rights of British America" from 1774, see *Notes*, Query XXIII, 304. Gassendi, whose Epicurean doctrines Jefferson admired, also cited Roman lawyers on this point, and saw it as evident that right is "more ancient than justice," the latter arising from a social contract (Schneewind, *Invention of Autonomy*, 268). As Jefferson could have learned from Lord Kames's studies on equity law, the Enlightenment-era notion of the equality of all human beings had long before turned equity into a special branch of jurisprudence that rectified common law when no exact statutes could be found.

6 TJ to Isaac H. Tiffany, April 4, 1819, *Jefferson Political Writings*, Appleby and Ball (eds.), 224.

7 TJ to Samuel Kercheval, July 12, 1816, *TJW*, 1397.

8 TJ to Robert Skipwith, August 3, 1771, *Papers* 1: 77.

9 As for Destutt de Tracy's importance to Jefferson, it is notable that Jefferson's sole criticism concerned the Frenchman's preference of a "plural over a singular executive." TJ to Destutt de Tracy, January 26, 1811, *TJW*, 1241–1247; TJ to William Duane, August 12, 1810, ibid., 1230. As noted earlier, Jefferson probably did not read Destutt de Tracy's books entirely because he was not "fond of reading what is merely abstract, and unapplied immediately to some useful science." TJ to John Adams, October 14, 1816, *AJL*, 491. Notably, Jefferson's appraisal of John Taylor's *Enquiry into the Principles of Our Government* from 1816 concerns only the chapter on "good moral principles of our government," for he had time to obtain only "a cursory idea" about the rest of the book. TJ to John Taylor, May 28, 1816, *TJW*, 1391–1392. In 1820, Jefferson assured Thomas Ritchie that he would read Taylor's *Construction Construed* "with edification, as I did his Inquiry." This may indicate that he eventually read Taylor's *Enquiry* entirely. However, much can be inferred from Jefferson's statement that the later book "is equally orthodox, I know before reading it, because I know that Colonel Taylor and myself have rarely, if ever, differed in any political principle of importance." Quotations, TJ to Thomas Ritchie, December 25, 1820, ibid., 1554.

10 TJ to William Ludlow, September 6, 1824, *TJW*, 1496–1497.
11 TJ to John Norvell, June 14, 1807, *Ford* 10: 416.
12 TJ, Response to the Citizens of Albemarle, February 12, 1790, *TJW*, 491.
13 TJ to Alexander von Humboldt, June 13, 1817, *Jefferson Political Writings*, Appleby and Ball (eds.), 221.
14 TJ to Samuel Kercheval, July 12, 1816, *TJW*, 1402.
15 In purely historical terms, the founding obviously meant different things to different founders. In studying Jefferson's understanding of the founding, one does not need to take sides between the so-called republican synthesis and the liberal and the neoliberal schools' interpretations about its "true" nature.
16 TJ to John Taylor, May 28, 1816, *TJW*, 1392.
17 Tacitus, *Annals* (4.33) as in Tacitus, *The Complete Works of Tacitus*, ed. by Moses Hadas (New York: The Modern Library, Random House, 1942), 162.
18 TJ to John Taylor, May 28, 1816, *TJW*, 1392.
19 TJ to Lafayette, November 4, 1823, *L&B* 14: 492.
20 TJ to John Langdon, March 5, 1810, *TJW*, 1218.
21 TJ to John Adams, January 24, 1814, *AJL*, 423.
22 TJ Major John Cartwright, June 5, 1824, *TJW*, 1495.
23 TJ to James Madison, February 17, 1826, *TJW*, 1513–1514.
24 On Mandeville, see Daniel Walker Howe, "The Language of Faculty Psychology in The Federalist Papers," in Ball and Pocock (eds.), *Conceptual Change and the Constitution*, 129. To convince oneself of the exceptional nature of Mandeville's famous thesis, one needs only to take a look at the Preface to the French *Encyclopedia*. There it was held evident that natural law is prior to all political associations to the effect that the statesman should always keep that law in mind. See D'Alembert, "Discours Préliminaire des editeurs," *Encyclopédie*, xi. [For a translation, see D'Alembert, *Preliminary Discourse to the Encyclopedia of Diderot*, transl. by Richard N. Schwab and Walter E. Rex (New York: Bobbs-Merrill, Library of Liberal Arts, 1963), 36.]
25 Quotations from *Notes*, Queries XVII, XVIII, 287, 289. On the general notion of corruption manifesting itself in effeminacy and passion for luxury in the founders' imagination, see, for example, Bernard Bailyn, *The Ideological Origins of the American Revolution* (Cambridge, MA: Harvard University Press, 1971), passim, e.g., 134–137.
26 TJ to the Marquis de Lafayette, February 14, 1815, *TJW*, 1360.
27 As a British political writer, Edward Forset, had argued in 1606, just as in medicine, it was important in politics to know "the constitution and complexion of the bodie politique." Gerald Stourzh, "Constitution: Changing Meanings of the Term from the Early Seventeenth to the Late Eighteenth Century," in Ball and Pocock (eds.), *Conceptual Change and the Constitution*, 38. On the quotation, see TJ to John Taylor, November 26, 1798, *Ford* 8: 480. By "patients," Jefferson here referred to those who sympathized with Adams's apparently anti-Jeffersonian measures during the recent "X.Y.Z. scandal," which concerned the French open demand of bribes from American negotiators. The incident preceded the so-called Quasi-War with France, 1798–1800.
28 TJ to P.S. Dupont de Nemours, April 24, 1816, *TJW*, 1388. The same notion was embraced in Montesquieu, *Spirit of Laws* (Bk. XIX, Ch. 21), 296. This commonplace ideal image of Solon as a constitutional reformer resulted from

Plutarch's writings. See, for example, Adam Smith's reference to Solon, *TMS* (Part VI), 233. Contrary to Solon, in Joseph Addison's *Cato* (with which Jefferson was well acquainted), Julius Caesar was viewed as the quintessential enemy of the republican form of government. See, for example, Eran Shalev, "Empire Transformed: Britain in the American Classical Imagination, 1758–1783," *Early American Studies*, Spring 2006, 112–146.

29 TJ to Samuel Kercheval, July 12, 1816, *TJW*, 1399.

30 TJ to John Adams, December 10, 1819, *AJL*, 549. To be sure, Jefferson occasionally praised the Roman Empire as free enough to allow Christianity to evolve. That view may have, however, rested on the assumption that the Roman political system was too corrupt to truly control anything.

31 TJ to John Adams, January 22, 1821, *AJL*, 570.

32 TJ to Marquis de Lafaeytte, May 14, 1817, *TJW*, 1407.

33 *Notes*, Query XIX, 290–291.

34 *Notes*, Query XVIII, 288.

35 *Notes*, Query XIX, 290–291.

36 TJ to Joseph C. Cabell, November 28, 1820, *Ford* 12: 170.

37 TJ to Doctor Thomas Humphreys, February 8, 1817, *L&B* 15: 108.

38 TJ to Joseph C. Cabell, February 2, 1816, TJW, 1381. For a similar use of these Aristotelian terms, see TJ to the Marquis de Lafayette, February 14, 1815, *TJW*, 1360.

39 TJ to Samuel Kercheval, July 12, 1816, *TJW*, 1403.

40 *Notes*, Query XVIII, 288.

41 James Madison, Federalist Number 51, *The Federalist Papers*, Rossiter (ed.), 325. Indeed, even the Madisonian, extended federal republic was to prevent a "rage for paper money, for an abolition of debts, for an equal division of property or for any other" wicked, sectionalist interest from pervading "the whole body of the Union." See The Federalist Number 10, ibid., 84.

42 Contrary to the Aristotelian three corrupt forms of government, Plato spoke of four imperfect forms of government among the Greeks. Sparta's military timocracy he considered the best of the four. The other three were the oligarchy of the rich in Corinth, the democracy of the poor in Athens, and the tyrannical form of government in Syracuse. See Plato's *Republic* (Book IX), Plato, The Republic, transl. by Desmond Lee, 2nd edition (Baltimore, MD: Penguin Books, 1974), 356–359.

43 On these elementary, although often misunderstood points, see, for example, Douglass Adair, *Fame and the Founding Fathers: Essays by Douglass Adair*, ed. by Trevor Colbourn (New York: W.W. Norton, 1974), 114–115; Arendt, *On Revolution*, 35–49; Lance Banning, *The Jeffersonian Persuasion: Evolution of a Party Ideology* (Ithaca, NY: Cornell University Press, 1978), 23–25; and the classic, J.G.A. Pocock, *The Machiavellian Moment: Florentin Political Thought and the Atlantic Republican Tradition* (Princeton, NJ: Princeton University Press, 1975).

44 TJ to Isaac H. Tiffany, August 26, 1816, *Jefferson Political Writings*, Appleby and Ball (eds.), 218. On the eighteenth-century idea "that politics may be reduced to a science," see Adair's interesting account of the founders distinguishing theirs from classical politics, Adair, *Fame and the Founding Fathers*, 93–106. On the same, see also Wood, *Creation of the American Republic*, 593–615. As for the historical linkage between the so-called Court and Country debate

and the Jeffersonian political thought, see, for example, Banning, *Jeffersonian Persuasion*, e.g., 194–206; Elkins and McKitrick, *Age of Federalism*, e.g., 6–29. In my view, the persistent scholarly disagreements about this issue (as well as about the proper definition of republicanism) often serve to obscure rather than to clarify Jefferson's personal views of politics and political economy.

45 TJ to Edmund Pendleton, August 26, 1776, *TJW*, 756.

46 TJ to John Taylor, May 28, 1816, *TJW*, 1392.

47 James Madison, Federalist Number 10, *The Federalist Papers*, Rossiter (ed.), 81.

48 TJ to Isaac H. Tiffany, April 4, 1819, *Jefferson Political Writings*, Appleby and Ball (eds.), 224 (emphasis added).

49 *Notes*, Query XIX, 290.

50 TJ to William Charles Jarvis, September 28, 1820, *L&B* 15: 278.

51 *Notes*, Query VIII, 211. On the essential connection of universal male suffrage to any genuine "consent" of the people as the proper authority of the state government, see TJ to John Taylor, May 28, 1816, *TJW*, 1393.

52 Judith Shklar, "Alexander Hamilton and the Language of Political Science," in Anthony Pagden (ed.), *The Languages of Political Theory*, 344. For an excellent account of the innumerable ways to understand the proper voting qualifications in early America, see Chilton Williamson, *American Suffrage from Property to Democracy 1760–1860* (Princeton, NJ: Princeton University Press, 1968).

53 As Jefferson kept lamenting, the Virginia legislature, for example, was "chosen by less than half the people," whereas the state should "let every man who fights or pays, exercise his just and equal right" to vote. TJ to Samuel Kercheval, July 12, 1816, *TJW*, 1396, 1398.

54 The quotation is historian Dabney's characterization of Randolph's view of Jefferson, Virginius Dabney, *Virginia: The New Dominion* (Charlottesville: University Press of Virginia, 1992), 217. In his last will, this archconservative plantation owner freed hundreds of slaves, an act that may bespeak grander benevolence toward slaves than Jefferson's position, even if in conveniently selfish terms. For Randolph nevertheless holding that "I am an aristocrat. I love liberty, I hate equality," see ibid., 204.

55 In his insightful study of the topic, David Mayer sees inescapable inconsistencies in Jefferson's constitutional thought, and eventually argues that purely historical considerations only gradually enter his thinking. On a historicized view of the concept of constitution, see especially Mayer's comparison of Jefferson's and Madison's views of the issue, David N. Mayer, *The Constitutional Thought of Thomas Jefferson* (Charlottesville: University of Virginia Press, 1994), 302–307.

56 On Jefferson's wishes in the summer of 1776, see Ellis, *American Sphinx*, 45–48.

57 TJ, Draft Constitution for Virginia, June 1776, *TJW*, 336–345. There is little question that general male suffrage was what Jefferson meant by his formulation that all freeholders "and all persons resident in the colony who shall have paid scot and lot to government" would be entitled to vote. In any case, his further suggestion to offer land to non-freeholders would have made all male residents in the state entitled to the general freeholder status. See Merrill D. Peterson, *Thomas Jefferson and the New Nation: A Biography* (New York: Oxford

University Press, 1975), 101. Many scholars have failed to grasp this central element of Jefferson's suggestion. In fact, Jefferson's draft says only that "The Senate ... members shall be appointed by the House of Representatives." TJ, Draft Constitution for Virginia, June 1776, *TJW*, 339. Obviously, the division of the legislature into two houses was a minor concern in comparison to the elections themselves taking place under general suffrage. Jefferson later explained the point in terms of a single "choice by the people" and – in obvious reference to the election of the Senate – the consequent opportunity to give "to those so chosen by the people a second choice themselves, & they generally will chuse wise men." TJ to Edmund Pendleton, August 26, 1776, ibid., 755.

58 *Notes*, Query XIII, 249.

59 On the various uses of the Latin term *constitutiones*, see Stourzh, "Constitution, Changing Meanings," 43. According to Jefferson himself, the term, "constitution," had referred to ordinary laws in the common-law tradition. *Notes*, Query XIII, 249.

60 Indeed, one of Jefferson's favorite authorities in legal studies, Lord Bolingbroke, had defined the constitution as simply an assemblage of customs, laws, and institutions of a nation, based on reason and directed to the public good. Stourzh, "Constitution, Changing Meanings," 43.

61 TJ, Draft Constitution for Virginia, June 1776, *TJW*, 345.

62 TJ to James Madison, October 28, 1785, *TJW*, 841–842.

63 As Madison summarized Jefferson's principle, "According to the laws of mortality, a majority of those ripe at any moment for the exercise of their will do not live beyond nineteen years. To that term then is limited the validity of *every act* of the Society." Madison to TJ, February 4, 1790, *James Madison Writings*, Rakove (ed.), 474.

64 TJ to James Madison, September 6, 1789, *TJW*, 959–964.

65 TJ to Samuel Kercheval, July 12, 1816, *TJW*, 1401–1402.

66 TJ to Samuel Kercheval, July 12, 1816, *TJW*, 1401–1402.

67 TJ to James Madison, July 14, 1793, *Ford* 7: 449.

68 TJ to General Thaddeus Kosciusko, June 28, 1812, *TJW*, 1266. Jefferson's expansionist reference to Canada, of course, pertained only to the easternmost parts of modern Canada.

69 TJ to John Adams, January 22, 1821, *AJL*, 570. For Jefferson speaking of "the foundations of our confederated fabric," see TJ to Thomas Ritchie, December 25, 1820, *TJW*, 1446.

70 On John Pickering's and Samuel Chase's impeachment trials, see, for example, Peterson *Thomas Jefferson and the New Nation*, 795.

71 See for Merrill D. Peterson's fairly similar account of the immediate foreign-policy concerns around the Louisiana Purchase, Peterson, *Thomas Jefferson and the New Nation*, 747–752. Oddly enough, even in Peterson's eyes, Jefferson's urging Congress to amend the Constitution so as to provide specific powers to the federal government to extend its borders and Congress's refusal to do so, proves Jefferson's, not Congress's, inconsistent reading of Congress's constitutional powers. See ibid., 775. Neither does Peterson appear to take seriously Jefferson's hesitancy about whether the purchase, even if a step toward extending the "empire of liberty" to the West, should ever lead to establishment of a continent-wide Union. See ibid., 773.

72 *Notes*, Query XIV, 264.
73 TJ to Jared Sparks, February 4, 1824, *TJW*, 1484. On "the patronage of our nation until the emigrants shall be able to protect themselves," see also TJ to Doctor Thomas Humphreys, February 8, 1817, *L&B* 15: 102–103. On freedmen's restricted capacity for "self-government," see, for example, TJ to John Lynch, January 21, 1811, *Ford* 11: 180.
74 TJ to Joseph Priestley, January 29, 1804, *TJW*, 1142. For the general argument that the Jeffersonian Democrats did not at all necessarily aim at a continental Union, see a brilliant summary of the historiography on early American diplomatic history, William Earl Weeks, "Historiography: New Directions in the Study of Early American Foreign Relations," *Diplomatic History*, 17 (1, 1993), e.g., 91.
75 TJ to James Monroe, October 24, 1823, *TJW*, 1482.
76 This retrospectively paradoxical view was shared by a number of founding fathers, particularly in their antipathy toward both the (presumably Federalist-minded) Cincinnati Society and the (Jeffersonian-minded) Democratic Republican Societies in the early 1790s. Even if the democratic clubs were viewed as private-study circles of radical politics rather than political organizations, they no doubt contributed to the later founding of the Democratic Party. See on the issue, Elkins and McKitrick, *Age of Federalism*, 457–465, 487, and an interesting collection of documents, Philip S. Foner (ed.), *The Democratic-Republican Societies, 1790–1800: A Documentary Source Book of Constitutions, Declarations, Addresses, Resolutions, and Toasts* (Westport: Greenwood Press, 1976). For evidence that at least by 1796 the federal Congress already voted on practically all issues according to the party lines between the Federalists and the Jeffersonian Democrats, see John F. Hoadley, "The Emergence of Political Parties in Congress, 1789–1803," *The American Political Science Review* 74 (1980), 777. (On Jefferson allegedly advocating some Tocquevillean wishful image of American society "in which the area of voluntary association took precedence over the formal realms of public policy," see Appleby, "Introduction: Jefferson and His Complex Legacy," 5.)
77 TJ to Jedidiah Morse, March 6, 1822, *TJW*, 1454–1457.
78 James Madison to TJ, October 17, 1788, *James Madison Writings*, Rakove (ed.), 421. Madison made the same point in the Federalist Papers, namely that subdividing the powers of government was aimed to secure "that the private interest of every individual may be a sentinel over the public rights." James Madison, Federalist Number 51, *The Federalist Papers*, Rossiter (ed.), 322.
79 For this proverbial witticism, see Becker, *The Declaration of Independence*, 234.
80 TJ to James Madison, January 30, 1787, *TJW*, 882 (emphasis added).
81 TJ to Edward Carrington, January 16, 1787, *TJW*, 880 (emphasis added). In fact, Jefferson's initial problem with justified rebellions can be found in his disagreements with the Virginia legislature, which enacted the state constitution on its own in the midst of the Revolution and justified it afterward on the basis that the people had not arisen in rebellion to oppose it. To no big surprise, Jefferson, who relied on peaceful political discourse as the very basis of politics itself, found such an argument totally absurd. See *Notes*, Query XIII, 249–250.

82 Aristotle, *The Nicomachean Ethics* (III, 3), 56. Jefferson's much-discussed criticism of Washington's huge peacetime army to suppress the so-called Whiskey Rebellion in Pennsylvania did not result from an embrace of a rebellion against the lawful government, but from his suspicions that the Federalists would use such an army to suppress all democratic opposition to the government. For an interesting discussion on these aspects of the Whiskey Rebellion, see Elkins and McKitrick, *Age of Federalism*, 479–488.
83 TJ to Edward Carrington, January 16, 1787, *TJW*, 880.
84 TJ Edward Carrington, January 16, 1787, *TJW*, 880.
85 TJ to Thomas Seymour, February 11, 1807, *Jefferson Political Writings*, Appleby and Ball (eds.), 273.
86 Madison, Federalist Number 48, *The Federalist Papers*, Rossiter (ed.), 311–312.
87 TJ to Edmund Pendleton, August 26, 1776, *TJW*, 757.
88 TJ to Albert Gallatin, June 26, 1806, *Ford* 10: 273.
89 *Notes*, Query XVIII, 288. On the emancipation plan, see Query XIV, 263–264.
90 In reference to this letter, Lucia Stanton speaks of Jefferson's goal of "reforming rather than ending" slavery. See Stanton 1994, 164. Garrett Ward Sheldon's statement that "except for a brief period in 1788–1789, Jefferson believed that the abolition of slavery must include the removal and resettlement of blacks in Africa," appears to rest on this single letter. See Sheldon, *Political Philosophy*, 133. As noted, it is questionable whether Jefferson ever thought that Africa could serve as an asylum for the entire slave population.
91 TJ Edward Bancroft, January 26, 1789, *Papers* 14: 492 (the brackets in the original).
92 TJ Edward Bancroft, January 26, 1789, *Papers* 14: 492.
93 *Notes*, Query VIII, 211.
94 In fact, Jefferson appears to have become truly aware of his unsustainable economic situation only around the year 1808. See, for example, Sloan, *Principle and Interest*, 218.
95 This is how Jefferson stated the case: "I had often thought on the subject you propose as to the mode of procuring German emigrants to take place of our blacks. To this, however, the state legislatures are alone competent, the general government possessing no such powers but those enumerated in the Constitution, and that of obtaining emigrants at the general expense not being one of the enumerated powers. With respect to the state governments, I not only doubt, but despair, of their taking up this operation, till some strong pressure of circumstance shall force it on them." TJ to J.P. Reibelt, December 21, 1805, *Ford* 10: 205.
96 TJ to Edward Coles, August 25, 1814, *TJW*, 1345.
97 For Jefferson's careful calculations on how five-sixteenths of "negro blood" still retains the racial status of mulatto, and three-sixteenths allows deeming the individual to be pure white, see Brodie 1974, 434. The law drafted by Jefferson stated, perhaps too simply, that "every person, who shall have one fourth part or more of negro blood, shall in like manner be deemed a mulatto." TJ, Bill No. 54, A Bill Declaring What Persons Shall Be Deemed Mulattoes, *Papers* 2: 476.
98 Quotations from Jefferson's Bill No. 51 (presented to the assembly on October 31, 1785), Papers 2: 470–471, 473n1–3. In the now famous *Howell v. Netherland*

case of 1770, the young advocate Jefferson served the then twenty-eight-year-old black man Howell, who was not a slave, but a servant born during his mother's involuntary servitude. Jefferson argued that Howell should be freed from his temporary bondage. Both Howell's mulatto grandmother and his black mother had reared their children under temporary bondage. In effect, Howell was under bondage not because of his race, but because of the original breach of race codes by his grandmother's mother. The young Jefferson appears to have considered temporary involuntary servitude inapplicable even to the black child further than the law explicitly required. The law of 1705 made a white woman's mulatto offspring servants until the age of thirty-one, but the later statute from 1735 bound even the second-generation children to the same condition, in this case, Howell's mother. (The later acts of 1748 and 1753 did not appear to change the contents of law, and they had been enacted after Howell's birth.) Jefferson thus attempted to end Howell's servitude on the basis that the law of 1735, even if it included the grandchild, should not be interpreted as applicable further than that. As he stated, lacking any precise stipulation, the law obviously "does not include the grandchild, great-grandchild, great-great-grandchild, &c. in infinitum." But Jefferson lost the case. The court decided to cling to the age of thirty-one, even with Howell. That the case was not about the legality of slavery itself is evident. Jefferson argued that the 1705 clause, which dictated that "children shall be bond or free, according to the condition of the mother," in fact "affected the children of slaves only." See *Ford* 1: 470–481.

99 Even if not the whole truth, there is a good deal of it in Eric Williams's classic statement that slavery "was not born of racism: rather racism was the consequence of slavery. Unfree labor in the New World was brown, white, black, and yellow; Catholic, Protestant and pagan" (Williams, *Capitalism and Slavery*, 7). Quite in line with the standards of the time, Jefferson's own revision of the state laws, from the late 1770s and early 1780s, included severe restrictions on white servants tied to temporal servitude until the age of twenty-one. White servants could be captured just like slaves if considered runaways. See Jefferson's revision of Virginia laws as in Bills No. 52 and No. 53, *Papers* 2: 473–475. Similarly, orphans could be "bound apprentice" until the age of twenty-one. See Bill No. 60, *Papers* 2: 487.

100 Egerton, *Gabriel's Rebellion*, 165–166.

101 Whereas the loopholes in the laws regulating slavery usually benefited the victims, the lack of control also produced such phenomena as professional slave hunters kidnapping and selling free African Americans illegally back to slavery. See, for example, MacLeod, *Slavery, Race and the American Revolution*, 22.

102 For example, historian John Chester Miller strongly condemns Jefferson's advocacy of streamlining slavery regulations all over the country, including Louisiana's older *code noir*. See John C. Miller, *The Wolf by the Ears*, 144.

103 As noted, the slave's right to hire his own time was made illegal in Virginia as early as 1792, and in 1808 the whole self-hire system was forbidden. In 1806, in an effort to put a stop to the growth of the freed black population, all newly freed slave men were required by law to leave the state of Virginia within twelve months. From 1812 onward, any free African American who happened to leave the state was prohibited from ever reentering it (on the legislation, see Egerton, *Gabriel's Rebellion*, 165–166). Jefferson's early drafts for slave codes

of Virginia from the 1770s already included many of these principles, although the state enacted such laws much later. Interestingly, Jefferson's Bill No. 51 (presented to the assembly on October 31, 1785) suggested that no new slaves could be brought to the state, for "Negroes and mulattoes which shall hereafter be brought into this commonwealth and kept therein a whole year, together, or so long at different times as shall amount to one year, shall be free." Jefferson clearly sought to restrict legal slavery and keep its expansion in Virginia within more precise limits. Such limits also concerned the free property rights of slaveholders. Bill No. 51 offered strict requirements for an individual master to emancipate a slave and included an implicit requirement to provide the freed slave the means to move out of the state. According to Jefferson's bill, "if such slave, so emancipated, shall not within one year thereafter, depart the commonwealth, he shall be out the protection of the laws." Thus, freed blacks could be enslaved anew if they failed to leave the state. These requirements were not included in the eventual law. See *Papers* 2: 470–471, 473n1–3.

104 TJ to John B. Colvin, September 20, 1810, *TJW*, 1231.

105 TJ, Opinion on the French Treaties, April 28, 1795, *TJW*, 423. Grotius, Pufendorf, and Vattel shared the doctrine that a change in the form of government cannot invalidate international treaties. On this, see, for example, Jefferson's excerpt from Grotius that "the same body remains, tho' the head is changed" in TJ on the French Treaties, April 28, 1793, *TJW*, 430.

106 TJ to Samuel Kercheval, July 12, 1816, *TJW*, 1399.

107 TJ to Diodati, August 3, 1789, *TJW*, 957.

108 Today, the state of Nebraska has a unicameral legislature.

109 TJ to Major John Cartwright, June 5, 1824, *TJW*, 1492. Also consider Jefferson's musings about the division of the legislature into two chambers by lot so as to disarm popular demagogues in either house while still providing "the benefit of time and separate deliberation." TJ to A. Coray, October 31, 1823, *L&B* 15: 486.

110 TJ to Samuel Kercheval, July 12, 1816, *TJW*, 1401.

111 TJ to John Taylor, June 4, 1798, *TJW*, 1049.

112 John Howe, "Republicanism," 71. In the midst of the Revolution and under the pressure of a good deal more conservative statesmen than the young Jefferson himself, he "could submit, tho' not so willingly" to the idea of state senators getting "an appointment for life, or to any thing rather than a mere creation by & dependance on the people." Jefferson was ready to make this compromise after explaining again that his proposition was to provide a statewide, single electorate to engage in the elections, after which the elect would turn themselves into two chambers according to their discretion. TJ to Edmund Pendleton, August 26, 1776, *TJW*, 755–756. Letting the elected choose the wisest clearly suggests that there was no other criterion for defining "wisdom" than human discretion.

113 TJ William Branch Giles, February 3, 1807, *TJW*, 1175.

114 TJ to Edmund Pendleton, August 26, 1776, *TJW*, 756 (the parentheses in the original).

115 TJ to Edmund Pendleton, August 26, 1776, *TJW*, 756. For Jefferson's allegedly "later" view that the state should "let every man who fights or pays, exercise his just and equal right" to vote, see TJ to Samuel Kercheval, July 12, 1816,

ibid., 1398. As for some scholars' contrary claims that Jefferson in fact became more reserved in his advocacy of equal suffrage over the years, it is notable that in his 1784 draft of the later Northwest Ordinance, Jefferson suggested universal male suffrage without any property or tax qualifications in the Western territories. That he would have later developed some hidden agenda to keep the extremely poor out of the ballot, as has been indicated by Chilton Williamson, for example, seems questionable. See Williamson, *American Suffrage*, e.g., 128, 138. In 1816, Jefferson still held it inexcusable that "one half of our brethren who fight and pay taxes, are excluded ... from the rights of representation, as if society were instituted for the soil, and not for the men inhabiting it." TJ to John Taylor, May 28, 1816, *TJW*, 1393. The principle had not changed to that of both paying "and" fighting, for a couple of weeks later Jefferson used the phrase "every man who fights or pays" to express the same idea. TJ to Samuel Kercheval, July 12, 1816, *TJW*, 1399.

116 TJ to Edmund Pendleton, August 26, 1776, *TJW*, 756.

117 *Notes*, Query XIII, 245.

118 Hamilton in the Constitutional Convention, Philadelphia, June 18, 1787 (the version recorded by Robert Yates) in *Alexander Hamilton Writings*, ed. by Joanne B. Freeman (New York: Library of America, 2001), 164.

119 For the Blackstone quotation as cited by Hamilton, see White, *Philosophy of the American Revolution*, 259. On the fact that, for example, Richard Price and John Adams shared the commonplace conviction that property qualifications are necessary in democracy, see ibid., 262–265. Or consider U.S. Supreme Court Justice Samuel Chase's statement from 1803 about Maryland's reform allowing universal male suffrage: "The change of the State constitution, by allowing universal suffrage, will, in my opinion, certainly and rapidly destroy all protection of property, and all security to personal liberty; and our republican constitution will [change] into a mobocracy, the worst of all possible government." Quoted in Dumas Malone, *Jefferson the President, First Term: Jefferson and His Time, Vol. 4* (Charlottesville: University of Virginia Press, 2005), 466.

120 *Notes*, Query XIV, 275.

121 Morris's statement on August 7, 1787, as in Madison, *Notes of Debates in the Federal Convention*, Koch (ed.), 402.

122 TJ to Jean Babtiste Say, February 1, 1804, *TJW*, 1144.

123 TJ to William Charles Jarvis, September 28, 1820, *L&B* 15: 278.

124 *Notes*, Query XIV, 274.

125 TJ to Edward Carrington, January 16, 1787, *TJW*, 880. About the seminal importance of a free press, Jefferson proclaimed that "the people may safely be trusted to hear everything true and false, and to form a correct judgment between them." TJ to Judge John Tyler, June 29, 1804, *TJW*, 1147. Although convinced that Europeans were not yet ripe for a truly "republican government," Jefferson emphasized that even under a monarchical government, the "only security of all, is a free press" because the "force of public opinion cannot be resisted, when permitted freely to be expressed." TJ to Lafayette, November 4, 1823, *L&B* 15: 491.

126 TJ, *Autobiography* (1821), *TJW*, 44.

127 TJ to Littleton Waller Tazewell, January 5, 1805, *TJW*, 1150.

128 See TJ to P.S. Dupont de Nemours, April 24, 1816, *TJW*, 1387.

129 TJ to Joseph C. Cabell, February 2, 1816, *TJW*, 1380.

130 For earlier, unnecessarily pejorative accounts of Jefferson's natural aristocracy, see, for example, Boorstin, *The Lost World*, passim., and May, "The Enlightenment," 52.

131 TJ to John Adams, October 28, 1813, *AJL*, 388.

132 John Adams in his *A Defense of the Constitution of Government in the United States of America*, as in Adams, *Political Writings of John Adams*, George A. Peek, Jr. (ed.), 138–139.

133 *Notes*, Query XIII, 245.

134 TJ to John Adams, October 18, 1813, *AJL*, 390.

135 For this alternative of "virtue and talent," see TJ to John Adams, October 28, 1813, *AJL*, 389.

136 TJ to Edmund Pendleton, August 26, 1776, *TJW*, 755.

137 TJ to P.S. Dupont de Nemours, April 25, 1816, *TJW*, 1385.

138 TJ to Joseph C. Cabell, February 2, 1816, *TJW*, 1380.

139 TJ to Samuel Kercheval, July 12, 1816, *TJW*, 1399.

140 TJ to Samuel Kercheval, September 5, 1816, *Ford* 12: 16n.

141 TJ to Samuel Kercheval, September 5, 1816, *Ford* 12: 16n. During the 1820 Missouri Crisis, Jefferson abhorred the possibility that the federal Congress "goes out of the Constitution to arrogate a right of regulating the conditions of the inhabitants of the states." TJ to Albert Gallatin, December 26, 1820, *TJW*, 1449.

142 TJ to James Madison, September 6, 1789, *TJW*, 959–960.

143 TJ to Samuel Kercheval, July 12, 1816, *TJW*, 1400.

144 Aristotle, *Nicomachean Ethics* (VI, 2), 139.

145 TJ to James Madison, October 28, 1785, *TJW*, 842.

146 TJ to James Madison, October 28, 1785, *TJW*, 841–842.

147 TJ to James Madison, October 28, 1785, *TJW*, 841–842.

148 TJ to James Madison, October 28, 1785, *TJW*, 841–842.

149 TJ to James Madison, October 28, 1785, *TJW*, 841–842.

150 Adam Smith's classic account of the historical development of the use of landed property began from the "slave cultivators of ancient times" to "tenants," and then moved on to "a villain enfranchised" (equaling the "metayer" with no own stock), to the "farmers properly so called, who cultivated the land with their own stock, paying a rent certain to the landlord." Adam Smith, as in *The Wealth of Nations, Books I-III* (1776), ed. by Andrew Skinner (London: Penguin Books, 1986), (Bk. III, Ch.2), 489–491.

151 TJ to John Wayles Eppes, June 12, 1813, *TJW*, 1282.

152 TJ to Robert Skipwith, August 3, 1771, *Papers* 1: 77. By the same token, Jefferson later argued that the British Act of 1650 "for inhibiting their [the colonies'] trade with foreign nations," began "parliamentary interference with the colonies, and produced that fatal precedent which they continued to follow." *Notes*, Query XIII, 238.

153 TJ's Report on Negotiation with Spain, March 18, 1792, *Ford* 6: 433–435.

154 TJ to James Madison, September 6, 1789, *TJW*, 959.

155 TJ to James Madison, October 28, 1785, *TJW*, 841–842.

156 On TJ's familiarity with Cato's theater argument, see TJ to Robert R. Livingstone, September 9, 1801, *TJW*, 1092. For an excellent introduction to

the complexities of the natural lawyers' views of property as compared to those of Locke, see Hont and Ignatieff, "Needs and Justice," in Hont and Ignatieff (eds.), *Wealth and Virtue*, 1–44.

157 TJ to Isaac McPherson, August 13, 1813, *TJW*, 1291. As early as 1789, Jefferson had suggested that copy and patent rights should expire in nineteen years. See TJ to James Madison, September 6, 1789, *TJW*, 964.

158 See Hont and Ignatief, "Needs and Justice," 1–44.

159 TJ to John B. Colvin, September 20, 1810, *TJW*, 1232.

160 According to Locke himself, all human laws "are only so far right, as they are founded on the Law of Nature" Locke, *Second Treatise* (§12), 275.

161 *Notes*, Query XIV, 269.

162 *Notes*, Query XIV, 263.

163 *Notes*, Query XIV, 259.

164 *Notes*, Query XIV, 259.

165 TJ, Bill No. 55, A Bill Declaring Who Shall Be Citizens of This Commonwealth, *Papers* 2: 477.

166 "If we strike out the 25,000 dollars for the services of the clergy" Jefferson suggests, the public expenses of the state would diminish considerably. *Notes*, Query XXII, 299.

167 For Jefferson's revision of the laws, see, as earlier, the following bills about the poor, slaves, guardians, etc.: No. 32, No. 51, and No. 60, *Papers* 2: 419, 470, 485.

168 TJ, A Bill for the More General Diffusion of Knowledge (1778), *TJW*, 365.

169 TJ to Samuel Kercheval, July 12, 1816, *Ford* 12: 8–9. On the idea of dividing the counties into hundreds, each having a court and militia and the task of taking care of the roads and the poor, see also TJ to John Tyler, May 26, 1810, *TJW*, 1226.

170 TJ to Joseph O. Cabell, February 2, 1816, *TJW*, 1381.

171 On the view that the concept of embargo referred to an act in preparation for defensive war and was hence distinguishable from commercial coercion into which it gradually turned in the Jefferson administration, see Burton Spivak, *Jefferson's English Crisis: Commerce, Embargo, and the Republican Revolution* (Charlottesville: University of Virginia Press, 1979), e.g., x. Regarding Jefferson hinting at the possibility of waging war against France in alliance with the British (both in 1803 and 1805), see Egan, *Neither Peace nor War*, 50. On Egan's quite straightforward judgment that it was Jefferson's greatest error while in office that he did not declare war on Britain, see ibid., 74.

172 TJ to John Langdon, March 5, 1810, *TJW*, 1218.

173 TJ, A Memorandum (Services to My Country, c. 1800), *TJW*, 702.

174 On Jefferson's advocacy of internal improvements, see Peterson, *Thomas Jefferson and the New Nation*, 856–858. Historian John Larson's account of this issue is a good deal more complicated. Larson admits that constitutional changes regarding internal improvements were recommended by Jefferson and by his Secretary of Treasury, Albert Gallatin. Nevertheless, Larson seems to think that Jefferson should have pressed the issue further, as if he could compel the federal Congress to take action. Larson's logic in this, however, seems questionable in light of the fact that Jefferson certainly could not (and hardly imagined he could) compel the Congress to amend the Constitution even when the

purchase of Louisiana was at issue. See John Lauritz Larson, "Jefferson's Union and the Problem of Internal Improvements," Onuf (ed.), *Jeffersonian Legacies*, 340–369. On Jefferson's call for the construction of interstate roads and canals as well as the establishment of a national university, and for a constitutional amendment, see TJ, Sixth Annual Message, December 2, 1806, *TJW*, 529–530. Even in Jefferson's often cited 1825 statement defiantly defending states' rights, he duly recognized the need for internal improvements, and argued that he would "give to the federal member, by a regular amendment of the constitution" the right to implement such improvements. He insisted only that each state would retain its jurisdiction to its share of such funds so as to avoid "the federal corruption" in appropriating the money. TJ to William Branch Giles, December 26, 1825, *TJW*, 1511. On Madison's famous call for internal improvements and on his subsequent veto of the federal Congress's Internal Improvements act because of the lack of the necessary constitutional amendment, see, for example, Madison's Seventh Annual Message in *James Madison Writings*, Rakove (ed.), 716–717; Madison's Veto Message to Congress, March 3, 1817, ibid., 719.

175 TJ to Joseph O. Cabell, November 28, 1820, *Ford* 12: 171.

176 TJ to Albert Gallatin, December 26, 1820, *TJW*, 1450. This letter was probably inspired by Jefferson's son-in-law and then Governor of Virginia, Thomas Mann Randolph. Randolph's moderate proposals (made in the same month) to the state legislature aimed to reduce the number of Virginia slave population by sending all emancipated slaves out of the state. Earlier the same year, Randolph had openly opposed "the new morality which tolerates perpetuity of slavery." Quotation in Dumas Malone, *The Sage of Monticello: Jefferson and His Time, Vol. 6* (Charlottesville: University of Virginia Press, 2005), 341.

177 Even when offering lip service to the African Colonization Society's attempts to send some freed slaves to Africa, Jefferson hoped that the "commercial advantages" of the plan would repay "its expenses." TJ to John Lynch, January 21, 1811, *TJW*, 1241. For Jefferson's insistence that he had never thought of Africa as a proper asylum for the entire slave population, see TJ to Jared Sparks, February 4, 1824, *TJW*, 1484. As for his earlier statements about Africa, it is notable that in his 1802 letter to Rufus King about sending slaves to Sierra Leone, Jefferson was concerned about "the expense of so distant a transportation" and ambiguously referred to both a few imprisoned slaves guilty of insurrection and to the idea of sending "emancipated negroes" to a settlement "nearer home than Africa." TJ to Rufus King, July 13, 1802, *L&B* 10: 326–330. Jefferson's 1801 letter to Monroe is an exceptionally clear account of Jefferson's views of the matter. It is also the only source, to my knowledge, to contain any fairly clear evidence that Jefferson ever thought of Africa as an asylum for more than a handful of rebellious slaves – and even there only with the provision "if all others more desirable should fail us." The most promising option was St. Domingo. As to Jefferson's expansionist hopes, his speculations about Anglo-Americans spreading all over North and South America as "speaking the same language, governed in similar forms, & by similar laws" were not meant to suggest that all Americans would end up with one common federation. This long-term, cultural rather than political, expansionist vision was the reason for Jefferson to prefer the Caribbean as the asylum for freed

slaves so as to avoid a racial "blot or mixture" on the continental Americas. TJ to James Monroe, November 24, 1801, *TJW*, 1096–1099.

178 Cf. *Notes*, Query XIV, 264 and TJ to Jared Sparks, February 4, 1824, *TJW*, 1485.

179 TJ to Jared Sparks, February 4, 1824, *TJW*, 1485.

180 Jefferson also thought that St. Domingo might be willing to pay for the passage, leaving "for the general confederacy, no expense but of nurture with the mother a few years, and would call, of course, for a very moderate appropriation of the vacant lands." The "very moderate appropriation" of land was probably meant for the young blacks to work on until capable of taking the trip. TJ to Jared Sparks, February 4, 1824, *TJW*, 1486.

181 TJ to Jared Sparks, February 4, 1824, *TJW*, 1487.

182 *Notes*, Query XIV, 264.

183 See, as earlier, TJ to J.P. Reibelt, December 21, 1805, *Ford* 10: 205. In the *Notes* it was stated that the children "should continue with their parents to a certain age," after which they would "be brought up, at public expense, to tillage, arts and sciences." It appears that "the public" was supposed not only to supply the vacant lands for the African-American youngsters prior to their deportation, but also to finance their elementary education. *Notes*, Query XIV, 264. As late as 1833, Madison spoke of the "purchase by the public of all female children," and further noted that the acquirement of an appropriate asylum and the replacement of slave labor would demand not only voluntary donations, but also "[l]egislative grants by the States" as well as funding from the sales of "the public lands held in trust by Congress." James Madison to Thomas R. Dew, February 23, 1833, as in the extract of the letter in Saul K. Padover (ed.), *The Complete Madison: His Basic Writings* (New York: Harper & Brothers, 1953), 327.

184 TJ to Edward Coles, August 25, 1814, *TJW*, 1345.

185 TJ to George Logan, November 12, 1816, *Ford* 12: 43.

186 Historian Lance Banning made this same distinction decades ago in his "Some Second Thoughts on Virtue and the Course of Revolutionary Thinking," in Ball and Pocock (eds.), *Conceptual Change*, 201–204. Quotation from TJ to Francis W. Gilmer, June 7, 1816, *Ford* 11: 534.

187 TJ to P.S. Dupont de Nemours, April 24, 1816, *TJW*, 1387. Again, the form of government was of minor importance. Jefferson did not scruple to support a constitutional monarchy in France so long as all its political powers were aimed at promoting "the happiness of the individuals who compose" the nation. TJ to Thomas Paine, July 11, 1789, *Papers* 15: 268.

188 John C. Miller, *The Wolf by the Ears*, 279.

189 TJ to George Logan, May 11, 1805, *Ford* 10:141–142. On Brannagan's letter to Jefferson, see Jefferson, *Catalogue*, ed. by Sowerby, Vol. II, 62.

190 TJ to John Adams, January 22, 1821, *AJL*, 570.

191 This is exactly the context in which historian Charles Griswold finds Jefferson's moral failure. In Griswold's words, the "danger is a danger to the means of self-government, not to its ends – but the means possess moral legitimacy only if they can be shown to lead to the ends (at least over the long term), and Jefferson did not show this with respect to the Missouri question." Instead, Griswold states, Jefferson used "a crude utilitarian calculus that dispenses with

the individual rights of the numerical minority altogether," (Griswold, "Rights and Wrongs," 207). At this point, Griswold, with many others, loses sight of Jefferson's progressive worldview, in which only free, representative democracy may bring about the desired end – namely, gradually evolving fuller respect for human rights.

192 For Coles's position as well as for a detailed account of Madison's dodging with the slavery issue, see McCoy, *The Last of the Fathers*, esp., 308–322.

193 TJ to Albert Gallatin, January 13, 1807, *Ford* 10: 339.

194 TJ to John Adams, January 22, 1821, *AJL*, 569.

195 TJ to N.G. Dufief, April 19, 1814, *TJW*, 1334.

196 It is good to bear in mind, for example, that many states required religious oaths from their public servants until the Supreme Court declared such practices unconstitutional in 1961.

Conclusions

1 TJ to John Adams, April 11, 1823, *TJW*, 1469.

2 TJ to John Adams, October 14, 1816, *AJL*, 492.

3 *Notes*, Query XIV, *TJW*, 273–274.

4 *Notes*, Query XVIII, 288.

5 *Notes*, Query XVIII, 288–289.

6 TJ to William Short, August 4, 1820, *TJW*, 1437.

7 TJ to Doctor Walter Jones, January 2, 1814, *Ford* 11: 375.

8 TJ to Peter Carr, August 10, 1787, *TJW*, 904.

9 TJ to Henri Gregoire, February 25, 1809, *TJW*, 1202.

10 See TJ to Samuel Kercheval, July 12, 1816, *TJW*, 1398. As for Jefferson's genuine belief in mass participatory democracy – or citizens' day-to-day exercise of control over their own society – this is the best summary of his understanding of politics: "Where every man is a sharer of the direction of his ward-republic, or some of the higher ones, and feels that he is a participator in the government of affairs, not merely at an election day in the year, but every day; when there shall not be a man in the State who will not be a member of some one of its councils, great or small, he will let the heart be torn out of his body sooner than his power be wrested from him by a Caesar or a Bonaparte." TJ to Joseph C. Cabell, February 2, 1816, *TJW*, 1380.

11 Quotation in TJ to William A. Burwell, January 28, 1805, *Ford* 10: 126.

Select Bibliography

The Adams-Jefferson Letters: The Complete Correspondence Between Thomas Jefferson and Abigail and John Adams, Lester J. Cappon (ed.), 2 Vols., Chapel Hill: University of North Carolina Press, 1959.

Adams, John, *The Political Writings of John Adams*, George A. Peek Jr. (ed.), New York: The Liberal Art Press, 1954.

d'Alembert, Jean Le Rond, "Discours Préliminaire des editeurs," *Encyclopédie ou dictionnaire raisonné des sciences, des arts et des métiers*, Tome premier, Paris, 1751.

d'Alembert, Jean le Rond, *Preliminary Discourse to the Encyclopedia of Diderot* (transl. by Richard N. Schwab and Walter E. Rex), New York: Bobbs-Merrill Co., Library of Liberal Arts, 1963.

American Colonization Society, "The Sixth Annual Report of the American Society for Colonizing the Free People of the United States; with an Appendix," (Washington DC, 1823), *The North American Review*, No. 42, January, 1824.

Aristotle, *The Nicomachean Ethics* (transl. by David Ross and revised by J.L. Ackrill and J.O. Urmson), Oxford: Oxford University Press (World's Classics), 1980.

The Politics (transl. by T.A. Sinclair and revised by Trevor J. Saunders), London: Penguin Classics, 1992.

Bacon, *The New Organon and Related Writings*, Fulton H. Anderson (ed.), Indianapolis and New York: Bobbs-Merrill Company, 1960.

Barbeyrac, Jean, "An Historical and Critical Account of the Science of Morality; And the Progress it has made in the World, from the earliest Times down to the Publication of Pufendorf's the Law of Nature and Nations," in Samuel Pufendorf, *The Law of Nature and Nations* [*De jure naturae et gentium*, 1672], (translated by Jean Barbeyrac), London: 1729, 1–68.

Burlamaqui, J.J., *The principles of natural Law: in which the true principle of morality and civil government are established* [*Principes du droit naturel*, Geneva 1747], (translated by Mr. Nugent, London, 1748), reprint: Clark, NJ: The Lawbook Exchange, 2003.

Brucker, Johann Jacob, *The history of philosophy* [*Historia critica philosophiae*] (translated by William Enfield), 2 Vols., London: 1741.

Catalogue of the Library of Thomas Jefferson, E. Millicent Sowerby (ed.), Vol. II, Washington, DC, 1953.

Cicero, *On Duties* [*De officiis*] (ed. and transl. by M.T. Griffin and E.M. Atkins), Cambridge: Cambridge University Press, 1991.

The Federalist Papers (by Alexander Hamilton, James Madison, and John Jay), Clinton Rossiter (ed.), New York: Penguin Books, 1961.

Hamilton, Alexander, *Alexander Hamilton Writings*, Joanne B. Freeman (ed.), New York: Library of America, 2001.

Hume, David, *Hume's Moral and Political Philosophy*, Henry D. Aiken (ed.), New York: Hafner Press, 1948.

Hutcheson, Francis, *A Short Introduction to Moral Philosophy* (Anonymously translated from Latin, Glasgow, 1747), reprint: Hildesheim, Netherlands: Georg Olms Verlagsbuchhandling, 1969.

An Inquiry concerning Moral Good and Evil (1725, 1726), in L.A. Selby-Bigge (ed.), *British Moralists: Being Selections from Writers Principally of the Eighteenth Century*, Indianapolis: Bobbs-Merrill, 1964.

Jefferson, Thomas, *Notes on the State of Virginia* (London, 1787), in Merrill D. Peterson (ed.), *Thomas Jefferson Writings*, New York: Library of America, 1984.

The Writings of Thomas Jefferson, Andrew A. Lipscomb and Albert Ellery Bergh (eds.), 20 Vols., Washington DC, 1903–1904.

The Works of Thomas Jefferson, Paul Leicester Ford (ed.), 12 Vols. (Federal edition), New York, 1904–1905.

The Commonplace Book of Thomas Jefferson: A Repertory of His Ideas on Government [Jefferson's Legal Commonplace Book], Gilbert Chinard (ed.), Baltimore: Johns Hopkins University Press, 1926.

The Papers of Thomas Jefferson, Julian P. Boyd et al. (eds.), Princeton, NJ: Princeton University Press, 1950–.

Jefferson's Extracts from the Gospels: The Papers of Thomas Jefferson, Second Series, Dickinson W. Adams and Ruth W. Lester (eds.), with an Introduction by Eugene R. Sheridan, Princeton, NJ: Princeton University Press, 1983.

Thomas Jefferson Writings, Merrill D. Peterson (ed.), New York: Library of America, 1984.

Jefferson's Literary Commonplace Book. The Papers of Thomas Jefferson, Second Series, Douglas L. Wilson (ed.), Princeton, NJ: Princeton University Press, 1989.

Thomas Jefferson: Political Writings, Joyce Appleby and Terence Ball (eds.), New York: Cambridge University Press, 1999.

Kames, Henry Home (Lord Kames), *Essays on the Principles of Morality and Natural Religion*, Edinburgh: 1751, Facsimile reprint: London: University Microfilfms International, Ann Arbor, MI, 1981.

(Lord Kames), *Six Sketches on the History of Man*, Philadelphia, 1776.

(Lord Kames), *Principles of Equity*, Edinburgh: A. Kincaid, 1760.

Law, Thomas, *Second Thoughts on Instinctive Impulses*, Printed for the author, 143 pp., Philadelphia, 1813 [Micprint 8, No 28918, University of Virginia].

Linnaeus, Carolus, *Systema Naturae* (Holmiae, Editio Decima, Reformata), 10 Edition, Vol. I, Holm, 1758.

Locke, John, *An Essay Concerning Human Understanding* (1690, 1700), Peter H. Nidditch (ed.), Oxford: Oxford University Press, 1979.

The Second Treatise of Government, in John Locke, *Two Treatises of Government* (1690, 1698), Peter Laslett (ed.), Cambridge: Cambridge University Press, 1994, 265–428.

The Works of John Locke, Vol. X, A new edition, corrected (London, 1823), reprint: Aalen, Germany: Scientia Verlag, 1963.

Madison, James, *The Complete Madison: His Basic Writings*, Saul K. Padover (ed.), New York: Harper & Brothers, 1953.

James Madison Writings, Jack N. Rakove (ed.), New York: Library of America, 1999.

Notes of Debates in the Federal Convention of 1787 Reported by James Madison, Adrianne Koch (ed.), Bicentennial Edition, New York: W.W. Norton & Company, 1987.

Montesquieu, Charles Louis Secondat, baron de, *The Spirit of Laws* (*L'Esprit de lois*, 1748), A Compendium of the First English Edition as translated by Thomas Nugent, London, 1750, David Wallace Carrithers (ed.), Berkeley: University of California Press, 1977.

Moral Philosophy from Montaigne to Kant: An Anthology, J.B. Schneewind (ed.), 2 Vols., Cambridge: Cambridge University Press, 1990.

Personal Slavery Established, By the Suffrages of Custom and Right Reason (Anonymous), Philadelphia, 1773.

Plato, *The Republic* (transl. by Desmond Lee), Second Revised Edition, Baltimore: Penguin Books, 1974.

Randolph, Sarah N. (ed.), *The Domestic Life of Thomas Jefferson: Compiled from Family Letters and Reminiscences by His Great-Granddaughter*, New York: Frederick Ungar Publishing Co., 1958.

Reid, Thomas, *Essays on the Active Powers of Man* (1768), *The Works of Thomas Reid*, Sir William Hamilton Bart (ed.), Eight Edition, Vol. II, Edinburgh, 1880.

An Inquiry into the Human Mind (1764), Timothy Duggan (ed.), Chicago: Chicago University Press, 1970.

Rousseau, Jean-Jacques, *The Social Contract and Discourses* [*Du Contrat Social*, 1762] (transl. with an introduction by G.D.H. Cole and updated by P.D. Jimack), London: Everyman 1993.

Smith, Adam, *The Theory of Moral Sentiments* (1759, 6th edition), ed. by D.D. Raphael and A.L. Macfie (The Glasgow Edition), Oxford: Oxford University Press, 1982.

The Wealth of Nations, Books I–III (1776), Andrew Skinner (ed.), London: Penguin Books, 1986.

The Wealth of Nations, Books IV–V (1776), Andrew Skinner (ed.), London: Penguin Books, 1999.

Stewart, Dugald, *The Elements of the Philosophy of the Human Mind* (1792), in *The Works of Dugald Stewart*, Vol. I. Cambridge: Hilliard and Brown, 1829.

Tacitus, *The Complete Works of Tacitus*, Moses Hadas (ed.), New York: The Modern Library, Random House, 1942.

Taylor, John, [of Caroline], *Construction Construed and Constitutions Vindicated* (Richmond: 1820), Reprint New York: A Da Capo Press, Plenum Publishing, 1970.

[of Caroline], *An Inquiry into the Principles and Policy of the Government of the United States* (Fredericksburg, VA, 1814), Roy Franklin Nichols (ed.), New Haven, CT: Yale University Press, 1950.

Thucydides, *The History of the Peloponnesian War* (translated by Greek by R. Crawley), London: J.M Dent & Sons (1910), 1940.

Tracy, Antoine Louis Claude, Destutt de, *A Commentary and Review of Montesquieu's Spirit of Laws* (translation by Thomas Jefferson et al., 1811), reprint: New York: Burt Franklin, 1969.

A Treatise on Political Economy to which is prefixed a supplement to a preceding work on the understanding or, Elements of Ideology, (translation edited by Thomas Jefferson, 1817), reprint: New York: Augustus M. Kelley Publishers, 1970.

Vattel, Emer [Emerich] de, *The Law of Nations: or Principles of the Law of Nature applied to the Conduct and Affairs of Nations and Sovereigns* [*Le droit de gens*, 1758] (translated by Joseph Chitty), Sixth American Edition, Philadelphia, 1844.

Wilson, James, *The Works of the Honourable James Wilson, L.L.D*, published by Bird Wilson, Vol. 1, Philadelphia: Bronson and Chauncey, 1804.

Witherspoon, John, *An Annotated Edition of Lectures on Moral Philosophy of John Witherspoon*, Jack Scott (ed.), University of Delaware Press, London and Toronto: Associated University Presses, 1982.

Wollstonecraft, Mary, *Vindication of the Rights of Woman* (1792), Miriam Brody Kramnick (ed.), Harmondsworth: Penguin Books, 1978.

Literature

Adair, Douglass, *Fame and the Founding Fathers: Essays by Douglass Adair*, Trevor Colbourn (ed.) with a Personal Memoir by Caroline Robbins and a Biographical Essay by Robert E Shalhope, New York: W.W. Norton, 1974.

American Legal History: Cases and Materials, Second Edition, Kermit L. Hall, William M. Wiecek and Paul Finkelman (eds.), New York: Oxford University Press, 1996.

Appleby, Joyce, *Capitalism and a New Social Order: The Republican Vision of the 1790s*, New York: New York University Press, 1984.

"Introduction: Jefferson and His Complex Legacy," in Peter Onuf (ed.), *Jeffersonian Legacies*, Charlottesville: University of Virginia Press, 1994, 1–18.

"Republicanism in Old and New Contexts," *The William and Mary Quarterly* 43 (1, 1986), 20–34.

Arendt, Hannah, *On Revolution*, New York: Viking Press, 1968.

The Human Condition (1958), Second edition, Introduction by Margaret Conovan, Chicago: Chicago University Press, 1998.

Ashcraft, Richard, "Locke's Political Philosophy," in Vere Chappell (ed.), *The Cambridge Companion to Locke*, Cambridge: Cambridge University Press, 1995, 226–251.

Ayers, Michael, *Locke: Epistemology and Ontology*, London: Routledge, 2001.

Bailyn, Bernard, *The Ideological Origins of the American Revolution*, Cambridge, MA: Harvard University Press, 1971.

Ball, Terence, "A Republic – If You Can Keep It," Terence Ball and J.G.A. Pocock (eds.), *Conceptual Change and the Constitution*, Lawrence: University Press of Kansas, 1988, 136–164.

Ball, Terence and J.G.A. Pocock (eds.), *Conceptual Change and the Constitution*, Lawrence: University Press of Kansas, 1988.

(eds.), Introduction in Terence Ball and J.G.A. Pocock (eds.), *Conceptual Change and the Constitution*, Lawrence: University Press of Kansas, 1988, 1–12.

Banning, Lance, *The Jeffersonian Persuasion: Evolution of a Party Ideology*, Ithaca, NY: Cornell University Press, 1978.

"Jeffersonian Ideology Revisited: Liberal and Classical Ideas in the New American Republic," *The William and Mary Quarterly* 43 (1986), 3–19.

"Some Second Thoughts on Virtue and the Course of Revolutionary Thinking," in Terence Ball and J.G.A. Pocock (eds.), *Conceptual Change and the Constitution*, Lawrence: University Press of Kansas, 1988, 194–212.

Becker, Carl L., *The Declaration of Independence: A Study in the History of Political Ideas*, New York: Random House (1922), 1970.

Bedini, Silvio A., *Thomas Jefferson: Statesman of Science*, New York: MacMillan, 1990.

Beeman, Richard, *The Penguin Guide to the Unites States Constitution: A Fully Annotated Declaration of Independence, U.S. Constitution and Amendments, and Selections from the Federalist Papers*, Walbaum, MT: Penguin Books, 2010.

Beeman, Richard R., "The American Revolution," in Merrill D. Peterson (ed.), *Thomas Jefferson: A Reference Biography*, New York: Charles Scribner's Sons, 1986, 25–47.

Beitzinger, A.J., "Political Theorist," in Merrill D. Peterson, *Thomas Jefferson: A Reference Biography*, New York: Charles Scribner's Sons, 1986, 81–100.

Berlin, Ira, *Slaves without Masters: The Free Negro in the Antebellum South*, New York: Oxford University Press, 1981.

Bock, Gisela, Quentin Skinner, and Maurizio Viroli (eds.), *Machiavelli and Republicanism*, New York: Cambridge University Press, 1993.

Boorstin, Daniel J., *The Lost World of Thomas Jefferson*, Boston: Beacon Press (1948), 1963.

Boskin, Joseph, *Into Slavery: Racial Decisions in the Virginia Colony*, Washington, DC: University Press of America, 1979.

Boulton, Alexander, "The American Paradox: Jeffersonian Equality and Racial Science," *American Quarterly* 47 (1995), 467–492.

Brinkley, Alan, Richard N. Current, Frank Freidel, and T. Harry Williams, *American History: A Survey*, 8th Edition, New York: McGraw-Hill, 1991.

Brodie, Fawn M., *Thomas Jefferson: An Intimate History*, New York: W.W. Norton & Company, 1974.

Burns, J.H. with Mark Goldie (eds.), *The Cambridge History of Political Thought 1450–1700*, Cambridge: Cambridge University Press, 1991.

Burstein, Andrew, "Jefferson and the Familiar Letter," *Journal of the Early Republic* 14 (1994), 195–220.

The Inner Jefferson: Portrait of a Grieving Optimist, Charlottesville: University of Virginia Press, 1996.

Jefferson's Secrets: Death and Desire in Monticello, New York: Basic Books, 2005.

Bushman, Richard L., *The Refinement of America: Persons, Houses, Cities*, New York: Vintage Books, 1993.

Cassirer, Ernst, *The Philosophy of the Enlightenment (Die Philosophie der Aufklärung*, 1932) transl. by Fritz C.A. Koelln and James P. Pettergrove, Princeton, NJ: Princeton University Press, 1979.

Chappell, Vere (ed.), *The Cambridge Companion to Locke*, Cambridge: Cambridge University Press, 1995.

Chinard, Gilbert, "Introduction," in Gilbert Chinard (ed.), *The Commonplace Book of Thomas Jefferson*, Baltimore: Johns Hopkins University Press, 1926, 3–65.

Colbourn, Trevor H., *The Lamp of Experience: Whig History and the Intellectual Origins of the American Revolution*, New York: W.W. Norton & Co., 1965, 1974.

Conkin, Paul K., "The Religious Pilgrimage of Thomas Jefferson," in Peter Onuf (ed.), *Jeffersonian Legacies*, Charlottesville: University of Virginia Press, 1994, 19–49.

Conrad, Stephen A., "Putting Rights Talk in Its Place: The Summary View Revisited," in Peter Onuf (ed.), *Jeffersonian Legacies*, Charlottesville: University of Virginia Press, 1994, 254–280.

Crisp, Roger and Michael Slote (eds.), *Virtue Ethics*, New York: Oxford University Press, 1997.

Cunningham Jr., Noble E., *In Pursuit of Reason: The Life of Thomas Jefferson*, Baton Rouge: Louisiana State University Press, 1987.

Dabney, Virginius, *Virginia: The New Dominion: A History from 1607 to the present*, Charlottesville: University Press of Virginia, 1992.

D'Amico, Robert, *Historicism and Knowledge*, New York: Routledge, 1989.

Davis, David Brion, *Slavery and Human Progress*, New York: Oxford University Press, 1984.

Dawidoff, Robert B., "Man of Letters," in Merrill D. Peterson (ed.), *Thomas Jefferson: A Reference Biography*, New York: Charles Scribner's Sons, 1986, 181–198.

Dunn, John, *The Political Thought of John Locke: An Historical Account of the Argument of the "Two Treatises of Government,"* Cambridge: Cambridge University Press, 1969.

"The Concept of 'Trust' in the Politics of John Locke," in Richard Rorty, J.B. Schneewind, and Quentin Skinner (eds.), *Philosophy in History: Essays on the Historiography of Philosophy*, New York: Cambridge University Press, 1984, 279–302.

Edling, Max, *A Revolution in Favor of Government: Origins of the U.S. Constitution and the Making of the American State*, New York: Oxford University Press, 2003.

Egan, Clifford L., *Neither Peace Nor War: Franco-American Relations, 1803–1812*, Baton Rouge: Louisiana State University Press, 1983.

Egerton, Douglas R., *Gabriel's Rebellion: The Virginia Slave Conspiracies of 1800 and 1802*, Chapel Hill: University of North Carolina Press, 1993.

"Race and Slavery in the Era of Jefferson," in Frank Shuffelton (ed.), *The Cambridge Companion to Thomas Jefferson*, New York: Cambridge University Press, 2009, 73–82.

Elkins, Stanley and Eric McKitrick, *The Age of Federalism: The Early American Republic, 1788–1800*, New York: Oxford University Press, 1995.

Elkins, Stanley and Eric McKitrick, "Institutions and the Law of Slavery: Slavery in Capitalist and Non-Capitalist Cultures" (American Quarterly. No. 9, 1957), in Peter Charles Hoffer (ed.), *Africans Become Afro-Americans: Selected Articles on Slavery in the American Colonies*, New York: Garland, 1988, 26–45.

Ellis, Joseph J., *American Sphinx: The Character of Thomas Jefferson*, New York: Alfred A. Knopf, 1997.

Fasolt, Constantin, *The Limits of History*, Chicago: Chicago University Press, 2004.
Finkelman, Paul, "Jefferson and Slavery: 'Treason against the Hopes of the World,'" in Peter Onuf (ed.), *Jeffersonian Legacies*, Charlottesville: University of Virginia Press, 1993, 1994, 181–224.
Fliegelman, Jay, *Declaring Independence: Jefferson, Natural Language & the Culture of Performance*. Stanford, CA: Stanford University Press, 1993, 1996.
Foner, Philip S. (ed.), *The Democratic-Republican Societies, 1790–1800: A Documentary Source Book of Constitutions, Declarations, Addresses, Resolutions, and Toasts*, Westport, CT: Greenwood Press, 1976.
Frankena, William, *Ethics, Second Edition*, Englewood Cliffs, NJ: Prentice Hall, 1973.
Freeman, Joanne B., *Affairs of Honor: National Politics in the New Republic*, New Haven, CT: Yale University Press, 2001.
"Dueling as Politics: Reinterpreting the Burr-Hamilton Duel," *The William and Mary Quarterly*, **LVIII**, (2, 1996), 229–318.
French, Scot A. and Edward L Ayers, "The Strange Career of Thomas Jefferson: Race and Slavery in American Memory, 1943–1993," in Peter Onuf (ed.), *Jeffersonian Legacies*, Charlottesville: University of Virginia Press, 1994, 418–456.
Gaustad, E.S., "Religion," in Merrill D. Peterson (ed.), *Thomas Jefferson: A Reference Biography*, New York: Charles Scribner's Sons, 1986, 277–294.
Gay, Peter, *The Enlightenment: An Interpretation, The Rise of Modern Paganism*, New York: W.W. Norton & Co., 1966.
The Enlightenment: An Interpretation, The Science of Freedom, New York: W.W. Norton & Co., 1969.
Gordon-Reed, Annette, *Thomas Jefferson and Sally Hemings: An American Controversy*, Charlottesville: University of Virginia Press, 1997.
"'The Memories of a Few Negroes': Rescuing America's Future at Monticello," in Jan Ellen Lewis and Peter Onuf (eds.), *Sally Hemings & Thomas Jefferson: History, Memory, and Civic Culture*, Charlottesville: University Press of Virginia, 1999, 236–254.
Gould, Stephen Jay, *I Have Landed: The End of a Beginning in Natural History*, Cambridge, MA: Harvard University Press, 2011.
Greene, Jack P., "The Intellectual Reconstruction of Virginia in the Age of Jefferson," in Peter Onuf (ed.), *Jeffersonian Legacies*, Charlottesville, University of Virginia Press, 1994, 225–253.
Griswold Jr., Charles L., "Rights and Wrongs: Jefferson, Slavery, and Philosophical Quandaries," in Michael J. Lacey and Knud Haakonssen (eds.), *A Culture of Rights: The Bill of Rights in Philosophy, Politics, and Law – 1791 and 1991*, Cambridge: Cambridge University Press, 1991, 144–214.
Haakonssen, Knud, *Natural Law and Moral Philosophy: From Grotius to the Scottish Enlightenment*, Cambridge: Cambridge University Press, 1996.
"From Natural Law to the Rights of Man: A European Perspective on American Debates," in Michael J. Lacey and Knud Haakonssen (eds.), *A Culture of Rights: The Bill of Rights in Philosophy, Politics, and Law – 1791 and 1991*, Cambridge: Cambridge University Press, 1991, 19–61.
Haakonssen, Knud (ed.), *Thomas Reid: Practical Ethics, Being Lectures and Papers on Natural Religion, Self-Government, Natural Jurisprudence, and the Law of Nations*, Princeton, NJ: Princeton University Press, 1990.

Handlin, Oscar and Mary Handlin, "Origins of the Southern Slavery Labor System" (*The William and Mary Quarterly*, No. 7, 1950), in Peter Charles Hoffer (ed.), *Africans Become Afro-Americans: Selected Articles on Slavery in the American Colonies*, New York: Garland Publishing, 1988, 199–222.

Helo, Ari and Peter Onuf, "Jefferson, Morality, and the Problem of Slavery," *The William and Mary Quarterly*, 60 (2003), 583–614.

Hoadley, John F., "The Emergence of Political Parties in Congress, 1789–1803," *The American Political Science Review* 74 (1980), 757–778.

Hochstrasser, T.J. and Peter Shröder (eds.), *Early Modern Natural Law Theories: Contexts and Strategies in the Early Enlightenment*, Dordrecth: Kluwer Academic Publishers, 2003.

Hoffer, Peter Charles (ed.), *Africans become Afro-Americans: Selected Articles on Slavery in the American Colonies*, New York: Garland Publishing, 1988.

Hoffer, Peter Charles, *The Brave New World: A History of Early America*, Baltimore: Johns Hopkins University Press, 2006.

Hont, Istvan, "The Language of Sociability and Commerce: Samuel Pufendorf and the Theoretical Foundations of the 'Four-Stages Theory'," in Anthony Pagden (ed.), *The Languages of Political Theory in Early-Modern Europe*, Cambridge: Cambridge University Press, 1990, 253–276.

Hont, Istvan and Michael Ignatieff, "Needs and Justice in the Wealth of Nations: An Introductory Essay," in Istvan Hont and Michael Ignatieff (eds.), *Wealth and Virtue: The Shaping of Political Economy in the Scottish Enlightenment*, Cambridge: Cambridge University Press, 1983, 1–44.

Howe, Daniel Walker, "The Language of Faculty Psychology in The Federalist Papers," in Terence Ball and J.G.A. Pocock (eds.), *Conceptual Change and the Constitution*, Lawrence: University Press of Kansas, 1988, 107–136.

Howe, John, "Republicanism," in Merrill D. Peterson (ed.), *Thomas Jefferson: A Reference Biography*, New York: Charles Scribner's Sons, 1986, 59–79.

James, C.L.R., *The Black Jacobins: Toussaint L'Ouverture and the San Domingo Revolution* (2nd, Revised Edition, 1963), New York: Vintage Books, 1989.

Jayne, Allen, *Jefferson's Declaration of Independence: Origins, Philosophy and Theology*, Lexington: University Press of Kentucky, 1998.

Koch, Adrienne, *Power, Morals, and the Founding Fathers: Essays in the Interpretation of the American Enlightenment*, Ithaca, NY: Cornell University Press, 1961.

Korkman, Petter, "Voluntarism and Moral Obligation: Barbeyrac's Defence of Pufendorf Revisited," in T.J. Hochstrasser and Peter Shröder (eds.), *Early Modern Natural Law Theories: Contexts and Strategies in the Early Enlightenment*, Dordrecth: Kluwer Academic Publishers, 2003, 195–226.

Lacey, Michael J. and Knud Haakonssen, "Introduction: History, historicism, and the culture of rights," in Michael J. Lacey and Knud Haakonssen (eds.), *A Culture of Rights: The Bill of Rights in Philosophy, Politics, and Law – 1791 and 1991*, New York: Cambridge University Press, 1991, 1–18.

Larson, John Lauritz, "Jefferson's Union and the Problem of Internal Improvements," in Peter Onuf (ed.), *Jeffersonian Legacies*, Charlottesville: University of Virginia Press, 1994, 340–369.

Lehmann, Helmut and Melvin Richter (eds.), *The Meaning of Historical Terms and Concepts: New Studies on Begriffgeschichte*, Washington, DC: German Historical Institute, 1996.

Lehmann, Karl, *Thomas Jefferson: American Humanist*, New York: MacMillan, 1947.

Lévai, Csaba, "A Moderate Reformer?" *Budapest Review of Books* 4 (1999): 198–202.

Levy, Leonard W., "Civil Liberties," in Merrill D. Peterson (ed.), *Thomas Jefferson: A Reference Biography*, New York: Charles Scribner's Sons, 1986, 331–348.

Lewis, Jan Ellen and Peter Onuf, "Introduction" in Jan Ellen Lewis and Peter Onuf (eds.), *Sally Hemings & Thomas Jefferson: History, Memory, and Civic Culture*, Charlottesville: University Press of Virginia, 1999, 1–18.

Long, David F., *Nothing Too Daring: A Biography of Commodore David Porter, 1780–1843*, Annapolis, MD: United States Naval Institute, 1970.

Lovejoy, Arthur O., *The Great Chain of Being: A Study of the History of an Idea*, Cambridge, MA: Harvard University Press, 1936, 1978.

McCoy, Drew R., *The Last of the Fathers: James Madison & the Republican Legacy*, New York: Cambridge University Press, 1996.

McDowell, John, "Virtue and Reason" (*The Monist* 62, 1979, 331–350.), in Roger Crisp and Michael Slote (eds.), *Virtue Ethics*, New York: Oxford University Press, 1997, 141–162.

McLaughlin, Jack, *Jefferson and Monticello: A Biography*, Lawrence: University Press of Kansas, 1977.

McPherson, J.B., *The Political Theory of Possessive Individualism: Hobbes to Locke*, Oxford: Oxford University Press, 1972.

MacIntyre, Alasdair, *A Short History of Ethics: A History of Moral Philosophy from the Homeric Age to the Twentieth Century*, London: Routledge, 1967, 1995.

MacLeod, Duncan J., *Slavery, Race, and the American Revolution*, New York: Cambridge University Press, 1974.

Maier, Pauline, *American Scripture: Making the Declaration of Independence*, New York: Vintage Books, 1998.

Malone, Dumas, "The Life of Thomas Jefferson," in Merrill D. Peterson (ed.), *Thomas Jefferson: A Reference Biography*, New York: Charles Scribner's Sons, 1986, 1–24.

The Sage of Monticello. Jefferson and His Time, Vol. 6 (1981), Charlottesville: University of Virginia Press, 2005.

Jefferson the President, First Term. Jefferson and His Time, Vol 4 (1970), Charlottesville: University of Virginia Press, 2005.

Marías, Julián, *History of Philosophy (Historia de la Filosofía*, 1966), transl. by Stanley Applebaum and Clarence C. Strowbridge, New York: Dover Publications, 1967.

Marx, Leo, *Machine in the Garden: Technology and the Pastoral Ideal in America*, New York: Oxford University Press, 1967.

Matthews, Richard K., *The Radical Politics of Thomas Jefferson: A Revisionist View*, Lawrence: University Press of Kansas, 1984.

May, Henry F., "The Enlightenment," in Merrill D. Peterson (ed.), *Thomas Jefferson: A Reference Biography*, New York: Charles Scribner's Sons, 1986, 47–58.

Mayer, David N., *The Constitutional Thought of Thomas Jefferson*, Charlottesville: University of Virginia Press, 1994.

Miller, Charles A., *Jefferson and Nature: An Interpretation*, Baltimore: John Hopkins University Press (1988), 1993.

Miller, John Chester, *The Wolf by the Ears: Thomas Jefferson and Slavery*, New York: New American Library (1977), 1980.

"Slavery," in Merrill D. Peterson (ed.), *Thomas Jefferson: A Reference Biography*, New York: Charles Scribner's Sons, 1986, 417–436.

Nash, Gary B., *Race and Revolution: The Inaugural Merrill Jensen Lectures*, Madison, WI: Madison House Publishers, 1990.

Neem, Johann M., "Beyond the Wall: Reinterpreting Jefferson's Danbury Address," *Journal of the Early Republic*, **27** (2007), 139–154.

Noonan, John T., *Persons and Masks of the Law: Cardozo, Holmes, Jefferson, and Wythe as Makers of the Masks*, New York: Farrar, Straus and Giroux, 1976.

Onuf, Peter S. (ed.), *Jeffersonian Legacies*, Charlottesville: University of Virginia Press, 1994.

Jefferson's Empire: The Language of American Nationhood, Charlottesville: University of Virginia Press, 2000.

The Mind of Thomas Jefferson, Charlottesville: University of Virginia Press, 2007.

Padover, Saul K., *Jefferson*, New York: Harcourt, Brace and Company, 1942.

Pagden, Anthony, "Introduction," in Anthony Pagden (ed.), *The Languages of Political Theory in Early-Modern Europe*, Cambridge, 1990, 1–18.

Palonen, Kari, *Quentin Skinner: History, Politics, Rhetoric*, Cambridge: Polity Press, 2003.

"Four Times of Politics: Policy, Polity, Politicking, and Politicization," *Alternatives*, **28** (2003), 171–186.

Peltonen, Markku, *The Duel in Early Modern England: Civility, Politeness and Honour*, Cambridge: Cambridge University Press, 2003.

Peterson, Merrill D., *Thomas Jefferson and the New Nation: A Biography*, New York: Oxford University Press, 1975.

Peterson, Merrill D. (ed.), *Thomas Jefferson: A Reference Biography*, New York: Charles Scribner's Sons, 1986.

Pocock, J.G.A., "States, Republics and Empires: The American Founding in Early Modern Perspective," in Terence Ball and J.G.A. Pocock (eds.), *Conceptual Change and the Constitution*, Lawrence: University Press of Kansas, 1988, 55–77.

Pocock, J.G.A. "A Discourse of Sovereignty," in Nicholas Phillipson and Quentin Skinner (eds.), *Political Discourse in Early Modern Britain*, Cambridge: Cambridge University Press, 1993, 377–428.

"Political Thought in the English-Speaking Atlantic, 1760–1790: The Imperial Crisis," in J.G.A. Pocock, Gordon J. Schochet, and Lois G. Swoerer (eds.), *The Varieties of British Political Thought*, New York: Cambridge University Press, 1993, 246–283.

Pocock, J.G.A., Gordon J. Schochet, and Lois G. Swoerer (eds.), *The Varieties of British Political Thought*, New York: Cambridge University Press, 1993.

Rakove, Jack, "Our Jefferson," in Jan Ellen Lewis and Peter Onuf (eds.), *Sally Hemings and Thomas Jefferson: History, Memory, and Civil Culture*, Charlottesville, University of Virginia, 1999, 210–235.

Rodgers, Daniel T., "Republicanism: The Career of a Concept," *The Journal of American History*, **79** (1992), 11–38.

Rorty, Richard, J.B. Schneewind, and Quentin Skinner (eds.), *Philosophy in History: Essays on the Historiography of Philosophy*, New York: Cambridge University Press, 1984.

Ross, Ian Simpson, *Lord Kames and the Scotland of His Day*, Oxford: Clarendon Press, 1972.

Rothman, Joshua D., "James Callender and Social Knowledge of Interracial Sex in Antebellum Virginia," in Jan Ellen Lewis and Peter Onuf (eds.), *Sally Hemings & Thomas Jefferson: History, Memory, and Civic Culture*, Charlottesville: University of Virginia Press, 1999, 87–113.

Saastamoinen, Kari, "Pufendorf on Natural Equality, Human Dignity, and Self-Esteem," *Journal of the History of Ideas*, 71 (2010), 39–62.

Samuelson, Richard, "Jefferson and Religion: Private Belief, Public Policy," in Frank Shuffelton (ed.), *The Cambridge Companion to Thomas Jefferson*, New York: Cambridge University Press, 2009, 143–154.

Sanford, Charles B., *The Religious Life of Thomas Jefferson*, Charlottesville: University of Virginia Press, 1992.

Schlesinger Sr., Arthur M., "The Lost Meaning of the 'The Pursuit of Happiness,'" *The William and Mary Quarterly*, 23 (1964), 325–327.

Schneewind, J.B., *The Invention of Autonomy: A History of Modern Moral Philosophy*, Cambridge: Cambridge University Press, 1998.

Schneewind, J.B. (ed.), *Moral Philosophy from Montaigne to Kant: An Anthology*, 2 Vols., New York: Cambridge University Press, 1990.

Schneewind, J.B., "Locke's Moral Philosophy," in Vere Chappell (ed.), *The Cambridge Companion to Locke*, Cambridge: Cambridge University Press, 1995, 199–225.

Shalev, Eran, "Empire Transformed: Britain in the American Classical Imagination, 1758–1783," *Early American Studies* (Spring 2006), 112–146.

Sheldon, Garrett Ward, *The Political Philosophy of Thomas Jefferson*, Baltimore: Johns Hopkins University Press, 1993.

Sheridan, Eugene R., "Introduction," in Dickinson W. Adams and Ruth W. Lester (eds.), *Jefferson's Extracts from the Gospels: The Papers of Thomas Jefferson, Second Series*, Princeton, NJ: Princeton University Press, 1983.

Shklar, Judith, "Review of Garry Wills's Inventing America: Jefferson's Declaration of Independence," *The New Republic* (Aug. 26, 1978), 32–34.

"Alexander Hamilton and the Language of Political Science," in Anthony Pagden (ed.), *The Languages of Political Theory in Early-Modern Europe*, New York: Cambridge University Press, 1990, 339–360.

"Montesquieu and the New Republicanism," in Gisela Bock, Quentin Skinner, and Maurizio Viroli (eds.), *Machiavelli and Republicanism*, New York: Cambridge University Press, 1993, 265–279.

Shuffelton, Frank (ed.), *The Cambridge Companion to Thomas Jefferson*, New York: Cambridge University Press, 2009.

Slauter, Eric, "The Declaration of Independence and the New Nation," in Frank Shuffelton (ed.), *The Cambridge Companion to Thomas Jefferson*, New York: Cambridge University Press, 2009, 12–34.

Sloan, Herbert, *Principle and Interest: Thomas Jefferson and the Problem of Debt* (Oxford University Press, 1995), Charlottesville: University of Virginia Press, 2001.

Smith, Henry Nash, *Virgin Land: The American West as Symbol and Myth*, Cambridge, MA: Harvard University Press (1950), 1970.

Spivak, Burton, *Jefferson's English Crisis: Commerce, Embargo, and the Republican Revolution*, Charlottesville: University of Virginia Press, 1979.

Staloff, Darren, "The Politics of Pedagogy: Thomas Jefferson and the Education of a Democratic Citizenry," in Frank Shuffelton (ed.), *The Cambridge Companion to Thomas Jefferson*, New York: Cambridge University Press, 2009, 127–142.

Stanton, Lucia C., "'Those Who Labor For My Happiness': Thomas Jefferson and His Slaves," in Peter Onuf (ed.), *Jeffersonian Legacies*, Charlottesville: University of Virginia Press, 1994, 147–180.

Stourtzh, Gerald, "Constitution: Changing Meanings of the Term from the Early Seventeenth to the Late Eighteenth Century," in Terence Ball and J.G.A. Pocock (eds.), *Conceptual Change and the Constitution*, Lawrence: University Press of Kansas, 1988, 35–54.

Sweet, Timothy, "Jefferson, Science, and the Enlightenment," in Frank Shuffelton (ed.), *The Cambridge Companion to Thomas Jefferson*, New York: Cambridge University Press, 2009, 101–113.

Kaija, Tianen-Anttila, *The Problem of Humanity: The Blacks in the European Enlightenment*, Helsinki: SHS, 1994.

Tuck, Richard, *Natural Rights Theories: Their Origin and Development*, Cambridge: Cambridge University Press, 1981.

Tully, James, *A Discourse on Property: John Locke and His Adversaries*, Cambridge: Cambridge University Press, 1980.

"Locke." in J.H. Burns with Mark Goldie (eds.), *The Cambridge History of Political Thought 1450–1700*, Cambridge: Cambridge University Press, 1991.

Valsania, Maurizio, "'Our Original Barbarism': Man vs. Nature in Thomas Jefferson's Moral Experience," *Journal of the History of Ideas*, **65** (2004), 627–645.

Weeks, William Earl, "Historiography: New Directions in the Study of Early American Foreign Relations," *Diplomatic History*, **17** (1993), 73–96.

White, Morton, *The Philosophy of the American Revolution*, New York: Oxford University Press, 1978.

Williams, Eric, *Capitalism & Slavery* (1944) with a new introduction by Colin A. Palmer, Chapel Hill: University of North Carolina Press, 1994.

Williamson, Chilton, *American Suffrage from Property to Democracy 1760–1860*, Princeton, NJ: Princeton University Press, 1968.

Wills, Garry, *Inventing America: Jefferson's Declaration of Independence*, Garden City, NY: Doubleday, 1978.

Wilson, Douglas L.,"Jefferson vs. Hume," *The William and Mary Quarterly*, **16** (1989), 49–70. "Jefferson and the Republic of Letters," in Peter Onuf (ed.), *Jeffersonian Legacies*, Charlottesville: University of Virginia Press, 1994, 50–76.

Wood, Gordon S., *The Creation of the American Republic 1776–1787*, Chapel Hill: University of North Carolina Press, 1969.

The Radicalism of the American Revolution, New York: Vintage Books, 1991. "The Trials and Tribulations of Thomas Jefferson," in Peter Onuf (ed.), *Jeffersonian Legacies*, Charlottesville: University of Virginia Press, 1994, 395–417.

Yack, Bernard, *The Problems of a Political Animal: Community, Justice, and Conflict in Aristotelian Political Thought*, Berkeley: University of California Press, 1993.

Yarbrough, Jean M., *American Virtues: Thomas Jefferson on the Character of a Free People*, Lawrence: University of Kansas Press, 1998.

Žižek, Slavoj, *Interrogating the Real*, ed. by Rex Butler and Scott Stephens, London: Continuum, 2006.

Zuckert, Michael P., *The Natural Rights Republic: Studies in the Foundation of the American Political Tradition*, Notre Dame, IN: University of Notre Dame Press, 1996.

Zvesper, John, "Jefferson on Liberal Natural Rights," in Gary L. McDowell and Sharon L. Noble (eds.), *Reason and Republicanism: Thomas Jefferson's Legacy of Liberty*, Lanham, MD: Rowman & Littlefield, 1997, 15–30.

Index

Lightning Source UK Ltd.
Milton Keynes UK
UKOW02f1235010616

275376UK00001B/147/P

9 781107 687721